COMMUNICATION IN AFRICA

A Search for Boundaries

COMMUNICATION IN AFRICA

A Search for Boundaries

LEONARD W. DOOB

New Haven and London, Yale University Press

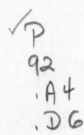

√ P
92
.A4
.D6

To David and Kathie Hovland
for
Carl and Gertrude

CONTENTS

PREFACE

This book tries to be faithful to its title and especially its subtitle. It deals specifically with communications in Africa in order to locate the significant boundaries of communication in general. For this reason the breathless hope can be expressed that its content may interest those seeking knowledge about Africa and that its approach may appeal to anyone concerned either with communication or with the systematic understanding of behavior.

Names of many African societies have not been standardized. Some were originally written down independently by Europeans from different linguistic backgrounds who inevitably followed their own informal system of phonetics. Since the number of a noun in many African languages is indicated by its prefix (for example, one man is a Muganda, two men are Baganda, the country is Buganda), Africans and their friends may use the plural form to refer to the people or the society, but now social scientists and others prefer the stem alone (in this illustration, Ganda). Local names, furthermore, sometimes compete with a more inclusive term. A famous society in Tanganyika has been called Chaga, Chagga, Dschagga, Jagga, and Wadschagga; and some of the people referred to as Kahe and Meru may be said to belong to the same grouping. In this book the African prefixes are omitted, and the forms adopted by Murdock (1959) have been followed even in quotations that use variants. In the References, however, the original spelling of the author has of course been retained.

For convenience the name of the nation or modern political entity occupied by each society is indicated. Unless the context demands a reference to the former colonial name, the country is the one existing and so officially designated at the end of 1960. "Congo" means the former Belgian colony (République *du* Congo), and not what was once part of French Equatorial Africa

(République *de* Congo). "Sudan" refers to the republic formerly known as the Anglo-Egyptian Sudan or the Sudan, "The Mali Republic" to the member of the French Community formerly referred to as the French Sudan or the Soudan.

The preparation of this study was supported in part by the National Academy of Sciences, National Research Council, under Contract No. DA-19-129-AM-1309, with the Quartermaster Research and Engineering Command, U. S. Army. This formal acknowledgment, though required, is not the least bit perfunctory: the sponsors are heartily and deeply thanked for providing complete freedom and stimulating encouragement. My colleagues in the interdisciplinary venture, especially Paul J. Bohannan and George P. Murdock, firmly and kindly urged me, when at the outset I felt bewildered and wanted to retreat, to carry on this search for boundaries. As a result I did return to Africa; I have surveyed available literature; and I have tried desperately to think. In addition, Professor Murdock has been most generous as a friend and adviser. In the summer of 1959 my stay in Ghana and Togo seemed fruitful to me only because Andrew Taylor and Godfried Mortty were graciously helpful; and so, too, in Nigeria were John W. Court, Haruna Adido Fulani, and Marjorie Lambert Lamond. At Yale University Emily Moore, in the role of research assistant *extraordinaire,* valiantly produced what eventually turned out to be sparkling hunches and rich material. Thomas M. Achenbach gathered, checked, and collated data far beyond the conscientiousness associated with his particular post. Jane V. Olson has functioned as a pleasantly sensible, efficient, and friendly editor. During the final months of the struggle, I have had joyful leisure in the compatible roles of Senior Faculty Fellow and Fellow generously created, respectively, by Yale University and the John Simon Guggenheim Foundation.

L. W. D.

Merano, Italy (Meran, South Tyrol)
January 1961

PROLOGUE

After some effort an experiment had been completed. Fulani school children in Zaria, Northern Nigeria, listened to four pieces of prose and indicated by making marks on paper whether they agreed or disagreed with the statements. Their papers were collected and then, a few minutes later and without previous warning, they were told to recall or try to recall the prose. In two of the pieces, the conclusion came ahead of the supporting arguments; in the other two, the arguments came first and were followed by the conclusion. Two equivalent classes were used so that each of the four statements could be presented under both conditions. The experiment thus sought to determine which of the two orders of presentation would more favorably affect the learning and hence the recall of the material.

A few days later an African official of the Gaskiya Corporation, a government-sponsored publishing house, listened carefully to the description of the experiment. He complimented the investigator and said he considered the problem very interesting. "But do you know," he said, "do you know what we find more important in our work? We never worry about whether we draw a conclusion before or after the arguments. What troubles us is the weather and the state of the roads." When the roads are flooded during the rainy season, he explained, lorries cannot deliver the newspapers of his company, and therefore people cannot be reached. "It doesn't really matter, does it, whether the conclusion comes first or last in an article which people do not see?" he asked.

Position-of-the-conclusion versus state-of-the-weather-and-the-roads—here are two variables from different universes. Ordinarily variables of this type are considered one at a time by assuming, explicitly or implicitly, that the others can be temporarily discounted or at least that they are weighted in a particular way. "Other things

1

being equal" is the conventional phrase that is attached. In this
way it is postulated that people perceive a communication before
a principle pertaining to position-of-the-conclusion can operate;
whether the communication is delivered by a lorry over flooded
or unflooded roads matters not.

There is of course nothing unique about using such a procedure
in the study of communication. Every discipline must restrict its
principles to specified conditions. Generalizations about centrifu-
gal force are not invoked when the body in question is at rest. An
expert on illumination whose advice is sought by management in
order to increase the productivity of workers simply must assume,
before using his knowledge, that the men are neither starving nor
on strike, that they are motivated for some reason to continue
working, and that they are performing operations whose efficiency
may be affected by illumination. His decision that illumination is
a relevant variable must then be empirically verified.

From a broader standpoint, the industrial expert wishing to increase productivity by any legitimate means approaches each new
situation not with a preconception of what affects production there
but with a list of variables which, past experience has shown, may
possibly be relevant. He does not necessarily expect a single factor
like illumination to be critical, but he cannot be certain that it is
not critical until he has empirically investigated the situation. If
illumination is "satisfactory" according to his criteria, he determines the other relevant factors that are operating; if "unsatisfactory," he may concentrate upon illumination alone; if "partially
satisfactory," he may try to alter not only illumination but also
some other condition or conditions.

But when the efficiency expert has a long list of factors like
illumination which *may* be relevant at the moment, he does not
necessarily engage in a prodigious amount of empirical labor to
discover in each situation which ones are critical and which noncritical. For in practice, many or most of the noncritical ones may
be eliminated at a glance: one ascertains quickly, impressionistically, almost slyly, whether a particular factor is in fact relevant
or irrelevant. Has the union been recognized? Is there a retirement
system? Is a bonus offered for increased output? Does some official
listen to the men's complaints? Are there adequate toilet facilities?

Can men park their cars close by? No detailed investigation may be needed to answer some of these questions.

In industry, and in most social situations, not one variable turns out to be critical but rather the interaction of many variables. The importance or the weight to be attached to one variable may affect the way in which the other variables function. If men desperately need money, for example, they may work relatively efficiently under unsavory conditions that otherwise would markedly reduce their efficiency. Here the high weight attached to one factor counterbalances the low weights attached to others. A variable that is sometimes critical may be neglected—that is, given a weight of zero—in one situation but not in another. One group of workers may function effectively even though their attempts to form a union have been frustrated, whereas another may strike unless the union is granted full recognition. In contrast, food is not a factor like the recognition of a labor union, for it can never be altogether neglected. Obviously men must earn enough to eat before they can work at all.

In a multivariant situation, therefore, past experience suggests the relevant variables; the one or more variables that are critical must be empirically determined; some variables may be eliminated at a glance from further consideration; after the general pattern has been appraised, principles that apply to particular variables in that situation can be employed.

The simple anecdote about the African official can now be viewed in much broader perspective. Let us suppose that the problem is to determine whether or not an issue of a newspaper will be effective. From past experience it is known that at least two factors are relevant: the state of the roads over which the lorry must go if the paper is to reach its potential readers, and the position of the conclusion in an editorial. The two variables are of varying importance. The road factor cannot be weighted zero: the lorry must arrive, however late, if the paper is to be read, and it clearly must be read if it is to be effective. The conclusion factor, past experience might suggest, is not critical: its position may possibly affect the precise effectiveness of the editorial, but some readers will be maximally affected and all readers will at least be minimally affected regardless of whether it comes first or last. By glancing at the road directly or by consulting meteorological forecasts, the investigator will know whether the road variable must be taken into account. If the lorry is expected to reach the community, principles pertaining to the position of the conclusion can usefully be applied.

The primary aim of this book thus quickly emerges: to indicate in some detail all the variables that have at least on one occasion affected communication in Africa and hence may do so again. Besides the state of the roads and the position of an argument's conclusion, what other variables are there? The article of faith and methodology should be apparent: unless the boundaries of the problem of communication in Africa—its parameters—have been carefully delineated, it is impossible to know exactly which factors may be relevant or to appreciate which factors can be eliminated by looking empirically at each new situation. What, in slightly different but repetitious words, are the other things which must be assumed to be "equal" before principles can be formulated and utilized? For the moment, therefore, the task is very humble and reminiscent of that of Linnaeus—the location and classification of critical variables.

Even on this level, however, it is possible to point to certain significant implications of the challenge at hand. First, since Africans and other ethnic groups who live in Africa are human beings, generalizations about them must apply in some measure to the rest of mankind. What the continent lacks in the environmental challenges that face people—for example, perpetual snow over great distances—is relatively unimportant. While it is true that environmental and cultural differences elsewhere must modify somewhat not the intellectual scheme derived from Africa but its application, it is well to remember that changing conditions always require some modification even within the nations of a continent, within the people of a nation, or indeed within the same person from time to time. There is nothing unique about Africa as such which demands unequivocally that the search for boundaries be based upon materials gathered there. Africa is the site of the quest because the area happens to interest this particular writer as well as some of the people who have paid his research bills. And yet Africa does have certain advantages that cannot be gainsaid. It is so different from the West that it automatically provides cross-cultural perspective and inspiration. It is so culturally heterogeneous—perhaps more so than any other area of the world of comparable size and population—that it overwhelmingly challenges and stimulates anyone who, literally or through the accounts of others, travels there and then assembles his afterthoughts. Modern mass media are just beginning to function in Africa and hence can be observed as they help change contemporary peoples. Resources and data are usually so sparse that the investigator is forced to exercise ingenuity and initiative, and thus to obtain new insights. Yes, if anyone would insist, the study could have gone on in Asia; but there seems to be no good reason for being apologetic about Africa as the site. The theme, then, is communication in Africa as a way of grasping communication and its problems throughout the world.

The other gain from such an approach has already been indicated: a variable once found to be important in the past becomes part of man's conceptual frame of reference and forever after cannot be completely ignored, even though it may be set aside at a glance. A tentatively definitive list of the variables underlying communication in Africa, consequently, can help to uncover the hidden or partially hidden assumptions that must be made before carrying on or analyzing communication anywhere. In research on communication it may seem more dramatic, for example, to discuss the relation between anxiety arousal and change in attitude; but, the mundane question now is, what conditions must be satisfied before a communication reaches people who then are made to feel or not feel anxious? When the boundaries of an area are located, at the very minimum men of action or research know what to look for.

The present book, in a sentence, searches for the critical variables and then seeks to determine tentatively whether within the boundaries thus established it is possible to include and to cope with many, perhaps most aspects and problems of communication in Africa and hence elsewhere.

The Singularity of Social Situations   This paragraph is set aside from the rest of the chapter and carries its title to emphasize as strongly as possible the following thesis: every communication is likely to involve a somewhat novel pattern of variables and thus to be surprising in some respect. Again and again, the novelist, psychiatrist, or blessed layman stresses the uniqueness of the single person with whom he comes in contact, and then expresses aesthetic pleasure or practical displeasure over that fact. Every natural situation—an ocean, a desert, a plateau, a mountain—also has some unique features or possesses a more or less distinctive operational problem. Likewise each social situation, whether in the past, the present, or the future—whether a slum, a paradise, or closer to the mean—is roughly singular and also unique in some respect. To understand, to analyze, often to survive, on the other hand, it is absolutely essential to be able to perceive regularity through intuition or principles; nobody can or would deny the importance of past experience or generalizations. And yet that experience and those generalizations serve usefully only to reduce the element of surprise, not to eliminate it completely. In social science, for example, almost no finding is ever perfect; in statistical terms, the standard deviation (the measure of variability) most probably is above zero. Except in the laboratory of a very precise natural science, no condition exactly approximates the one which must be postulated to test or apply a principle. The existence of such singularity, it is being argued, is no reason to be discouraged or to justify the trite, bland assertion that you cannot ever be completely "scientific." Of course you cannot be, if by scientific is meant achieving absolute certainty. Some empiricism is necessary to discover, if only at a glance, what variables are likely to be critical. More empirical investigation is needed when the variables believed to be relevant are to be weighted. In addition people, alas, are imperfect, and hence they are likely to formulate imperfect principles and not to include within the boundaries they establish all the variables that should be included. Finally, the best of data in the social sciences or in any area of change grow old, must be continually revised, and consequently at any moment in time are somewhat unparalleled. The fact of singularity should not cause tears to flow, for tears are both irrelevant and useless. Instead the acceptance of the fact enables analysis and practice to proceed more realistically. Other things are never quite equal, and it is foolish to think they can be. Here, at any rate, is the faith that sustains the present undertaking.

The Variables   At a bare minimum at least two factors must be considered in analyzing or understanding communication: the communication itself and the audience, the people who receive the communication. Even for a captive audience, such as children in a school who must perceive a communication, more conceptual tools are needed. Before the communication reaches the audience of students, five stages demand analysis; one begins with the communicator and what he would achieve:

I. *Communicator.* The origin of virtually every communication is a human being, and usually more than one person is involved in the transmission. The teacher in the classroom is the last in a series of communicators. Other people have first given him information: the writer of the textbook he uses, the principal determining the curriculum, the school board sanctioning the school and perhaps deliberately affecting the content and manner of teaching, etc.

II. *Goal.* The communication is delivered to achieve some kind of goal. That goal may be consciously formulated; for example, the teacher wants his students to learn arithmetic. Or it may be quite or utterly unconscious; he wants them to learn arithmetic but, without realizing it, he would also simultaneously assert his own superiority by displaying greater knowledge.

The communicator seeks to attain his goal by means of one or both of the following media:

III. *Basic media.* He expresses himself through media which flow directly from his goals and which are perceived by the audience in his presence. The teacher talks to his students, he listens to them, he praises and he punishes them with words and also by moving his eyebrows and wrinkling his forehead.

IV. *Extending media.* He reaches his audience even though he is distant from them or completely absent. The same lesson can be studied by students outside the class from their own notes and textbooks; or the teacher uses flamboyant or humble audio-visual aids.

The media or medium reaches the audience at some location and is subject to certain regulations:

V. *Site*. The communication arrives at a specific place whose characteristics do or can affect the reactions of the audience. The students hear the teacher in a classroom that has good or bad acoustics and ventilation; they are seated in rows or around a table; their number is large or small. The textbook may be read in class, in a study hall, or at home.

VI. *Restrictions*. For many reasons conditions exist which inhibit or facilitate the transmission of the communication. The teacher rejects what he considers to be a promising pedagogical technique because his students are too immature or the school board too conservative. The perfect textbook remains unsold when the distributing facilities of the publisher break down.

Now the communication—delivered by a communicator to achieve a goal through a medium at a particular site—can be considered in its own right:

VII. *Communication*. The actual contents as determined by some informal or formal method of analysis elicit a certain response. In the classroom, the same sentences, whether they are spoken by the teacher or appear in the textbook, convey or attempt to convey identical information which perhaps can be specified independently of the potential or actual audience. What is in the textbook, the school board asks, before it is adopted for use?

The communicator is ready to communicate to an audience previously affected by momentary experiences:

VIII. *Mood*. Prior conditions produce temporary feelings and responses in the potential audience. Before or after an important holiday, for example, students are likely to be excited and hence not in an especially propitious mood. Temporal factors operate here. How long, for example, is the communication? The teacher knows that he is restricted by the length of a given period into which, therefore, he must fit the specific lesson; but that lesson must also consume a given amount of time—or space—if its essentials are to be transmitted. A substitute teacher, who appears before a class only once or twice, has certain advantages or disadvantages as a communicator which the regular teacher enjoys or tolerates.

At length, it may now finally be presumed, people are exposed to a communication whose communicator (I) seeks to achieve a goal or a set of goals (II) through a medium or media (III, IV) at a particular site (V), in spite of certain restrictions (VI), by means of a message (VII) that reaches them in a specified mood (VIII). What happens then? When communication occurs, the following processes must be differentiated:

IX. *Perception*. The contents of the communication are perceived. The basic problem here is to account for the perception by means of attributes of the communication, the ongoing drives of the recipients, or both. Ordinarily, for example, many forces or groups compete for people's attention; then, after attention has been gained, there are likely to be slips 'twixt the goal or the content of the communication and the comprehension of the audience.

X. *Reactions*. After perceiving a communication and after comprehending its contents more or less accurately, people respond to their new impressions. Predispositions from the past are evoked, and the audience may then grow disturbed or pleased. How can these predispositions be located, how can the ensuing internal responses and processes best be described and analyzed?

XI. *Changes*. The effects of the communication may range from zero to a profound influence upon action. In between are gradations of change that are covert and that may have momentary or subsequent effects upon overt conduct.

One variable remains. So far the communication, as it were, has been cast upon an audience by a communicator and that audience responds or fails to respond in some specified way. To what extent are those reactions communicated to the original communicator?

XII. *Feedback*. The reaction of the audience to the communication is or is not conveyed to the communicator and, if conveyed, is or is not transmitted adequately.

"*Who* says *what*, through what *channels* (media) of communication, to *whom* and with what *results?*" This justly famous statement (Smith, Lasswell, and Casey, 1946, p. 121; italics theirs) has now been extended by adding critical variables that a single sentence cannot be expected to include. The impetus to present a broader, more general approach came from the writer's restlessness during World War II when it became obvious to him that innumerable nonpsychological assumptions had to accompany his previously outlined plan of analysis (Doob, 1935) before success-

ful psychological warfare could be waged. What later emerged
were attempts to make these assumptions very explicit, first by
improving and refining the basic psychological concepts (Doob,
1948), next by outlining what was hoped to be an exhaustive list
of the logically conceivable strategies of psychological warfare
(Doob, 1949–50), and then by adducing the principles behind the
operations of a very practical man, Propaganda Minister Goebbels
(Doob, 1950). An interest in African problems has served to
strengthen the conviction that almost any theory in social science
worthy of utterance must be tested cross-culturally (Doob, 1957c
and 1957d).

The schema of the present book, moreover, has profited from
the lucid analysis provided by Hovland and Janis (1959, p. 4) in
their review of the "major factors in attitude change produced by
means of social communication." Resemblances between their approach and the present one are not accidental but as deliberate as
conscious adoption can be. As investigators, however, they are primarily concerned with establishing an intellectual framework sufficient to embrace data gathered by means of experimentation.
Since experimentation relies rather exclusively on captive audience, they concentrate upon people's reactions and pay little or no
systematic attention to the factors determining whether or not a
communication reaches an audience and the reasons for its particular form and content (I–VI).

The proposed boundaries of communication, the twelve variables, have been put together in the accompanying diagram. The
relation of any one variable to all the rest may be conveniently
noted by the reader either now as he recovers from his first contact with the present cosmic approach to communication or in
later chapters as he wishes to take a bearing in the midst of an
African-type jungle. The arrows on the large circle that go consistently in a clockwise direction signify that ordinarily communication can be viewed as a process which begins with a communicator (I) and ends and then perhaps begins all over again with
feedback (XII). The twelve variables have been arranged in four
groups of three, within each of which double arrows would suggest that interaction occurs. The grouping, though tentative, is
deliberate: most but not all of the important theoretical relation-

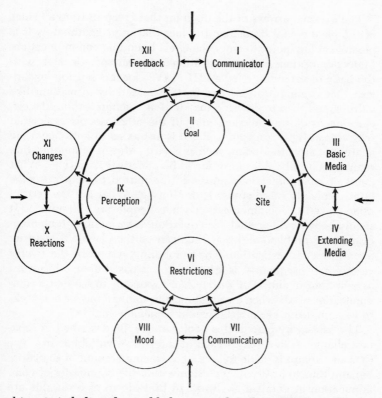

ships, it is believed, are likely to involve the variables within a given group. Quickly and hence a little flippantly, an example can be seized from each trio. The goal of the communicator (II) depends in large part on himself and his position in the society (I) as well as upon what he has learned about the audience in the past (XII). The site at which an audience is located (V) influences the kinds of basic media to be employed (III) and may or may not require extending media (IV). The contents of a communication (VII) are affected by all sorts of taboos or restrictions (VI) and by the mood of the audience (VIII). Whether or not changes occur in people (XI) can be traced to the way in which they perceive (IX) and react to (X) the communication.

The external arrows of the diagram that creep in from all sides of the page would dramatize the fact that most legitimately it is possible at any point to enter the circle bounding communication. Many descriptions of communication in African societies start with the basic or extending media (III or IV); for it is sensible to suggest that communications can be transmitted by a medium like a drum, and then to describe the kinds of communication, the circumstances of transmission, and all the other details associated with this intriguing medium. But it is just as sensible to begin the analysis at any other point, such as X (e.g., Must a communication refer to cultural values in order to be effective?); II (e.g., What kinds of communications must be transmitted to help the tribe hunt elephants successfully?); or VI (e.g., What are the restrictions placed on communication when people are illiterate?). It should be self-evident that each question raises an important, often fascinating problem and that each can be the place of departure for a proper investigation. The numbering system of the twelve variables, consequently, is arbitrary but is based upon a historical assumption: in almost all instances it is possible to see that a communication starts when a communicator, deliberately or not, seeks to communicate because he would achieve a goal.

The expository plan of this book can now be described. A separate chapter is devoted to each of the twelve variables. In every case an attempt is made to give a convincing account of the variable and thus to justify its inclusion within the boundaries of communication. A detailed analysis and breakdown of a variable are provided in order to suggest very concretely the kinds of operational definitions that are required. Communication theories are, or perhaps should be, based upon subcategories like these. The categories and subcategories are numbered and lettered in conventional fashion: upper-case roman numerals for the twelve variables; upper-case letters for the principle subdivisions or headings within each chapter; and arabic numerals, lower-case letters, and lower-case roman numerals for finer distinctions. For the sake of convenient reference and cross-reference, the first three and sometimes also the fourth of these symbols usually appear at the left-hand margin where the category is first mentioned. The main outline is brought together in the Table of Contents.

Almost all subcategories are illustrated by data from at least one African society, in order to demonstrate that, in that instance, the variable is indeed critical. With very few exceptions, the society is located south of the Sahara; in fact, *the word* Africa *as used throughout this book always refers to sub-Saharan or "black" Africa* and hence excludes the predominantly Arab countries of North Africa whose cultures are so different from those found in the south.

The illustrations vary in length and quality for a number of reasons. Some of the subcategories are so self-evident that they demand little or no documentation, whereas others are so murky that details are essential. Sometimes the length depends on available material: it is tempting to be long-winded when you have something to say, or at least something that you yourself consider fascinating, and just as obviously it is better to be quiet when you have little or nothing to report. A number of the illustrations are sheer speculation, as is quite proper in a treatise that would open and not close avenues to future research.

Material on communications in Africa is lamentably scarce, for not until recently has the rubric become sufficiently fashionable to encourage research and reports. Three sources of information have been extensively exploited. First, the activities of missionaries as described by themselves are exceedingly useful: so much of their work involves communication and, being humble and sincere men and women in a noble service, they usually provide revealing and honest documents. Occasionally the impression may be gained that the work of the missionary is being evaluated in a basic way. Such is not the intention. The reasons for the success or the failure of a mission definitely relate to the problem of communication; and these reasons can be induced and analyzed without deciding whether missionary work is good or worthwhile.

The second source of information is anthropology. Often the conceptual outline guiding field work includes categories eliciting data related to communication. Or anthropological data can be mercilessly twisted, as the reader will soon note, to make them relevant. One critical point concerning ethnographies must be raised here: if no reference is made to an institution or a practice in a published report, can one conclude that the institution or practice does not exist in the particular society? Unfortunately, the answer is no, one cannot draw such a conclusion. For the omission may mean not the absence of the institution or practice but the failure of the anthropologist to note its presence. Under these circumstances, it is not possible, with present knowledge, to offer any idea concerning the distribution of communications systems or practices in African societies. One cannot try to associate "talking" drums or public meetings with some other cultural factor until there is adequate knowledge of the societies in which the communication factor and the other cultural factor appear or do not appear. This deficiency will persist until anthropologists and other competent observers spend as much time observing communication as they have kinship and agriculture in the past.

Often throughout these pages the tone in which the data and contentions of missionaries and anthropologists are reported may sound a trifle critical. Indeed, if that is the sound conveyed, then the communication has been deviously successful. But the purpose of the criticism is lofty: to indicate the inadequacies of a report or an observation so that all information about communication can be carefully appraised in the terms here provided and so that better information can be obtained in the future. The present writer insists he is never consciously sadistic, he has liked and also respected many of the missionaries he has met, and some of his best friends are anthropologists. From personal experience, moreover, he knows that data about Africans are likely to be imperfect: arbitrary decisions must be made in selecting the societies to be investigated, truly random samples of African informants can seldom be located (except in schools and in other organizations that provide captive audiences), interviewing and testing demand special patience and skill, and measuring devices from the West are not likely to be suitable or valid without extensive modification (Doob, 1957d; 1960a, pp. 41–8). Current evaluation, nevertheless, must be mercilessly derived from the edicts of scientific method.

The third type of material, statistical and journalistic reports, is viewed with equal skepticism and detached objectivity. Government documents, especially those on so-called community development and fundamental education, are valuable, even though they are written not without some ulterior motive. Anecdotes are cited, not because they may be amusing—and there is nothing criminal about being amusing—but because they too serve the theme that what happens once may happen again. Often these data provide little more than a preliminary hunch concerning the situation at hand. In Africa, however, one must be grateful for the smallest bits of information, and then be prepared to use them as clues or symptoms from which limited inferences can be drawn. The exploratory and hence inconclusive pilot studies of the present writer are noted frequently and at some length: "noted," because they were conducted in order to obtain new insights and to record the difficulties that arise when the experimental method is assayed in field work; and "at some length" whenever they are being reported here for the first time.

The observers of Africa, being so numerous and scattered over time, have naturally adopted no uniform way of reporting their findings. One not picayune stylistic decision has had to be made: whenever possible Africans and African societies are described in the present tense. This tense is the one most frequently employed by anthropologists, except when discussing events before their own arrival in Africa, and hence it requires fewest changes when citing their publications. The practice, whether used by them or anyone else, is misleading if it gives the impression that the observations of a few years ago are still valid and that no changes have occurred in the meantime. Usually it is impossible to state whether the situation being reported has or has not persisted until the present; to do so, another investigation would be needed, and—since there is always some publication lag—an infinite regress soon appears. This annoying point becomes quite crucial when two societies are being compared: the difference or the similarity may be a function of the different time at which the observations were originally made. Perhaps the past tense might be more accurate, but that tense often sounds awkward. "Swahili was spoken in Kenya"—nonsense, it still is spoken. The present writer scrupulously cites the publication date of his sources in the text; hence in each instance the reader himself can hazard a good guess as to how recent the information is, particularly if he takes publication lag into account by subtracting at least two years from the indicated date. The past tense is invoked, however, when a historical point is being made; when an author using that tense is quoted; and when the sensibilities of Africans might be disturbed were the impression to be given that a custom from the somewhat distant past (e..g., human sacrifice) persists into the present.

This Prologue may now be summarized in a rather formal statement: when on one occasion, in the same or in a different society, or in the same or a different context, a particular variable has been shown to play a critical role in communication, thereafter that variable must be at least tentatively explored and can never be completely disregarded. The principle would stir the conscience of anyone concerned with communication. At your peril you disregard one or more of the dozen variables—and, for that matter, the subcategories too. Ideally an investigation of each variable and subcategory is demanded. Actually glancing often suffices to determine that one or more of them is or is not critical in the singular situation at hand.

I. THE COMMUNICATOR

The analysis of communication begins with the communicator since as a human being he usually initiates the process. Of course the source need not be human—the height of mercury in a barometer conveys information. Eventually, however, an interpretation of information from such a source is made by a person who thus transmits the information to himself and often to others.

I.A *Identification* When one man talks to another or addresses a public meeting, it is immediately clear that he is the communicator. But when some very general change in a society has been affected in large or small part not by one communication but by a long series of communications over time, then it may not be possible to identify all the communicators who have been involved. The communications and, except for the end result, the reactions of the audience also remain elusive. In theory the relevant data might have been collected by omniscient investigators; in fact they rarely have been. Thus the communicator who has persuaded a particular African to change from traditional to Western clothes could doubtless be ascertained, but not the thousand and one communications during the past fifty years which really enabled the present communication as the last in the long series to be successful. Communicators, then, can be most easily identified in connection with a discrete communication.

Known communicators may be described in all the ways that can be applied to people anywhere. Sociologically, however, it seems essential to suggest their *status in the society*.

I.A.1 They are male or female, young or old, skilled or unskilled, bright or stupid, members of an upper or a lower group, etc. Relevant, therefore, becomes the entire social structure of their society and their position therein,

17

for obviously people's reactions to them and usually the kinds of opportunities to communicate fluctuate with that structure and position. One set of categories extremely useful for changing African societies and unquestionably applicable anywhere is that of (a) *insiders* and (b) *outsiders*. Insiders are people from the same group as the audience, and any definition of group that has functional meaning within the society may be used. Outsiders do not belong to the audience's group. In Africa insiders are the traditional communicators within the indigenous society and range from chiefs to commoners. Outsiders are of the indigenous type when they come from other communities of the same society or from other traditional societies; or they may be clearly non-African in origin and in contemporary culture or appearance. In the latter category, besides Europeans, are Arabs, Hindus, Moslems, Lebanese, Syrians, Chinese—in brief, people who in Africa are so often grouped together as "Asians" or "Asiatics."

Insiders with comparable technical ability, according to many observers, are likely to transmit more effective communications than outsiders. "It is becoming increasingly important," a conference of colonial officers once concluded, "to produce African films and newsreels (preferably in color) with an African cast or African advisers, for they alone fully understand the Bantu character" (Belgian Congo, 1958a, p. 2). Insiders, the contention is, know their own people and hence can anticipate and later validly appraise their reactions (Doob, 1960a, pp. 125–30). Still, outsiders in Africa often control the powerful mass media that reach, however ineptly at first, larger audiences.

People themselves frequently make the distinction between insiders and outsiders. Europeans, it may be assumed, are almost always identified by Africans as outsiders since they differ perceptibly in so many respects, ranging from skin color to the hallmarks of formal education. Sometimes an effort is made to diminish somewhat their strangeness by fitting them into the prevailing structure of the society, but doubtless the distinctiveness never disappears so long as the real difference in status—and possibly also in physical appearance—remains. A well-liked person is initiated into the clan. Missionaries and government officials are given friendly nicknames like "Father-take-it-easy," "Mother-peace," "Mr. Talks-talks," "Mr. Know-everything," and "Mr. Thinks-first," which thus specify one of their attributes or functions.

Important outsiders in contemporary Africa are Africans who migrate from one area to another in search of temporary or permanent employment. At the new site they are likely to disseminate, through their appearance, their speech, their manners, their actions, and sometimes intermarriage, information concerning themselves and their society. If they return home, they inevitably carry to their kin information from the new locality. According to one estimate, the number of people moving into the territory of the Ganda in Uganda is roughly 100,000 per year; and the contribution of these migrants to the population of various Ganda counties varies from as low as 4 per cent to over 50 per cent. This particular population movement is "from districts with lower earning possibilities, fewer opportunities for cash crop production and, in some areas, more severe communal obligations, to a wealthy country which has developed rapidly and has had land available for settlement." On the whole, however, these migrants remain relatively "isolated" from the villages in which they settle: they lack both status, which depends largely on kinship, and political authority, which stems from descent and land ownership (Richards, 1954, pp. 1, 95, 220–3).

———◆◆◆———

The communicator must also be located with respect to his *position in the communication network:* he may initiate a communication, act as an intermediary between a communicator and the audience, or at first function as an audience and later retransmit the communication he has received. The persons or person beginning the communication at a given moment is the *initiator.* In an ultimate sense no one ever begins anything, for he is always continuing a communication that is part of the social heritage. Pragmatically, however, it is clear that someone, as it were, speaks up, and the conversation goes on from there.

I.A.2

I.A.2.a

Chiefs in very authoritarian societies who initiate most of the politically important communications cannot completely neglect the predispositions of the audience. Traditionally among the Zulu of South Africa, the powerful king did not declare war until he had called together his councilors, most of whom also were leaders of regiments. Without "their advice and concurrence it would have been unwise for even the despotic Zulu king to act." If they disagreed, he summoned "a different lot," for some concurrence was "essential" (Krige, 1936, p. 267). Clearly the initiative to communicate belonged to the king, but he exercised it with some discretion.

I.A.2.b

An *intermediary* retransmits a communication which otherwise cannot reach the audience directly from the initiator; his own role as an audience to that initiator is considered relatively unimportant. The chief's drummer beats the drum but only when the king tells him to do so.

Unquestionably the outstanding illustration of the culturally stereotyped intermediary in West Africa is the "linguist," or spokesman for the chief. In societies with this institution, the chief does not address his followers directly nor do they reply to him at a public meeting. In theory he speaks first, the linguist standing next to him repeats the words to a follower, the follower replies, and then the linguist passes that reply to the chief. It thus appears superficially as though the linguist is superfluous: he tells people what they have probably heard the chief say, and he reports to the chief what the chief himself has heard them say. Anyone who has observed a linguist in action, however, is most impressed with the actual functions that he does in fact discharge.

First the linguist symbolizes the power and sacred character of the chief. He stands as a barrier between a sacred or semisacred man and the nonsacred followers. A chief who is really great possesses a whole team of linguists. The very presence of the linguist thus communicates information to the audience—as well as outsiders—concerning status in the society (IV.B.3.g).

The delay that passage through the linguist introduces into the give-and-take communication between the chief and his followers in the face-to-face situation can be helpful to both parties. Each hears the message a second time and is less likely to misunderstand it. And, while the repetition occurs, each has time to reflect upon his reply (Westermann, 1935, p. 17). Delay may be further increased by the stammer which, according to tradition, some chiefs are supposed to display (Danquah, 1928, p. 41).

Sometimes the linguist may not bother to repeat or paraphrase what the chief has said but merely state, at the completion of the chief's message, a customary epilogue, "So says the king." Usually, however, he is more than a puppet or an intermediary: he rephrases, sharpens, or condenses the words of his superior, or he may inject "some of the celebrated witty and philosophical reflections (which linguists are known for) to the credit of both himself and his chief" (ibid., pp. 41–2). In some societies he may advise the chief during the conversation and even participate directly in the negotiations (Westermann, 1935, p. 217).

The linguist's role of being more than an intermediary may be further extended. He may act as the chief's messenger to minor officials. He may be authorized to represent him in his absence or during an illness. He may be dispatched as a messenger to another chief or subchief and act as the sole negotiator with him. Among the Mende of Sierra Leone he occasionally supports the chief financially; and he may function as the regent chief at the time of an interregnum. In that society, he probably acts as a scapegoat to deflect some aggression away from the man he serves: when people wish to criticize the chief, they may instead impute bad qualities to his linguist, or in any case they are likely to submit their complaints to the servant rather than the master. These functions of a sounding board as well as of a personal adviser are so well recognized that in some areas the nickname of the linguist is "wife of the chief" (Little, 1951, pp. 196–7).

In Mende society another type of linguist acts as intermediary not between people and their chief but between the audience and a woman who is impersonating the spirit of a female secret society in an elaborate dance. The dancer communicates to her "interpreter" a series of signs by means of a whip of stiff grass; hence the audience may in fact be dependent upon the intermediary for the decoding of the message. Like the chief's linguist, the interpreter has more than one function: she watches the dancer very carefully in order to "adjust any disarray in dress which might give away the spirit's human identity" (ibid., p. 252).

Many African societies also prescribe intermediaries in connection with courtship and marriage negotiations. Under what cultural circumstances do particular societies use and others not use such intermediaries? The question is intriguing, but for the moment unanswerable since, the writer feels, data from too few African societies regarding the point have so far been reported. Instead, as frequently happens with anthropological materials at the outset, only a high degree of variability can be demonstrated. First, when does an intermediary between prospective bride and groom (or their families) actually function? He may serve exclusively during courtship: among the Yoruba of Nigeria, the man proposes marriage through "a reliable and interested person," preferably an older woman, whom he selects and then rewards with gin, kola nuts, and money; and she retains an interest in the pair after their marriage (Ajisafe, 1924, pp. 51–2). Or he may act to arrange the dowry after there has been direct communication and agreement between the man and the woman. Among the Rundi, the man proposes "without asking anyone else"; if accepted, he entreats his parents to provide the bride price; and, if they are willing, he sends a "matchmaker" to the parents or closest relative of the girl (Meyer, 1916, p. 106). Finally, the intermediary may carry on both courtship and marriage negotiations. Among the Bemba of Northern Rhodesia, the boy's parents tell an emissary that they desire their son to marry a particular girl; he then conveys the information to the girl's parents and plans the details (Labrecque, 1931, pp. 211–12).

Is it absolutely mandatory to employ an intermediary to communicate the wish to marry? In some societies, it appears, the answer is definitely yes. Among the Kikuyu in Kenya, a boy who falls in love with a girl is not permitted to tell her directly that he loves her or to "display his affection for her in public"; instead the declaration is eventually delivered by one of his best friends in his own age group (Kenyatta, 1938, pp. 165–6). Another observer, however, thinks that in more recent times the boy in that society privately proposes to the girl, and then follows through with a prescribed ritual which includes as intermediaries solely the pair's families (Leakey, 1952, pp. 13–15). In other societies the custom of using an intermediary exists but is followed only under certain circumstances. Among the Ashanti of Ghana, someone else is called in when the girl is too shy to reply directly (Danquah, 1928, p. 146).

Finally, when an intermediary is used, who is he? Again there is no uniformity. His relationship and status may be very formally prescribed; among the Tiv of Nigeria, he is the son of a man who has married into the clan of the man's mother (East, 1939, pp. 112–12). His standing may be indefinite: among the Wolof of Senegal, a friend, a family slave, or a cross-cousin is used (Gamble, 1957, p. 66). Or he may have status not because of lineage but for social reasons. Among the Mossi of the Mali and Voltaic Republics, where the prospective husband may exercise the initiative, the intermediary is "a person who is on good terms with the elders of the girl's village" (Delobsom, 1932, p. 174).

I.A.2.c   Like an intermediary, a *recipient-disseminator* also receives information from the initiator and then retransmits it to the audience, but he reacts to the information he receives before passing it on and alters it somewhat. In fact, no communication ever ceases when once it has affected someone; for that person, until he dies, communicates what he has received in some form, and his own behavior is likely to be influenced by it and to influence others.

Throughout the continent, especially in West Africa, markets are an extremely important institution for the selling and buying of goods. They occur daily, on a definite day of the Western week such as Saturday, or on a regular cycle such as every four or five days. The large numbers of people who come together undoubtedly seek not only to accomplish their economic objectives but also to meet friends and to be generally stimulated by the always colorful and noisy social situation. Most people who attend, therefore, must be considered communicators who receive and also disseminate information. As they report news and express their opinions, they also hear news and opinions from others (see also V.D).

Observers of communication systems in Africa point again and again to the importance of the recipient-disseminator, especially in connection with printed matter. Information concerning communications in various Ghanaian towns and villages, for example, has been collected by a sociologist and his students. The introductory parts to three questions on their schedule are as follows:

> 11. Are there any individual persons in your village who buy books and newspapers and magazines for themselves regularly, but who lend them freely to others who want to read? . . .
>
> 12. Are there certain people in the village who keep very well informed about what is going on in the world and who share their knowledge and information with others? . . .
>
> 13. Are there any places in the village where people gather every evening and where people who read tell other people what they have read in newspapers and magazines? [Drake, 1959]

Usually particular kinds of communication are transmitted through routes that are conventionally and hence well established within a society. On a formal level, for example, the procedure for disseminating news in the West is clear-cut: someone notifies a journalist, he collects the facts and writes the story, and then the story is transmitted through print, radio, or television. The informal mechanisms are often difficult to establish not because they lack a structure but because their very informality makes them less conspicuous and hence less amenable to research. Among the Amhara of Ethiopia, "communication 'by grapevine' is still the major method of dissemination of news, rumor, and entertainment." Feudal lords use a formal mechanism which consists of transmitting written notes through messengers who may be taught a secret musical note so that they can establish their authenticity.

The informal but more popular channel involves people who are members of what the anthropologist calls secondary groups. Members of such groups may visit each other without formal arrangement, they may be called upon to stand personal bond for one another, and they are likely to act as negotiators in preliminary marriage arrangements. As friends they frequently exchange visits to share barley beer and bread, and thus they act as recipients and disseminators of news. Or one man hears a bit of news which he then uses as an excuse for visiting and sharing the beer and bread (Messing, 1957, pp. 487–8, 500).

The way in which the audience rather than the investigator identifies the communicator is an important datum in the flow of communication. For identification influences their opinion of him; the opinion in turn may determine whether or not they receive his communication and then how they react to it. Here is the first link in a long chain.

I.B

Attitude toward the Audience The communicator's attitude toward members of the audience may affect his total behavior with reference to them, including the communication he delivers. They then may glimpse his feelings toward them and be affected by what they observe or infer. Broadly, the *feelings* may be considered (a) *favorable,* (b) *unfavorable,* or (c) *neutral.* The attributes are expressed qualitatively but are meant to suggest points along a quantitative continuum of varying length.

I.B.1

Next among the attitudes of the communicator it seems useful to suggest two kinds of prestige the audience has in his eyes. First, there is their general *prestige as people;* does he, for example, respect them or does he rather feel contemptuous toward them? Three degrees of prestige may be distinguished: (a) *high,* (b) *medium,* and (c) *low.* In most situations, presumably in any society, forms of communicating are affected by the difference in status between communicator and audience. If the speaker has a mighty superior as an audience, his tone will be deferential; he may employ special honorific

I.B.2

terms; and he may even follow different grammatical rules (e.g., her ministers address the Queen of England not in the second but in the third person).

Secondly, people's *prestige as an audience* must be taken into account: does the communicator think them receptive, bright, cooperative? Again the ratings in this respect may be (a) *high*, (b) *medium*, or (c) *low*, also considered to be points along a continuum.

I.B.3

The weights attached to the three subvariables affecting the communicator's attitude toward his audience may be quite independent. He may like them and know that they are important within the society but feel that his message is beyond their technical competence. He may dislike them and still respect them as people and as an audience for the topic at hand. He may even like and doubly respect them, or quite the reverse.

———•———

At this point the first of numerous references to Christian missionaries in Africa is being made, and therefore two introductory notes are struck. These dedicated men and women are so numerous in Africa and represent so many different religions and cultural backgrounds that they cannot be grouped together for purposes of making some generalization, or at least it is most risky to do so. The danger, nevertheless, is occasionally braved in order, on the basis of personal contact and from a reading of their reports, to suggest possible, not certain, trends. Then for easier cross reference and in the tradition of missionary writing, the clumsy but mnemonic device of capitalizing the terms used to specify the trends is employed.

Missionaries seem to have at the present time a Respectful Attitude toward African custom and tradition. "Simply to rue and to condemn questionable amusements," a team surveying mission in 1953 has stated in connection with the enthusiasm toward football that Africans display, "is no answer to the natural human needs which cry for suitable satisfaction" (Bates et al., 1954, p. 71). And yet they would not work as hard as most of them do unless they also believed that African religions must be replaced by Christianity. Even a very liberal critic of missionaries, who in one sentence states that "the task of the missionary is not to destroy native culture but to teach people to consecrate it to the service of God," immediately writes in the very next sentence that "that which is incompatible with the message of salvation must go" provided that it can be "supplanted by something richer and more satisfying" (Nida, 1952b, p. 34). At least with respect to religion, therefore, missionaries admittedly have a low opinion of their audience; theirs is really not a Respectful Attitude but an Attitude of Respect-with-Reservation.

In addition, the attempt to understand Africans is likewise qualified. Missionaries give the impression that, although they sincerely respect all men in their own right and for their divine spark, they show consideration for African beliefs and customs for no intrinsic reason but because they are seeking to locate the predispositions they must utilize in the attainment of their crusading goal. Thus the same team quoted above, after admitting that African boys require "suitable satisfaction," immediately suggests that "camps, festivals, and great assemblies meet with hearty response, and could, with imagination, serve much more widely the purposes of the churches in the community." Elsewhere, they say that "description of Hebrew customs, the sacrifices, the legal provisions" in the Old Testament "entrance many students in the resemblances to elements of African life"; therefore these sections of the Bible provide "excellent points of contact for great teachers" but are also "perils for lesser teachers" (Bates et al., 1954, p. 60). The Understanding being sought is not Pure, it is Useful.

Unquestionably some missionaries would comprehend African values not merely to be able more effectively to combat or to change them but respectfully to help incorporate them into a distinctive African type of philosophy or religion. A student of missionary work considers it significant that it is now "the custom" in Western countries to use the word *communication* rather than *approach* in describing the problems of missions. For "approach," he thinks, "expresses the attitude of the outsider, who tries to find an entrance into an alien world and thus to establish some sort of contact"; in contrast, " 'communication' implicitly confesses a given solidarity, taking one's stand *in* the world and as part of the world *of* the other, not over against that world, howsoever sympathetic this may be meant" (Kraemer, 1956, pp. 60–1; italics his). In fairness to some of the older missionaries, it must be immediately added, words like those just quoted may have a modern twist, but their sentiment is not completely new. "It pains me to witness two very strong tendencies on the part of good men of the present epoch," a member of the Indian Civil Service, interested in missionary work in Asia and Africa, wrote before the end of the nineteenth century, "which I cannot but with all humility pronounce to be erroneous." The first tendency was "the wholesale, and inconsiderate, condemnation of Non-Christian forms of Belief" and the second was "the idea . . . that we have no sooner got rid of these Non-Christian Beliefs, than some form of real Christianity will occupy the vacuum, and the customs, traditions, and familiar notions, of millions of men, will be washed off the slate of the minds of men" (Cust, 1891, pp. v–vi).

The degree to which there is correspondence between the communicator's attitude toward the audience on the one hand and the actual state of that audience, their attitude toward him, or their conceptualization of his attitude toward themselves on the other is a fascinating problem in its own right which will be mentioned more fully under the heading of feedback (XII). At this point it is necessary to emphasize the possible consequences of communicating, subtly or crudely, that attitude to them. In Northern Rhodesia, Africans are reported to have two images of Europeans which correlate very well with the attitudes possessed and displayed by two different groups of Europeans toward them. The first image pertains to missionaries and government officials whose unselfish actions and feelings have given them the reputation of being "benevolent" fathers; the second concerns settlers who in promoting their own interest have an unfavorable view of Africans because they consider them to be either potential or actual economic rivals, or uncivilized "monkeys just down from the trees." One African has said of a European missionary, "He is not a European; he is a missionary" (Powdermaker, 1955, pp. 433–4). Communications from the two groups must be similarly discriminated by African audiences.

I.C   *Capabilities* Communicators differ with respect to
I.C.1   the *resources* they command. At one extreme the
          prototype of the weak communicator may be a small
boy who has only his voice and body to use, and perhaps a pet animal to assist him. At the other end is the strong government information bureau with vast paraphernalia at its disposal. The actual resources of the communicator, to be considered
below in detail (VI.B), consist largely of money or its equivalent,
access to relevant media of communication, and suitably trained
personnel. These factors usually are interrelated but must sometimes be distinguished, especially in Africa. A communicator there
may have ample funds and a printing press, for example, but lack
trained people to operate the plant.

It is obviously expensive to employ modern mass media in order
to reach large audiences. In Africa, as in any area where those
media are just developing, an extremely useful device is the mobile
cinema van. A truck carries to remote communities or regions a
small group of technicians as well as apparatus consisting of a
motion picture projector, a public address system, a phonograph,
a radio, and—to supply the power—a gasoline- or kerosene-oper-
ated generator. In addition to transmitting information straight-
forwardly by such equipment, the unit can serve other functions.
It may be used as a health or veterinary center or as a school to aid
campaigns involving literacy and the improvement of crops. Its
crew may collect as well as disseminate information, such as still
or motion pictures or tape recordings. But these vans are costly
and so "lack of funds hinders their widespread use and development for education purposes" (Film Centre, 1949, p. 38).
Most African governments have official information services
which constitute in large part their communication resources on a
day-by-day basis. Generally each service has press, photographic,
and radio sections that transmit materials either directly to people
through the appropriate media or, more usually, indirectly to privately owned or other government-controlled media, which may
then accept or reject the official or semi-official releases. Some-

times, too, there is a film unit that produces motion pictures for local and overseas consumption. The personnel consists of people who have had practical experience and who, because of the nature of their jobs, are acquainted with the details involved in the mass media of communication, such as the names, addresses, probable importance of those media as well as any changes that may have recently occurred. The bureaus perform a public-relations function for government not only by distributing releases but also by advising officials concerning the statements or speeches it would be advantageous for them to make or the action they should take; and they arrange press and radio conferences for them (Doob, 1953).

For a variety of reasons it may be presumed that the number of mass media will continue to expand in Africa during the next decade and that many or most of them will be established by government or be under government control. The media symbolize to African officials the Western civilization which, for better or worse, is their model. During a transition period when a small elite dominates a newly independent country, power can be retained by appealing directly to large groups of people, or certainly by preventing the opposition from doing so. Then some outlet must be provided for nationalistic, patriotic impulses. Thus the official announcement concerning the creation of a "regional radio service for Nyasaland" by the Federation's station in Northern Rhodesia in the spring of 1960 indicates that "the financial and technical problems involved in establishing a full-scale regional service in Nyasaland are being examined" and that recording studios have already been opened there (Federation of Rhodesia and Nyasaland, 1960, p. 9).

Newly created or expanding organizations seeking to influence large audiences must literally create their own resources. To circulate a new religious journal, its publishers obtained the names of the 300 agents of a daily newspaper already in existence, and then sent them a copy of the first issue accompanied by the request that they become official distributors in their areas (Shaw and Shaw, 1956, p. 33). Outsiders with financial resources can consult a variety of published sources to locate necessary equipment and personnel in an African country. In a "Handbook of Commerce and Industry" that has been "designed primarily for the use of business visitors to Ghana" and published by the appropriate Ministry of Government in 1958, there are lists of companies together with their addresses. Some probably maintain media of communication in order to reach customers (e.g., insurance companies); others, such as newspapers and advertising agencies, are directly concerned with communication. Census figures in a publication of this type are of unknown validity and quite out-of-date; population figures come from a census that was then ten years old (Ghana, 1958). Sometimes, therefore, to obtain the most recent and reliable information, the potential communicator from the outside must conduct his own investigation of available resources.

Americans in particular favor that direct approach and so, when they would found or improve an organization to communicate with Africans, they usually send a team of "experts" on the grand tour. The investigators, accompanied always by cameras and sometimes also by tape recorders and even wives, arrive in Africa frequently knowing nothing more about the countries than their approximate location on the map. They confer with the relevant African and European officials, and thus disturb the smooth functioning of government, education, and industry. Eventually, they issue a report which, however potentially useful, unfortunately is likely to be out-of-date before it is duplicated and circulated privately in a conspicuous manner. A team of experts, constituting the Audio-Visual Deputation of the National Council of the Churches of Christ, for example, toured many African countries and then compiled a document which lists by country the names and addresses of specific missionaries as well as the "mission" and "non-mission" use of audio-visual aids (RAVEMCCO, 1953). The fact that such a deputation was sent to Africa suggests that information so collected was not otherwise available to missionary bodies in the United States and that it could not be obtained through other sources in Africa. Most unlikely in this instance but otherwise all too frequently, American delegations have been known to disregard existing information in order to be sent to Africa on an expense account and thus have, in the glorious phrase that only a country as recklessly wealthy as the United States could afford to coin and then by deed illustrate, their own "look-see."

Aside from the resources of the communicator, it is necessary to know something of his *past experience*, if any, with the same or similar audiences or with any aspect of the process of communication. To a certain extent such experience determines how successful he is likely to be in the future. Part or most of this experience becomes valuable, however, only when there is valid feedback from previous communications (XII).

I.C.2

The importance of past experience is explicitly recognized in many African societies which accord high prestige to older people just because of their age. "In the old days" among the Luo of Kenya, for example, the authority of the elders "was the head and font of power in the tribe, and the exercise and enjoyment of this power became the chief interest of a man's life as his years increased and his sons grew up and took from his shoulders the family duties and cares of his earlier days" (K. C. Shaw, 1932, p. 39). Competent authorities, including the Luo themselves, once advised the present writer to obtain an interpreter who would be as old as possible; older informants, they said, would be reluctant to talk in front of a young man.

Past experience may increase the communicator's actual skill in the use of the mass media to produce change, partially by enhancing his self-confidence: he becomes convinced of his own ability to communicate and he believes more strongly in the objective to be attained. To combat a disease attacking cocoa trees in the Gold Coast (now Ghana), for example, the Community Development Department there first organized courses and trained personnel who thus became well acquainted with the kind of technical information they were to disseminate. Only after achieving competence and confidence did they begin actual work with the farmers (anon., 1955).

Writing under the auspices of the Department of Social and Industrial Research of the International Missionary Council, one critic suggests that missionaries entering Africa have seldom had the correct kind of background and experience for the work confronting them. Instead they usually come from an urban area and have a corresponding point of view and corresponding interests. Then at mission schools "they are trained in the arts, theology, and many of the sciences, but rarely in agriculture," and so they are ill prepared "to give many of the finest elements of Western culture to a people whose main interest and destiny in life is farming" (Davis, 1933, p. 333).

An outsider can infer that a communicator has had successful experience in the past by observing his current operation. Suppose, for example, a communicator a decade ago wished to reach a group of Africans in Northern Rhodesia and Nyasaland through the use of books. He could have observed there a Joint Publications Board which published books only for Africans both in English and in vernacular languages; he could have noted that some of the latter were translations but others were original creations; he might have been impressed, too, with the fact that the books ranged in subject matter from pamphlets on games and songs to grammars and dictionaries (G. H. Wilson, 1950). Obviously, if he could enlist the help of such an enterprise, he would solve most of his communications problems through its organization and experience. At the present time, however, such an outsider would of course have to determine whether the bureau still exists and, if it does, how it now functions.

————◆◆◆◆◆————

The communicator may be characterized in yet another way— the *importance* to him *of his motive to communicate.*

I.C.3   An extreme contrast can be drawn between incidental and dominating motives, between which consequently all motives to communicate may be said to fall. The motive is (a) *incidental* when the communicator, while discharging a traditional or occupational role, transmits a communication as part of the sequence of acts. It is (b) *dominating* when, for reasons associated with his role as socially defined or his personality as it develops, he particularly emphasizes communication. In Western society, the factory worker may talk while working because he is sociable or because he must originate or respond to communications that enable him to cooperate with his fellows, but his principal motive is to perform his productive task. A journalist, on the other hand, is professionally preoccupied with the problem of communicating.

Since the attainment of virtually any goal demands some form of communication (II.A), it seems evident that a high proportion of communication springs from motives incidental to the attainment of noncommunicatory goals. A member of the Mbuti society of pygmies in the Congo communicates news concerning his discovery of a beehive by blowing upon a pipe a tune which imitates the song of a bird (Garlanda, 1957). The communication here is incidental to obtaining and sharing the honey.

Likewise it is easy to find in any society situations in which the motive to communicate dominates. Among the Ganda of Uganda, for example, an early observer indicates the conditions that once prevailed at the court of the king. Before contact with the West and the establishment by the British of a form of indirect rule, his reception hall was the highest court of the land to which chiefs came or were summoned almost daily. In this council "anyone might speak; indeed several people would often be talking at the same time." There, too, "the most weighty matters of State were mixed up with the most trivial conversation, which latter was intended to amuse the court, and to keep those present from being dull." The motive to communicate in such an atmosphere must have been exquisitely central, not only because it was important to win a particular case or to curry favor but also because during these sessions "life and death were treated as of little moment; the king might cause any one of his chiefs to be bound, detained, or put to death at his pleasure" (Roscoe, 1911, pp. 258–9).

Nowadays African leaders in independent countries devote a major part of their energies to communicating with one another and with the general population. Communication is a dominant preoccupation of political leaders in any modern state; this new elite, however, must not only operate the machinery of government but also teach others the techniques and transmit the new values of the changing society. Of course, too, they are not without personal ambitions which cause them to publicize their own virtues. Some of their communication skill they have acquired by being educated in the manner of the West, a type of education that usually deliberately fosters such ability. Indeed one observer thinks they are so "small in number" and "powerful in political character" because "the limitation of facilities for the provision of higher education in British tropical Africa" has given that particular advantage to them and not the masses (L. J. Lewis, 1949, p. 325). The ability to communicate and the capability of doing so, therefore, are coveted attributes.

II. THE GOAL

The primary aim of this chapter is to suggest that communication is involved in the attainment of any human goal. In the first place, what is communicated as such helps people achieve goals, a process hereafter called "instrumental" or "purposive" communication. Hunters whisper instructions to one another as they stalk game. Then, secondly, the striving for and the achievement of the goals themselves communicate information not only to those concerned directly with the goals but also in all probability to a wider audience; and this process is dubbed "consequential" communication. The stalking of game by the hunters indicates to outsiders, for example, that food is scarce. Very deliberately, therefore, communication is being defined most broadly in order to argue, perhaps demonstrate, that diverse phenomena are reducible to the same conceptual schema and thus in one or more respects may be considered conceptually and methodologically identical.

II.A *Types* Admittedly it is exceedingly boring to try to classify human goals, because they are so numerous and because the attempts to do so are legion. Still the unpleasant, trite task cannot be avoided when there is an interest in distinguishing types of communication and when communication itself is re-

II.A.1 ferred to goals. A painless twofold division is proposed.

The first type of goal is called *primary:* it involves the bare survival of people and includes the activities usually referred to as economic. First, note can be made of the *role* performed by communication in connection with such basic goals. A man, for example, sows seeds on his

II.A.1.a land; his goal is a bountiful harvest. He uses (i) *instrumental communication* when he calls his family

36

together to go out into the fields; and while there, he gives them instructions concerning planting or cultivating. Such communication is likely to arise from an incidental rather than a dominating motive (I.C.3): the man's communication is dedicated to the crops, not his audience. Then there is (ii) *consequential communication* as a result of the farming activities. Someone else sees the man and his family walking in a given direction and concludes that they are on their way to cultivate their fields. Whether he simply draws the conclusion or decides to act on the information (for example, by plundering their homes while they are away), that other person is responding to a communication. Or a stranger passes by, notes the cultivated fields, and is able to infer that human beings and not nature must have grown the crops or that one type of horticulture is followed rather than another. The same man may acquire considerable information about the inhabitants by looking into their tool sheds. Here the motive of the original communication, whether incidental or dominating, may be unrelated to the way the activity eventually is interpreted. A scientific discipline based entirely upon consequential communication is archaeology, which makes skilled inferences concerning the behavior of people who no longer exist on the basis of physical artifacts from the past.

II.A.1.b Next, the *nature* of the primary goals can be distinguished by means of a convenient threefold division: (i) *body-sustaining* (food, drink, drugs, etc.), (ii) *body-protecting* (clothing, shelter, etc.), and (iii) *tool-obtaining* (devices through which the body-sustaining and -protecting goals may be attained). Again, these subcategories are neither original nor sacrosanct: they would only serve as aids in the analysis of communication.

Communicating in connection with body-sustaining goals is frequent during hunting since often more than one person participates. A simple illustration comes from the Nkole of Uganda. Traditionally, when a king decided to hunt, he dispatched messengers the night before to warn people of the impending event. The next day hundreds of his followers went out early with their dogs to serve as beaters. By midmorning, accompanied by a number of assistants, he stationed himself in an advantageous position toward which the beaters drove the game so that he could "shoot them with arrows or throw spears at them, or even spear them down if they passed near him" (Roscoe, 1923, p. 162).

Obviously a king need not be the reason for having elaborate instrumental communication in hunting. Among the Acholi, also of Uganda, the head of a clan who exercises ownership rights over the hunting tract communicates to surrounding families his intention to stage a hunt by placing branches from a particular bush in front of a local shrine. Then a meeting is held at which each person is assigned a position on the outside of a great circle, whose diameter may be eight miles or more. As the hunt begins, the men light grass fires to signify the fact that they have attained their positions and are turning inward. The fires also serve the purpose of frightening the animals toward the middle of the circle as its area is gradually contracted. Horns are sounded when an animal is killed, for the prize must be divided in accordance with certain rules: the killer and those who have assisted him obtain specified parts of the animal, and the owner of the tract as well as other people of importance may also demand various cuts (Upper Nile, 1946, pp. 178–81).

According to another account, the fire that is similarly used among the Lunda in the Congo also communicates information to the animals being hunted:

> As soon as the men who were with me saw a column of black smoke billowing up to windward, each set fire to the end of his rope and, turning his back on his mate, ran to the station nearest to him, trailing the burning rope and paying it out as it burned shorter. In a surprisingly short time the circle of fire, several miles in circumference, was complete. The men explained to me that it was very important that the circle should be completed without delay because many of the bigger game were quick at recognizing their danger and, as soon as they saw any smoke at all, rushed for the nearest gap and escaped [Fisher, 1948, p. 36].

The Ganda suggest how instrumental communication pervades the making of an important tool, in this instance a mode of transportation. Traditionally there are two types of boats: one is dug out of a single tree and used as a ferry and for fishing; and the other is made from planks, is much larger, and therefore can carry many more people greater distances. Undoubtedly considerable communication between builders is required as the large trees are felled, as the trunk is dug out with tools or carefully burned for the smaller boats, and as the wood is smoothed and fastened together for the larger ones. Part of such communication must involve mundane requests and responses among those cooperating; and the communication may well be more completely structured when specialists give orders in working on the bigger boats. In addition, certain stereotyped communications are called for in building and sailing. Before a tree may be cut down and work can begin, a medicine man is consulted, for the tree is possessed of spirits and hence must be offered a goat or fowl, and sometimes beer and cowry shells as well. Men must refrain from sexual intercourse during the initial part of the construction; but when the boards are cut and brought to the water, a normal life may be resumed. Boat building thus affects social relations and the communications attending them. When the boat is ready for launching, a shrine for "the spirit of the canoe" is constructed on the shore; a goat or fowl is killed in the boat and its blood, to which beer is added, is poured over the shrine. One of the first fish caught is offered to the shrine. Before a long journey, people go to a god's shrine to seek his blessing. Finally, communication, often through songs, occurs among the dozen or more paddlers of a large boat who must coordinate their labor (Roscoe, 1911, pp. 37, 385–90).

The attaining of primary goals is so important and so time-consuming that it is often accompanied by other forms of communication which are not directly instrumental and hence are of the purposive type to be described in the next section. For this reason many changes in the general communication pattern of a society stem from changes in such basic activities. People in Southern Nigeria, for example, have been consuming more meat, some of which is supplied by Northern Nigeria and by surrounding territories or nations. Most of the cattle are driven to Kano, the capital of the North, after having passed through "the hands of many middlemen until they are purchased by agents of the rich Hausa traders"; then they reach the South by various routes (Birkett, 1952b). The simple, superficial description of the new market suggests innumerable contacts between the Africans who produce, who drive, who purchase, who repurchase, and who eventually market the cattle and meat; and it can be assumed that more than trade is discussed during some of the meetings. And the increased demand for meat has made it all the more necessary to combat the diseases that have ravaged herds in the past. "Cattle immunization camps" have been established to inoculate the animals (Birkett, 1952a). At these camps the herders presumably exchange information and gossip as they arrive, await their turn, and then often remain overnight. Their initial suspicion concerning immunization, no doubt springing in large part from the love of cattle that is so characteristic of people in the area, has been largely overcome by the success of the technique; hence the camps are added to sites (V.A.1) at which communication can occur. In these ways new opportunities for selling cattle have increased communication in Northern Nigeria; and it seems probable that as a consequence of the change herdsmen and traders have become acquainted with additional products, such as those displayed at the great markets of the North, which thereafter they seek. Here, then, is an illustration of the interplay between economic and communicative forces.

II.A.2   The second type of goal sought by people is called simply *social*, for the emphasis is upon affecting other people. The motive to communicate is usually not incidental but dominating (I.C.3). From the standpoint of the communicator, the *role* of such communication could well be called instrumental as previously defined (II.A.1.a.i) but, as a result of its central role, it is honored with the special term of (i) *purposive communication*. The farmer asks his son to fertilize the land in a particular way not only to produce an improved crop (instrumental communication) but also because he hopes that the activity in which the lad engages will somehow either help his character or improve his knowledge of agricultural techniques (purposive communication). No new concept is needed to describe the information conveyed by purposive communication to the outside observer; (ii) *consequential communication* may again serve. The farmer's insistence that his son scatter fertilizer as he himself prescribes may indicate that the man is head of a patriarchal family or that he wishes to crush the child's initiative.

II.A.2.b The *nature* of social goals is indicated by the following classification: socializing, governing, inter-

II.A.2.b.i group, and emotive. *Socializing goals* are involved in all forms of training, such as child-rearing, general education concerning the rules and values of a society, puberty rites, occupational instruction, etc.

———•·•———

The communication announcing the birth and sex of a child may but need not necessarily have some effects upon him. Among a segment of the large Amhara society in Ethiopia, the placenta of a male child is buried inside the house to the right of the door but that of a female on the outside and to the left (Bas-Work, 1957). The child may or may not be told later that his parents adhered on his behalf to the customary practice, but he is likely to assume that they have. No doubt can exist among the Mbuti pygmies of the Congo on this score, it would seem, since there the umbilical cord is buried under a newly planted tree which then becomes the abode of his protector-spirit (Garlanda, 1957). Presumably the tree forever after communicates appropriate information to him and his kin.

The later communications in socialization may be either purposive or consequential. Among the Ibo, near Oron in Nigeria, girls around the age of 15 go through a period of "fattening" which lasts for one to three years. During that time they are placed in seclusion so that they can be given general domestic instruction (Ema, 1940). Unquestionably the communicators must appreciate the fact that they are teaching the girls the proper ways of the society. Bozo children in the Mali Republic, on the other hand, play a game in which one child tries to pierce a hidden target with iron points while one of his comrades does what he can to hinder him (Griaule and Ligers, 1955). The child providing the distraction probably is merely enjoying himself, but as a consequence he is also helping to train his friend to hunt and fish under unfavorable conditions similar to those that will confront him in the future.

The very last ceremony for a person—his funeral rites—not only indicates his death but also communicates other information about him as well as about the values treasured in the society and the postulated nature of the afterlife. A feature characterizing rites in some African societies involves "doing things in reverse, or backwards, or with the left hand." For example: among the Nandi of Kenya, the eldest son puts his clothes on inside out after the death of his father; among the Soga of Uganda, men and women dress in the clothes of the opposite sex; in Dahomey, dances at a funeral are performed anticlockwise. Perhaps, it is thought, the practice results from the belief that in the afterlife the usual order of things is reversed (Jeffreys, 1949b). If this is so—and the theory sounds much too simple—then the symbolic actions during the funeral serve to reinforce and sustain that belief among those witnessing them.

II.A.2. b.ii   *Governing goals* refer to practices whose aim is to enforce the regulations learned for the first time during socialization; the communicator or the enforcing agency may thus be the political apparatus of government in a very formal sense, a smaller unit such as a clan or a peer group, or indeed the community as a whole which is sometimes vaguely called "public opinion."

In various ways the facts and subtleties of a society's structure are regularly communicated to people. Rites attending circumcision, for example, may serve such a function. Among the Soruba in Dahomey, the young men about to be circumcised are brought before a central altar where "elders arrange them in ritually prescribed positions, according to the order of seniority of their lineage within the clan, and of their family within the lineage." Only on this occasion is the clan's hierarchy thus "reproduced in its entirety"; even at a funeral mere fragments of the clan assemble. Those being circumcised undoubtedly can fully grasp the information thus being communicated to them, for they are not children but adults around the age of twenty-five. Their learning is further reinforced by the fact that they undergo the unforgettable "bloody rite" in an order that strictly follows the same hierarchy: the climax of the ceremony comes at the end, when the man who belongs to the oldest family of the oldest lineage is circumcised (Mercier, 1951). The others present at the rite also have an opportunity to observe the hierarchy and thus to be impressed once more by the way in which their society is structured.

Attached to rules governing behavior, it would seem likely, are modes of communication that supply appropriate rewards for obedience and punishments for disobedience. When a society fosters virginity for unmarried girls, the question might be: Is there a system of communication that informs relevant people whether or not a girl at marriage is in fact a virgin? Among the Luo in Kenya, a marriage is consummated in the presence of witnesses, though without orgasm. Immediately an examination is made of the man's genitals for traces of the hymen. If they are found, the bride's sister shouts the tidings to a singing party of girls who have remained outside the hut; that party then enters and beats the groom, saying, "You have killed our sister." They and the young men sing together all night. The next morning they return home, singing and carrying the hymen. Finally, they enter the bride's homestead and throw ashes toward her father and mother (Evans-Pritchard, 1950, p. 134). This account obviously reveals a considerable amount of communicating which, among other things, publicizes the bride's virginity and hence the value of the governing regulation. It almost looks as though the Luo seek deliberately to communicate warnings to unmarried girls to remain technically intact. In this instance the speculation receives informal confirmation from the fact that the Luo hold a complete marriage (one in which a child has been born) in such high esteem that it is continued, as it were, after the death of one of the partners by means of the sororate and levirate.

In other groups valuing virginity, information about the bride's condition may be communicated in less violent ways, as three societies in Nigeria indicate. Among the Hausa, the husband who discovers that his bride is not a virgin proclaims "her shame to the entire town by breaking a pot outside the house." Among the Yoruba the man sends white cowries to the girl's mother if he finds her "chaste," discolored ones if not. Among the Bolewa the message to the mother which signifies virginity is "a gift of sheep" (Meek, 1925, v. 1, pp. 188–9).

Communication plays a major role in the use of social sanctions to enforce customary ways of behaving, first because the nature of the offense must be made known to members of the group and, secondly, because one of the punishments, social ostracism or social disapproval, involves in effect the withdrawal of communication or the use of a communication which itself is punishing. Among a group of pagan Nupe in Nigeria there is a "semireligious" institution through which disputes are settled. A husband may complain of his wife's conduct at a meeting in the chief's house and ask that she and any other wrong-doer be taken to task. If they are found guilty, a chief's representative "mounts on stilts and appears among the people after dark, proclaiming their evil deeds, and receiving propitiary offerings of goats and fowls" (Temple, 1922, p. 331). Among the Kikuyu of Kenya a neighbor who does not help in the construction of a house or kraal which, according to tradition, must be started and completed within a single day, finds himself "socially boycotted for his individualistic attitude." It is said, too, that a Kikuyu youth, in engaging in premarital sexual play with a girl, does not dare try "to loosen her garments during the night" when they are together: if he does, the girl "generally reports the matter to all her friends in the district, . . . the matter is taken to the age-group meeting," and the man "would be ostracised by his friends and would be debarred from having [a similar sexual experience] with other girls, as they would not trust or have confidence in him" (Kenyatta, 1938, pp. 78–9, 160).

II.A.2.
b.iii

Intergroup goals are really special forms of governing goals that involve groups clearly recognized as outsiders. The out-groups may range from the family in the neighboring hut to a nation overseas. The activity, correspondingly, may include a simple visit or a complicated war.

The formal provisions of a society for receiving visitors and strangers affect the kind of communication with outsiders. Among the Nkundo of the Congo a traveler seeking shelter allegedly hears the following hospitable communication from his host: "Here is your house; here are your wives." The greeting is not perfunctory, for the wives indeed are said to be turned over to him temporarily. If the host is monogamous, he nobly "leaves his house and his spouse at the visitor's disposal and goes to bed elsewhere alone" (Hulstaert, 1938, p. 33). Among the Ashanti in Ghana, hospitality, and hence suitable communication, is given "on the strength of membership in the same clan" (Busia, 1951, p. 86); such a practice characterizes many other African societies. Ashanti hospitality, which includes both food and lodging—but no temporary wife—is summarized concisely in a proverb: "When the porcupine is going to visit the porcupine, he does not take any food with him" (Rattray, 1916, p. 69). The Ganda in Uganda believe that any passer-by who appears while people are eating must be invited in and asked to share the food: "the proverbial height of meanness is that of a person who provides against this contingency by eating behind closed doors." At almost any time of day, moreover, a Ganda visitor traditionally receives some food either to eat immediately or to take away with him (Mair, 1934, pp. 22, 137).

Wars too have their forms of purposive communication. Moslems in Northern Nigeria who formerly fought among themselves customarily warned their enemies of an attack in advance, for a sudden surprise was considered "an unfair trial of strength." It almost looks as though such communication may not have occurred with complete enthusiasm, since "often" the messages were phrased in metaphors as if to conceal their meaning somewhat without succeeding completely in doing so. "The chief of Dadui may get some puddings ready, and we shall bring him milk to mix with them and all partake together," the Fulani once said in a message just before attacking that chief. He replied, "If you are men, come, for I have meat all ready. Bring the sauce and we shall eat together" (Meek, 1925, pp. 300–1). Then, after that outburst of mildly coded psychological warfare, the battle began.

	The fourth and final type of social goal is called
II.A.2.	*emotive:* these goals involve the sometimes vague but
b.iv	clearly important impulses concerning his feelings,

ideas, philosophy, status, etc. which the individual himself would express or have others strengthen and which appear to bring immediate satisfaction in their own right (cf. Ogden and Richards, 1936, p. 149). They range from simple courtesies that are spoken when acquaintances meet to protestations of eternal love or hate.

A very personal communication of the emotive type may be expressed through a special medium like poetry or through a particular communicator like a troubadour. Among the Yoruba in Nigeria, each person has his own praise song with which people greet him on special occasions. Cult groups there also have songs which use distinctive tone qualities produced by the human voice (Beier, 1956).

The "safety-valve" feature of some institutions in any society is a clear-cut illustration of a function that emotive communication can perform. The headman among the Fort Jameson Ngoni in Northern Rhodesia, for example, has innumerable responsibilities to the chief and the administration on the one hand and to people within his own village on the other. To satisfy those superordinate to himself, he frequently if inadvertently evokes the hostility of his subordinates. Ordinarily villagers do not express their hostility, but supress it until a culturally approved occasion arises. During a ceremony at which the deputy of a new headman is installed, they seize the opportunity to rid themselves of the repression by stepping forward and hurling accusations and insults at the headman: "Now you tell lies here . . . and you often brew and do not give beer to the people." After being thus overtly aggressive, the villagers symbolize their guilt, perhaps, by contributing a gift to the headman (Barnes, 1949, p. 105). Presumably, these people thus voice disapproval of their leader and simultaneously also their willingness to obey him; hence the emotive satisfaction derived from communicating hostility in an ambivalent manner makes them more cooperative citizens.

The emotive function of magic is sometimes easy to comprehend, at other times more elusive. The medicine man in a society must be a communicator with prestige, for otherwise he would not be consulted. The audience seeks the goal he would help them attain, but evidently requires from him an emotive increment. This personage among the Sukuma in Tanganyika gives a potion to a lover and says, "If you have executed my orders exactly and if you used the medicine as I told you, the girl will not resist your courtship. Now go and look for the girl; do not be afraid of her; she is under the spell of the medicine." A man receiving such a communication under these circumstances is likely to have his "self-assurance" improved, and this change alone may bring him success. Likewise the audience in the same society must feel favorably disposed toward the medicine man who asks their ancestors to produce rain; in this instance the approval may not prove efficacious in fulfilling the wish but may bring temporary, emotive solace during the drought. In fact he uses a cautious phrasing, which may or may not be noted by the audience: "Now bring plenty of rain, so that we may all recuperate, corn and cattle may thrive, and men may have children" (H. Cory, 1949, pp. 25–6).

Some emotive communications seem to be rather unemotional reflections of people's hard-won philosophy. A bishop of the Methodist Church reports hearing a congregation in Africa sing its own slightly revised version of Handel's Hallelujah Chorus. The original line, "He shall reign forever and ever," has become, "Nobody works like Him" (Ledden, 1959, p. 3). Such a change means perhaps that the Africans have difficulty understanding Handel's thought, or—more likely—that they see fit to project upon Him an attribute considered most important among themselves, the ability to work and work.

Finally it must be emphasized that emotive communication may occur in connection with primary goals. Men commonly stage festivals of thanksgiving when the harvest is in, as they do in the region of the Upper Volta (Arnould, 1949). They thus react to and inter-

pret their own deeds which under propitious conditions represent
the attainment of a primary goal; they use consequential communication to celebrate the victory.

————◆••◆————

As this section concludes, the tentative nature of the discussion
concerning goals must again be emphasized. At the very least, attention has been called to an important problem, that of finding
the goal in any communication. When it is asserted, as government
information bureaus often do, that their goal is communication as
such, language is being abused or used stealthily. For communication serves some purpose, and in this instance presumably communication occurs on a wide scale in order to induce an audience
to believe in the communicator's impartiality, his generosity, or
some trait that he would advertise.

Intention So far no clear-cut distinction has been
made between the conscious goal of the communicator and the goal which he in fact seeks or manages
II.B
to achieve by means of the communication. Person A
praises person B. If the praise be considered a form of purposive
communication, then A may or may not be fully aware of what he
is doing. In the first instance, his goal may be the ostensible one
of conveying a message that will please B; in the second instance,
he may "really" wish to injure B but, since he does not recognize
his own hostility, he transmits sweet words in order to continue to
conceal that hostility from himself and perhaps too from B. Next,
if A's deliberate goal is to praise B, his actual communication may
or may not be successful (IX.D.1). For B may receive the communication as praise or as idle flattery. Finally, if A's praise and
B's reaction are viewed as a form of consequential communication,
once more the goal achieved may or may not be the one deliberately
sought by A. Thus the communication might convey to the by-
stander the existence of a friendly relation between A and B—and
A as well as B would concur. Or it might suggest to him that the
people of this fair land prefer to engage in empty talk rather than
to prepare for a nuclear war. Poor A, poor B: their simple conversation has certainly now been made to appear hopelessly complicated.

Actually, though, nothing too complicated is proposed, for the discussion may be quickly brought to a climax by stating that in any communication there can be two types of goals, intended and unintended. By *intended goal* is meant the one which motivates the communicator and which he can report to himself or to others. The physician advises his patient: there is no trace of sadism in the communication, he truly wants him to get well. Ordinarily most communication is thought of as being dedicated to an intended goal. At the other end of the continuum is the *unintended goal*, which must be postulated, it should now be evident, in order to be able to take into account not only unconscious motivation but also many instances of consequential communication. The present writer has previously suggested that the unintended consequences of propaganda (a nasty word now replaced by the fashionably more attractive and broader term "communication") are frequently much more important than the intended ones (Doob, 1935, pp. 71–89; 1948, pp. 245–50). There may possibly be a relation between the communicator's motive for communicating (I.C.3) and his intended goal. If that motive is dominating, the communicator may be more sensitive regarding both the goals he would achieve and those he unintentionally attains; but then again his very zeal may make him overlook some consequences of his own communications.

II.B.1

II.B.2

————•————

Goals, conscious or unconscious, are never easy to ascertain even with the communicator present. The laboriousness of psychoanalysis and other psychiatric techniques bears witness to this sad or happy circumstance. The difficulty increases when the communicator cannot be examined directly and also when the communication is culturally stereotyped. The Nyakyusa of Tanganyika enjoy spending some of their evening hours spinning riddles; mothers and grandmothers specially favor them because they think they foster the intelligence of children (Busse, 1957). From such an ethnographic account it is impossible to say whether riddles are liked for educational reasons or whether, being liked for some other purpose, they are said to serve an educational objective. Indeed the intended goal of some who pose riddles may be sheer amusement, and for them the pedagogical function is unintended.

Among the Mende in Sierra Leone, the junior wife of a man uses a number of symbols to communicate the fact of her pregnancy. She wears a piece of "white shirting" about three yards long; she attaches to her clothes a bell; she always carries a knife. Why does she do these things? One can only guess from the ethnographer's account that, if asked point-blank, she would provide a supernatural explanation: a soothsayer has advised her to use the cloth, the bell warns off spirits, the knife symbolizes the fact that she is now regarded as a warrior. And yet it seems evident too that, intentionally or not, this junior wife is communicating information about herself that has other goals. The pregnancy brings her more respect; if people do not observe her pregnant condition directly, the shirting, the bell, and the knife will inform them. Maybe, furthermore, potential lovers must be made aware of her condition, and her husband must be dramatically reminded of it, since intercourse with a pregnant woman is taboo (Little, 1951, pp. 132–3, 147). Thus, if these interpretations are correct, the expressed intentions of the woman may not indicate all the functions the symbols actually perform.

In apparently marked contrast to the sweet naiveté of the junior wife among the Mende who may be unable to verbalize the goals she achieves are the words spoken or written by modern technicians when they discuss their plans for carrying on public relations or information programs. Slick, self-conscious formulations of goals are well known in the West both in industry and government; they are now beginning to appear with increasing frequency in Africa. The professional communicators of a large oil company operating in West Africa have stated their objective as follows: "To communicate the significance of oil to a developing society; to prove the identity of [the company] with, and its determination to serve, all that it properly can in African emergence; to demonstrate its desire to foster the scientific approach and spread technical information towards better living." Of course no official of the corporation would deny that the more general goal behind the subgoals so beautifully clothed in flowery phrases is to remain in business and to sell oil at a profit. He would also agree no doubt that the organization favors a particular kind of social order and that he himself has his own reasons for working in Africa, for seeking status and position within the company, and so on.

Communicators who are self-consciously aware of the goals they intend to achieve are also likely to locate a prospective audience most deliberately. The memorandum of the oil company suggests that, to achieve its subgoals, "the educated population as a whole should form the main target during an initial period [for two reasons]: first, their growing power to mould decisive opinion in an Africa whose field of choice in external associations is inevitably widening; second, their tendency to concentrate in centers of education or industry where they are accessible physically as audiences." And then a few pages later the analysis coolly notes a danger in working exclusively with the elite: "the peasant as well as the proprietor" in West Africa is acquiring the right to vote, and may be offended if the company concentrates exclusively upon educated people. For this reason, it is also recommended that "the mass audience or selected sections of it should be regarded as an important objective of a later phase."

Similarly a self-conscious communicator deliberately seeks the kinds of communications that will achieve his goals. In some instances, however, a very special problem arises: the communications themselves are so intimately linked to the goals that they cannot be altered even when feedback (XII) subsequently reveals that they are not so efficient as they might be. Here is the ancient struggle between means and ends which in Africa occurs frequently in the field of missionary activity.

Missionaries of course are acutely aware of their intended goals: Africans must be saved first by being converted, subsequently by following a way of life and a form of worship in accord with the rules of the particular church. The new religion, however, is accompanied by communications that are alien to Africans; regardless of their Attitude toward, and their Understanding of, their audiences and regardless too of their own backgrounds (I.C.2), these religious communicators must decide the extent to which modifications in the ritual they advocate are desirable or necessary in order to achieve essentially spiritual ends. Is their communication policy one of Flexibility or Inflexibility? Opinion among them, according to an African sociologist, "is sharply divided on the question of Africanizing Christian worship." Opponents of Africanization wish to avoid "a return to African paganism" from which their converts have been ostensibly saved, but the proponents believe that "if Christian worship is to mean anything to the majority of African Christians, it must not be presented and practised in a *foreign* garb" (Nketia, 1958, p. 59).

Hymns and church music suggest the problem in more concrete terms. Christian worship permits music, but what form should that music take in African churches? The music and the words to the songs can be left unchanged, and frequently are. Obviously, with such a technique little is then communicated to the African audiences. Translations of the words are difficult, the same sociologist points out, because African languages do not have the Western metrical forms: those now used, consequently, sound like a "peculiar hymn language" which Africans accept "as a special ritual language of the Church." Then Western melodies ignore two features of African songs: the imitation of the rhythm of speech and of the intonation of words. If special music in the African manner were permitted inside a church, percussion instruments, especially drums, would have to be substituted for the organ or piano. For Africans, however, drums mean bodily movements, "from simple wagging of the head to vigorous dancing," which form of emotive communication obviously cannot be tolerated in a Christian church: "I am concerned with its propriety for worship rather than with its cultural value" (ibid., pp. 62-3). What, then, should be done? The proposed solution is not a Flexible compromise but one demanding rather Inflexible adherence to the intended goal of the church. "Much experimentation will be required before new patterns are established," the writer says somewhat vaguely; even then, such experimentation "should be encouraged outside the church," so that "the regular period of worship will not be disturbed" (ibid., p. 64).

The case for Flexibility is not new; years ago, for example, the wise explorer and administrator, Sir Frederick Lugard, called for a different approach to missionary work:

> Is it not possible . . . to introduce some measure of adaptation in the teaching of religion by selecting those qualities

in the African mind most in harmony with Christian ethics, and such tribal traditions as have in them a nucleus of good, grafting upon them the cuttings which shall bear a better fruit? . . . In such matters as do not affect the vital principles of Christian ethics, the religion of the temperate zone and of a civilized environment might be relaxed in its adaptations to the tropics and conditions of African life [Lugard, 1926, pp. 152–3].

The Attitude of Respect-with-Reservation bursts out: "In such matters as do not affect vital principles of Christian ethics."

Some observers of missionary activity feel that the Inflexible Policy of adhering rigidly to Western forms within the church stems from a "superiority complex." This means, one missionary says, that "consciously or subconsciously we know that we inherit a superior civilization" and hence "we are anxious to share with others the benefits we enjoy." In the long run, therefore, "we expect our converts to conform to our mode of life, to adopt our institutions, our conventions, to worship God with our form of ritual, and to take over our architecture, our music, and even perhaps our language." This particular critic lashes out against such a view; he believes that "Christianity and our civilization are not identical" (E. W. Smith, 1946, p. 15).

There are mission groups, therefore, which deplore the Inflexible Policies of their predecessors. Whether or not Flexibility produces or results from a more Respectful Attitude toward Africans need not be debated here. Rather it seems perfectly clear that such groups stand ready to alter radically many but not all of the communications which might attract their audience into the fold. They utilize the modern mass media in behalf of Christianity, as a brief survey here indicates.

> With the peoples of the world becoming increasingly aware of their national and cultural heritage, Christianity must be presented, stripped of its "Western packaging." For centuries Christ has been painted as a Westerner. Many of the teaching pictures used in African Sunday schools show a blue-eyed Jesus surrounded by blond children.

The quotation is taken from a descriptive leaflet of RAVEMCCO, the Radio, Visual Education, and Mass Communication Committee

of the Division of Foreign Missions of the National Council of the
Churches of Christ, an organization whose long list of supporting
organizations begins with the African Methodist Episcopal Church
and ends with the Young Women's Christian Associations. To de-
Westernize Christianity and also simultaneously to stimulate and
reinforce missionary activity, this group fosters both research in
and the use of audio-visual devices throughout the areas where
the missionaries of its sponsoring organizations normally function.
The training of "national Christian leaders" is accomplished either
by bringing outstanding Africans to the United States or by establishing courses in African countries. Special films and filmstrips are
produced and suitable ones are noted and promoted. Here is the
organization's description of a filmstrip of 26 frames called "The
Prodigal Son in Africa":

> Using drawings set in modern Nigeria, the strip interprets the
> words of Luke 15:1, 11–24. The son (in singlet and shorts)
> leaves his father (in Yoruba robes) and travels (by bus) to
> a city, where he spends his money on modern luxuries and
> entertainments. After his period of destitution and laboring
> on the land, he returns and is welcomed by his father, who
> prepares for feasting.

The same catalogue says, in part, concerning the "use" of this strip:

> The strip is HIGHLY RECOMMENDED for use in most parts of
> Africa and, with suitable explanation, outside Africa. . . .
> Possibly the most effective way of using [it] is to follow the
> short script, utilising only the words of Scripture. . . . A de-
> tailed talk at the end is probably preferable to attempting
> to elaborate the story as originally told [Hubbard, 1959, p. 27].

The other medium of special interest to RAVEMCCO is radio.
In a letter of May 20, 1960, asking missionaries and others in Africa
to fill out a questionnaire concerning radio and religion in each
area, the following goal has been declared:

> Mission leaders in America stated at a recent Consultation
> on "The Church's Use of the Mass Media Overseas" that the
> Church must use the broadcasting opportunities "if the in-

creasing world population is ever to hear the Christian Gospel, and if Christian 'thought' leaders (persons influencing the ideas of others) are to be able to communicate with their non-Christian countrymen."

The Sudan Interior Mission owns and operates Station ELWA, located in Monrovia, Liberia, which reaches wide areas of the continent because of its very high power, 50,000 watts. The writer has listened frequently to the station and has the impression that the "packaging" of the Gospel is completely "Western." Perforce the language used is English—or sometimes French—but most of the speakers are Americans or from the United Kingdom and present as orthodox and hell-fire an approach to Christianity as if they were talking to people in the hills of Tennessee or in Hyde Park, London. Only the media, not the communications which serve the Lord's purposes, have changed.

This particular section on missions has been adducing, it should now be evident, material which inexorably leads to the posing of an unanswerable question: when the Serpent of modern media is thus encouraged to enter the Garden in which missionaries toil, must not an unintended consequence be the changing of the intended goals which have always been sought and sometimes achieved?

III. BASIC MEDIA

A communication from a communicator to an audience is transmitted through a medium in which a message from the former is encoded in such a way that it can be decoded by the latter. Any event, object, or device whatsoever, therefore, can serve this purpose, provided that at least one person, the audience, has learned to attach some significance to it. The event functioning as a medium may be one over which both the communicator and the audience have no control, as when it is established that the battle will begin the moment darkness sets in. In common parlance a dark cloud conveys to a person information concerning pending rain; actually there has had to be a human communicator in the past to give meaning to the phenomenon—perhaps the man himself who does the interpreting, more likely people in his society long dead whose wisdom in this respect was transmitted to him by his parents while he was a child. In consequential communication, furthermore, there may be little or no congruence between the significance attached to an event by the original communicator and the one now attached to it by the audience. The most casual observation of spoken language immediately suggests that all the sounds of which people are capable, including clicks and tones, may be used to convey information. The number of media and the use to which they are put, consequently, are almost unlimited.

A straightforward distinction among media must be clearly stated at the outset in terms of the communicator's location with relation to the audience: he may be present, distant, or absent. When he is *present,* he is heard, seen, touched, or smelt directly by the audience; the prototype here is the everyday give-and-take situation in which people converse with one another directly. When he is *distant,* he is present during the communication but, since he cannot be perceived directly, one or more of his attributes are not transmitted; the man's voice is heard through a megaphone, telephone, or radio without his being seen, touched, or smelt. When he is *absent*, he also cannot be perceived directly but one or more of his attributes can be; the words come from a tape or a newspaper. The distinction here is based upon the actual state of affairs, not the conceptualization of the audience. The listener who knows that the voice on the tape was recorded months ago may forget that fact by becoming absorbed in the performance, or the one who has not been told that the voice on the radio is taped may think the communicator less distant than he actually is—in either case the communicator is factually absent.

The media employed by the communicator who is present shall hereafter be called *basic media,* for a profoundly simple reason: they are the original modes of communication between an infant and his mother or any of the human beings in his surroundings. Throughout life, too, the words, the gestures, the clothes, and the actions of a person all convey information and can be directly perceived by others in face-to-face contacts. Media which do not demand the actual presence of the communicator are herewith baptized *extending media,* for what they do is to extend the range of the original message in time or space. A special type of extending medium is a *channel* of communication which by itself transmits no message other than that contained in a basic medium or in another extending medium. Suppose I would have you eat prunes for breakfast. I use a basic medium: I tell you to your face to do just that. I use an extending medium: I leave a note for you which contains the important message. I use an extending medium that is a channel of communication: I telephone you about the prunes. I use two extending media, one of which is a channel of communication: I write out a message which is telegraphed to you. The relation between these terms and another term in common use, viz., *mass media,* must be mentioned to complete the nasty task of definition. Mass media like the press and radio are extending media, but not all extending media are mass media: my advice over the telephone about prunes, be assured, is directed to you, not the whole country.

———— • • ————

These fine distinctions become quite useless if inadequate data are reported. The following information concerns the Ashanti of Ghana:

> In every village the commoners had an association of their own. They did not hold regular meetings, but whenever any matter of importance was discussed by the elders, *it became known* and was talked about. The commoners would meet to discuss such matters [Busia, 1951, p. 10, italics added].

Undoubtedly only basic media are involved here: news of the elders' discussion must have been spread by word of mouth. It is conceivable, however, that the commoners may have established some sort of channel in order to transmit the news efficiently. One person might be delegated to inform a specific person, the latter would have the responsibility of transmitting the message to a third person, etc., until finally the commoners assembled. In the above quotation, therefore, the statement, "it became known," is unclear.

———————— ◄••••► ————————

Basic media are discussed in the present chapter, extending media receive their comeuppance in the next chapter. The attributes that can be utilized to characterize both kinds of media will first be quickly specified, after which the media can be examined. The number of the media in both chapters ought really to dispel the erroneous notion that speech and writing are the only or the really important ones and hence also to extend perspective.

	Attributes In analyzing a medium in a particular
III.A	context the first attribute to be noted is the actual *relation between the basic and the extending media*.
III.A.1	Three categories are involved: basic medium, extending medium that is a channel, and extending medium

that is not a channel. Since any one of the three can either be present or absent, eight logical possibilities arise: $2 \times 2 \times 2 = 8$. In fact, four of the eight can be quickly eliminated because they are incompatible with reality as here defined in a situation in which communication actually occurs: all three simultaneously present *or* absent; only a channel present with the others absent, or only a channel absent with the others present. The four remaining combinations, then, are the following (a √ means the medium is present, an x that it is absent):

	Basic	Extending	
		CHANNEL	NONCHANNEL
1.	√	√	x
2.	√	x	x
3.	x	√	√
4.	x	x	√

The above schema may prove useful if two operational points are made explicit. When a given communication is directed to different audiences, one or more combinations may occur. A man talking to a small committee is using only the basic medium of speech(no. 2); if simultaneously his words are broadcast by radio, the basic medium of his speech also goes into a channel (no. 1); if a copy of the speech is read later by someone, the extending medium of writing functions (no. 4); and if that speech is printed by the press, again the same extending medium is used but this time through an established channel (no. 3). Secondly, it is quite possible to discuss and analyze a medium out of context without reference to the above combinations; thus, although radio is used as a channel only to transmit from basic media and as such conveys no information except as a consequential index of the society in which it functions, its problems as a channel can be portrayed in their own right. In this and the succeeding chapter, consequently, the media are discussed one at a time as if they were operating alone, the way the basic medium does indeed operate in no. 2 and the extending in no. 4.

The remaining four attributes are presented as dichotomies in order to speed up the exposition, but the division in each instance should be thought of as extreme points along a continuum. Each medium, then, has some kind of *relation to reality*. Reality is deliberately left undefined, except to state that the criterion to be used in the analysis of communication is not metaphysical but is the referent of the message conveyed by the medium. Thus the object that in

III.A.2

English is symbolized by the vocal vibration "chair" or a condition
like "comfort" resulting from a chair is reality. This relation to
reality fluctuates between the iconic and the symbolic. When the
relation is *iconic*, the medium is able to represent in
miniature or in essence the reality being communicated (cf. Morris, 1946, pp. 191–2). The audience
must do very little decoding: people react to icons
roughly the way they do to reality because they instantly perceive
that the icon is not reality but like it. "Continuous functions" are
thus communicated: qualitative changes or differences are conveyed as they are perceived in the absence of the medium (Ruesch
and Kees, 1956, p. 8). An iconic form of writing is the pictograph,
which shows objects, people, and actions with little distortion except of course that the representations are smaller, must be conventionalized somewhat, and lack a third dimension. Mass media
like radio and television offer icons of the performers and their
basic media.

III.A.2.a

In a *symbolic* relation, the medium is able to suggest reality because, not through any necessary or
inherent connection but through custom and habitua-
tion, the symbol arouses responses very similar to
those evoked by reality itself. In different words: the association
between symbol and referent is more arbitrary than that between
icon and referent. Almost all words are symbols in this sense: the
few in a language that are onomatopoetic can be said to represent
sounds iconically. A symbolic form of writing uses a system of
phonetics that is based not on an inherent but a conventional,
arbitrary connection between letters or words and their referents.
An ideograph is partially iconic since it directly represents an object or person, but it is also symbolic since the reference is not to
the representation but to what the representation stands for. Metaphors and similes, though they may contain iconic elements, are
basically symbolic: the connection between the two phenomena
that are being, respectively, implicitly and explicitly compared
must come from experience devoted to the learning of the meaning
as such. A young man among the Sonjo in Tanganyika who decides
not to marry his fiancée communicates his change of heart by
sending her a broken twig (R. F. Gray, 1960, p. 41). The girl of

III.A.2.b

course can immediately observe that the twig is broken, but the fact that a broken twig in that context signifies a broken betrothal is a conventionalized response that is far removed from what is directly perceived and that has had to be deliberately learned in the past.

III.A.3
Next it is important to investigate the *versatility* of a medium: what kinds of information can it transmit? Ultimately a medium can be no more versatile than the messages which communicators put into it or those which audiences can extract from it, but intrinsically two extremes may be noted. First, a medium may be said to be (a) *relatively versatile* when it can transmit a large number of thoughts, objects, relations, etc. Obviously language is extremely versatile since the essence of almost anything, except perhaps for feelings, can be reduced to speech or writing. (b) A *relatively unversatile* medium can transmit a more finite number of communications. The human skin falls into this category: since its surface is restricted, only a small amount of information can be painted, incised, or tattooed thereon.

III.A.4
Media also differ with respect to the *permanence* of the communication they transmit. When once it has been employed to transmit a communication, (a) a *relatively permanent* medium can either never or never easily be employed again for other messages. The piece of marble is carved; the figure that emerges cannot quickly be altered, nor is it likely to be replaced by another figure. In contrast, (b) a *relatively impermanent* medium may be employed again and again to transmit different or new information. The sounds of the human voice disappear the moment they are spoken, but they can be made more permanent by being recorded or written down.

III.A.5
The medium's *relation to the audience* is the final attribute to be noticed. That relation may be (a) *personal:* the medium is of such a type that it can reach only one person or a very homogeneous group. In this category falls a "private" language known to a few people, or a letter addressed by one person to another. (b) An *impersonal* medium reaches many people simultaneously or eventually over a period of time. Speech when addressed privately to one individ-

ual is thus personal, but when used in a public meeting it becomes impersonal.

III.B   *Types*   The first media to be considered are quite *direct:* they are part of human equipment everywhere
III.B.1   and transmit information without the aid of channels of communication or of mediating or intervening
III.B.1.a   mechanisms. The relatively versatile, impermanent human *voice* is the obvious starting point. First there is (i) *speech,* some aspects of which are considered under language (VI.C); and songs are included as parts of music (III.B.1.d.iv). Certain very deliberate movements of the body, such as the sign language of the deaf and gestures with very specific meanings, belong under this category since they are direct substitutes for speech (but see also III.B.1.c.ii).

————————

Aside from the words that are spoken, speech has other attributes that can convey meaning. Among the Azande in the Congo and Sudan, for example, men indicate respect by speaking in a low voice in the presence of superiors or in front of an oracle (Evans-Pritchard, 1937, p. 299). A loud voice, on the other hand, may be used not to transmit an unsubtle message but merely to be certain of reaching an audience. At the opening of a new bridge among the Tiv in Nigeria, the fetishes at both ends were once asked to kill any person "who evacuated on the bridge, who willfully damaged it, or who shed blood" upon it. Intentionally or not, the communicators here seemed also interested in having the warning heard by the spectators, for they issued it "publicly, in a high, loud voice" (Bohannan and Bohannan, 1957, p. 619). A general manner of speaking, furthermore, may be so highly prized that he who displays it communicates flattering consequential information about himself. The Tiv place a premium upon "oratory," which probably includes the ability both to hold an audience and to discuss problems judiciously (Bohannan and Bohannan, 1958, p. 95). The Wolof of Senegal consider "verbal wit" at the top of the "lesser social qualities" that have prestige (Gorer, 1935, p. 38).

————————

III.B.1.
a.ii

By *nonspeech sounds* are meant: belch, cough, cry, groan, grunt, hiccough, howl, hum, shout, sneeze, sob, ululate, whistle, yodel. These sounds all spring from the throat and the mouth. Other parts of the body, moreover, can provide meaningful sounds: hands are clapped, feet are scraped, footsteps reverberate, fingers are snapped, and then from a nether region can come rumblings for which there is no polite, non-Victorian term in English. Many of the sounds enable people to communicate at greater than normal distance without using an extending medium.

Two observations must be made about nonspeech sounds. First their use in a society is likely to be regulated. In one community among the Ashanti of Ghana, whistling in the town takes its place as tabooed behavior along with cutting up fish to be sold in the market or the marriage of a priest to a priestess (Rattray, 1929, p. 314). The medium may also be prescribed: Mende women in Sierra Leone clap their hands when approaching the camp of the men's secret society in order to give warning of their presence (Little, 1951, p. 118). Then, secondly, just as laughter need not mean that a person is happy but, as in Japan, may signify embarrassment, or just as some people in America cry when they are happy (Hall, 1959, p. 150), so the meaning attached to sounds fluctuates from society to society. Among the Fanti of Ghana, for example, the interpretation given a simple sneeze by a second person depends upon the location of the sneezer and the significance attached to that location. Every individual, it is believed, has a good- and a bad-luck side determined by order of birth and the sex of one's siblings. If a boy is followed by another boy, the older child's back and his left side are unlucky; for him a sneeze from either of these positions means bad luck. In addition, if he sneezes harder through the nostril on his unlucky side, he knows that someone is speaking ill of him or planning ill for him (Lantis, 1940, pp. 150–2). Among the Thonga of Mozambique hiccoughing signifies either that the person is bewitched or possesses magical power (Junod, 1927, v. 2, p. 520).

At first glance it may appear that shouting should be called a loud speech sound rather than a nonspeech sound. In fact, though, more may be involved in shouting than simply raising the voice. Vowels in the Bantu languages of South Africa are said to be few in number but more important than consonants and also to possess "great carrying power." This linguistic property that encourages shouting is likely to be exploited at dawn, for then frequently there are low-hanging clouds which function as "a great sounding board from hill to hill across the valley beneath." The hills, furthermore, are inhabited, and so there is an audience at that time to receive the communication. Thus shouting here means using a special kind of language under particular atmospheric, topographic, and social conditions. Likewise whistling as a subtle form of communication is reported to be used by people with a tonal language; even among them "conversation is confined to more or less set phrases which can be whistled" (Goodwin, 1937, pp. 230–3).

All people speak, save the completely dumb, yet even the latter transmit information by means of the *inevitable appearance of the body*. "Inevitable" here would suggest that deliberate human intervention may change the body somewhat or affect the rate of change, but basically little can be accomplished. Appearance from this standpoint can be traced to two sources, genetic and acquired.

III.B.1.b

The *genetic* factors in a person's appearance, being determined at birth, are essentially unalterable and are utilized by others (and often by the man himself) as a consequential communication. The following are the outstanding media: skin color; somatotype, including height, weight, shape of head, size of any organ, type of hair, bodily proportions; aging, including the condition of the skin, hair, muscles, etc.; and pregnancy. Pregnancy a genetic condition? After becoming pregnant—certainly an acquired process—the appearance of the woman is determined by factors over which she has little or no control. All four media can be directly perceived; whether or not valid information is conveyed through them is without doubt a crucial question. Probably other attributes—blood type, temperature, respiratory rate—convey much more valid information, but

III.B.1.
b.i.

they are excluded here since they can be measured only indirectly and usually only by specialists.

Again and again Africans seem to prefer one type of skin color rather than another. Generally of course the preference can exist only when the society has had contact with people whose skins in fact are of a different hue. This attribute, besides usually evoking an aesthetic response, also conveys information about the individual's social background or character traits. Here are two excerpts from the life history of a Hausa woman:

> Then the Tejani [a Fulani group] came, they came from the edge of the river far away, the Christians had driven them out so that they came to our town, to Zarewa. . . . They came into the town and rested. Some had lost their legs, some had no arms, some were ill; some rode horses, some came on foot. . . . They were light people with reddish skins, all ruling Fulani; their wives had fine clothes. They weren't like Mai Sudan's people [another group]—those were Gbari, very black—these were beautiful people. . . .
>
> She was light-skinned, like my mother; my mother was very beautiful and light-skinned. Look at me—black, like my father! [M. F. Smith, 1954, pp. 66, 75]

Undoubtedly every aspect of aging can be used as a source of information not about the physiological process that is involved but about the person or some outside event. Even the arrival of teeth can convey significant information. The Lovedu in South Africa believe that a child has evil power within him if his upper teeth appear before his lower, if his molar teeth appear first, or if his teeth in general appear irregularly. Such a child should be killed, but nowadays he is treated by a native doctor and later is warned never to bite anyone (Krige and Krige, 1943, pp. 70, 218). The Nkole of Uganda are also disturbed when the first teeth come through in the upper jaw, for this is considered to be a bad omen for the parents; hence the child is cared for by a relative until he loses those teeth. In addition the death of the father before the first teeth are cut requires both the mother and the child to leave home, for they may not be seen until those teeth put in an appearance (Roscoe, 1923, p. 114).

Pregnancy obviously communicates the fact of conception, and has special significance for the woman. In many, perhaps most societies she changes her diet, her work habits, her social activity, and hence the kinds of communications she receives and transmits before the birth of the child. Her condition may also act as a signal to produce changes in the husband's behavior. Among the Tallensi in Ghana, for example, a man with a pregnant wife is supposed to be living under a "strain"; hence he may not participate in funerals, he may not cut a new bush farm, and he may not kill "certain mystically dangerous animals" in the chase (Fortes, 1949, p. 163).

III.B.1.
b.ii
Acquired factors include all the tell-tale changes in appearance resulting from people's way of life. They are too numerous to list, but brief reference can be made to some of them by including in parentheses the kind of consequent information about a person which each of them in Western society may possibly convey: calloused hands (manual occupation); wrinkled brow (frequently worried, perplexed); stooped shoulders (age); sun-tanned, rugged skin (outdoor work); well-developed muscles (athletic occupation); perpetually erect posture (soldier, policeman).

Among the Amhara of Ethiopia a high-status person like a noble, priest, or elder assumes a "stoic appearance" very contrived in so many respects that obviously it must result from years of patient cultivation:

> The jaw muscles are relaxed, the mandible slightly dropped, the eyes half-closed but alert, breathing very quiet, the voice in even tone (in contrast to the strident whine of the argumentative peasant . . .). The body expresses almost the permanence and immobility of a statue, as if the high-status person could not be surprised or dismayed by anything, certain that all things due him will come to him. . . .

In walking, nobles of the old school walk somewhat slowly, somewhat heavily, as if in formal procession. Members of their retinue carry their cane, overcoat, etc. By contrast, laborers carrying heavy burdens walk catlike, largely on the instep, and fairly fast [Messing, 1957, pp. 521–2].

A truly mysterious combination of genetic and acquired characteristics produces in each society another inevitable physical attribute fully worthy of separate attention: *attrac-*

III.B.1.   *tiveness,* or the unique quality of personal magnetism,
b.iii   sex appeal, glowing health, charm, etc. that clearly
           make some people more outstanding or desirable than
others, from the standpoint of their admirers. What is a beautiful woman? Or why do most, possibly all, women appear beautiful on some occasions?

The characteristics of women which make them sexually attractive are frequently noted, no doubt not only because each society has its own standards but also because outside reporters from the West are men. Four illustrations, culled from a modest collection, suffice to suggest how culturally tenuous standards of beauty can be. Among the Azande of the Congo and Sudan, beauty is conveyed by these attributes: "a certain age, pendulous breasts— young girls often tie theirs down and are heard sighing, 'Oh, if my breasts would only fall!'—and a full habit of body" (Larken, 1926, p. 20). Frequently Africans, like the Hausa woman quoted above, place special emphasis upon skin color in judging beauty. In spite of the fact that many Zulu have "a relatively light skin," according to a careful anthropologist, they hold "dark" complexions "in highest esteem" (Krige, 1936, p. 370). Other attributes, however, usually are added. Among the Thonga in Mozambique, a beautiful woman is characterized by "tall stature, strong limbs, and well-developed breasts," and men prefer a face that is "elongated" rather than "broad" and a complexion that is "light" rather than "very dark." The last-named preference is said to be related to the fact that "the white or yellow races are regarded as superior, and a Native laying claim to any European or Asiatic blood is proud of it" (Junod, 1927, v. 1, pp. 182–3). Among the Bambara of the Mali Republic, men are "not unmoved by the beauty of a woman's form," they find "a coppery skin" more attractive than one of "ebony black," and they are "displeased" by "a face pitted by smallpox or a bosom covered with scars." Their personal tastes, however, do not guide them in selecting a wife, for she is considered "primarily a source of pleasure and profit" rather than an aesthetic object bringing joy to behold (Henry, 1910, p. 199).

Attractiveness of course need not be defined sexually but can be formulated in other terms. Among the Fulani in Northern Nigeria, "a striking resemblance" between a first-born son and his deceased grandfather by itself conveys information to the boy's parents and also causes them to communicate with the child in a distinctive manner. The resemblance is fitted into the category of reincarnation and the boy is then conspicuously respected by his parents, who sometimes even call him "father." Otherwise, when the first child is thought not to look like that ancestor, he is treated most impersonally, in fact often neglected (Meek, 1925, v. 1, p. 235).

III.B.1.c The *body movements* that convey information to an audience may be considered relatively involuntary

III.B.1. or voluntary; they are easier to photograph than to describe (Ruesch and Kees, 1956). In the first place,

c.i *relatively involuntary* movements include facial expression, eye shifting, dilation of pupils, muscle twitching, changes in breathing, tics, jerks, and scratching which occur spontaneously and usually without the awareness of the communicator. Temporary changes in the appearance of the skin fall into the same category: flushing, pallor, sweating, drooling, rising of the hair, etc.

Everywhere, it would appear, bodily changes convey to people information not intrinsically connected with what is perceived but arbitrarily and symbolically attached to it. Among the Hottentots of South Africa, the itching of a woman's or young girl's breasts means that "my son, my cousin, or some near relation, will soon arrive" (Hahn, 1881, p. 87). A traveler in Somaliland once reported that, at a temperature of 118° F. in the shade, the noses of some of his men began to bleed. When asked why this was happening, they replied cheerfully, "Oh, Allah makes our noses bleed to cool our heads" (Swayne, 1900, pp. 36–7). On the other hand, sometimes reflexes can be appraised quite realistically. "No one was permitted to cough, or sneeze, or blow his nose in the court" of an authoritarian king of the Ganda in Uganda lest the monarch, considered particularly susceptible, catch cold (Roscoe, 1911, p. 259). Realism, finally, may be mixed with symbolism. In order to bring together "the hearts" of Zulu warriors being prepared for battle through a series of intricate ceremonies lasting a few days, not more than four warriors at a time had to vomit into specially prepared holes. Here, as it were, was an unusual movement of the body which by its very unusualness may have helped symbolize the seriousness of the situation. Since vomiting is not a voluntary movement but a series of reflexes that must be triggered off by some intervening processes, the warriors drank a mouthful or two of an emetic concocted for them by the war doctors of the king (Krige, 1936, p. 269).

III.B.1.
c.ii

The *relatively voluntary* movements refer to gesturing, posture, contrived facial expression; position of body; movement of any organ; spitting, nose-blowing, urinating, excreting. Scratching, which made an appearance under "involuntary" movements, must be welcomed here too, since people deliberately eliminate itches. No doubt because most of these movements are also part of the "silent language" of communication (Hall, 1959), they have not been studied extensively and hence cannot be referred to systematically. While it may be true, for example, that the physical propinquity of two speakers can convey an emotion or an attitude to themselves or a cultural rule to an outside observer (Hall and Whyte, 1960), the problem of finding meaningful measures of the distance between them, so far as the present writer can tell, has not even been mentioned. Similarly postures can be variously described: a person may be standing, leaning, sitting, lying, rising, falling, etc. His movements, too, possess an unknown number of attributes, such as speed, agility, and grace. In the West careful investigation has shown that small variations of such movements are related to people's enduring personalities (Allport and Vernon, 1933), but in the present discussion the information they convey about the momentary mood and the culture are emphasized.

Only a quick glance at African societies is needed to appreciate the tremendous number of relatively voluntary movements that are used to transmit information. The fuller accounts of prevailing customs in this respect provided by some observers may be a function either of their interest in the subject or of a real emphasis within the society on such forms of communicating. Likewise only a brief reference may reflect the investigator's indifference or the society's; unfortunately, as indicated in the Prologue, negative instances cannot be interpreted unless explicit guidance is provided. Here, for example, is a brief summary of movements that convey information among the Amhara of Ethiopia. Anger is shown by the wide opening of the eyes, by biting the lower lip or finger, by a knit brow, or by "a furious, intent stare"; melancholy by a wrinkled face; timidity and respect in the young by "turning the eyes to the dust"; impatience by rapidly shifting the glance; and greetings or acknowledgment of superordination by rhythmic handclapping. In commercial relations, a buyer and seller signify agreement by waving their right hands up and down and then touching each other's palms with the fingers stretched away. Master and servant sit differently: the master pushes his body way back as if to show that a special effort is required to rise; the servant, on the rare occasions when he is permitted to sit in the master's presence, must "sit lightly" (Messing, 1957, pp. 520–1, 574). There is no way of knowing whether the Amhara have a richer or poorer repertoire of such movements than other people.

Unquestionably, no uniform set of meanings is attached to particular body movements, as can be seen when the problem is viewed in cultural perspective. Among the Mbundu of Angola, for example, it might appear that any outside observer ought to be able to comprehend certain gestures. Throwing a mat on the ground and laying the head on one's hands indicates sleep; or fingers are used to signify various numbers. But what is the meaning of the gesture that suggests the stroking of an imaginary bear? Or one in which the head is bent forward with eyes wide open and tongue out? Or one in which the left arm is held up with the fist closed and, while that fist is shaken, the wrist is grasped by the right hand? Clearly an outsider would be foolhardy to guess the meaning of such esoteric signs. He would have to be told that they mean, respectively, an inquiry concerning the health of one's father; a very insulting way of saying "You are a fool"; and extreme anger, so strong that adequate words cannot be found to express one's feelings (Hambly, 1934, pp. 252–3).

The *faux pas* reported by missionaries and other travelers in Africa are indeed evidence that the meanings of movements cannot be transferred from one society to another without running the risk of misunderstanding. Thus the warm gesture of patting a child's head or indicating the height of a plant or animal by a horizontal extension of the hand is considered in some societies to be an evil attempt to cast a spell upon the child, plant, or animal so that growth will cease at the height indicated by the pat or the extension (A. Fraser, 1932, p. 5). Pointing to objects with the index finger in certain areas of Central Africa is a "crude and vulgar" gesture; the polite way to point is by sticking out the lower lip (Nida, 1952b, p. 12). Africans who have frequent contact with Europeans often grow tolerant when outsiders violate their etiquette. The present writer sat with his legs crossed in front of the chief of an Ewe community in Ghana; later he apologized, after learning that the gesture showed disrespect; the chief smiled and indicated that he knew the impoliteness had been unintended.

The messages communicated by voluntary bodily movements are often intimately linked with extremely important values of the society. In particular there is a right and a wrong way to conduct one's body in order to demonstrate respect, but again that way varies and may be displayed in different social contexts:

Ashanti of Ghana—it is insulting to use the left rather than the right hand for gesticulation (Rattray, 1929, p. 164).

Chaga of Tanganyika—children receiving or giving something to an older person are expected to clasp their outstretched right hand with their left one; they must offer seats to old people who enter a hut (Raum, 1940, p. 175).

Ganda of Uganda—inferior people receiving or giving something to a superior person must use both hands; if it is necessary to hold the object in one hand, then the free hand must touch the arm of the hand holding the object (Roscoe, 1911, p. 44).

Luo of Kenya—while speaking, a man and his mother-in-law must turn their backs to each other (Evans-Pritchard, 1950, p. 141).

Mende of Sierra Leone—anyone approaching a chief, including the younger members of his own family, must bend his body, place his hands on his knees, and uncover his head (Little, 1951, p. 192).

Some, perhaps most bodily movements convey information not only to others but also to the communicators themselves. In addition to participating in the vomiting ritual previously mentioned, Zulu warriors about to go into battle also chewed a particular plant which they then spat out in the direction of the enemy. This action they felt would cause the enemy "to make mistakes." No doubt the gesture helped the spitter and his marching contemporaries more than it harmed the enemy. Besides spitting and vomiting, these warriors strengthened themselves in other ways. When summoned to war, they donned a special war dress and would "leap about as if fighting, in order to 'get up steam'" (Krige, 1936, p. 268).

Since the symbolic significance of voluntary movements seems on the whole to be quite arbitrary, it is not surprising to discover that the process of establishing the symbolic link may be extended another step: a gesture can replace words which are themselves symbols, and symbolic words can replace a gesture. The Ashanti in Ghana provide an illustration of the first relation, the Mossi in the Mali and Voltaic Republics, of the second. Among the Ashanti, the way to abuse or slander a paramount chief is to use certain stereotyped phrases ("the child of a fool") or to invoke a special oath ("May your ancestral spirits chew their own heads"); such utterances were once punishable by death. The same abuse or slander may be conveyed by a simple gesture, which consists of "closing the hands, placing the closed fists together, and holding up the thumbs" (Rattray, 1929, p. 310). Among the Mossi, gratitude is expressed by saying "My head is in the dirt." The words represent the custom of demonstrating gratitude by bowing so low that the head is actually pressed into the dirt, "so humbled does one feel because of the graciousness of another" (Nida, 1952a, pp. 134–5).

III.B.1. c.iii

The third and final form of bodily movement to be considered is a special type of voluntary movement requiring, let praise be uttered, no formal definition: *dancing*.

After surveying some of the literature (most of which seems to be either romantic or arty), the writer feels tentatively that competent observers agree on two points concerning dancing in Africa. First, dancing is important and occurs frequently. Africans allegedly "dance for joy and they dance for grief; they dance for love and they dance for hate; they dance to bring prosperity and they dance to avert calamity; they dance for religion and they dance to pass the time" (Gorer, 1935, p. 289). Then, secondly, dancing is always linked with other expressive forms: "In the African village singing, clapping, dancing, and drumming are not separate entities, but may be said to constitute one homogeneous art form" (Hailey, 1957, p. 67).

There is, however, less agreement concerning the precise functions performed by dancing, especially with relation to communication. One promising theory suggests that dancing is "an important factor in maintaining the sense of group solidarity" (Krige, 1936, p. 336). This hypothesis need not exclude other functions simultaneously served, such as expressing aggression or communicating—and stimulating—sexual desire. Undoubtedly the fruitful approach is to appraise the medium in each social context. The same writer, for example, indicates that Zulu hunters once danced both before and after the hunt. In advance, they entered "the cattle-kraal of the master of the hunt, where they danced round, boasting of their prowess and stabbing imaginary bucks." Afterwards those who had distinguished themselves received the approval of all as they danced about (ibid., pp. 336, 341–2). Without additional information, without knowing exactly how the dancers themselves felt on the two occasions, it may be reasonable nevertheless to think that before the hunt "solidarity" and morale-building were the important goals, but that later the communication from the audience to the dancers became more significant than the feelings of in-group membership conveyed among themselves. In a different society—the Bemba in Northern Rhodesia—dancing is "for amusement" and also to show respect. The latter feeling may be vividly communicated by the soloist who, while singing and "with vitality and dash," dances in front of the person he would honor (Richards, 1956, p. 59). Like other forms of bodily movement and especially those involving the entire body, dancing must convey to the dancer himself a variety of feelings about himself that he may not ordinarily verbalize.

The people who are permitted to dance on special occasions or in a particular way are usually specified within a society. Men, for example, are likely to have their own dances that are different from those reserved for women. Among the Wolof of Senegal, who have a large number of dance forms, low-caste women may "act in an outrageously flirtatious manner, make risqué remarks, and when dancing perform the indecent actions and postures for which Wolof dancing is notorious." In contrast, high-caste girls generally do not dance in public, and when they do, their dancing is "very restrained" (Gamble, 1957, p. 75).

Each person communicates with himself, sometimes by talking aloud, sometimes by thinking, and sometimes by experiencing, as it were, his own body and its processes. Such communication may be sufficient unto itself; the communicator is his own audience. Often, however, this communication emerges from the person because, for example, he also expresses himself in front of others.

III.B.1.d   *Creative* communication is included under the heading of direct media because at least at the outset the
communicator communicates without the assistance

III.B.1.   of mediating devices, even though eventually he may
d.i   employ some.

The first form is called simply *imagination*. People work out good or evil deeds, wise or stupid plans, partial or complete philosophies for themselves. Also, directly and without mediating devices, according to the view in some societies, a man's thoughts, feelings, or dreams are affected by and can affect other people.

Among the Nuer in the Sudan the curse of a man is believed to be effective if he has in fact been wronged. He need not overtly utter the curse under these circumstances, "he has only to think it." That thought, moreover, does not have to be clearly formulated in imagination, "a mere feeling of resentment arising from a genuine grievance being sufficient to cause injury to the person who has occasioned it" (Evans-Pritchard, 1949b, p. 291). Here the communicator is convinced that his own imagination, without external aid, is the medium of communication. Since others share the belief, they undoubtedly try to refrain from committing the kind of act that may lead to an overt or nonovert curse. The consequence, then, is a method of social control that happens to be phrased as a form of communication.

Devices for decoding dreams often are standardized in a society so that the dreamer, when he awakens, has at his disposal a set of meanings to be assigned to his recollection of the dream content. The following schema exists among the Fanti in Ghana (Lantis, 1940, p. 157):

dream content	*decoded*
a cow	a witch is after you
a horse	an enemy is seeking you
a dead person	long life for the one dreamed of
a person dressed in white	death is coming soon to the one dreamed of

fish (when dreamed by a woman)	you will become pregnant
flying	prosperity
picking up money	debt or unusual spending
forcibly being deprived of money	you will get money

III.B.1.
d.ii

The second creative form is *fiction* (including po-etry): any story which, though influenced by histori-cal events, transforms those events either consciously or not; which is transmitted by a communicator to an audience; and which may be perpetuated by tradition or print.

Without doubt folk tales must be considered serious forms of communication. In the first place, they help transmit to each gen-eration factual information about the society as well as many of its values. The moral of an enduring folk tale reflects the view of respectable people. Usually, however, their emotive function is more apparent. According to one observer, African folk tales "offer a means of release for pent-up emotions." When an apparently weak character triumphs over a powerful chief, the listener may think of certain chiefs in real life whom he does not completely cherish, and thus "he rejoices in the whacks they are getting by proxy" (E. W. Smith, 1940, p. 70).

Dramatic evidence on the last point comes from the Akan peo-ples of Ghana. There the storyteller begins by disclaiming the truth of the tale: "We don't really mean to say so; we don't really mean to say so." Having thus formally absolved himself of respon-sibility, he relates a tale dealing with ordinarily sacred subjects such as gods, fetishes, ancestors, chiefs, the sick, and sexual matters in a profane manner and sometimes too with ridicule. During or after its recital, the effectiveness of a story can be increased by the entrance of actors who realistically and cleverly impersonate the characters being described. Formerly anyone with a grievance against a contemporary or even against the king could vent his aggression through a thinly disguised tale; he would avoid directly implicating himself not only by claiming similarly that he was reciting a make-believe tale but also by not using personal names. Another way of achieving the same goal involves "vituperation by proxy." The person with a grievance has a friend accompany him to the house of the man against whom the hostility is to be expressed. The two pretend to quarrel; during the charade and obviously within earshot of the intended audience, the aggrieved person assails his friend "with every kind of abuse" (Rattray, 1930, pp. x–xii).

A well-established folk figure is a useful ingredient to add to a new communication in the same society. A reference to him is likely to attract attention and hence induce people to perceive the communication (IX.A.3.a). Then, when the responses clearly associated with him are evoked, they aid the audience in comprehending and learning the content of the communication (IX.D.2.b; X.A.1.b). A number of years ago, for example, the Uganda press popularized a cartoon character named Kapera, whose antics eventually made him symbolize incompetence and inefficiency. Later he appeared as the foil in an instructional film which attempted to teach the correct methods of planting and growing cotton (Spurr, 1950). As will be indicated subsequently (IX.A.3.b), however, there is danger in the use of such a technique: people may enjoy the character but not learn the serious message that he is supposed to help communicate.

III.B.1. d.iii	Next there is *drama* (including puppetry): the reproduction of fiction by one or more actors whose total behavior resembles the behavior of the real or imaginary characters in some type of setting.

Like folk tales, folk drama also communicates information and values, and certainly serves an emotive function. Among the Mende of Sierra Leone, for example, most of the secret societies provide a form of simple drama which, while entertaining, also signalizes some important ceremony such as a funeral. An actor impersonates a spirit by wearing a wooden mask and a cape of raffia that covers his entire body, because it is "absolutely essential" that no part of him be revealed. Accompanied by attendants and followers, he moves about the community, squats in various "grotesque poses" in front of the houses of important people, and there resorts to "miming and mimicry" to convey his message. Those who wish to maintain a high social standing give gifts of money to the spirit's entourage (Little, 1951, p. 251).

This form of communication appeals almost instantly to most African audiences. Traditionally, the Fang of the Gabon and Cameroon Republics had no theater until contact with the West. Now they have devised "short farces" that resemble morality plays or the satirical sketches of "our cabaret revues" and that show "no hesitation in scoffing at the authorities" (Alexandre and Binet, 1958, p. 127). Crusading governments, therefore, have also used folk drama. In Ghana, for example, educational goals, such as those pertaining to public health, literacy, or the control of cocoa-tree pests, are sought by means of a simple, rather spontaneous form called "vernacular" or "village" drama. An official may suggest the theme for a play, but thereafter people from the area who work for a government department and who are not professional dramatists or actors contrive the plot and its elaboration. One such plot is described briefly as follows: "An eligible young man, offered the choice by their father, chooses the plain rather than the beautiful of two sisters because she is literate; the beautiful one promptly joins a literacy class" (Pickering, 1957, p. 180). The plays, unlike centrally produced motion pictures, contain local allusions and, lest the audience protest or titter, the action on stage follows local etiquette. Thus the actor portraying a messenger must greet a chief exactly as people in the village greet their chief, or else they groan or hoot. A play is rehearsed, but no effort is made to achieve professional perfection. Obviously the entire production is inexpensive, and these dramas are said to be extremely popular. At the end of the play, some of the audience are in a mood to carry on a discussion related to the plot's educational theme (anon., 1956; G. Brown et al., 1959).

III.B.1.
d.iv

The final medium of creative communication—*music*—is too complicated to be discussed in any detail. Obviously the communicator who plays an instrument or sings may be present, at a distance, or—in a recording—absent. Musical instruments may or may not be accompanied by speech in the form of singing or by body movements in the form of simple gestures or elaborate acting. Music may be realistically or impressionistically iconic, or emotively or intellectually symbolic.

While music in Africa, like music everywhere, serves a number of functions, most authorities agree with what might appear to be an extreme view, to the effect that traditionally "music infuses all the activities of the African from the cradle to the grave" (Hailey, 1957, p. 67). Vocal and instrumental music is likely to be included in most ceremonies and to add an emotive component. Singing frequently accompanies normal work activities, and so not only improves esprit but also through its decisive rhythms promotes the coordination of those who are working together. An expert has indicated that among the Hutu in Ruanda there are recognized

> at least twenty-four general social song types, as distinguished from religious songs, including those played by professional musicians for entertainment, songs for beer-drinking, war, homage to a chief, hunting, harvesting, and general work; songs sung at the birth of a child or to admonish erring members of the society, to recount a successful elephant hunt, to deride Europeans; songs of death, vulgar songs, and others. Further, within each of these categories subtypes can be distinguished: certain songs are sung when taking a new canoe from the place where it was constructed to the water, when paddling against a strong current, or to make the paddlers work better together [Merriam, 1959, p. 50].

At this traditional level there is usually no sharp line between performers or communicators and the audience, for virtually everyone is performing and everyone is listening. As the music of African society is affected by musical styles and techniques from the West,

skilled musicians become the performers and the audiences begin
to assume a more and more passive role (Hailey, 1957, pp. 68–71).
These musical forms from outside sometimes are combined with
indigenous forms; in Ghana, for example, the music known as "high
life" reflects certain African rhythms and Western dance-band
music in such a way that its appeal is now "intertribal" (Nketia,
1957). These changes, as consequential forms of communication,
convey information about the acculturation of African societies.

Songs can serve the same function as any other kind of speech,
except that their musical element makes them more easily perceived under many circumstances and their traditional character
is likely to render their message impressive. Among the Chaga of
Tanganyika, for example, singing directed at children is employed
"to publish the disgrace of an age-mate or to mock him for being
stupid," and riddles which serve the function of warning others
are often sung (Raum, 1940, pp. 221–2). Among the Nguru of the
same territory, the ethics of the society is summarized in songs,
which are therefore learned during an initiation period. The songs
themselves, moreover, are associated with distinctive figurines
made mostly from clay or wood, so that thereafter a rule of conduct is symbolized by two stimuli, a song and a figurine (A. Cory,
1944).

---◆◆◆---

A direct form of communication which traditionally speaks
louder than words but which uses words as well as every conceivable body movement in the human repertoire and every object or device in the environment is *action*. The components of action are so many that it must be con-
III.B.1.e   sidered a medium in its own right. Consequential
communication (II.A.1.a.ii and 2.a.ii) involves action:
attaining a goal in itself conveys information to other people. Sometimes, moreover, action is a form of purposive communication
(II.A.2.a.i): the action achieves the social goal, as when a mur-
derer is executed to convey to people the punishment associated
with a particular crime. Modern public relations counselors stress
that the reputation of a company may be affected more by its
policies and deeds than by its advertising.

Almost any action can be subtly interpreted by people who have been taught its meaning. A man who breaks a cooking pot is what? Clumsy, inefficient, nervous, aggressive—out of social context the action as such is impossible to interpret. Among the Shambala of Tanganyika the deed, when carried out ritually, means that the person is committing symbolic suicide (Moreau, 1941). Obviously only an insider could provide the correct interpretation. Or the kind of food a man eats may indicate whether in this respect he is conforming to traditional or European standards; in many parts of Africa—since food habits change very slowly—the eating of European food is likely to reflect a high degree of acculturation.

From Africa, as from elsewhere in the world, come reports indicating that sometimes the actions of the communicator become the communication that is more influential than his formal message. Thus during World War II a mobile propaganda unit of the East Africa Command toured Northern Rhodesia and Nyasaland in order to show how African soldiers lived and were trained, to demonstrate the modern paraphernalia of war, to explain war aims, and thus in the last analysis to encourage "an intensified war effort by the civilian population." The European officer in charge reports that the real value of the demonstration lay "not in the formal display, but in the conduct and speech" of the African soldiers when they were "off parade." Informally, for example, they helped drill local police units (Dickson, 1945, pp. 10–11).

More often than not actions are difficult to interpret, especially when communicator and audience come from different cultures. African soldiers, in the propaganda unit just described, demonstrated during the formal performance methods of physical training by vaulting, tumbling, and forming pyramids. Their agility and coordination was sometimes explained by spectators as a form of magic. "Those white men have changed our men into boneless individuals," one African said (ibid.). Misunderstandings of action may have more serious consequences. Two missionaries attached to a Methodist mission in Northern Rhodesia once camped near an African village on the banks of the Zambesi River. After dark they strolled into the village where one of them, having a special interest in buildings, paid particular attention to the way the village was constructed. He then deliberately and publicly communicated to his associate by sketching with his stick upon the ground what he considered to be the plan of the place. From the standpoint of the two Europeans, here was a simple social communication, and nothing else. The consequential interpretation of the Africans, however, was different: the men must be sorcerers because they acted like sorcerers. They entered the village after dark, approached a house, drew figures on the ground, and uttered sentences—all actions performed by a sorcerer when he would predict and thus produce his victim's death. These two outsiders are said only narrowly to have escaped the death sentence to which they were therefore immediately condemned (E. W. Smith, 1946, pp. 33–4).

So far the media of communication that have been considered emanate directly from the communicator. Now attention may be turned to the artifacts and devices that are employed as media in their own right or as supplements to the direct media. A warrior, for example, can communicate ferocity by wearing a special uniform, without the help of any other medium; or he may simultaneously convey the same impression by the uniform and a war dance.

III.B.2   *Changes in the appearance of the human body* are deliberately produced for the sake of communicating information. The communicator is considered to be the person on whose body the changes occur; hence the changes themselves are classified as basic media here rather than as extending media in the next chapter. In fact, parents and others in authority often are the communicators who require the bodies of children and other subordinates to be altered, but thereafter those with the changed bodies communicate information directly. The changes may be alterations *of* or *on* the body.

III.B.2.   (a) *Changes of the body,* all of which are relatively permanent, include those on the *skin:* scarification or
a.i   cicatrization, tattooing.

--- • • ---

Scars are observable so frequently throughout Africa that it is necessary to discuss in some detail the kind of information which is thus conveyed. The best summary would seem to be that they are not like a printed sign or badge which unequivocally communicates one or more facts to people who know the coding system but that, when interpreted cautiously, they always transmit some valid information.

Can one deduce from a person's scars the society to which he belongs? The writer once informally tested the proposition with an African who claimed that he could identify people in this way. The two of us walked together through a market in Kaduna, where Africans from many societies in Nigeria trade. I casually pointed to a dozen men, one after the other, who had facial scars. My African friend in all instances named a society; then he and I politely verified the claim by speaking to the person and asking him to tell us the name of his tribe. In eleven instances out of twelve, he was correct. Certainly, however, he may have been responding simultaneously to other cues in the person's appearance, such as his clothing or his skin color.

A keen observer believes that in some parts of West Africa "one can *often* tell where a person comes from by his facial cicatrizations." Note the word "often," italicized by the present writer: "always" has not been used. For the same observer also suggests that the following seemingly distinctive scar is visible on the faces of people coming not from one but from four different societies: "a slashed scar . . . running diagonally downwards from the bridge of the nose across one or both cheeks . . . often embellished with a neat tracery of tiny incisions . . . spreading in herring-bone lines over the forehead and down the neck" (Fortes, 1945, p. 16). The societies, however, are all in Ghana, closely related to one another and in many instances living side-by-side; hence this carved badge may distinguish them, if not from one another, at least from other societies. Likewise some observers point out that similar scars are used in different societies; for example, "the tribal marks of the Kagoro, Moroa, Ataka, and Kaje are *practically* identical, being fourteen or fifteen vertical lines down the cheek, and sixteen to twenty-two vertical lines on the forehead" (Meek, 1925, v. 1, p. 47). Once more the qualifying adverb in italics, again supplied by the present writer, may be significant, for clearly there is variability in the number of lines which may or may not be correlated with the particular tribes. In addition, the five societies all inhabit the same area, the plateau section of Nigeria, and are so closely related that one expert groups them under a single category (Murdock, 1959, p. 91).

On the other hand a number of factors make the identification of a person's tribe from his scars either impossible or difficult. Whole societies no longer use scars, because they associate them with the days of slavery. Within almost every African society there are some people, usually as a result of missionary influence, who do not have their children scarred. Then sometimes—among the Tiv of Nigeria, for example (Bohannan, 1956)—"style changes" in scars occur from one generation to the next. Finally, some scars may be made only "for personal gratification" and hence cannot be associated with a particular society (Basden, 1938, pp. 330–1). For similar reasons, as a study in Southern Rhodesia suggests (Gilfand and Swart, 1953), tattooed skin must also be cautiously interpreted when it is used as a clue to the individual's society.

Within a particular society, however, it is clear without any doubt at all that scars convey unequivocal information. Although the Tiv, as indicated above, do have fashions in scars, they "definitely associate . . . different types of scars with different ages of men" (Bohannan, 1956). Likewise, the Ibo of Nigeria, who may be scarred for purely personal satisfaction, know that one scar in particular, the "winged solar disk" is definitely "a sign of status, rank, or nobility." If arrested, a person with such a scar is never handcuffed; and it is taboo for him to perform a menial task, such as carrying a load on his head (Jeffreys, 1951). Among the Nupe of Nigeria ancient kings and, later on, minor chiefs could be easily identified by the six slight cuts below their mouths (Meek, 1925, v. 1, p. 49). An anthropologist who has worked in this society is so certain that the scars convey specific information that he has included as an appendix to his report a series of diagrammatic faces showing the "tribal marks of Nupe sub-tribes," both the "traditional" and the "modern" ones (Nadel, 1942, pp. 405–6).

The material cited so far indicates that scars symbolize permanent status or rank within a society. They may also function to indicate a change in status. Among the Lala of Nigeria, a girl's "passport to marriage" is a series of three sets of scars incised at different times during special ceremonies. While an infant, she has her abdomen scarred around the navel. At puberty her arms and the back of her neck are scarred. Finally, a year later during a festival at the start of sowing, scars are made upon her buttocks and thighs. A special woman executes all three operations and is rewarded, on the last occasion, by a gift of two hoes from the girl's father and one of corn and beer from her mother (Kirk-Greene, 1957).

It is to be suspected that, since scarring is usually extremely painful, the symbol thereafter communicates an appropriately strong message. "By far the most important event in the life of a Nuer boy" in the Sudan, according to an anthropologist, "comes when he has about reached the age of puberty. His people decide that he must have the tribals marks cut when the cold wind blows." The cutting is an "ordeal": the operator starts at the center of the forehead and extends each of six cuts up to or past the ear; the cuts are so deep that blood flows freely. The boy must be brave: usually he "lies absolutely still, for a show of fear on his part would bring ridicule from the girls and women that would be hard to bear, and if he moves it will mean that the cut will not be straight and he will always have to wear a scar that will proclaim to any Nuer that he flinched while the tribal marks were being cut." Thus he communicates his bravery both at the moment and forever after. It is considered, furthermore, a "great honor" for the mother to undergo the same operation after six or seven of her sons have been scarred (Huffman, 1931, pp. 29–34).

When the operation is optional, there is no way of knowing whether only the brave agree to the ordeal or whether the ordeal makes them brave, but the scar as a symbol or symptom of bravery remains. In fact it is reasonable to wonder whether the severe test of courage and endurance demanded of the Ibo elite, who are incised with the winged solar disk mentioned above, may not have accounted in part for the wild desperation formerly shown by men with such scars when captured by slave dealers. An anthropologist once asked some Tiv whether scarification is painful. "Of course," he was told, "of course it is painful. What girl would look at a man if his scars had not cost him pain?" (Bohannan, 1956).

Quite unabashedly in one society, the Nkundo in the Congo, tattoos are reported to serve a most obvious and direct "sexual" function. First, the tattooed figures on a woman's body are "placed in such a way that they converge toward the sexual organs." Although women wear clothing nowadays, they apparently still successfully communicate their sexual attractiveness by, "at some time, for some reason or another," uncovering the tattooing in the presence of men (Hulstaert, 1938, p. 67). Possibly in the same society, as the report describes two other societies in the same province, the suggestion is offered that the appeal of these markings may not be completely aesthetic: the tattoos are raised on the skin and are "very exciting" to men "essentially as a result of the very pronounced movements of the woman during the sexual act" (Maes, 1924, p. 190).

By and large, it may be concluded, scars and tattoos are likely in most African societies to have real significance in communicating information to the bearer and to his contemporaries. Many Africans feel deprived unless they are properly marked, just as a woman and her associates among the Luo in Kenya believe that she cannot bear children until she has been tattooed in a traditional manner (Hobley, 1903, p. 353). The outsider, in brief, has not a simple but an intriguing medium that can be cautiously decoded.

III.B.2. a.ii
The body may be changed by the *piercing* of ear lobes, nose, or lips, through which some symbolic or decorative object is usually inserted or tied.

Since this device does not appear to occur so frequently in Africa as the scarring and tattooing of the skin, the hypothesis is advanced that its presence but not its absence may be a more reliable, or less ambiguous, clue to the identification of the bearer's society. Then within a society it must be a mark of respectability or acceptability. Anthropological reports, however, merely indicate the existence of the custom and seldom suggest the ascribed or real reason for its appearance; hence only scattered illustrations, without the usual penetrating analysis, are quickly given below.

"The distinguishing mark of the whole Zulu nation" in South Africa is said to be their pierced ears. The piercing occurs before puberty at a special ceremony marked by feasting and merrymaking. A person with unpierced ears was once considered to be "foolish and childish and good-for-nothing" (Krige, 1936, pp. 81, 375). Not all but "many" members of the Luo society in Kenya have "about" fifteen small holes pierced along the outer edge of the ear; in each hole there is inserted a brass ring with a blue bead at its outer extremity (Hobley, 1902, p. 31). Among the Chaga of Tanganyika, the father perforates the right ear lobe, the mother's brother the left; thereafter the lobe is said to "belong" to the piercer (Gutmann, 1926, p. 8). Among the Fang in the Gabon and Cameroon Republics, a hole for attaching ornaments is pierced through the septum of the nose between the ages of three and eight (Tessmann, 1913, p. 18). Nuer girls in the Sudan have a hole in the center of their upper lip in which they sometimes wear a blade of grass, a flower, or a small piece of wood, but more usually "a nail with the point sticking outward" (Huffman, 1931, p. 9).

———◄•••►———

Another set of relatively permanent changes upon the body are *deformations* (including minor excisions) of ear lobes, genitals, head, neck, teeth, umbilicus. Ear lobes are included here to indicate that they may be not merely pierced but also extended gradually by weights hanging in the holes until they begin to approach the shoulders. The appearance of the head may be changed, for example, by an indentation of the forehead caused by frequently wearing across that part of the head a band at the ends of which burdens are suspended. The neck may be lengthened by a series of rings that are added, one at a time, over years. The umbilicus may be ruptured, so that it protrudes beyond the abdomen; or, as among the Mende of Sierra Leone, children "pluck at it" in an effort to distend it (Staub, 1936, p. 24).

III.B.2.
a.iii

The circumcision of young boys and men and, to a lesser degree, the excision of young girls and women are such frequent practices in Africa that, even when the changes are not concealed either by clothes or anatomy, they probably are not an unambiguous symbol of tribal membership. Perhaps the practice serves or could serve this function only when it exists in one society and not in another close by. In Ghana, for example, according to an African anthropologist, the "only one fundamental difference" between one group of peoples (Ga and Adangme) and another (Twi, Ashanti, and Fanti) is that men among the former are circumcised and among the latter they are not (Danquah, 1928, p. 1). But of course the important point here is whether or not the people actually use—or before Western clothes or clothes in general became popular, once used—the "fundamental difference" as a medium of communication, and no data about this are provided.

The presence or absence of circumcision may be useless in identifying membership in a society for other reasons: like scars and tattoos, the practice is not uniform in every society and changes over time. In Northern Nigeria, for example, all Moslem societies but only some pagan ones circumcise. Some of the pagans, moreover, once followed the custom and then abandoned it; and "within the limits of a single tribe we may find groups that circumcise and others that do not" (Meek, 1925, v. 2, p. 83). In samples of 100 males in each of two very closely related societies, the Wambu and the Sambu of Angola, 24 per cent of the former and 100 per cent of the latter were found to be circumcised. Corresponding figures for dental mutilations were 26 and 44 per cent; for pierced ears, 5 and 4 per cent; and for tattoos, both nil (Sarmento, 1951). It would be important to know whether any significance is attached either to those who do not display the sign when they come from a society where many people do (e.g., dental mutilation among the Sambu) or to those who display it when most of their contemporaries do not (e.g., circumcision among the Wambu).

Since the genitals are the medium, however, it is not surprising to find that attitudes toward circumcision and excision are frequently very intense. In Ghana the two societies mentioned above that do circumcise consider the operation to be "an indispensable mark of manhood," those that do not regard it "as an abominable practice" (Danquah, 1928, p. 1). Within a society, moreover, circumcision often conveys two kinds of information. First, since the operation is either the climax of, or is accompanied by, a series of other rituals, it signifies that the individual has reached a certain stage of maturity or has been successfully taught the traditions of his group. Among the Kikuyu of Kenya, according to the famous anthropologically trained leader of that society, circumcision of a boy or excision of a girl "signifies that the individual operated upon has been given, during the course of the pre-initiation ceremonial dances and songs, all the essential information on the laws and customs of the tribe" (Kenyatta, 1938, p. 155). Then, secondly, being circumcised is evidence that the individual has been able to endure the pain inevitably associated with the surgery; circumcision, like scarring, is often regarded as an ordeal during which the person must demonstrate bravery or restraint by not crying or protesting.

When a society possesses a distinctive theory which explains circumcision and excision in other terms, then presumably the occurrence of the operation communicates additional information. Among the Bambara of the Mali Republic, for example, the bisexuality of every human being is considered to be "fundamental"; thus "the boy is feminine in his foreskin, the girl masculine in her clitoris." By removing through circumcision and excision these "organs of the opposite sex," the child is helped "to attain the sex to which it is apparently destined" (Dieterlen, 1951, pp. 70–1). Other variations in the operation are reported, but their meaning to the people themselves may not be disclosed. What significance, for example, do the Zulu of South Africa attach to another kind of surgery upon the penis which apparently became the vogue after a strong leader abolished circumcision? Or why do they consider it "a filthy habit" to allow the pubic hair of young men and women to grow? (Krige, 1936, pp. 116–17, 375).

Information concerning other deformations of the body by Africans is so scanty that it can be only guessed that they perform the same communicative function as circumcision. In three neighboring societies of Kenya (the Chuka, Embu, and Mbere) the two upper incisors are chipped, but in a fourth in the same area (the Kikuyu) teeth are not chipped or filed (Middleton, 1953, p. 58). Presumably disfigured teeth merely indicate that a person is not a Kikuyu. It would be interesting to discover under what circumstances more than one deformation is employed as a hallmark.

◄••►

III.B.2.
a.iv

The appearance of the human body may be permanently affected by the *removal of one of its parts,* such as an arm, an eye, a finger, the genitals, a foot, the nose, one or more teeth, or the tongue.

•—•

At puberty the Luo of Kenya and the Chaga of Tanganyika extract, respectively, the four and the two front teeth (Roscoe, 1915, p. 283; Raum, 1940, p. 301). Here is a clear-cut coding device to distinguish members of the two societies—or the dead on a field of battle—provided no other society in the area employs the same system and provided, too, the tradition is followed to perfection. In this instance both the Luo and the Chaga add other distinguishing signs, such as piercing their ear lobes in different ways. Like most permanent changes of the body, the extraction of the teeth serves to alert the community to the person's change in status. Afterwards the gap in the mouth communicates to the Chaga that the boy expects "a certain economic independence and the right to wider social contacts"; no one, for instance, objects to his presence at beer parties. The lad himself may aim toward another glory: "he who can spit higher [through the gap in the teeth] is praised and his mutilation admired" (Raum, 1940, pp. 301–2).

The removal of any other part of the body is such a radical step that it seems to occur only as a form of punishment. Some Hottentots of South Africa, however, are reported to cut off one finger of a child at birth; perhaps in this way they present a sacrifice or offering to a supreme being in order to avert illness (Hahn, 1881, p. 87). The more common situation is illustrated among the Ashanti of Ghana where, it is reported, mutilation "sometimes took the place of capital punishment." The cutting off of the entire external ear or of a piece of it was the punishment for displaying impertinence toward an official or chief; cutting off the lips for "tale-bearing and abuse," especially if the chief were involved; cutting off the nose for having the reputation of being "conceited, disrespectful, swaggering"; castration for entering the women's apartments and seeing one of the chief's wives naked (Rattray, 1929, pp. 376-7). People were thus informed of a man's conviction and reminded of the prevailing punishment but, unless each mutilation was really limited to a particular misdeed, somewhat ambiguous messages were communicated until the precise reason for the mutilation could be learned through some other source. Usually among the Ganda of Uganda an adulterer was punished by being killed. If spared, he paid a fine of two women—at least those who could afford the women did so—and also he "lost a limb or had an eye gouged out, and showed by his maimed condition that he had been guilty of a crime" (Roscoe, 1911, p. 261).

III.B.2.
a.v

The ultimate change in the human body is *death*, including suicide. Aside from showing that the person is dead, a corpse may communicate the cause of death. It may suggest the possibility of contagion from germs or spirits. And of course it provokes grief, guilt, or satisfaction among the survivors.

The kind of information conveyed by a corpse is best shown by the way it is handled during burial ceremonies. Among the Ganda of Uganda, only the corpse of a suicide is feared, and hence his "ghost" must be destroyed so that it will not cause "trouble." Usually the suicide has followed custom by hanging himself on a tree or in a house. The tree must be chopped down; the house taken down. Then both the tree or house and body are dragged to a distant place and burned. Those performing the task must wash their hands with sponges made from plantains and burn the sponges on the pyre. These ceremonies seem to remove all traces of the deed so that others may not be reminded of it; for example, the Ganda fear to live in a house in which a suicide has occurred "lest they too should be tempted to commit the same crime." While passing by, women are supposed to throw grass or sticks upon the site of the pyre "to prevent the ghost from entering into them and being reborn" (Roscoe, 1911, p. 20).

------------◆◆◆◆▶

(b) The *changes on the body* about to be discussed are usually impermanent. A glance around the world, or even at any one society immediately confirms the impression that human ingenuity in this respect is boundless; nevertheless certain broad categories are easily distinguishable. First come *cosmetics* on III.B.2. any part of the body: painting, staining, powdering, b.i oiling. Primarily this medium is a visual one, but often an olfactory element (perfume, scent) is added. No doubt because sexual impulses can be so easily conditioned, cosmetics frequently are employed to convey the suggestion of availability or desirability.

------------◆─◆─▶

Ethnographers are prone to report the cosmetics which Africans use in courting, perhaps because they are accustomed to observe and respond to this medium in their own society. A Zulu male in South Africa finds favor with a girl when his body is "well ornamented, and his skin smooth and sleek from the grease with which he carefully anoints himself on festive occasions." So far only part of the story has been told, for he also sprinkles "his body lavishly with scented powder, sometimes even painting his head or body with colored spots or patterns." After all this, he dons his best bead ornaments (Krige, 1936, pp. 370, 374).

With or without the sexual element, cosmetics may serve other functions. The Zulu dandy described above must be clearly identifiable as a Zulu to outsiders less interested in his charm and more concerned with locating him. Likewise when a male among the Nuer in the Sudan uses the ashes from cow manure to powder his body until it appears greyish white, to polish his teeth, and—if he follows the fashion of keeping his hair long instead of cutting it short or shaving it entirely except for a distinguishable tuft on top

—to bleach his hair a light bronze, he must be deliberately publicizing his own attractiveness to insiders and unwittingly his tribal identity to outsiders (Huffman, 1931, pp. 2–3). Three or four months beforehand, Kikuyu boys in Kenya communicate their approaching initiation ceremony by moving about the countryside singing and dancing. In addition, their appearance is distinctive: they wear special clothes and other ornaments, provide themselves with shields and rattles, and paint the exposed parts of their bodies. The painting varies "considerably" but is constant in one respect: the legs and the abdomen are always painted "with an indentated pattern in a white pigment" (Routledge and Routledge, 1910, p. 156).

III.B.2. b.ii — Another way to change the human body is through *clothes,* broadly defined here to include both the presence and absence of all types of apparel from hats and shoes to dresses and pants.

In Africa, no doubt like everywhere in the world, almost any conceivable attribute of the communicator may be transmitted by means of the type of clothes he wears or his manner of wearing them. Is the woman a prostitute? Among the Bwaka of the Congo, only prostitutes cover their breasts with clothing (Nida, 1952b, p. 16). Is she married and, if married, is she pregnant? Among the Zulu of South Africa, girls who have not reached puberty use the color white; unmarried ones have a distinctive loincloth; married women wear "a short leather skirt reaching from the thigh to the knees" and displaying all colors in addition to white; and married women before the birth of the first child and thereafter during each pregnancy wear "a skin tied at the back below the armpits, concealing the breasts and abdomen" (Krige, 1936, pp. 370–2). Is the person literate? Among the Mende in Sierra Leone who are not Creoles or educated, the literate wear shoes and stockings, the illiterate go barefoot (Little, 1951, p. 265). Did the man's dead father have prestige? Among the Tallensi of Ghana, as the oldest son of an important man addresses those assembled at the funeral

of his father; as he holds in his hand a large red cock while recapitulating the noble accomplishments of that father; and as he beats
the cock to death against the walls and hurls it to the spectators
with the challenge that it be taken by anyone who would dare
claim an equally impressive record of achievements, he wears upon
his head a "ceremonial plumed helmet of straw" (Fortes, 1949,
p. 180). Is the man superior or inferior? Among the Amhara of
Ethiopia, the dominant person may signify his desire to protect or
shield a subordinate person such as a younger person or a female
by a bodily gesture which includes his clothes: he lifts part of the
toga off his own body and covers the head and shoulder of the
subordinate (Messing, 1957, p. 519). Once more, it should be evident, the answers to questions like the above vary with the society;
clothes may indeed help make the man, but their particular significance must ever be singularly comprehended.

------◄•••►------

	Another way to change the body is by concentrating
III.B.2.	upon *hair* only: coiffure, shaving (including beard
b.iii	and mustache), depilation.

------•-•------

In Africa hair as a medium of communication seems less versatile than clothes, although through trial and error over generations ingenious coding devices have been evolved. There is, in
the first place, a proper way to treat the hair, which of course
fluctuates considerably from society to society. The Mongo in
the Congo groom their beards and mustaches "with great care,"
but they pluck out "every last hair" on the rest of their body, including their eyebrows and eyelashes (Maes, 1924, p. 172)—to
spot a Mongo in the Congo ought to not take longo. There are
fashions in hair dress among young Zulu men and girls, for the
styles there vary by date and district. The Zulu language itself indicates how expressive coiffure is, for it has one distinctive word
for what in English must be translated as "topknot worn by women
as a sign of marriage" and still another word for what must be
called the "head-ring of a married man." A second communication
can be added to the husband's head-ring by placing in the hair a

gall bladder; then all Zulu know that "the wearer has had a goat killed in his honor at some kraal to which he has been sent as a messenger" (Krige, 1936, pp. 371, 378), no doubt a priceless bit of information for a Zulu. Among the Nkole of Uganda, a man shaves his head once a month but leaves a tuft for his king, another for his father, and sometimes a third for his children; if one of these persons dies, the tuft representing him is shaved away. Women there follow a similar coding system. Then, in addition, all the body hair of married men and women, except for the head patches, is likewise shaved off; and a bride's hair is similarly eliminated, "except that on the pubes, which [is] pulled out by her mother, a very painful process" taking several days to complete (Roscoe, 1923, pp. 76–7, 131).

III.B.2.
b.iv

The fourth change on the human body can come through the use of *ornaments and insignia*, between which no sharp line need be drawn. In common usage, ornaments serve an aesthetic function, and insignia some communicative function. Ornaments, though they are used emotively, are also consequential communications: they can provide information about the wearer's status. And insignia that help people distinguish one another and hence contribute to the stability of a society can certainly be aesthetically satisfying.

There seems to be literally no end to the objects employed in Africa to communicate information about the wearer. Beads, whether imported or manufactured locally, are used in many societies (Bloomhill, 1957). A leopard's tooth signifies royal rank or membership in a royal family among the Mende in Sierra Leone (Little, 1951, p. 190); an ostrich feather in the hair signifies the killing of a man in battle among "certain tribes" of the Somali (Swayne, 1900, p. 11); wearing rings of the entrails of an elephant, sea cow, or rhinoceros on the arms signifies the killing of the first animal of that type among the Nama Hottentot of South Africa (Schapera, 1930, p. 307); and—it may be said unperfunctorily—and so on. Instead of composing a catalogue, a number of points may be briefly made. As ever, it would be interesting to know *why* from a historical standpoint particular significance is attached to an object, but such information is seldom provided. Early Europeans, according to one of them who wrote in 1673, for example, gave the leader of the Hottentot group just mentioned a copperheaded cane, and ever since such a cane has been regarded as "a distinguishing badge of authority"; and common soldiers there carry a club with knots at the top, their officers one without knots (Ten Rhyne, 1933, p. 135). Then the communicative function of each object can only be understood adequately when people's reaction to it is known, as it seldom is. The white ostrich feather, again mentioned above, is rejected by other Somali tribes, which consider it to be a "crude and vainglorious" form of ornamentation (Paulitschke, 1888, p. 38); why? Finally, some ornaments and insignia are presented to their audience in special ways. A total impression may be created not by a single decoration but by a complicated pattern; among the Akan peoples of Ghana, for example, a paramount chief can be distinguished from a lesser chief on an important occasion by the state umbrellas, the drums, and the attendants accompanying him; by "the size and quality" of the emblems attached to those attendants; and by a general and "extraordinary" display of beads, gold, and other jewelry (Danquah, 1928, p. 26). Among the Ganda of Uganda, the keeper of the king's umbilical cord literally keeps it as a symbol in the background, he does not wear it (Roscoe, 1911, p. 235). O tempora, O mores!

IV.   EXTENDING MEDIA

All the media considered thus far, let it be repeated, are called basic because the communicator is present. Now the communicator must recede: first he remains at a distance; then he disappears altogether and may in fact never be known. His message, however, is extended over some distance and over periods of time; pity him not.

The first task here is the same as that in the previous chapter: to specify the *attributes* of each medium. That task, however, can be dismissed at a glance, for it has already been completed: the attributes of the extending media are exactly the same as those of the basic media—no new dimension is needed and the concepts of the previous chapter suffice (III.A). One reminder, though, may not insult the reader's memory: often no extending media are used in communicating; they are not always a part of the communication process.

IV.A

Before plunging crudely ahead into a detailed description of the extending media, let there be a dignified, humanistic pause to raise, without supplying an answer, a fascinating question already mentioned in passing and forever unavoidable: why is it that a society possesses some media of communication and not others; or why does a medium exist in some societies and not elsewhere? To date, historical investigations of the communication media have not provided decisive data. Treatises on the origin of speech or language necessarily can be only speculations. Historical accounts of particular languages are largely descriptive and indicate that linguistic forms depend on a variety of factors, some of which are broad (natural environment, tradition, contact with outside languages), others specific (a shift in pronunciation, perhaps to avoid ambiguity or effort; the style of an important leader).

Likewise the history of modern mass media, such as printing and radio, is well documented in the West but has been almost completely neglected in other areas such as Africa. As these media diffuse to the rest of the world, the phenomenon of differential receptivity in various societies or groups could be investigated directly.

In the absence of provocative historical accounts, a correlational method might be tentatively useful. One illustration can be briefly suggested. Here is a description of the land inhabited by the Tumba, who live in the Congo and who can convey very subtle information on their "talking" drums:

> There are no hills, and the dense tropical rain forest covers the whole country. It is impossible to see for a distance greater than the length of a village except up and down the river. Under these conditions the only way to convey a message by signals from one village to another without a messenger is by sound [Clarke, 1934, pp. 34–5].

The theory here seems to be that, if the assumption is made that people in neighboring villages wish to communicate, they are likely either to devise or borrow drums to do so when the terrain excludes the use of a visual device and makes ordinary travel difficult. Is this so? Clearly empirical investigation of many societies is required. Suppose, then, some relationship were established: the percentage of African societies with such drums would turn out to be significantly greater in the presence than in the absence of the postulated habitat. Unless exactly one hundred per cent of the societies having that habitat and exactly zero of those without it actually possessed the drums, the conclusion would have to be drawn that at least one other factor is also associated with them. No doubt, as suggested subsequently, drums can "talk" only when the drummer and his audience have a tonal language. Thus a two-factor theory would emerge, based on type of habitat and language. And it is also likely that each society singularly accepts or rejects the drums. Such an approach, it would seem, is more provocative than decisive, and so—alas—is the whole historical problem, which forthwith, therefore, is gently and respectfully cast aside, though it refuses to be neglected.

IV.B   *Types* One kind of extending media may be called *instantaneous channels* because they are de-
IV.B.1   vices which only increase immediately the distance over which a message travels without affecting appreciably its content. Two subdivisions seem necessary, both of which are given jargonistic names in order to suggest their mode of functioning. First, there are *secondarily iconic* media which represent in miniature or with little dis-
IV.B.1.a   dia which represent in miniature or with little distortion not the primary referent but either the basic or the extending medium through which the referent originally has been expressed. Speech is a basic medium for thought, and a clear telephone circuit iconically transmits directly not the thought but the speech in which it has been expressed. Among these media a distinction can be drawn between (i) *amplifiers*—megaphones, public address systems; and (ii) *electronic channels*—telephone, radio, television.

Instantaneous communication over a distance may also be through *secondarily symbolic* media. Here the origi-
IV.B.1.b   nal message cannot be transmitted until it has been encoded through a set of symbols, which therefore represent not a primary referent but a medium of communication. The thought is expressed in a sentence, and then the sentence must be thrown into the Morse code before it can be transmitted on an old-fashioned telegraph instrument. The media can be broken down by sense modality: (i) *tones and noises*—bells, drums, gongs, horns, rattles, shots, telegraph, tom-toms; and (ii) *visual devices*—beacons, fire, flags, lights, smoke. Naturally these media may function for the benefit not only of a distant audience but also for those who are in the presence of the communicator. The sound from the drums is heard by people across the valley as well as by those close enough to see the drummers.

———•———

In the interest of fair play and to demonstrate an open mind, the present writer feels obliged conscientiously to report the following: an overseas member of the Royal African Society and a commander of the Italian Air Force are convinced that information is sometimes transmitted at a distance in Africa, not through any of the media mentioned above, but through telepathy. "Some natives," they say, "have a sixth sense either lost to or undeveloped in the European" (Brownlee, 1937), and they supply anecdotal evidence. A duty has been performed; on to drums.

Drums communicate information at a distance either by signaling or "talking" (see especially Carrington, 1944 and 1949). In signaling with a single drum an arbitrary meaning is assigned to a particular sequence or combination of notes so that the instrument becomes a secondarily symbolic medium. Or a set of drums may be employed, each drum associated with a particular kind of message. The drums themselves are then distinguished on the basis of pitch, timbre, and volume. The highest sounding drum of all in the collection among the Akan peoples of Ghana, for example, is beaten only on urgent occasions to summon people to the chief's house; another to assemble councilors for a meeting; and another to announce the king's dinner hour and "when he goes to the toilet." Some of their drums, moreover, can transmit a series of distinctive messages which are appropriately coded (Danquah, 1928, pp. 52–4). In this respect, then, drums are no different from any instrument on which sounds can be produced. In fact, they sometimes are part of a repertoire of other instruments, each of whose notes come to have special significance in the society. Thus among the Ibo of Nigeria innumerable messages may be transmitted without using the human voice:

1. A drum which looks like a water pot and is made of baked clay is played regularly by young girls who are passing through the preliminary stages of marriage, and is used to accompany chants; it may also set the rhythm for dancing.

2. A whistle about the size of a billiard ball, usually made from clay, occasionally wood, produces shrill, piercing notes which serve to sound alarms and transmit messages during skirmishes and wars.

3. Ivory horns, carried only by chiefs, produce notes that can vary in length and are of two tones. Long messages may be transmitted, but usually the instrument is played only for purposes of display.

4. Whistling with the lips or by means of grass stems or hol-

low stalks of leaves transmits general information quite "freely." Those not addressed may be unaware of the transmission since the notes sound as though they were coming from birds.

5. A reed six inches in length has shrill and piercing tones, which are emitted when men work in groups and are supposed to increase their energy.

6. Large tom-toms, which are cylinders of wood, can be heard for five miles and are used to call meetings, at sacrificial festivals, and for making some official announcements.

7. Small tom-toms, which are reserved for the king, are either like the large ones or have stretched across one end a piece of skin that used to come from people flayed alive for the purpose (Basden, 1938, pp. 357–60).

In addition, at least one group of people in this society makes use of a bull-roarer, an instrument which goes back to paleolithic times and hence perhaps is widely diffused throughout the world (Jeffreys, 1949a).

"Talking" drums, on the other hand, reproduce the tonal pattern of a sentence in the proper sequence and hence are somewhat secondarily iconic as well as secondarily symbolic. For vowels two distinct tones are produced by striking either one of two lips on an all-wooden drum (sometimes called a gong or a slit-gong) or a pair of drums with skin tops. Consonants may be approximated by attaching to the drum a jangling metal snare that gives rise to harsh, jarring, or discordant notes. Unquestionably, available evidence suggests, this type of drum language is or can be so frequently employed in Africa because many African languages themselves are tonal—that is, differences in the pitch of the same sounds have different meanings. On the drum, therefore, the tonal value of each syllable of a word or phrase is quite realistically reproduced.

With such a system of drumming it is almost never possible to transmit directly a thought or sentence from common speech. For one thing, many words in each language have the same tonal pattern. They are distinguished from one another only when they are accompanied on the drums by other words which together can produce a relatively distinct pattern. Thus in one African language the words for moon and fowl have exactly the same pattern; hence for moon one long phrase is drummed ("the moon looks down on the earth") and for fowl another ("fowl, the little one which says *kiokio*"). In brief, not words but "the tonal patterns of characteristic short phrases" are encoded. Then the idea behind the sentence to be transmitted is usually reduced to one of the sequences in the spoken language that is so common or stereotyped that people are likely to recognize it. The speech of the talking drum, however, need not always consist of such sequences: information concerning relatively unique events occurring for the first time can be transmitted by combining the old and established phrases into new patterns.

The important subjects for which drummers and audience among the Ashanti have stereotyped holophrases are: "(1) the calling up of any particular chief by name; (2) notice of danger, an enemy, fire, etc.; (3) death of a noted individual; (4) approach of Europeans; (5) summons to take up arms on declaration of war; (6) pieces drummed at . . . festivals . . . which constitute a complete drum-history of the particular clan." Elsewhere, in addition to chiefs, other important people and sometimes ordinary commoners have their distinctive drum names so that messages to or about them can be easily recognized (Goodwin, 1937, p. 234; Rattray, 1923, pp. 252–8). In some areas drum names have three parts: one characteristic of the person, another of his father, and another of his mother's village.

The medium of "talking" in this manner—which also is used in shouting, whistling, and on certain types of instruments, such as a horn or a lute—clearly transmits information at a distance but somewhat laboriously. Thus among the Kalai of the Gabon Republic, the sentence, "The missionary is coming up-river to our villa tomorrow; bring water and firewood to his house," is translated as follows into drum language:

> White man spirit from the forest of the leaf used for roofs comes up-river, comes up-river, when tomorrow has risen on high in the sky to the town and the village of us. Come, come, come bring water of [a specific type] vine, bring sticks of firewood to the house with shingles high up above of the white man spirit from the forest of the leaf used for roofs.

In addition the message must include opening and closing signals, the drum names of the communicator and the audience, and a number of repetitions to insure comprehension; all together, about ten minutes elapses (Carrington, 1949, p. 39). In that society, in fact, messages as long as twenty or thirty minutes are reported to be "frequent."

Among the same people, furthermore, the "maximum distance" at which a single drum can transmit a message is estimated to be about twelve miles. Of course the same message can be retransmitted by another drummer after it has been received, but only provided he wishes to do so and provided that he and the second audience can comprehend it. For the talking drum speaks to no one who has not practiced the coding system and who is not acquainted with the language of the society (Goodwin, 1937, p. 235). There is no intercultural drum language extending beyond the area or region to which people's language has diffused unless there is agreement that the drum language of one society shall prevail (Danquah, 1928, p. 21) or also—as reported in two instances—unless the drum languages of the two societies, aside from personal names, are more similar than the spoken languages (Clarke, 1934, p. 34).

Instantaneous channels extend the distance over which a communication travels; *preserving transmitters* increase the period of time during which a communication can reach an audience. A preserving medium need not always be a channel; handwriting, for example, may be considered an extending communication when one man writes to another. The first subdivision here again may be called (a) *secondarily iconic:* motion pictures (with or without sound) and recordings in any form. They preserve basic or extending media which communicators have utilized; some selection and distortion is inevitable, but the original medium remains more or less intact. The other category is best referred to as (b) *visual* since this modality is utilized and since the media preserve the original situation less iconically. Even the most "naturalistic" representation is likely to contain some interpretation by the communicator or his agent. Visual media may be two- or three-dimensional, and

IV.B.2

they include also devices for display. The follow-
IV.B.2.   ing *two-dimensional* media are noteworthy: photo-
b.i   graphs, drawings, cartoons, paintings, filmstrips, posters, graphs, flannelgraphs, wall pictures.

The problem of whether Africans, through lack of experience,
react differently to the representation of three dimensions on a
two-dimensional surface is discussed subsequently (IX.D.2.c);
here it is sufficient to quote without comment from a missionary
the kind of anecdote that frequently circulates:

> Even pictures are hard to understand, as one realized watch-
> ing an African woman standing before a photograph of a
> Greuze [a French portrait painter] head and gradually dis-
> covering that it *was* a human head. She discovered in turn
> the nose, the mouth, the eye, but where was the other eye? I
> tried by turning my profile to explain why she could only see
> one, but she hopped round to my other side to point out that
> I possessed a second eye which the other lacked! [A. Fraser,
> 1932, p. 38]

In passing, too, the point must be made that it would be useful,
from a practical standpoint, to have for each of the media being
discussed a concise, accurate summary of its advantages and disadvantages for particular audiences in Africa. Such a summary,
however, does not exist: data are either unavailable (e.g., size and
composition of an audience served by each medium) or unknown
(e.g., relative effectiveness of the various media for transmitting
certain types of information). The simpler media can be more
easily pigeonholed, or at least manuals attempt to characterize
them briefly. Here is a description of a flannelgraph, as well as rec-
ommendations concerning its use, that comes from officials in
Ghana:

> Flannelgraph is a set of distinctly cut and brightly colored
> pictures backed with cheap flannel which can stick easily to
> such fluff background as blanket, flannel, and also beaver-
> board or rough hardboard. . . . Flannelgraph is most useful

in the teaching of specific topics to groups of 20 to 30 people but of little or no use in a large rally situation. It has the advantage of being transportable, durable, artistic, and captivating, as well as being an incentive to the class to participate in the work which is being done. Its use facilitates also concentration of attention on one point at a time and makes recapitulating easy. It is inexpensive and easy to prepare. However, it is only effective if the user is conversant with it, active and able to show initative in adapting it to local needs; and it is essential, in order to avoid boredom to the class, not to use the same picture over and over again [anon., 1959a, p. 24].

The temptation to find exceptions to such crisply stated rules is positively overwhelming, but it is resisted for two reasons: the flannelgraph, though important in limited contexts, is not likely to save either the body or the soul of many Africans; and many, perhaps most, busy fieldworkers like to follow boldly stated rules, not ones hedged with bothersome, accurate qualifications.

IV.B.2.   Other visual media are *three-dimensional:* models,
b.ii   masks, statues, casts, footprints.

Models are considered by the missionary quoted a page or so ago to be "most satisfactory" for teaching Africans because the three dimensions of real life are in fact present to be perceived. In addition, when they are put together, in whole or in part by the audience, they convey iconically the situation they are supposed to represent. To improve transportation in Africa, missions are urged to encourage students to make in the classroom "small models of different modes of transportation suited to highways." The technique of road construction can be learned on a small scale by building useful roads on the approaches to the mission stations and on its own grounds (Davis, 1933, p. 335).

Masks and statues are forms of emotive communication, for they are consciously or unconsciously designed not only to represent a real or imaginary referent but to convey dramatically ideas and feelings about that referent. The overpowering statement just made reflects the best which the present writer can squeeze from the views of critics of African masks. One student, for example, suggests that the carvers of masks are not indifferent to natural forms but are seeking to simplify or abstract those forms in order "to express the spiritual world of belief mirrored in the natural world." Members of an unspecified African audience, he implies, know that the dancer they watch is wearing a fetish mask which he has donned in a special hut, but the mask also reinforces their "faith in fertility" (Underwood, 1948, pp. 4, 10, 11). The mask, perhaps, arouses more or less uniform responses among those trained to interpret it in the traditional manner. Another theory argues that masks "always" have two functions: disguising the wearer and "presenting another being." The first function is especially important for secret societies whose members must try to conceal their identity. Then the wearer of the mask may become convinced or would convince his audience that a new spirit has temporarily taken possession of his body. Both functions are served simultaneously when masks are used "for instilling fear into women and children" (Schmalenbach, 1954, pp. 143–8). Among the Ibo of Nigeria, "common belief held that the dead communicated with the living" through masks; and among the Dan of the Ivory Coast, the masks seem through their tranquil appearance to welcome the "spirit of a benign ancestor" rather than to evoke fear (Riley, 1955, pp. 60–4).

IV.B.2.
b.iii
Certain *mechanical devices* display visual media and thus function as channels for disseminating them: bulletin boards, picture frames, chalkboards, billboards, and epidiascopes.

In most parts of West Africa, owners or drivers are fond of painting mottoes or proverbs on their trucks. The goals to be achieved by such communications seem to be varied: advertising the fact that the "mammy wagon" can accommodate paying passengers; providing general advice to mankind; or expressing the pride or anxiety of the owner who, though pleased with his occupation and the vehicle, is likely to be worried about his future and his financial stability. One observer has reported a religious theme in the mottoes to be seen near Ibadan, Nigeria: "No King as God," "God is God," and "God save me" (G. Parrinder, 1953, p. 205). Drivers in Ghana, however, when questioned by a psychiatrist, demonstrated that they were revealing "unconsciously" their "sentiments and character-traits" in selecting the inscriptions and were not merely providing their audiences with helpful information or religious injunctions. Indeed, the investigator noted, the general public also usually understood the emotive nature and content of the cryptic messages. Here are a few examples (Field, 1960, pp. 134–45):

Inscription	*Translation*
Help is God.	God has helped me to get this lorry: human beings haven't.
Some are crying and some are laughing.	I am laughing because I have been able to buy a lorry, but other people are crying because they can't.
All in vain.	I am well protected, so if envious people plot my downfall, they won't succeed.
Kill me and fly.	If you do me any harm, you won't escape.
Cry for life.	I have got a lorry, but now I cry to get a living out of it.
Women are woe to men.	If you spend your money on women, you won't be able to pay for your lorry.

———◆◆◆———

IV.B.2.c *Writing and print* are also preserving transmitters, and assume many forms: (i) notes, letters, tablets; (ii) handbills, leaflets, pamphlets, booklets, books; (iii) magazines; (iv) newspapers; (v) signs, posters, placards, billboards; and (v) teletype, hellschreiber, any form of facsimile transmission. All the subcategories are self-explanatory except perhaps the last, which merely indicates channels for distributing printed and other visual materials to distant places. The actual form of the writing or the print, rather than its content, may be a consequential communication. Graphologists believe they can make valid deductions concerning a writer from various attributes of his writing. Print type may be used as an index of the communicator's affluence, aesthetic taste, or culture.

———•••———

The importance of a given medium of communication can sometimes be appreciated most easily by considering some of the problems that arise when it is absent in a society. Before contact with the East and the West, only two African societies—the Vai and the Mum, both in West Africa—had their own written script (Hailey, 1957, p. 79). Without writing, it was difficult, for example, to send a message from one community to another. Among "southern Bantu" a messenger upon arriving at his destination had to establish his authenticity by means of some symbol provided by the communicator who dispatched him; one chief sent along his own dagger for that purpose. Then the message itself was listened to most carefully and repeated, lest a misunderstanding arise (Goodwin, 1937, p. 242).

In the absence of writing, moreover, permanent records can be kept only by relying on men's memories or upon some mnemonic or mechanical device. For this reason, traditional history in Africa frequently distorts the past and, according to experienced observers (e.g., D. Fraser, 1928, p. 135), contemporary news there becomes virtually "unrecognizable" within weeks. Not for a moment is it being suggested that written records guarantee accuracy, for instances in which the past and the present are distorted in the written communications of the West are all too numerous. On subjects concerning which they might reasonably be expected to be informed, the present writer trusts some African friends in the bush more than he does most metropolitan tabloids and one popular news magazine in the United States. Nonliterate peoples, it seems fair to say, nevertheless, are battling unfavorable odds in trying to preserve the past (XI.C).

The fact that so many African societies by themselves contrive or accept indigenous devices for recording information is evidence that they independently recognize the need for some system that promotes accuracy. Among the Ganda of Uganda, tax collectors tally each hut by means of a cowry shell; they are responsible for avoiding any discrepancy between the number of shells and the pieces of barkcloth or the cattle that constitute the tax (Goodwin, 1937, p. 243). In the same society a messenger with several items to remember cuts off bits of sticks and ties them into a bundle; then he throws away a stick as he delivers each message (Roscoe, 1911, pp. 41–2). Some Kikuyu mothers in Kenya plant trees at the birth of a child and thus for a while can keep track of his age (Routledge and Routledge, 1910, p. 11). The Chaga of Tanganyika assign to each child a notched stick elaborately carved with numerous complicated symbols; and many of his duties and responsibilities are taught by means of those symbols. Thus the first lesson, represented among some of the Chaga by its own symbol on the stick, "deals with the protection of feces from misuse for magical purposes" (Gutmann, 1932, p. 29). Among the Nama Hottentots of South Africa a woman keeps track of gestation by making a cut in a pole of her hut after the first new moon following knowledge of her pregnancy; thereafter "every successive new moon is similarly marked, until the ninth cut has been made, when preparations are taken in hand for the delivery" (Schapera, 1930, p. 261). Among the Fang peoples of the Gabon and Cameroon Republics the meanings assigned to two systems of communication, one using bundles of little sticks and the other "une sorte de pictographie," are known to everyone but have esoteric significance to the initiated (Alexandre and Binet, 1958, pp. 124–5). Finally, again and again incidents like the following are reported, which show how pathetically eager some Africans are to utilize print for the sake of accuracy. At the end of a course on child welfare in West Africa, a "group of semiliterate African women" asked for copies of the instructor's charts before returning to their remote villages: "We wish to teach other women how to keep death from the door of the hut," they said, "but without copies of these lessons we shall make mistakes and forget" (J. Davis et al., 1945, p. 182).

Throughout modern Africa, moreover, people have become dependent upon writing, especially letters, so much so that the oc-

cupation of professional letter-writer is a popular one. These somewhat literate scribes work either full- or part-time at their trade;
some have their own offices devoted completely to this function,
others are located within shops having primarily some other purpose, and still others congregate at an appropriate public site, such
as a post office, and there squat as they receive dictation or read
aloud. "The enormous bulk of native correspondence in the African
post offices," a missionary suggests, "proves how links have been
formed which connect the village life with the wanderers who have
travelled thousands of miles in search of work" (D. Fraser, 1928,
p. 139). Clearly, it would seem, the drift of African males away
from home to find temporary or permanent work has set up a new
need, which the postal service can uniquely satisfy. As ever,
though, the cause-and-effect sequence may not be so simple. For
the existence of the service may have helped produce "the wanderers" who might not otherwise leave home or leave it so readily if
they knew they were to be cut off completely from their families
or if they could not send them, through the same postal system,
some of the money they earn in distant places.

Undoubtedly, this section may conclude, the most revolutionary
change in the communication system of Africans as a result of contact with the West has been the introduction of the phonetic system of writing and its accompanying tools.

------◆◆◆◆------

IV.B.3   The important media here grouped together and
called *consequential* are artifacts serving two functions. First, they enable people to achieve primary
and social goals (II.A.1 and 2). Then, after being
created, they transmit information about the communicators and
their society, and they may thus affect prevailing communication
patterns. In a basic sense, this category restates the traditional
archaeological assumption that whatever men do and create provides information about them.

IV.B.3.a   Some consequential media, in the first place, spring
from *body-sustaining* activities: agricultural, hunting,
fishing, and pastoral practices, and the animals and
plants that are utilized.

Contrast the pastoral methods of two societies. Among the Rundi of Ruanda-Urundi the cattle feed in pastures and are kept within the inner fence of the household at night. Only in the dry months are they driven into the "fresher pastures of the mountains" (Meyer, 1916, pp. 21, 42). The Somali of Somalia, on the other hand, must range over "wide distances in the search for pasture and water" (I. M. Lewis, 1958, p. 246). These different practices reflect of course the physical environment: the Rundi inhabit a relatively fertile area, the Somali a desert-type region. But perhaps centuries ago the methods could also have been influenced by the cultures which the people moving into the area brought with them. Now, however, there can be no doubt that the "permanent" dwellings of the Rundi and the "nomadic" hamlets of the Somali affect the social relations and the kinds of communications prevailing in the two areas.

IV.B.3.b   *Body-protecting* media include arrangements of buildings within the community; building type; furnishings. Clothing could just as well be mentioned here as under changes on the human body (III.B.2.b. ii). A more detailed breakdown is required for each of the subcategories; under building type, for example, must be included not only the function of the structure (dwelling, shop, church, government office, etc.) but also the decorations, seating arrangements, acoustics, etc.

To suggest the importance of the consequential media of communication, let it be assumed in fantasy that a complete stranger is approaching a village in Africa; that he has an encyclopedic knowledge of African ethnography; but that he does not know where in Africa he is at the moment. Under these circumstances, what kinds of information are conveyed to him by the buildings of the village before he observes or has any contact with its inhabitants? In the first place, he might be able to deduce the identity of the society from the arrangement of the buildings in the village and from their modal style. A Ganda village, for example, is not built according to a regular plan. It has no open or public place at which by deliberate design people are supposed to assemble. Instead, "each house stands by itself, among its own bananas," seldom within shouting distance of the neighboring dwellings (Mair, 1934, p. 15). In contrast, Nuer huts and windscreens in the Sudan are arranged much closer together, in a semicircle or a complete circle with their backs to the prevailing winds (Evans-Pritchard, 1938, p. 69). The carefully and skillfully built houses of the Nuer, moreover, are cylindrical in form and have conical roofs (Westermann, 1931, p. viii); whereas those of the Ganda, though formerly round, now are generally square or rectangular, usually with overhanging roofs made of thatch (Mair, 1934, pp. 16–17). Surely the stranger using such consequential media would not deduce that a village belonged to the Ganda when in fact it was inhabited by Nuer.

The same outsider may also be provided with information enabling him to distinguish between communities within a society. Among the Bemba of Northern Rhodesia, the first buildings in a village that usually attract attention are the granaries, most of which are around the outer edges of the community. They are reported to be "the measure by which the prosperity of a village is largely judged." As media they transmit information most efficiently. "Many huts with a few grain bins" signifies "few adult male householders in the community"; "cracking walls or uprights eaten by white ants" means "supplies are running low." If the stranger entering the village really is as omniscient as has been assumed, he will respond like "a native" who uses in effect the condition of the granary as a consequential medium to decide whether the building is full or empty. Such a person says of the owner of the granary: "If she had more than a couple of baskets of millet left, she would get her husband to mend the roof again" (Richards, 1939, pp. 84–5).

Next the gifted outsider might wish to make deductions concerning the function of a particular building. First, he can note its location. The Bemba, for example, "usually" build men's club houses at the end of a village (ibid., p. 120); the Tiv of Nigeria "usually" place a smithy on the outskirts of a village (East, 1939, p. 62) and a reception hut inside the oval of the houses composing the compound (Bohannan, 1954, p. 3). Then the appearance of the house can serve as a consequential medium. A "flimsy" shelter of grass among the Nuer means that the hut is used only in the dry season; whereas "massive byres and well-built huts" are for the rainy season (Evans-Pritchard, 1938, p. 69). The sleeping hut of the Tiv has only a single entrance, but the important house in which men meet and in which palavers may be conducted has four entrances diagonally opposite each other (East, 1939, pp. 53, 64).

Finally, the postulated omniscience of this extraordinary audience would provide him with information about people in the community. Still without assistance from anyone, he ought to be able to find the chief's residence. In Bemba country he would not even look for a chief in a village having from thirty to fifty huts, for chiefs live only in communities with "several times" that number (Whiteley, 1950, p. 23). The house of a Ganda chief can easily be distinguished, for it is surrounded by a fence of intertwined cane. Inside or outside the fence are usually other government buildings, like a courthouse, prison, and rest house for visitors. Formerly such an establishment was located on a hilltop in order, for security purposes, to command a good view; now it is often closer to the main road so that ready contact with British officials can be made (Mair, 1934, pp. 17–18). Innumerable telltale characteristics of a house offer clues concerning the occupant's status. A corrugated metal roof among the Ganda is clearly a sign of affluence (ibid., p. 17), as indeed it seems to be for most African people. Among the Nuer a "smooth and even" roof symbolizes either the skill of the owner or the wealth that he must have in order to be able to hire a skilled roofer (Huffman, 1931, p. 16). Older men among the Bemba preempt "good sites such as small eminences or ant-hills" and live in huts that tend to be large and well built; and the size of a person's village garden reflects the age and status of the occupant (Richards, 1939, pp. 120, 271).

Our friend, the stranger, may now be dismissed because he has served his function of showing how the buildings of a village unwittingly are consequential media. A fact previously withheld to prevent him from becoming either discouraged or cocky, however, must be disclosed: in seeking social goals, people may deliberately construct a building in a particular way so that it may be there-after a medium of communication. The owner of the hut wants the metal roof not because it provides better or safer protection than one built from thatch but solely because it will bring him prestige among his peers. The clearest illustration in Africa, per-haps anywhere, is the distinctive style of churches, temples, or mosques. When one enters an African city like Ibadan (G. Par-rinder, 1953, p. 66), for example, the many mosques which are immediately visible indicate clearly that Islam is important in that area of Nigeria. There is little danger of confusing a mosque and a church.

IV.B.3.c   *Tool-obtaining* media refer to any sort of hand tool or machine.

The method of constructing a tool may identify the society from which it comes; here are observations concerning hoes in Northern Nigeria:

> As we advance toward the south, the soils become increasingly heavier, and heavier types of hoes are used, each district em-ploying a characteristic type. . . . The wooden handle is generally set at an angle of 45° to the blade, but one may see pagan hoes (e.g., the Makangara) where the angle is as sharp as 15°. The handles are generally fitted to the blades by the socketing method, but Yoruba hoes are commonly tanged; while among many of the pagan tribes (e.g., the Angas and Sura) the handles are made fast to the iron midrib by a fibre binding [Meek, 1925, v. 1, p. 127].

In addition, the blades of the hoe used on the western side of the Niger are half the size of those favored on the eastern side (Basden, 1938, p. 301). The consequential vocabulary of a hoe in Nigeria, it thus appears, consists of weight, size, blade angle, and method of attaching the handle.

IV.B.3.d *Physical objects* other than buildings that protect people, tools, and decorations and insignia upon the body are also extending media. The boundary between the objects being considered here and those previously considered is thin and almost indistinguishable, but worth retaining. For there is a difference between a building used as a dwelling and one used as a tomb; between a hoe and a ceremonial baton; and between a ribbon on the chest and a flag upon a pole.

A brief survey of objects having a communicative function suggests that they range from those serving only that purpose to those serving other purposes simultaneously. Sometimes a report does not specify the exact functions. Thus among the Mende of Sierra Leone, parents are sent a piece of tobacco when their daughter has been initiated into the female secret society (Little, 1951, p. 127). Certainly the leaf communicates the good news, but then what happens to it? Is it kept as a kind of certificate or, having served its destiny, is it then smoked like any ordinary tobacco?

Usually, however, cosmic doubts of this sort do not arise. Memorials, for example, are completely dedicated to communicating their messages. Among the Ibo of Nigeria, conical mounds of earth decorated with small pots and covering the remains of goats that have been killed in a special ceremony are in fact shrines for the goddess whose aid is invoked to secure children (Basden, 1938, p. 167). Although it is clear that the mounds serve only a communicative end bestowed upon them during the ceremony, nevertheless, it is not certain how people continue to react to them. Are they thus powerfully reminded of the goddess or do they allow the mound gradually to fade into the landscape without forcefully serving its original purpose any longer? Among the Amhara of Ethiopia, on the other hand, the conical piles of rocks visible along the countryside must eventually lose their communicative power. Originally they commemorate a battle or the resting place of a saint, but their form becomes unrecognizable when passers-by alter the shape and size by adding small rocks. In addition, they bear no inscriptions, in order "to prevent an evil spirit . . . from fastening onto the name and doing harm" (Messing, 1957, p. 488).

The noncommunicative function of an object may be apparent but most unimportant. On certain occasions a chief uses as a seat the holy stool that symbolizes the authority of the office he holds, but its role as a piece of furniture is secondary. Among the Ashanti of Ghana a king never dies, for his spiritual soul returns to the Supreme Being and his physical soul remains bound to his stool (E. G. Parrinder, 1956). The symbolic function of an object, moreover, may come to replace its earlier purpose. Among the Nuer in the Sudan, a spear brandished in the right hand is no longer a warlike gesture but signifies the vitality of the person and his lineage (Evans-Pritchard, 1953). Ceremonies involving food and drink may provide both sustenance and symbolism. Among the Ibo the serving of kola nuts by the host to the guest at the outset of a visit points to good relations between the two, provided that a complicated ritual is first followed. After many salutations, the host puts a nut to his lips, "thus signifying that it is about to be offered in good faith" and also that he himself is "free from malice" (Basden, 1938, p. 162).

Noticeable in many of the illustrations just cited is the fact that an object comes to serve as a communication medium only after a ceremony or ritual has invested it with a meaning it had not inherently possessed beforehand. The association, however, may be established without formality. Lectures on home economics in Africa, for example, are advised to depend during a cooking demonstration upon utensils that have been deliberately borrowed from the homes of members of the audience. For if the demonstrator uses her own "perfect little models," the women might attribute her success to those objects and be convinced that without them they themselves could not succeed (Moomaw, 1957, p. 22).

IV.B.3.e   *Attributes of objects,* such as color, shape, size, and texture, are considered consequential media because by themselves, almost regardless of the context in which they are embedded, they convey information.

Among the Ashanti of Ghana, the color of the symbolically important stool mentioned above is changed from white to black when people wish to perpetuate the memory of a wise ruler. Then it is placed in the stool house where it assumes the status of "a treasured heirloom" and also that of a sacred "shrine": the help of the departed is invoked on special occasions (Rattray, 1923, p. 92). The new color, therefore, helps to remind people of the chief's death and of the new role to be performed by his stool. The Zulu of South Africa seem to cultivate the circular form for their kraals and for the clothes and coiffure of their women; and so a sample of Zulu women who had little meaningful contact with Europeans tended to prefer a crudely drawn circle rather than a square or a triangle (Doob, 1960a, p. 199). Here circularity may be a consequential medium that either communicates to outsiders and to Zulu a cultural preference or identifies in some instances a Zulu person or artifact.

IV.B.3.f *Money,* either in the form of blatant currency or subtle property, transmits information about the wealth and purchasing power of the owner.

Unquestionably the one form of wealth most clearly associated with Africa is cattle. This currency, like any other, is valued first of all because its possession confers prestige upon the owner. Among the Nkole of Uganda, who are fairly typical of cattle people in this respect, "a man was considered poor or wealthy according to the number of his cattle, and the places of the chiefs when assembled before the Mugabe [king] were arranged according to the size of their herds" (Roscoe, 1923, p. 2). Then, although very often the cattle bring joy as animals, almost in the way the stereotyped miser is supposed to obtain satisfaction from counting and fondling his gold, they are also used to obtain other desirable goods and, very frequently, a wife. Among the Tallensi of Ghana, a woman is "usually" espoused when a man agrees to pay the bride price of four cattle immediately or their equivalent in installments. The woman thoroughly approves of her cost; she indignantly refuses a man who has not paid at least a portion of the bride price. In her view, not to be paid for is an insult, "placing her on the level of a casual lover and exposing her to the taunts of her co-wives of the lineage" (Fortes, 1949, p. 86).

Those wise in the ways of Africans—almost all Africans, many anthropologists, some European colonial servants, and various missionaries—look upon bride price not as a crude way to buy a wife but as an important part of the marriage contract which contributes mightily to the stability of the African family. Among the Mende of Sierra Leone, the woman's relatives who have received part of the bride wealth retain "an interest in keeping the marriage intact"; if the marriage crumbles, they may be called upon to return money already spent. Likewise the man's relatives would have the two live in love and harmony, for they lose not only "the general services" of the wife but also part or all of their own contribution to the man's marital expenses if she runs away; as a result of that contribution, they have "a say over the treatment of the girl" and thus "sometimes" may be able to restrain a husband or his other relatives if they treat her harshly (Little, 1951, pp. 160–1). When the wealth that has passed from one family to another takes the form of cattle, the constant presence of the animals must serve to remind the contractors of their privileges and obligations: four cattle grazing with the rest of the herd constitute a more obvious and certainly a more attention-demanding symbol than money in the bank.

———————◄••►———————

IV.B.3.g *Bodies of other people* are consequential media when they function like an object attached to the communicator and communicate information about him. A leader's status or power can be inferred from the size of his following. The fertility of a person is shown by the number of children. A wife may provide a clue to the husband's mobility, clan, or good judgment. No earth-shaking claim is being made: people are known to a certain extent by the company they keep, seek, or create.

The number of dependents seems to be a universal symbol of importance, at least in Africa. Thus the "greatness in power and affluence" of a chief among the Ashanti of Ghana is suggested by the number of linguists he can maintain (Danquah, 1928, p. 43). Since in virtually every African society polygyny is the ideal attained only by relatively few males and since women have important economic roles to perform in addition to their usual duties and functions, the number of wives a man possesses generally signifies unequivocally his status in terms of his society's values. "Customary law of marriage provides that a man may have as many wives as he can support," the Kikuyu anthropologist reports of his society, and "the larger one's family, the better it is for him and the tribe" (Kenyatta, 1938, p. 174). As every man knows, moreover, a wife's symbolic attributes do not detract at all from her charm.

The human body, whether in action or dead, conveys information. In Northern Nigeria, the present writer was told in 1959, casual contact between important people gives rise to all kinds of rumors. Let an emir and a district officer be seen walking down a road, and people begin to anticipate the official edict which much later will be made known to them. In parts of southern Africa and Angola ritual murder is said to be committed to obtain supernatural power from the dead person's soul either directly by killing him or afterwards by eating, or making an amulet from, some special part of his body (Estermann, 1958). The trophy thus conveys the increase in power both to the person himself and his associates. Similarly among twenty-seven head-hunting societies of Northern Nigeria which were once observed, "the acquisition of an enemy's head [was] the young man's passport to manhood." Without such a head in his possession, "his social status [was] no better than that of a girl, and no girl would marry him." In some societies, moreover, the head communicated the desired information only if it had been obtained under prescribed and hence proper conditions, just as a soldier in Western society is supposed to win his medal in battle and not buy it from a pawnbroker. Among the Igala, for example, wounding and then beheading an enemy did not count; a "direct blow in a stand-up encounter" was required—and then the dead man's spirit had to be appeased yearly by pouring pullet blood over his skull. Among the Anaguta, on the other hand, any kind of head sufficed, even one from a body shot by someone else (Meek, 1925, v. 2, pp. 51–2).

———◆◆◆◆▶———

IV.B.4   The final group of media, *natural phenomena*, may seem at first glance to stretch the definition of communication beyond the breaking point. For in truth reference is made here to any kind of object or event not under direct human control which transmits information to an audience. Such information is conveyed as a result of the past experience of some communicator who may or may not be the same person or persons as the audience. The man to whom a rainbow portends pending death may have laid the foundation for such an interpretation through an experience none of his contemporaries have had; hence he is both communicator and audience, and others do not react to a rainbow as he does. On the other hand, the significance attached to this natural phenomenon may spring from a tradition within the society; then the original communicators, the men and women who found that rainbows mean pending death, are undoubtedly unknowable. In these two senses any cloud, any plant, any animal, any event must be considered a medium of communication. Why not? The broad approach, it should be evident, would emphasize again that the omnipresent proclivity of people to attach meanings to virtually every aspect of their surroundings indicates that they are utilizing whatever information they can to help themselves. And the process of obtaining information is the same whether the final medium in a long chain of singular events is a newspaper or a cloud in the sky.

———•—•———

The literature of Africa teems with instances of natural phenomena being employed as media as now defined. Typical is a report concerning the Gogo of Tanganyika, who believe that the position of a chameleon's tail conveys important information: a raised tail is a good omen for a traveler, but a curled-up one is such a bad sign that the traveler must return home. The latter communication also brings bad luck to the animal, for it is then killed (Carnell, 1955). Perhaps everywhere some special significance is attached to the soil, on which people are dependent for all or most of their food. Among the Tallensi in Ghana, for example, everyone stands "in awe" of the earth, for which in consequence there is a special cult with its own shrines. The earth is not supposed to be desecrated by having blood shed upon it, nor the shrines despoiled by sounding in their neighborhood the alarm signal that summons men to arms (Fortes, 1945, p. 176).

Two chapters on the media of communication cannot be concluded without raising a question previously left unasked: since so many media are usually at the disposal of a communicator, what determines the choice of a medium for a specific communication? This question, like all others involving the interrelationship of the variables within the boundaries of communication, can be answered ultimately only in terms of all the other factors comprising the circle unveiled in the Prologue. In this instance, though, more specific factors seem pressingly important. The choice of medium certainly depends in part upon its availability, its suitability for the communication to be transmitted, and perhaps too upon the communicator's interest in the medium as such. Drums cannot be sounded in a society which does not possess them, they will not be used to transmit a message which cannot be encoded into their "language," and they may not be heard if the communicator develops a personal aversion to them. To anticipate the existence of one of these precipitating conditions is an occupation fascinating in its own right but probably beyond the scope of the analysis of communication as such. The servant of the chief beats the war drums only when there is a war; it is too much to ask that the war be predicted for the sake of specifying when the drums will be struck. Or if the scar on the man's chest is visible only when he takes off his shirt, some other discipline, please, must assume the responsibility of forecasting when he doffs it.

It would be dreadful, finally, to leave the impression that communications always reach people in the neat little package of a single medium. Obviously the communicator sometimes does indeed use only a drum, a public address system, or a radio transmitter; but frequently, too, he resorts to a barrage of media. In addition, many communicators may be functioning simultaneously. Consider, for example, the following description of contemporary Africa:

> Today it is not possible to live in Africa and to be indifferent to political questions. In the most remote villages there are some who have travelled to the town or plantations or mines for work and have brought back news of the great changes that are taking place. The most backward tribes are affected by community development plans, and their chiefs are confronted by new problems of social change. Wherever there is a man who can read, there the newspapers will somehow find their way. Rumors of fear and tensions penetrate along every bus and lorry route; the ferment of change is carried in every basket of goods along the paths linking the market places with the peasant homes [J. Taylor, 1957, p. 7].

The journalistic report exaggerates a bit no doubt, but it does suggest that communications about change in Africa are numerous and are transmitted variously. In such a situation no analyst can ordinarily identify with precision and certainty either the communicators or the audiences. The significant role of communication in hastening social change, however, is clear.

V. THE SITE

A communication always reaches people at a particular site. Even in the simplest conversation the site may affect their reactions. Two persons conversing indoors hear each other easily in the absence of distracting sounds; they talk leisurely and at length, in part because they are comfortable. The same two people, discussing the same topic outdoors, react differently: a howling breeze makes comprehension difficult, requires them to speak loudly and distinctly, and causes them quickly to stop communicating. Likewise the listener to a radio program may be swayed by the speaker when he is alone but may be uninfluenced when other listeners in the room hoot derisively.

Obviously people can communicate at any kind of site. Only the dead are completely silent or unreceptive. The living, even when asleep or unconscious, transmit and receive information in sites ranging from the bottom of the ocean to ever-increasing heights in the air or from the largest banquet hall to the most intimate bed. This chapter would not and cannot classify sites, rather it suggests the effects of any site upon certain factors relevant to communication.

Size of the Audience   The number of people accommodated at a site is important for many reasons. First, it may determine the extent of the communicator's effectiveness at a given moment or over a period of time. Then sheer quantity can be influential; so-called mob hysteria is more likely to be displayed by a large group of people than by a handful. The communicator himself faces different problems in composing and transmitting his communication as the size of the audience increases; and feedback from a few is usually but not always easier to obtain than from many. What attributes of the site, then, are likely to affect size?

V.A

The first attribute is the actual *location* of the site. In a crude sense it is necessary to specify only the exact location; the market is at the crossroad, the meeting house is in the center of the town, etc. In fact, though, the coordinates are significant only as they locate the site with respect to an audience of a potential size. That size in turn is a function of *population density*. It seems unquestionably true throughout the world that denser urban areas, in comparison with less sparsely settled rural areas, contain a greater number of media and sites at which communications are transmitted. For practical reasons, printing plants, radio stations, and meeting halls are almost always found in cities and not in the country, and so the latest news from outside circulates there more quickly and perhaps in greater quantity. Similarly government officials find it less productive to work in or travel to sparsely settled areas.

V.A.1

V.A.1.a

———•———

Accurate and up-to-date population figures for most of Africa, including almost all urban areas, are usually lacking, as a result of which it is virtually impossible to estimate or anticipate with any precision the potential size of an audience for a mass medium at a particular site. Still, crude estimates are frequently sufficient for most purposes, especially since other factors besides population density affect the actual size of the audience. In Nigeria, for example, about half the population lives in the Northern Region, which has a density of 85 people per square mile; whereas in the other two smaller regions of the country the corresponding figure is between 400 and 500 (Pilkington, 1956, p. 219). The possible error in such figures, though substantial, cannot be sufficiently large to cancel out the great contrast between the Northern Region and the other two, a contrast that can serve as the starting point for understanding or transmitting communications in Nigeria. There and elsewhere in Africa figures on population density must take into account significantly large areas that are uninhabited, such as deserts and sections infested by the tsetse fly.

———••►———

Whether or not people who live in a region will actually go to a site, such as a market or a meeting house, depends also upon its accessibility. Accessibility in turn can be viewed geographically or socially. By *geographical accessibility* is meant the actual distance people must travel or the effort they must expend to reach the site. Whether they attend the market or the meeting can be affected by its distance from their home; in contrast, they must cross only from one side of the room to another to turn on a radio set.

V.A.1.b

Here and elsewhere (VI.A.1 and 2), the problem of physical transportation becomes most relevant to communication: travel to a site often depends on available transportation. Particularly in Africa the airplane has brought sensational changes because so much of the continent has been—and still is—either inaccessible by railroads, roads, and waterways or inconvenient and time-consuming to reach (Stamp, 1953, p. 195). These changes, however, do not necessarily make new communication sites available to more Africans but instead bring more outside communicators and communications to them at old sites. For relatively few Africans have ever used a plane; but mail and printed media and people from the outside reach them in increasing numbers. To be sure, new sites have also been made more accessible by improved roads, by the phenomenally great increase in the use of the bicycle and the public bus, and by the growth of towns and cities in which the new mass media are conveniently located and where meetings occur. Details concerning these changes need not be recited, but clearly the traditional pattern of communicating with people outside one's immediate community has dramatically changed. Formerly, for example, there was relatively little moving about from place to place: communication sites were within the community, unless the society itself migrated or unless herding or war produced a group which in the course of their occupation became the conveyors and receivers of information. The following description comes from Somalia around 1880: "As he travels through the countryside, either following his herd or driving his animal in the caravan, the Somali, talkative creature that he is, never fails to call out to persons that he meets, to greet them, and if possible to question them. If there is time, they will squat down for a while and confide news to each other" (Paulitschke, 1888, p. 33). Not soon (VI.B.3) but in the distant future, if such a Somali continues to travel, he will carry a transistor radio.

————◄••►————

V.A.2 The second kind of accessibility, *social accessibility*, suggests the rules and regulations which enable some people and not others to be present at a communication site. An outsider does not participate in an intimate family discussion within the home unless he is deliberately invited to do so. Those unable or unwilling to pay the admission charge may not enter the theater. Women or children are not permitted to observe a ritual. The social organization of a society and in particular its method of regulating land tenure restrict the kinds of people who may have access to significant sites under specified conditions.

————•—•————

Typically, only members are admitted to the site at which secret societies in West Africa transact their affairs. Among the Mende of Sierra Leone, for example, the sacred bush of the principal society is usually adjacent to the town and engulfed by high cotton trees "that create an appearance of both majesty and mystery." In the center is a clearing where the founder of the bush and other notables in the past are buried. Formerly the special rites establishing the site included the sacrifice of a man and woman who were then buried "in a standing position" (Little, 1951, p. 247). Members who know that they alone have the privilege of being present at such a site are likely to be in a mood to respond favorably to the communications they receive during the society's rituals and deliberations (VIII.E).

A site can become socially inaccessible because it is too small, and a small site may be selected deliberately to limit the size or the activity of the audience. Among the Nupe in Nigeria, weeks and even months of discussion often pass before a decision can be reached concerning who should be given a vacant or a new title. First the elders come together in small groups in their own houses. Then later, after reaching "a more advanced stage" in the discussion, they meet in the house of people of higher rank and, still later, they finally congregate at the house of the chief:

> As always in meetings of this kind the assembly gathers in the entrance hut of the house; the younger men sit near the outer door, the elder men on the inner side of the hut. . . . The meetings . . . are quiet and dignified, the discussion flows slowly, no loud word is spoken; the younger men are mostly silent, only the elder ones take part. If controversies or disagreements occur, they are never apparent in the discussion itself [Nadel, 1942, pp. 49–50].

The site of the discussion, a hut with limited capacity, places the younger men in a less advantageous position on the outside. The entire procedure thus clearly favors the older men, who in fact rule a Nupe community.

As already indicated in the brief allusion above to the airplane in Africa, another way to increase the size of an audience is through the *mobility of the communicator:* he literally moves V.A.3 to the mountain because the people living there can or will not come to his site in the distant valley.

Any of the media that can transmit communications at a distance (IV.B.1), such as drums or smoke, are in effect being used by mobile communicators. The prototype is the town crier whose message reaches people no matter where they happen to be. Among the Tallensi of Ghana, a characteristic alarm call is sounded from the flat roofs of their houses when someone dies or the assistance of a neighbor is needed (Fortes, 1949, p. 49).

Throughout Africa a shortage of trained personnel makes it necessary for many communicators from the outside to serve at more than one site when it is impractical or undesirable to expect the audience to travel some distance to reach a central place.

Often, for example, the leader of a local church is a layman, but an ordained clergyman appears there and at a number of other churches on the same Sabbath or else only on certain Sundays of the month. Each church, even with a part-time minister, can serve important functions within its own community; thus among the rural Amhara in Ethiopia, these small churches are said to be "the most potent" of influences, one symptom of which is the fact that "every church is the center of a radiating system of small paths . . . chiefly used by people coming to service" (Buxton, 1949, pp. 169–70). Similarly, in the field of medicine, centralized hospitals and dispensaries service smaller units in outlying districts through visiting medical assistants and nurses. In this way not only are the ill spared a trip to the medical center but the local population as a whole benefits from the information concerning sanitation and public health transmitted by the experts during their visits to the community (J. Davis et al., 1945, p. 147).

V.B   *Composition of the Audience* The site at which a communication is received usually affects not only the size of the audience but also its composition, which
V.B.1   can be viewed in terms of homogeneity and the reciprocal attitudes of the members. With *homogeneity* is likely to be positively correlated meaningful experiences in the past, strong identification and sense of loyalty, and hence a readiness to respond to and with the group's values. At
V.B.2   some sites people may have strong positive or negative *reciprocal feelings;* at others—the proverbial bus stop—they may be quite indifferent.

Since people always belong to innumerable groups, ranging from the family to very informal organizations, and since they are likely to respond differently when one group rather than another is "salient" for them—that is, when they are conscious of their membership—the effectiveness of a communication may depend in part upon the group to which at the moment they refer their behavior. Their consciousness of membership in one group can be traced to at least three principal factors. First, is the group important to them? If it is, they are more likely at a given moment to be thinking about it or to be concerned with its affairs. Secondly, is there an allusion to the group in the communication itself? Obviously they may be reminded of their membership by such a reference. Thirdly and relevant to the discussion, regardless of the importance of the group to them and regardless of allusions to it in the communication, are they at a site associated with such a group? If the communication reaches them, for example, when they are at the club's meeting place, they are very likely to react to it, in part at least, in terms of that club's values. At the site, moreover, they may be required to behave in ways that remind them of one particular group or, at any rate, that create within them a special mood (VIII.B.4). To attend a meeting or participate in some ceremony, people may wear special clothes, the sight of which recalls the purpose for assembling.

Some forms of communication are likely to be used only in certain types of groups. Among the Azande of the Congo and Sudan "a shrill ululation" is "a sign of joy." A woman may cry out in that manner when she is alone, but a male will do so only at sites harboring groups of a particular composition: men must be with other men who simultaneously utter the wail; youths must be at work upon the chief's crops and must also wish to show that they have not abandoned the job. The men would no more think of suddenly shouting when not in such a group than "an Englishman would, alone, utter three cheers" (Larken, 1927, p. 97).

Different sites within a community may attract different audiences and hence be associated with different sorts of communications. In the market towns of the Amhara in Ethiopia, there are three classes of "public facilities for relaxation." High officials and nobles never go to any one of the three and so can be disregarded in noting the composition of the communicators and the audiences. First, the "teahouse" is "fully respectable"; it is for men only—even the waiters are male—and draws traders, clerks, minor officials, and police detectives, who reportedly discuss "business matters and events of the day." Then the "barley-beer house" is "fairly respectable" for commoners and lower classes. It is operated by women; lodging is offered, accompanied if the patron wishes by a "temporary wife." Finally there is the "mead house" where the communication is doubtless on an elementary and basic level; the owner here is a woman who offers her patrons only entertainment and sexual pleasure (Messing, 1957, pp. 539–40).

By and large the most significant communication site in any society must be the home, for there basic socialization occurs within the family. "Family" in the West suggests a relatively small and homogeneous group since the institution here is of the nuclear, monogamous type: one man, one woman, their children, and perhaps a few scattered relatives. In Africa, on the other hand, the number of communicators and the size of the audience in the family are likely to be greater, first because families tend to be of the extended type (and hence more relatives reside together) and secondly because polygyny, the marriage of one man to more than one wife, "preponderates to an overwhelming extent, prevailing in 88 per cent of a representative sample of 154 societies drawn from the continent at large." Even though, as previously indicated (IV.B.3.g), the polygynous ideal is not realized by all males in a society, still the different kinds of communications fostered by such a family form are suggested by the anthropologist whose statement has just been quoted:

> Africans have discovered means of making the institution work to the satisfaction of both sexes. No woman lacks a male provider. No polygynous wife has trouble finding a helper or a baby sitter in time of need. Since the first wife normally enjoys for her lifetime a position of superior authority and prestige, every woman knows in advance of her marriage what her future status will be and has no fear of being superseded. Since men almost universally establish each of their wives in a separate dwelling and endow them individually with land and livestock, sources of friction are reduced to a minimum. Custom normally requires the husband to treat each wife with equal consideration, to eat and sleep with each in regular rotation, so that no married woman suffers public humiliation through any overt manifestation of favoritism [Murdock, 1959, pp. 25–6].

Knowing that a society is polygynous, however, does not provide precise information concerning the kinds of communications that actually occur among members of a family, since within a polygynous framework the mode of regulating communications may be most varied. At one extreme are the Tallensi of Ghana, where the family is the locus for the critical communications of a man's entire existence. For there his home is "his castle in the psychological rather than the material sense." More specifically:

> It is the center and fount of his major interest, his dominant purposes, his deepest emotional attachments, and his whole scheme of values; it is his shelter, his storehouse, the stage of his life's drama. The Tallensi, unlike many African peoples, have no age sets or initiation schools. A person grows up and receives his entire education at home. If he practises a craft, such as leatherwork, or is a diviner, his home is his workshop or consulting place [Fortes, 1949, p. 46].

Under such circumstances a "familiarity, almost a camaraderie" exists between child and parents, especially the father. Thus a relaxed communication pattern emerges: the child may address his father directly by name, he may argue with him, and he may contradict him "politely." In addition, communications in this kind of family appear numerous and frequent. No topic is "tabooed or barred by etiquette." Regardless of his age or infirmity, an elder hears about everything that occurs in the house, and he is asked for his consent "before anything is done in his name, as everything that pertains to the family or lineage must be." No one goes anywhere without telling the head of the family. At the same time there is privacy, too, within the group, which means that under certain conditions communication does not occur. In the joint family, husband and wife have their own sleeping room, but they eat separately, each with one or more of their children. A well-behaved young wife is expected to be "self-effacing and deferential" toward her husband as well as toward his father and adult brothers. Certain ritual activities are discussed only by father and son. Communication with outsiders, moreover, is strictly regulated. Even closely related neighbors may never know the exact quantity of the food supplies within the household. A visitor who is a relative or friend must call out the name of the person he would see, one who is a stranger must say "excuse me"—and then each waits outside until he is asked to enter (ibid., pp. 80–1, 181, 196, 205, 249).

In contrast, the Mende of Sierra Leone, although they too have polygyny, assign to their secret societies "many of the functions which the family performs in other parts of West Africa," most significantly "the training and general 'socialization' of the young" and also the transmission of knowledge and beliefs in "certain religious and quasi-religious spheres" (Little, 1948, p. 1). Presumably, therefore, many communications delivered at the home among the Tallensi are transmitted and received at the site of the secret organizations among the Mende. Differences in the sites and the audiences present, as well as in the two cultures, must produce appropriately different kinds of communications. The Tallensi and the Mende must also have dissimilar expectations concerning the communication patterns and functions of their homes.

———◆◆◆◆———

V.C *Interaction* Almost always some interaction between communicator and audience or among members of the audience occurs at a communication site.

Such interaction may be absent when the communicator cannot be perceived (a faraway drum) or is absent (a recording) or when the audience is a solitary person. The problem of this section is to determine the attributes of sites that affect interaction. A concrete case at the outset can alert the reader to the difficulties that arise when the give-and-take of large-scale communications is the object of attention and analysis. The event is a culturally stereotyped dance that took place in a Kikuyu community of Kenya in 1903. The account is given in the order reported by the observer; large sections are summarized rather than quoted for the sake of brevity.

"The whole countryside assembled," he begins, "betwixt two hilltops, 80 yds. wide by 250 yds. long, surrounded in parts with the remnant of the primitive forest." The audience divided itself by sex, with the men and boys at the two ends and the women at the two sides of the dancing ground. The performing warriors first came together in a valley out of sight of the audience.

In this setting the performance began when a boy burst through the crowd to announce that a Masai raiding party was attacking. More news concerning the threat was added by a young warrior who arrived "in a lather of sweat and in an exhausted state." A war song could be heard in the distance, and then the warriors themselves "soon appeared from among the trees as a long single file, faultlessly accoutred and moving in a conventionally stealthy way." As they approached the chief, they announced through their leader that no anxiety need be felt, they could well protect everybody. Similar words were spoken to the entire audience, as the men executed a series of marches and countermarches.

> Finally the General Officer Commanding left the arena unobserved and took up a position behind the spectators at one end of the ground. . . . Suddenly, at his shout, the wall of spectators broke and separated on his either hand, and down the slope he came like a whirlwind, a magnificent specimen of savage manhood, with his shield half raised and his spear poised, each of which he slightly raised still more as he sprang with a yell into the air at intervals of about 30 yards. . . . Numbers of the warriors thus independently burst into the arena, and were received by the women with rounds of applause, which varied considerably in degree according to the popularity of the individual. Applause was given by the women throwing one leg forward and then inclining from the waist, whilst at the same time they feigned as it were to throw their handkerchiefs, in the form of a bouquet of leaves, to the favored individual. . . . When a woman has made her complimentary remarks anent the individual, she joins her fellows in uttering the peculiar cry of lu-lu-lu-lu-lu-lu, rendered as a descending scale, which has a liquid sound like water gurgling from a calabash [Routledge and Routledge, 1910, pp. 180–2].

This dance lasted about an hour and a half and clearly offered the audience an opportunity not only to have reaffirmed their faith in the warriors who were demonstrating symbolically their prowess but also to communicate to them varying degrees of approbation. It should be evident that some of the dramatic interaction could occur as a result of the properties of the site: the space large enough to accommodate "the whole countryside"; the valley close by where the warriors first assembled; the trees from which the dancers emerged; and the close contact between the audience and the dancers. Other factors of course contributed to the effect, such as the traditional character of the motif behind the performance, the skill of the dancers, the uniforms and weapons that were displayed, etc. In a rather singular manner, consequently, an apparently effective performance was rendered. Out of such singularity, however, a few essential ingredients can be glimpsed.

First of all, it is relatively easy to isolate certain mundane but important *mechanical aspects* of the site: (a) *acoustics,* or *distance* between communicator and audience or between members of the audience; (b) *illumination;* (c) *comfort,* including ventilation, heat or cold, protection from rain or sun, seating arrangements, etc.; (d) *devices,* such as platform, rostrum, audio-visual aids, etc.; and (e) *aesthetic qualities.* Some of these factors, it should be understood, may be of no great moment in some situations; but they loom large, for example, in planning a meeting hall from an architectural standpoint. Cultural elements also intrude here, especially in connection with what has been blandly called "comfort."

V.C.1

The habitation patterns of people are relevant to communications not only because they can serve as consequential media, as has been indicated (IV.B.3.b), but also because as the site of everyday communications they affect the kind of interaction likely to take place. The houses of the Bemba in Northern Rhodesia are placed so close together that "each villager can see or hear most of what goes on next door." Communication among these people is further facilitated by the fact that, since "life is lived almost entirely in the open" (including, for example, cooking), they inadvertently transmit a great deal of information about themselves which living indoors ordinarily conceals (Richards, 1939, p. 121).

In contrast, such communication between neighbors is likely to be less informal or inadvertent among the Ganda: almost every house there stands at such a distance from the next that it is usually difficult for one person to shout to his closest neighbor (Mair, 1934, p. 15). The Nuer of the Sudan are between the two extremes: their houses are separated by a considerable distance, ranging from "about a hundred yards to over a mile," so that they generally remain isolated, as they prefer to be, while retaining some contact with the neighbors whose help is needed at times in the cultivation and harvesting of crops (Howell, 1954, p. 184).

A straightforward illustration of the acoustical properties of a site comes from the Chaga of Tanganyika. These people, like many other Africans, know that, especially during the dry season, their huts can be quickly destroyed or ruined by fire. At night they post no watchman, nevertheless, because special circumstances of the site virtually guarantee that those asleep will hear anyone who cries that "somebody's home is on fire." Their huts have no foundation to "break the sound waves." Since they sleep only on an animal skin there is no "sound-breaking layer" between them and the ground. Their bed of course is hard and hence their sleep is likely to be frequently interrupted. They are, as it were, constantly alert to hear the shout; "the whole body of the sleeper . . . becomes a sort of receiver of the earth waves" (Gutmann, 1926, pp. 586–7).

People are likely to choose as a site even for a simple social conversation one in which they are comfortable. Among the Yoruba of Nigeria the informal communication associated with what the observer calls "lounging" occurs on the "street verandahs" of chiefs. The verandahs, on both sides of the main entrance, are made by extending or projecting the roof beyond the building. Such a structure provides protection from the sun and rain and also, since the chatting generally occurs "in the afternoon, at the cool of the day," makes people feel that they have placed themselves at a site which separates them from customary activity (Johnson, 1921, p. 98).

Sometimes traditional African societies have constructed sites which deliberately set off communicators from the audience. Among the Ibo of Nigeria, for example, an open space said to be "the property of the local god" is usually put aside to serve as a market, a playground, and the place for public meetings. Many of the areas are shaded by large trees, and some have "galleries constructed of whole trunks of suitably sized trees, or large branches fixed in forked uprights at each end," so that "seats rise in tiers and provide good accommodation for spectators watching a wrestling or other display" (Basden, 1938, p. 150).

Most mass media from the West function properly in African communities only at special sites. The mobile cinema van, for example, might seem at first glance to be geographically carefree. In a sense all that is needed is to erect a temporary screen for receiving the projection and to place the loudspeaker of the projector and the public address system near that screen. Experienced officers, however, indicate that a number of other problems must be satisfactorily resolved. One technician, after directing film demonstrations totaling over a thousand hours before roughly two million Africans, offers very specific advice. In order to attract an audience in the first place and also to plan a longer tour of the equipment itself, arrangements should be made with the local communities some time, even months, in advance. Only a few announcements are needed, since news of the performance is likely to travel quickly. A site should be selected so that "the rear of the van can face the direction of the town, on ground which very gradually slopes up from the van." People from the town are attracted by the sounds from the van in such a position, and also those arriving late stop as soon as they see the pictures sufficiently well. The space itself should be large and open. Chairs for the chief and administration officers should be provided about 30 yards from the screen. Small children arriving before the performance should be bunched together between the chairs and the screen. Viewers should not be offered benches, for they may stand on them and thus obscure the screen from others (Sellers, 1955).

V.C.2

The interaction at a site depends also upon the *rules* that people must or would follow there. Ordinarily in Western society, for example, men do not tell jokes to one another while waiting in a church for a funeral service to begin. The rules originate with the groups utilizing the site but often may come to be associated in people's mind with it rather than the group. Although proper behavior in a church stems from the standardized procedures of the service and from beliefs concerning respect for the religious institution, the physical structure evokes quiet and reverence. The rules functioning at a site may be thought of as (a) *relatively flexible* or (b) *relatively inflexible*. In a church the rules are relatively inflexible; in the living room of an American family they are likely to be relatively flexible and indeed to fluctuate with the moods and composition of the group assembled there.

In Africa the difference with respect to flexibility of rules and hence of communication patterns can be easily suggested by continuing to refer to the church and another site, in this case the public market. During the religious service of a Western denomination, little variation in communication usually occurs. Different hymns are sung, different sections of the Bible are read, but they are all within a standard frame of reference. Sermons of course vary considerably in delivery and content, and many churches follow the custom of inviting guest ministers from other communities to preach; again, however, the general goals sought by such communications can be largely anticipated by the congregation and the outside observer from a knowledge of the particular church's creed and principles. In contrast, the kind of communication to be heard in a market cannot be so easily predicted, for there the rules permit almost any topic to be discussed by whoever is participating in the transaction of the conversation. At a market, too, the audience and the communicators are likely to be much less homogeneous than those at a church, for many markets attract people from a large number of different societies.

The people assembling at a site at a given time are subject to some kind of regulation. Before, during, or after meals, for example, people may communicate with one another, in fact some of the most intimate and important communication of a family is likely to occur at the dinner table—*among people in the West*. In Africa, quite different rules may be followed at the dining site. Often the members of a household who share meals are carefully specified. Those who eat together among the Hausa of Nigeria are persons of the same sex and generation (M. G. Smith, 1954, p. 270). In two other societies the same distinction is observed but with an additional restriction for the head of the family: among the Mongo of the Congo, he eats only with his grown son, friends, or male relatives (Hulstaert, 1938, p. 265); and among the Tallensi in Ghana, he eats only with his youngest child (Fortes, 1949, pp. 223, 249). Among the Mossi of the Voltaic Republic, people of different sex do not eat together, but the relationship of those sharing food varies with the season, the time of day, and the size of the living compound (Tauxier, 1917, p. 230). Among the Yoruba of Nigeria, however, there seems to be no set of rules prescribing eating companions: "some men eat alone; some eat with their wives and children; and some eat with their friends." Very good friends eat together each day if possible. While eating, however, communication for some of the group is restricted, since "at meal times it is considered bad manners for anyone except elders to talk" (Bascom, 1951, p. 52).

Large public meetings in Africa are usually held outdoors, for the generally benign climate enables the community to spare itself the expense of constructing a meeting hall. The audience squats or sits upon the ground in scattered or well-ordered positions. The communicator may stand at a place where he is clearly visible and audible; and sometimes, in West Africa, the chief is seated upon a sacred stool. Often these meetings take place under a large tree so that everyone is protected from the sun and, up to a point, from the rain. The rules governing debate range from the relatively flexible to the relatively inflexible. At the former extreme are the public meetings among the Menabe section of the Tanala society in the Malagasy Republic, at which there are "no rules of order, no minutes," and also "no proceedings for opening or closing the session." No vote is taken; instead each problem is "threshed out" until those assembled feel that an agreement has been reached (Linton, 1933, pp. 147–8). At the other extreme are the Ewe of Ghana and Togo, whose traditional meetings appear to have been governed by parliamentary procedure that must have delighted and inspired the German anthropologist providing the following description:

Order rules the meetings. Nobody speaks except at the invitation of the chairman or the speaker or after receiving permission to speak at his own request. The person speaking begins with [an Ewe phrase], after which there is general silence. Interruptions are prohibited, and are censured or are penalized on the spot with a fine. At the conclusion of a speech or at a pause, however, approval or disapproval can be expressed. The address of an important person is acknowledged at the end by a flourish of the court band that is present. Speaking time is not limited, and abundant use is made of this privilege. Addresses of from two to three hours duration are not rare. . . . If the chairman suspects that a speaker in his defense has departed too much from the truth, he suddenly has the band interrupt the address with a vigorous flourish; if after this interruption the speaker immediately finds the thread of his argument, then that is a favorable indication of his trustworthiness [Westermann, 1935, pp. 221–2].

In contrast, order prevails at a Kikuyu trial in Kenya when a case is contested by what appears to be a much simpler method: two people cannot speak simultaneously because "the club of the first speaker is passed on from one to another of those who desire to express their views, and no man is allowed to address the assembly till he holds it in his hand" (Routledge and Routledge, 1910, pp. 205–6).

Forms of behavior may also be viewed in terms of the sites at which the rules permit, prescribe, or proscribe their appearance. Usually some kind of greeting is required when a new person enters a group or, for that matter, when two people meet and thus form a group. The entry or the greeting in Africa is frequently very subtle—or at least it appears or should appear subtle to outsiders from the West who usually only exchange rather meaningless inquiries concerning each other's health. In the first place, many African languages contain forms of salutation that cannot be quickly or perfunctorily recited. In the traditional Ganda manner, person A asks person B, "How did you pass the night?"; person B replies, "Well"; A hums; B hums; A and B hum in unison. Then the process is reversed with B asking the question first and with the unified hum at the end. Thus, as it were, the first verse ends. But there are many other verses ("How is the news?" the second one usually begins) which follow the same pattern and which must be used on formal, and sometimes also on informal, occasions. Next, after the opening greeting has been exchanged, in most African societies it is not possible to approach directly the business in hand. The custom may require harmless chitchat—the way Americans, after the perfunctory remarks about health, make equally perfunctory ones about the weather—or the exchange of gifts. A missionary reports from Nyasaland the ritual through which strangers must go even before the first greeting is exchanged. They walk into the village and silently sit down outside the cattle kraal. No one seems to notice them. After perhaps ten minutes have passed, the chief and his councilors leisurely approach and seat themselves in a position facing the outsiders. They first talk to one another, then finally the chief turns to the guests and begins the greeting with, "We see you." At that point the councilors and everyone in the vicinity repeat the sentence in a very friendly manner (A. Fraser, 1932, p. 47).

The sites associated with forms of behavior cannot be specified when the situations in which that behavior is displayed have in common only the relationships between people. What, for example, is a probable reaction of Chaga adults of Tanganyika when a growing child "flies into a rage, when he lies or steals, when he is recalcitrant or violates the code of etiquette, when he makes an ass of himself, when he is cowardly"? Obviously such antisocial behavior is not confined to the family's hut or the outdoors. Also what may happen when the same child is "worried or grieved or pained or again when merry and overjoyed"? Such moods can occur at many different sites. In all these instances, the older person is likely to quote some traditional proverb that offers the comment or advice finding favor in the society (Raum, 1940, p. 217).

Behavior and the communication accompanying it may be tolerated at some sites but not at others. Among the Azande of the Congo and Sudan, for example, a boy who flirts openly with a girl under normal circumstances is "reprimanded and abused," but he has at his disposal a series of discreet communications which he may employ with social approval toward a girl dancing with her female friend and which are said to lead often to "sexual connection." In this instance, therefore, the site of a dance is the cue to "sexual play to a moderate and discreet extent" (Evans-Pritchard, 1928, pp. 457–8).

In analyzing communication, it should now be evident, a rather common but very arbitrary line must be drawn between historical and nonhistorical materials. The rules which prevail at a site must be known if the process of communicating there is to be understood. The nonhistorical situation is thus accepted without historical inquiries concerning the reasons for the existence of particular rules (cf. IV.A). Thereby interesting insights are overlooked, sadly, as an illustration from a certain section of Ibo society in Nigeria quickly suggests. An association of Africans meets there every three months in order to collect dues and to discuss and approve policies concerning loans, road construction, education, funerals and inheritances, trade, thefts, recreation, etc. The proceedings are governed by parliamentary procedures reflecting, an anthropological analysis suggests, a fusion of traditional and European customs. In accordance with European practices, meetings are held on Sundays, offices are like those in a European association, the organization has a constitution, and records are kept. At the meetings the language spoken is Ibo and, as the Ibo pattern demands, respect is shown for age in seating arrangements and meetings are closed with a blessing. Members follow the traditional method of reaching a decision through informal discussion until arriving at consensus, but now the executive rather than the older men dominate the meeting and also, contrary to custom, younger men often disagree with the presiding officer (Ottenberg, 1955, pp. 6–10). But why, the neglected historical question must be, have the Ibo evolved this particular pattern?

V.D *Communication Function* A final attribute of a site is a very general one, viz., its normal communication function. Is it a site at which the principal goal of the communicator and the audience involves communication? Men assemble at a hunting site to shoot game, and their communications, if any, are dedicated to that end; but they expect to listen to other people and perhaps to speak themselves when they attend a meeting of their community in its town hall.

In Africa, as in the rest of the world, special sites are set aside for communication. In the manner of the boarding school of the West, African youth may be segregated from all or part of their community and placed in an institution whose primary purpose is to communicate the beliefs and values of the culture. Among the Ngoni of Northern Rhodesia, a boy is removed from his family around the age of six; thereafter, until his marriage, he lives with his contemporaries in a special hut. From the viewpoint of his society, various purposes are thus served, each of which has its own elaborate series of communications. In the first place, he acquires the essential facts about his physical environment and the herding of cattle as well as the values associated with self-defense and mutual aid that are prized by his people. Formerly a knowledge of the attributes of a good warrior was also a part of the curriculum. In addition, he is separated from the influence of women and non-Ngoni influences. Finally, he learns to cooperate with his own age mates and to show deference to those superior in age and therefore, in this society, in power and strength (Read, 1960, pp. 91–5): The first function, receiving knowledge and skill, could doubtless be accomplished without the dormitory, but the others seem to be facilitated by having the communications and interaction occur at this particular site.

The problem of attracting people to a site specializing in communication (IX.A) is well illustrated by the formal museum. On the one hand, it may be argued quite convincingly that the museum in Africa can be a "specialized visual aid" which uses devices like models and dioramas "to make explanations clearer or to give three dimensional reality to collections" and thus to promote the learning and recall of materials in the fields of health and technical assistance as well as arts and crafts (Daifuku and Bowers, 1956, p. 4). On the other hand, many of the very people who need the instruction do not live in urban centers where such museums are usually located. When they do visit the town or city, they have more urgent or less serious missions to perform. Museums, however, can be attached to the formal educational system, for then some captive audience of pupils is assured.

Throughout Africa an extremely important institution is that of the market, which is usually located in or close to a village or town. Some markets are open every day of the week; others—especially the traditional ones in West Africa which existed prior to contact with the West—have a cycle of their own which may be every three, four, five, or seven days. Obviously the ostensibly primary function of a market is economic: some people bring goods to be sold or exchanged, others come to buy. Anyone who has closely observed a particular market, however, notes innumerable functions that are also performed there. A Ngoni market in Nyasaland, for example, enables leaders to strengthen their ties with ordinary people. The paramount chief's office has a postal section in which stamps are sold and letters sent and received. The chief himself, his wife, and other officials stroll through the market and accept petitions from one and all; since he and his wife normally can be addressed only through intermediaries, "the ordinary people . . . are gratified at being able to see and greet the Chief, and they speak warmly of his condescension at walking among them thus freely." The appeal court of the chief is opened the day before the market assembles. Then here and in other markets one notes "the prevailing good humor of a market-place, the interchange of gossip, chaff, and prices across the stalls, the aesthetic pleasure in displaying the goods for sale, the friendly rivalry quickly established between buyer and seller" (Read, 1938, pp. 45, 51).

The same anthropologist also observes in connection with the market she is describing that "news and gossip from the rest of Nyasaland and from farther south is exchanged when the mail lorries arrive with their load of passengers." Others make the same point concerning the market as a communication site; among the Rundi of Ruanda-Urundi, for example, "the market is the place where people meet, inspect merchandise, and observe other people, gossip, hear and pass on news items, drink *pombe,* discuss business and non-business matters, and where they do many things which are useful and many others which are superfluous" (Meyer, 1916, p. 76). Undoubtedly, therefore, people at markets receive and transmit miscellaneous information, but it has not been possible for the present writer to determine in detail or with any precision the nature of its content.

In markets of the Ewe in Ghana and Togo and of the Hausa and Fulani in Northern Nigeria it seems patently evident that people talk a great deal. One young girl who arrived at an Ewe market in a crowded lorry was carefully shadowed in the interest of scholarly research. She began talking, and listening, before she entered the market's gate. Within a period of ten minutes—the duration of the research—she spoke with more than twenty people: some she greeted perfunctorily, others she talked to for a few moments concerning relatives and friends. No political or cosmic thoughts were aired. In fact, most of the conversations in these particular West African markets, additional unsystematic eavesdropping reveals, pertains to the problem at hand, buying and selling and especially bargaining over prices. Other topics include all the problems people might be expected to discuss, such as health, weather, and even politics. A very crude estimate for one market in Zaria indicates that somewhere between 5 and 10 per cent of the conversations surreptitiously sampled are on nonmarket topics. The writer would immediately caution himself and others concerning a possible ethnocentric bias: whereas people in the West and especially readers of this book are likely to keep themselves occupied and to avoid long periods of complete solitude or, in contact with others, of silence, it may be that many Africans are perfectly content to be unoccupied except by their own feelings and thoughts and sense of well-being. It thus appears that sellers in a market often stand or sit for many minutes without engaging in any activity whatsoever.

At African markets people come from some distance either on foot or especially on crowded trucks and buses. For this reason communicators and audience represent many communities and often, especially at the large markets, many different societies. In some areas a number of markets have their cycles so arranged that they occur on successive days; hence traders and others can function within a circle of more than one market. The market site, consequently, offers one of the few opportunities for communications to move from one community or society to another. In addition, flirtations occur and rendezvous are arranged, sometimes even across cultural lines. Most modern markets display not only locally produced vegetables as well as fish and meat but also cloth, clothing, drugs, hardware—in fact many or most of the reputable and disreputable modern trinkets and tools that do not depend upon electricity or motors. Africans thus perceive an aspect of civilization.

It has not been possible, however, to devise any plan of research that isolates the influence of the market from other sites at which information is disseminated. First, samples among the Ewe and the Hausa-Fulani were almost never able to reply to direct questions concerning what happens to them at market other than by mentioning activities involving buying and selling. Information-getting or -sending is so incidental that it is forgotten, and Africans quite naturally report only their economic transactions when asked, "What did you do at market yesterday?" The direct question, "What did you hear at market?" produces the reply, "I don't remember" or just "Nothing." A pagan Fulani woman answered the query about the people with whom she had spoken at the market with mock indignation: "Of course, I spoke to no man; I speak only to my husband."

Also, it is not feasible to attempt to compare those who have just been to market with those who have not gone, or those who habitually go with those who seldom go, because the groups differ in other respects besides their contact with the market. If the market is at some distance, for example, older people may not be able to make the journey; afterwards if they appear to know less about events, their age rather than their failure to go to market may be responsible. Finally, the hypothesis that those who have been to market are likely to disseminate what they have heard there cannot be verified because people do not keep track of the source of the news they spread or hear. In brief, therefore, it appears futile and unnecessary to try to document the importance of African markets for communication, but one feels a little uncomfortable at not being able to do so.

VI. RESTRICTIONS

A man may easily and quickly track down a friend to report news to him, but ordinarily, especially for the mass media, there are barriers to overcome before a communicator or his communication reaches the audience. The brilliant idea has to be made practical. The barriers of communication arise for reasons that are clearly natural, economic, and social. The primary emphasis of this chapter is to highlight the restrictions in great detail, but the approach is not altogether negative: restrictions cannot be mentioned without implying or stressing the smooth flow of communication when they are absent or avoidable.

VI.A *Nature* In modern times natural forces that cannot be controlled directly have often been circumvented. Heat comes with summer, but buildings can be air-conditioned. Circumvention is likely to occur in more civilized areas; hence a discussion of communication in Africa serves to recall some of the restrictions more or less successfully combatted by communicating systems in the West. The

VI.A.1 beginning here is at a truly basic level, viz., *meteorological factors*.

VI.A.1.a The temperature, humidity, precipitation, and wind pattern normally prevailing at a site are summarized by the concept of *climate*. People living in areas characterized by extreme climates react differently to some communications or to some aspects of them than do those in more temperate zones, but for the moment the only basis for such a belief is common-sense speculation. Are people in an extremely hot climate more or less patient, are they more or less alert, are they more or less impulsive? What a pity that the questions cannot be answered, and in part no replies are forthcoming because inevitably, whatever the influence of climate upon behavior, cultural factors simultaneously are of some importance and hence are methodologically confounding. Without question, however, climate has a direct effect upon many of the media of communication. Different problems from those existing in the far north or the far south must be faced in constructing a meeting hall in the tropics. On the one hand, the building need not be so sturdily built and no provision for glass in the windows or for heating facilities is necessary; but on the other hand, appropriate materials have to be found which can withstand insects and fungus growths.

The indirect effects that climate in the tropical sections of Africa has upon communication seem reasonably clear. Certain diseases, such as malaria and trypanosomiasis (sleeping sickness), tend to flourish there, and they in turn produce fluctuations in people's moods (VIII.B.3). Sustained work, especially when the humidity is high, is possible only during the early and late hours of the day; the long siesta and other devices to escape the midday sun shut people off from most communications, certainly from those requiring prolonged concentration or imaginative activity. Europeans in Africa waste large slices of time discussing climate and weather.

Some of the restrictions that climate places upon communications can be inferred from a knowledge of the simple climatic facts. Thus the Kikuyu in Kenya have two harvests each year (Routledge and Routledge, 1910, p. 40), but the Wolof in Senegal only one (Ames, 1959, p. 225). The people in the two societies, consequently, have different routines; in one the preoccupation with the harvest and hence the enforced isolation from irrelevant communications occurs twice annually and in the other once.

In most parts of Africa insects, together with mold and mildew, play havoc with books and other printed media. In recommending certain formulas to be applied to books with a paintbrush, a writer in West Africa points out that insects and rodents not only are attracted by paper but they also find "apparently appetizing substances" in the other materials used in a book. Glues and pastes that are derived from organic materials are devoured. Even certain dyes with which book cloth is colored is "palatable, at any rate to cockroaches" (Harris, 1956).

◆◆◆◆

Aside from their possible effects on people's mood (VIII.B.1), abnormal *weather* conditions, especially excessive rain or snow, can adversely and seriously affect the transportation facilities on which communication depends, as well as the media themselves. Floods prevent trains and cars and people from delivering necessary supplies; and newspapers and other printed materials may not reach their audience. Communicators may be unable to adhere to schedules. Members of the potential audience may refuse or be unable to travel. Bad storms can cripple certain media directly: when electric power fails, printing presses, photographic laboratories, radio stations and receiving sets, and telephones cease functioning.

VI.A.1.b

◆━━◆

Almost a decade ago a geographer stated that "it would be too much to say that the drier parts of Africa have now a network of roads, but, except in the rains, most parts can be reached by automobile." Then he immediately added: "The qualification 'except in the rains' may include a period of 6 or even 8 months in parts of tropical Africa" (Stamp, 1953, p. 184). Any kind of operation in Africa that depends upon highways must recognize the vast difference between the dry and the rainy season as well as the marked fluctuations within those seasons. Each year more roads and better ones are constructed throughout Africa, but "all-weather" highways are still likely to be blocked by continuous rains or flash floods. In the experience of the present writer, especially in West Africa, an outstanding hazard to transportation during the rainy season is the absence of bridges over streams which normally are dry and hence are left unbridged in the interest of economy.

◆◆◆◆

VI.A.1.c   *Electrical disturbances* make radio reception difficult or impossible.

The frequency of electrical disturbances in Africa is only one of the reasons why the more satisfactory form of broadcasting, medium-wave, that is ordinarily used in Europe and America is "economically out of the question" there. In addition, radio waves along the ground are hampered by the African bush and by mountains. Then the population is so scattered that signals must travel a comparatively long distance. As a result most broadcasting in Africa is by short-wave and, as every short-wave listener knows—especially in Africa—reception is "never completely reliable." For this type of wave suffers the disadvantage of "fading and distortion caused by periodical changes in the ionosphere which result in variations between day and night, between summer and winter, and over the eleven years of the sunspot cycle" (Welsh, 1951, p. 237).

VI.A.2 The second natural factor affecting communication is the *terrain,* the influence of which upon radio transmission has just been mentioned. Otherwise terrain facilitates or inhibits people's opportunities to circulate, and especially their transportation systems. For paths and roads must conform to the terrain, or else the terrain must be expensively altered, for example, by digging or blasting. Ordinarily it is difficult to construct roads in extremely mountainous country, as a result of which people from different areas may not establish contact with one another and printed media may not be efficiently distributed by foot, bicycle, or truck. Enclaves of relatively isolated communities still exist in almost every part of the world. Similarly terrain affects the construction of railroads and airports, and may produce hazards for approaching and departing planes. Likewise waterways and deserts can help or hinder transportation.

It seems unnecessary to document the fact that land-bound means of transportation in Africa are unreliable and usually difficult. The condition of African roads has been delicately mentioned above; they may not be the worst on this planet, but in justice to them it is claimed that they offer stiff competition for the distinction. Railroads, with few exceptions, run only from coastal ports to the interior and do not connect with lines from other areas; they are almost always heavily congested since the demand upon them is great, their equipment is likely to be old, and more often than not they have only one track. Trucks and buses have become extremely important for both short and long hauls; but of course they cause an additional strain upon the system of highways. Airplanes are increasing in number and significance. Almost all African rivers are navigable for short or relatively short stretches during certain months of the year; they are allegedly utilized over greater distances or more continuously only by certain species of skillful fish. Lakes, with the notable exception of the great lakes in East Africa, play a minor role. By and large, therefore, both experience and the literature suggest, people and goods can be shipped to almost any place in Africa, but usually at some expense and, if an ethnocentric adjective be permitted, after excruciating delays.

The Sahara Desert, ordinarily and justifiably considered an obstacle, merits special attention as an avenue of transportation and communication because of its "crucial role in history as an artery of trade and cultural diffusion between the Mediterranean region and Negro Africa." According to one concise summary, "old caravan trails crisscross it in every direction, following routes where dependable sources of water succeed one another at the shortest maximal intervals." The traffic, it is thought, has gone on since the early part of the Neolithic period. During the centuries, trade has followed the desert routes, with the result that "the products of Africa" and those from "the ancient seats of civilization" have been almost continuously exchanged (Murdock, 1959, p. 127).

Again and again accounts of African societies prior to contact with Europeans suggest that the barrier to travel and to the exchange of information was not the terrain or the inadequate roads and paths but hostility between indigenous groups. Rather typical is the following observation that has been made by an African: "Before the French occupation, the Moaga rarely left his village because of the dangers on the roads, frequented in those days by bandits. . . . There was little contact even between adjoining villages" (Delobsom, 1932, p. 248).

---◆◆◆---

VI.A.3   Those *natural resources* used in the manufacture of communication media and their accessories constitute a limiting factor, especially in the development of modern mass media. On a simple level, it can be pointed out that obviously animal skins must be procurable to construct certain types of drums. If the resources are lacking, then they must be imported, usually at some trouble and expense. Cultural factors operate simultaneously: the resources may exist but they may not be exploited either because they have not been discovered or because people lack the skill or the interest to do so.

---•---

A technical tome is needed to try to assess both the actual and —much more important—the potential natural resources of Africa that are being or will eventually be utilized in the construction and operation of the mass media. Clearly the continent is rich in mineral resources, but their exploitation for communications depends upon political, economic, and general cultural factors For the moment, therefore, it is sufficient to note that virtually all Africa, except the Union, is severely restricted in this respect: almost every single piece of equipment demanded by the mass media must be imported from some European country or from America. Likewise the electricity needed for those media is almost always expensive both in absolute and relative terms, because most African countries are just beginning to develop their natural sources of power.

---◆◆◆---

VI.A.4   The power and versatility of a medium (III.A.3 and 4) depend upon *limitations* inherent in its nature or, at a given moment, upon the way it has been constructed. Even under ideal conditions, the sounds of the largest drum can reach only a limited distance; and, as has also has been indicated above with great perspicacity (III.A.3.b), you cannot carve, paint, or tattoo a society's encyclopedia of knowledge upon a single person's skin because there just is not sufficient space. The same point can be made about the mass media *after* they have been built. The limitations of an electrically illuminated sign include the fact that the light cannot be seen around a corner unless there is some kind of reflecting surface; the power system, the fixture, or the bulbs permit an electric current of specified strength; the distance at which the sign's message can be read depends upon atmospheric conditions and ultimately, no doubt, upon the eyes of the particular audience. A radio or television transmitter, though versatile enough to transmit almost every human sound or gesture, can be expected to reach only a specified area that is a function of the power provided by its transmitter. Many of these restrictions upon media, like those stemming from terrain, may be temporary and can eventually be alleviated by improved inventions. Thus a transistor radio consumes much less electricity than a set with tubes, and hence in this respect has overcome one of the restrictions from which battery-powered receivers heretofore suffered.

VI.A.5   Finally, there are natural restrictions resulting from *human abilities* when confronted with a particular medium of communication. Most of these abilities, limited of course by cultural factors too, cannot be delineated in absolute or precise terms, but the fact remains that the human nervous system and the human body everywhere are subject to restrictions. Unlike X rays, eyes cannot penetrate an opaque object. Only a finite number of digits, letters, or words can be grasped at a quick glance, however great the practice fostered by the person or his society. Some theoretically possible coding systems turn out to be impractical because they are too complicated to be comprehended. Fatigue eventually sets in when a long communication demands sustained attention. Older people are less or—perhaps rarely—more likely to grasp the point of a communication than younger ones. The activity intervening between one communication and the next—so-called retroactive inhibition—can have a profound effect upon receptivity to the second communication. By and large no relationship has been established between intelligence as measured by an intelligence test on the one hand and susceptibility to communications as measured in experimental studies on the other hand, at least in the United States (Hovland and Janis, 1959, p. 237); but the reaction of American soldiers to some types of films has been shown to vary with their educational status (Hovland, Lumsdaine, and Sheffield, 1949, pp. 160–75).

Evidence indicates that Africans possess a general ability or intelligence no different from that of any other group, but that their performance on tests designed for people in the West may often be inferior since they lack the relevant training or experience (Doob, 1960a, pp. 170–5). The variations in training or experience, however, have at the moment profound effects upon communication. At the beginning of a long interview, for example, the present writer once read to a sample of 98 Ganda males an article on the control of soil erosion which allegedly came from a local newspaper. Immediately afterwards he asked whether they agreed or disagreed with the point of view therein expressed: "Those people who do not cooperate [with the program of government to check erosion] must be severely punished." Less than two hours later and without prior warning the men were asked to recall as much as they could of the communication. The same procedure was followed in South Africa with a sample of 91 Zulu, except that the article pertained to nutrition and stressed the fact that "tasty food is not necessarily good food." A comparison of highly educated Ganda with those less well educated or having no education at all in the Western sense reveals that on virtually every criterion the memory of the former was better than that of the latter: fewer of them recalled nothing at all from the article or confused it with some other communication; and of those recalling the article, more of the highly educated remembered important details. Similar results appear for the Zulu sample, in a comparison of those living in urban and in rural areas, with respect to quantity but not quality of recall. In both societies, finally, the ability to recall the content of a communication is significantly and positively related to a number of other correlated factors besides education: knowledge of English, adherence to Christianity or Islam rather than a traditional African religion, and rejection of traditional African beliefs (Doob, 1957b).

Africans actually seeking higher education in the tradition of the West are often confronted with limitations which in the long run may be overcome only when they and other Africans have been able to obtain that education. The student who must also help his family cultivate the land is tired at night when he should and would study. His home, moreover, may lack adequate illumination: the candles and kerosene lamps so prevalent in Africa are not easy to read by, and the pressure lamps that offer good light are relatively expensive to buy and to operate. Perhaps not for decades will electricity be fed into most African homes, and then only when enough Africans, in spite of such handicaps, attain the educational level enabling their countries to generate cheap electric power and to provide educational opportunities detached from economic responsibilities.

Costs The costs of communication include the time and money required not only to manufacture the apparatus that is needed to produce, transmit, and receive a communication but also to select and train whatever personnel are required to utilize it. If the time and money have not been previously invested, potential communicators are confronted with corresponding deficiencies which they themselves may or may not be able satisfactorily to overcome. Thus an audience cannot be reached by radio if there is no station within their range and if they have no receiving sets; with a gargantuan budget, the station may be built and the sets distributed, but before the station begins operating or the people actually receive the sets, the deficiency is paralyzing.

VI.B

An examination of published figures on the mass media in Africa establishes several points relevant to costs. First, since those media are expensive and since the African states are all relatively poor, the continent as a whole compares unfavorably with the rest of the world regarding both the number and the distribution of mass media. Almost any compilation of UNESCO offers evidence to support such a conclusion, whether one turns to figures on letters and telegrams sent and received, books published, newsprint consumed, number and circulation of daily newspapers, films produced and exhibited, or radio and television stations and receivers (UN, 1959).

Then, secondly, published figures are not necessarily accurate or up-to-date. Circulation data are usually difficult to obtain in any Western country—they may be carefully guarded for purely commercial reasons—but the situation in Africa is often complicated by the failure to keep adequate records and always by the rapid changes within the media themselves. Another UNESCO survey, this one of news agencies, newspapers, motion picture houses, and radio stations in every country of the world (UNESCO, 1951), looks more valid than it probably is: figures come from member governments which sometimes are more interested in their reputations than in accuracy. A definitive survey of the press in Africa under private auspices undoubtedly presents the best available information at the time of publication and in theory at least provides the facts concerning each publication that need to be known: name and place of publication; frequency of appearance; language; estimated circulation; name of editor and publisher; orientation and influence; and date of founding (Kitchen, 1956). A glowing account of the various journals and newspapers published in the Congo and the organizations that service them (Belgian Congo, 1958b) appears to be most useful, at least was useful before the withdrawal of the colonial power in 1960.

Similarly, the United States Foreign Broadcast Information Service periodically issues definitive manuals listing the broadcasting and television stations of the world. The following data are supplied, when possible, concerning each station: location by country and city; call letters; name used "in lieu of or in addition to call letters"; ownership; power in watts; wave length in meters; frequency in kilocycles per second; miscellaneous facts, which include future plans, programs carried, associated stations and networks, alternate frequency, daytime and nighttime operation, etc. But again it is virtually impossible to keep such information up-to-date. Under "frequency," for example, the editors themselves say that "due to propagational conditions, interference by other stations, jamming, malfunction of transmitter, reallocation of frequencies by a country or convention, or for some other reason, stations may use frequencies which are at variance with this publication" (U.S. Foreign Broadcast Information Service, 1959, pp. i–ii). In addition, the technical information, though basic, of course does not indicate for a particular station what audiences can be reached under the given conditions of the terrain and the atmosphere, or how popular the station is.

The conclusion must be drawn that published data on mass media in Africa provide only preliminary glimpses. Anyone who would utilize existing media or personnel must do his own market research on the spot. There is no substitute for the empirical approach.

--------◆◆◆◆▶--------

VI.B.1   Certain *production* costs are met in order to initiate
          a communication. In the first instance some consid-
VI.B.1.a eration must usually be given to the *training and/or
          hiring of personnel.* The brilliant conversationalist
may have attended no formal school, but his brilliance comes from years of informal practice. The linguist of a chief (I.A.2.b) and almost any technician attached to the mass media, such as an engineer in a radio station or a linotype operator, receive much more formal training.

--------◆•◆--------

Not unexpectedly there is in Africa a dearth of trained personnel for the mass media. This state of affairs may be inferred, not too riskily, from the condition of the media themselves: those media are poorly developed and poorly distributed, as just indicated, and hence people are not motivated to become technicians, nor are many opportunities offered to develop and exercise the appropriate skills. One publication of UNESCO, for the year 1952–53, lists the places in the world where "education for journalism at higher institutions of learning" can be obtained. Of the 645 institutions on the list, 550 are in the United States, 1 in the United Kingdom, and 2 in Africa. Both of the latter are in Egypt

(UNESCO, 1954). Men and women, however, can become good reporters without being trained formally at such institutions; hence the presence or absence of the schools does not begin even to suggest the number of available journalists in a country.

When technicians are not available, outsiders must be imported or local people must be trained. Colonial powers in Africa have tended to favor the former policy for the more skilled positions and the latter for the more menial ones. As African countries in the British areas approached or approach independence, however, the Colonial Office has sought to speed up the process of educating Africans for all types of position. The film unit of that office, for example, attempted, with funds provided by the Colonial Development and Welfare Act, to increase the supply of African technicians capable of producing films for so-called fundamental education through a special training program. In one six-month course, three Nigerians and three Ghanaians were taught the technical aspects of motion-picture photography and direction; the creative problems in dealing with scripts; and the essentials of thinking "analytically in the way that film directors and script writers must" (Lods, 1951, pp. 85–6).

Mission groups are interested in the establishment in overseas areas of "Christian colleges" at which students are trained in the Christian tradition and in some instances prepared for the ministry. It appears, according to a "Check List of Overseas Protestant Colleges and Universities," that most but not all of these institutions follow the same sectarian lines as in America and Europe. Without such educational institutions, it is stated, "Christianity cannot hope to win the increasingly numerous and significant intelligentsia of awakening peoples and aspiring nations" (Fenn, 1960, p. 3).

———◄••►———

VI.B.1.b A second unsubtle but critical cost in producing communications involves *equipment*. Such a cost is usually associated with the modern mass media but, when more than the human voice or a gesture is employed as a basic medium, some kind of capital investment is necessary, even if it means only skinning a cow to make a drum.

Included in the category is everything from a pencil to a television camera.

There seems to be no doubt that in Africa films locally produced are likely to be more effective than those from the outside, or at least run the risk of committing fewer blunders. A group of experts maintains that "local material" is always beneficial: "local fables, traditions, and customs should help to produce a link between the film and the audience" (Film Centre, 1949, p. 93). Again and again films are reported to fail because they are not adapted to the audience at hand. An educational picture produced in Nigeria and aiming to instruct mothers there on how to bathe a baby offends women in Uganda: a child, they say, should not be shown naked, and his head must be washed first, not last (Spurr, 1952, p. 38). Even what appear to be universally acceptable cartoons can cause trouble. Some Congo soldiers during World War II, meeting Donald Duck for the first time, threw stones at the screen because they thought they were being ridiculed. "Animals don't talk," they shouted; "whoever saw a duck in uniform?" (Bever, 1952, p. 6). Motion pictures, according to an official interested in mass education, have special value in stimulating Africans to improve their own communities by showing them that successful measures have been undertaken by people immediately recognizable as belonging to a neighboring society (Chadwick, 1949). Films must obviously be adapted to "the experience and interest of the group" (Prosser, 1951). Unless producers are really acquainted with "indigenous culture and symbolism," their films may attract an audience but contribute little of permanent value (Little, 1949).

The rub, though, is the cost of a local production, especially in African countries lacking trained technicians and adequate budgets. Are there compromises through which somehow the economies of centralized production can be achieved? The Central Film Unit in Salisbury, Southern Rhodesia, has produced 70 color films in four years, mostly of the silent type; their objective is to assist "in the development of Africans" (UNESCO, 1955). If a film on baby-bathing presents problems when exhibited in another African country, then surely the suitability of each picture on such a list must be determined in the light of local conditions and the goal of the communicator. This is not to say that no film from a central stockpile can be shown in many African societies; caution seems necessary. In fact, one investigator has offered films from that very unit to audiences in four different Nigerian societies; first he observed their reactions during the projection, then later he interviewed or gave questionnaires to some of them. His data reveal that these films as well as some from other sources without exception elicited diverse reactions in one or more of the different societies. One picture must serve as an illustration: "The Two Farmers," produced in color by the unit, runs for 17 minutes and seeks to encourage African farmers to follow the advice of government agricultural units. A commentary in the language of the audience was provided in each case. A sequence in which dismay is expressed by a cooperating farmer named Tanganai at the price of a cart he would buy provoked laughter among the Yoruba, the Ibo, and the Birom, but not among the Hausa. Here is the investigator's own account of the data he obtained in the subsequent interviews:

Yoruba

The film, like all films about farming, was enjoyed by this audience in which the majority of men were farmers. They did not find it difficult to understand, except for the sequence showing Tanganai's farm being marked out; all audiences among the four peoples found this obscure.

Hausa

The audience and even the professional commentator seemed to have difficulty in understanding details of this film. The story was followed easily, but the way in which the farm was laid out and the reasons for it were not grasped.

Ibo

Again, there was interest in a film about farmers, but the few people who saw it and who could be interviewed later seemed not to have derived any benefit from it. Their own environment is harsh enough for careless farming to bring its own punishment, and land so short that neglect of it arouses public disapproval. . . .

Birom

Many of the people understood that Tanganai had listened to the Agricultural Assistant, and had been told how to improve farming, and that Washoma [the noncooperator] had refused advice and had had a poorer crop; but what advice Tanganai had been given they had no idea at all. They were entertained by the film, but did not draw any lessons for themselves from it, and farmers did not feel that they had much need of a cart [Morton-Williams, 1953, pp. 19, 102–8].

Other ways of affecting economies in adapting films to particular societies have been devised. In the investigation just reported, a local commentator functioned during the showing of the film; thus the original English commentary of "The Two Farmers" was simply turned off. To avoid having to employ an extra person whose remarks during the film are likely to be a little uneven in any case, it is possible to produce a silent motion picture with an unrecorded sound strip on which anything may be inscribed, as on regular sound tape. If the film itself is satisfactory, then the commentary can easily, inexpensively, and once and for all be recorded in the language and with all the necessary modifications demanded by the culture; but of course the picture remains unchanged.

Film strips are sometimes offered as a solution, for they cost little to produce and certainly can portray local conditions: "How to make your own film strips" and "How to use the kerosene projector" are the titles of articles appearing in the journal called *African Women* (Phelan, 1956). Such strips, however, have a limited range and, it has been suggested, lack the moving dynamic qualities of the motion picture: "How can we get him [the African] to accept a picture of the rapids of a river if the water is motionless?" (Bever, 1952, p. 64). It appears, therefore, that the problem of producing films perfectly acceptable in Africa from a cultural standpoint is not likely to be solved in the near future. As the countries prosper economically, they will be able to afford more local productions; and, more importantly, as cultural differences slowly disappear or become less significant under the pressures of nationalism and of increased contact with the West—if they do—African audiences will be to that extent more similar and hence a little less inclined to respond differentially to a central production.

Similar points can be made in connection with any mass medium of communication: while it is desirable to have a medium adapted to the audience of a particular society, it may not be economically feasible to do so. On radio which almost always reaches people from many different societies simultaneously, program directors can only set aside certain programs for particular language or cultural groups. The compromises that have been proposed—for example, the use of low-power relay stations, some of which might be seasonally mobile (Terrisse, 1959)—have so far turned out to be neither popular nor practical.

VI.B.2   Another type of cost, again especially associated with mass media, springs from *transmission*. All the instantaneous channels and the preserving transmitters (IV.B.1 and 2) require equipment or energy to extend the range of the communication in space or time. Someone must pay for the public-address system enabling the chief to reach a larger audience or for the postage needed to transport the book from the printer to the shop where it can be purchased.

The natural factors already mentioned increase the cost of transmitting communications in Africa. In addition, the poor distributing facilities which result from these conditions keep consumer demand relatively low, and a low demand in turn increases still further the distribution costs. The number of literate Africans interested in books, especially in remote areas, is likely to be so small that truly adequate bookstores are not economically feasible. Such people, an observer in Ghana reports, do not often send for books from urban distributing centers unless their urge to read is exceptionally strong. Salesmen and others, consequently, must be trained to reach these "potential customers" (Mason, 1951). It may be true that "every settlement of any size has a book store" in the areas of West Africa now or formerly controlled by the British, but these shops "primarily" sell school supplies (Lancour, 1958, pp. 4–5). Ho, the capital town of one region of Ghana, had two bookstores in the summer of 1959. One, owned and operated by Africans, advertised fourteen titles written in chalk on a black slate placed outside the entrance in the following way:

Train and Test—Teachers Copy	The Technique of Sex
Love Works Wonders	Tales from Shakespeare
The Coral Island	Four-Figure Mathematical Tables
A Woman's Temptation	Civics for Self Government
Modern French Course	Landmarks of World History
Animal Farm	A First Atlas Method
Biological Drawings, Bks. 1 & 2	Fundamental English, Books 1 & 2

The other bookstore, like so many excellent ones in "British" areas of Africa, belonged to a mission group whose interest in the distribution of books was motivated by more than economic gain. Perforce the manager of such an enterprise distributes and publicizes only those publications not at variance with the ideals and objectives of the church organization directly or indirectly providing the subsidy.

Another way to distribute books of course is through libraries. Considerable progress is reported from the English-speaking areas of West Africa, where the number of libraries and the size of their collections are increasing—increasing in fact faster than the number of well-trained librarians needed to administer them (Lancour, 1958, p. 26). Sometimes mobile "library vans" extend the geographical range served by the central institution.

Mission groups producing printed materials for Africans, it was once reported, too rarely effect economies by cooperating with one another in solving problems of distribution (J. Davis et al.,

1945, p. 193). Such groups, however, are seldom if ever affluent, so that all possible economies are achieved within each organization, generally through the use of ingenuity and by modifying or amplifying existing channels of distribution to meet the problem at hand. When a religious journal previously published in English in Nigeria decided to begin a similar publication in French, its publishers surveyed various areas in West Africa where that language was used by the colonial powers. Léopoldville, in the Congo, was finally selected as headquarters because a press and central bookstore of several Protestant missions already existed there and could aid in the printing and distribution of the new periodical; in addition, printing costs were less. In Nigeria itself the same publishers persuaded Moslem vendors to distribute their very Christian journal through the simple expedient of offering them a "small commission" to do so. They also found zeal to be as efficient as money: when the principal of a large school in Lagos refused to permit the sale of the journal, a young convert sold the papers directly to his fellow students (Shaw and Shaw, 1956, pp. 33, 54–5, 89).

In contemporary Africa the most persistent as well as the greatest effort to change adults comes from government, and usually therein from a special department containing the phrase "adult education" or "community development" in its official title. A number of years ago, for example, the government bureau in what was then the Gold Coast was asked to carry on the following campaigns which, in broad outline, are quite typical of those conducted in many other areas of Africa: to inform people concerning the functions of government so that they would more willingly pay their taxes; to instruct farmers in the diagnosis and cure of certain cocoa-tree diseases; to induce owners to inoculate their cattle against rinderpest; to persuade certain farmers to use manure and others to grow rice as a cash crop; and to stimulate various communities to introduce an extensive series of public health measures. Radio and what were called "normal methods of publicity" were believed to be inadequate since, in the absence of distributing and transmitting facilities, they could not reach the illiterate or the inhabitants of isolated areas, the very audiences requiring the "education." The problem could be solved, it was hoped, through personal contact and especially through demonstrations by "mobile mass education teams." The following quotation from an official release suggests how costly it is to prepare distributing facilities and to train personnel *before* a campaign is able to get underway:

> A large-scale campaign requires at least six month's preparation, since special films and film strips have to be made. Posters, handbills, discussion sheets, etc. have to be prepared, translated into five or more vernacular languages and printed. Teams have to be given special training or even be specially recruited since they must have sufficient knowledge of the subjects they are covering to be able to deal with the discussions and questions of the villagers. The field staff of other Departments concerned also needs some instruction in Mass Education methods in so far as some of them accompany or are in close liaison with the teams in the villages. Then again, the village dramas have to be thought out and practised; transport, time-schedules, and equipment must be planned and literature distributed before the Campaign can start on a given date [Department of Social Welfare and Community Development, 1956, p. 1].

VI.B.3   The final costs are those occurring after the communication has been produced and transmitted, and they may be called *reception* costs for the consumer. People may be eager and able to read the book or the magazine that is available to them in the shop close by, or they may covet the radio set or the phonograph a dealer shows them, but they may lack the funds to make the purchase.

Undoubtedly the illustration is an extreme one, but the following is a description of the radio sets in what was then, in 1956–57, the Somaliland Protectorate:

> Few people can afford to buy their own wireless receivers and, in an effort to reach the nomadic people of the interior, some 250 wireless sets have been distributed to villages, local

authorities, and [rural police]. There is no form of wireless licensing in the country and an accurate assessment of the number of privately-owned wireless sets is not possible, but it is estimated that there must be at least 2,000 [Great Britain Colonial Office, 1959, p. 41].

For most Africans the costs of the mass media run too high. In Ghana, for example, the rent for a "radio-diffusion" box—a speaker attached by wire to a centrally located receiver and capable therefore of receiving only the government station to which that receiver is tuned—has been 7 shillings sixpence (about one dollar) per month, payable in installments six months in advance. To cut or eliminate the costs for the individual consumer, therefore, official and unofficial substitutes have been devised. A radio-diffusion box or a radio is placed in a public building, such as a school or meeting place. A few people in the community subscribe to a newspaper and read it aloud to groups of illiterate contemporaries. Since there is so much sharing, it is extremely difficult to estimate the real circulation of a medium. The number of radio-diffusion boxes, for instance, does not begin to indicate the true size of the audience; over a decade ago, it was estimated that each of these loudspeakers attracted at least ten people in what was then the Gold Coast (Williams, 1950). The same kind of multiple listening, viewing, or reading occurs of course in any country, but its importance may be greater in Africa (I.A.2.c).

———————◆•••▶———————

VI.C   *Society*   Within every society there are conditions which facilitate or inhibit communication. Like those springing from nature and from costs, they may be circumvented or altered, though the suspicion may be voiced that often if not always they offer greater resistance to change. It is indeed easier to blast a tunnel through a mountain that separates two societies than it is to persuade the inhabitants to learn each other's language. Even the most factual report sometimes indicates the social barriers confronting the mass media; a publication of UNESCO listing the mass media by country also includes the important if mundane restrictions suggested by import duties, currency regulations, and censorship edicts (UNESCO, 1951).

The restrictions imposed by a language upon all its speakers will be discussed under another heading (VII.A.2). Here another linguistic problem can be considered in some detail, that of *linguistic knowledge* within a society or an audience.

VI.C.1 Two questions must be raised: aside from their own language, what other language do people know, and are they literate? These are the kinds of questions that ordinarily do not have to be mentioned when communication is studied in a Western society, for there other languages are unimportant and it is safe to assume that most people are literate. Neither assumption is valid in Africa. First, then, consideration is given to *knowledge of nonindigenous languages.* No doubt this factor becomes real anywhere when an

VI.C.1.a outsider wonders whether he can use his own language in front of a strange audience; will they understand him? Of course translations can always be made from one language into the language of the audience, but the process, besides being time-consuming and expensive, may produce subtle changes in meaning.

———•—•———

African languages are difficult to classify and locate, it will be seen (VII.A.1); in addition, "one can only hazard a guess at the exact number of vernacular languages spoken in Africa." According to the some source, for example, "in Nigeria, the Cameroons, and certain other regions, languages exist about which practically nothing is known" (UNESCO, 1953, p. 16). In Nigeria three languages are spoken by less than two-thirds of the population; "no one knows how many different languages" are used there, although 80 is considered to be "a very moderate estimate" (Enemo, 1948, p. 191). This linguistic mélange is especially acute in urban areas in Africa, which often attract representatives from many linguistic communities. The situation clearly creates special problems for communication. In the Christian churches of one city, for example, Sunday services must be conducted successively in five or six languages; elsewhere hymns must be announced "with numbers for three books, each in a separate language" (Neill, 1950, p. 24). Anyone using mass communication in Africa, consequently, must carefully select his language, and it is highly likely that some members of the audience will not comprehend his message.

Although some Africans understand or speak more than one language, the error must not be committed of assuming that one African language is so similar to the next that the learning problem can be easily solved. An African educator suggests, for example, that "it is almost as hard for a Yoruba to speak Ibo or Hausa as it is for him to learn to speak a European language" (Enemo, 1948, p. 191). In addition, the prestige and hence the influence and persistence of vernacular languages, if anything, has increased since World War II. They are closely identified with nationalism. They have been employed in teaching adults and especially in increasing the number of literates. And in former and present British areas they have become "acceptable subjects of study for School Certificates and university-entry requirements" (L. J. Lewis, 1949, p. 334). A UNESCO report estimates that at the start of the fifties there were 91 languages being used in the schools of those areas (UNESCO, 1953, p. 17).

A lingua franca in Africa assumes one of three forms: a mixture of languages, generally African; an African language known in more than one society; or a European language. Members of the audience or enough of them must obviously be acquainted with the other language if it is to serve its purpose. No one of these attempts to solve the problem of intercultural communication is entirely satisfactory, as a brief survey will now indicate.

According to the same UNESCO source just cited (ibid., p. 20), the principal linguae francae of Africa are the following: Arabic (Somalia); pidgin English (Sierra Leone, Nigeria, British Cameroons); Jukun (two provinces of Nigeria, British Cameroons); Bari (southern Sudan); Lozi, Bemba, and Nyanja (Northern Rhodesia); Hausa (Northern Nigeria, elsewhere in West Africa); and Swahili (four territories of East Africa, eastern Congo). In the middle Congo alone, three trade languages have been distinguished: (1) Bangala, a crude language having few inflections, irregular forms, and a poor vocabulary and used largely between Europeans and Africans and to a lesser degree among non-Bantu societies; (2) Lingala, a more highly developed language but used only by a few people and showing no tendency to spread; and (3) Mangala, a language with a typically Bantu structure, including a simplified tonal system, and, though not the language of any one tribe or district, used extensively by Europeans and those Africans whose native tongue it resembles (Guthrie, 1943).

These languages raise problems. By definition they cut across linguistic boundaries, but understanding is often superficial and nuances may be missed. Or consider the difficulties of Swahili. First, the language itself differs from area to area; as it moves in and up from the coast of Kenya and Tanganyika, it becomes more and more "emasculated," with the result that in northern Uganda and parts of the eastern Congo "it is essentially a highly simplified means of communication for individuals of widely differing groups; pruned of all refinements, its link with the coast is a tenuous one" (Whiteley, 1956, p. 343). In a given area Swahili keeps changing by borrowing words from both Arabic and English; the Arabic word for school, *chuo,* is generally used to refer to a Koranic school, but the word *skule* or *shule* has appeared to refer to a school in which roman characters are taught (Gower, 1952, p. 154). The language with which it competes and which influences it, furthermore, varies from country to country; in many parts of Uganda, it is the Ganda language; in Kenya, English; in parts of the eastern Congo, both French and Lingala. In that same section of the Congo, Protestant and Catholic missions disagree concerning the kind of Swahili to be taught. The prestige of the language fluctuates: it is high in Zanzibar and Pemba but low in Kenya (Whiteley, 1956, pp. 347–50).

By and large, authorities agree, the deliberate attempt to improve communication by producing a standardized lingua franca from several related languages has not been successful (UNESCO, 1953, p. 21). Somehow people must feel the need for another language before they spontaneously adopt it, as they have Swahili or, very rapidly since the start of the century, Mangala. The language of the conqueror or of the most powerful or numerous people in the area, such as that of the Ganda in some parts of

Uganda or of Hausa in West Africa, may be used for purposes of everyday communication and may even become the mother tongue of some people. Another society's language has all the disadvantages of a lingua franca and may also have the additional one of being associated so definitely with an outside group.

Another solution to the linguistic problem in Africa is to employ a European language—English, French, Afrikaans, Portuguese, Spanish, or German—as the lingua franca and even as the official language of the country. So far these languages in general are understood adequately only by the educated elite; the majority of the people do not learn them or learn only a limited number of working phrases. In fact those Africans whose knowledge of a European language remains fluent and serviceable are likely to be atypical with reference to occupation or some other form of previous or continuing contact. To spread this linguistic ability more widely some countries, such as Ghana and many of the former French colonies, are requiring that the official or unofficial European language be the medium of instruction even in the lowest grades; and then sometimes the vernacular language is studied as another school subject. Unfortunately, however, the level of instruction is not high, because of a scarcity of well-trained teachers; and one often hears an almost unintelligible accent in English being unwittingly conferred upon pupils by a well-intentioned teacher. The present writer has the impression that linguistic facility, even of university graduates, quite quickly deteriorates unless there is the opportunity or necessity constantly to practice the language. It is also argued that too thorough training in a foreign language is undesirable: even though a language such as English may have a better developed technical vocabulary, a greater capacity for some kinds of literary expression, and a larger literature in general than even the richest and most flexible African language, it remains for Africans a second language in which they never can hope to express themselves as "easily and naturally" as their own culture demands (Hopgood, 1948).

Various efforts have been made to simplify English so that as a lingua franca it may be learned and used more readily by Africans. Available has been Basic English, the system in whose vocabulary of 850 words most ideas and propositions can be adequately if sometimes a bit lengthily expressed. One editor in South Africa has constructed a vocabulary of one thousand words by selecting them from written sources and then testing them on African school children; also some are English words which have already crept into the African languages of the country (e.g., *box, police, school, railway*). The first five words on the list are *afternoon, air, airplane, animal, ant;* and the last five are *wave, whip, whistle, wipe, work* (Roux, 1942). For purposes of communication on an elementary level, inevitably the foreign language becomes spontaneously simplified: the easiest possible words and the shortest possible sentences are used in order to tell the servant to prepare the tea, or to inform the master that the tea is ready. But more than rudimentary, so-called "kitchen" forms are needed to express subtle ideas and feelings. Two European writers with publishing experience in West Africa issue a warning that seems to the present writer to have, except for the last phrase, face validity:

> Adult Africans do not think as children. Just as children's stories and newspapers are childish to adults in the homelands, so they are to adults in Africa. Adult Africans think profoundly and with maturity, but in a *limited vocabulary* [Shaw and Shaw, 1956, p. 34; italics theirs].

A lingua franca, especially a European language, comes to be valued not only as a means of communication but also as a symbol of learning or status within the society. In Sierra Leone, for example, indigenous languages, a Creole language, and English all exist side-by-side. Creole is virtually a lingua franca in towns "on the railway line," but many people living in villages do not understand it; for this and other reasons a village is regarded as a place only for "the socially subordinate members of society." To achieve higher status, consequently, ambitious Africans seek to learn Creole. The people who use Creole among themselves and thus strengthen their own "feeling of cultural and group solidarity" object to mobility through language: they themselves consider the language a sign of their own status, and realistically they seek to retain a monopoly on it since thereby they have access to desirable jobs, especially in government. They also dislike being addressed by other Africans in English. That language from their viewpoint is associated with "the ruling European class" and hence "the native man" who speaks it in their presence is trying to claim "social superiority" over them (Little, 1951, pp. 105–6, 256, 264–5). Here, then, are social barriers to removing the linguistic barrier.

The conclusion must be drawn from this discussion that in the foreseeable future the voices of Africa will remain numerous and communication through language, though it will gradually improve, will continue to be restricted by the polyglot state of affairs.

Europeans who seek to communicate with Africans in their own language face difficulties that can be briefly described. If a European is to communicate with Africans, it is perfectly obvious that he will profit from knowing their language. At the very least they will feel pleased that he has gone to the trouble to learn it; ordinarily, they know very well, they have been expected to learn his language. Then he will be able to detect firsthand the nuances and subtleties which escape all but the best trained and most conscientious interpreters and which in fact sometimes must be experienced in order to be fully appreciated. The obstacles in the way of learning an African language, however, are formidable. First, as suggested above, some of them have not yet been described; and often those which have been studied do not have adequate grammars or dictionaries for foreigners. Even if the outsider is using African informants in their own setting and even if he forces himself to be utterly dependant on Africans who do not speak his or any European language—the technique used by the conscientious anthropologist who dumps himself into the bush—his progress is likely to be slow. For, as a learned missionary has indicated, "mastering an African language is no light task" —and he adds in lay terms:

Most are tone languages in which slight changes of pitch or intonation distinguish different meanings. The structure is usually at least as complex as Latin. A typical Bantu language will have about ten classes of nouns in the singular and seven in the plural. These correspond roughly to genders. They are distinguished by different prefixes that are attached to related pronouns, adjectives, and verbs. The Bantu verb has an abundance of moods and tenses; but its special wealth is a bright array of suffixes each of which gives a new twist of meaning to the word. By this means a single basic word can be refashioned by a skilled speaker into scores of derived words, each with its own shade of meaning and its full range of grammatical forms [Carpenter, 1959, p. 36].

Most Europeans in Africa have or at least feel they have other more important objectives to attain, and hence are convinced that they cannot afford the time which learning the language requires. No matter how eager and willing the African speaker of the language is, furthermore, he is not likely to know the best methods for teaching his language to a stranger; in fact he may have no conception whatsoever of pedagogy for this purpose. Until recently too, most Europeans in Africa segregated themselves so successfully from Africans that they had little or no opportunity to practice an African language except in connection with elementary matters pertaining to the household and the office (I. C. Ward, 1937). Also, the person confronted with an African language is not inspired by any of the extra benefits which are promised him when he learns a European language. The speakers of the African language are confined to one society; unless he learns a lingua franca, the European finds that his painfully acquired knowledge is useless or next to useless among Africans from other societies. And of course nobody speaks an African language except in Africa. No or virtually no printed literature exists in any African language; hence a knowledge of the language does not make available new riches in literature, philosophy, and science as is true of any European language. The restriction here is indeed a mighty one!

———◆◆◆———

VI.C.1.b   Linguistic knowledge includes also the ability to read and write; for printed media and for communicating in writing, the *literacy* rate can be important, especially in areas outside the West.

The problem of illiteracy is more acute in Africa than in any other area of the world. In 1957 UNESCO provided estimates of the percentage of adult illiteracy; an adult is defined as a person aged fifteen and older. The figures for Northern America were 3–4 per cent, those for Asia 60–65 per cent, Africa 80–85 per cent. African countries or regions reaching the highest rate of 95–99 per cent were Angola, French Equatorial Africa, French West Africa, Mozambique, and Spanish West Africa. The lowest figure of 70–75 per cent was estimated to be in Uganda; and the next lowest—75–80 per cent—in the Gold Coast and Kenya (UNESCO, 1957, pp. 15, 32, 38–40). Considerable variability exists within a given region; thus it is thought that approximately 85 per cent of the total population in English-speaking West Africa is illiterate, but the figure drops to about 50 per cent in Lagos, the capital of Nigeria (Lancour, 1958, p. 5). All such figures must be constantly revised because of the tremendous educational strides being made in many African countries. The number of junior and senior primary school pupils in Northern Nigeria is reported to have risen from 66,180 in 1946 to 176,894 in 1956 (Northern Nigeria, 1957, p. 23). Additional information about such a threefold increase, however, is needed before a corresponding rise in the literacy rate can be meaningfully postulated. What degree of proficiency do the children in fact attain? After leaving school, is their ability reinforced or, since the numbers attending school in this vast region are relatively small, is that ability allowed to lapse?

Among officials almost everywhere in Africa there is enthusiasm for formal education but really starry-eyed ecstasy for teaching adults how to read and write. The now famous inventor of a very popular technique for instruction in reading has stated the case in glowing words:

Printed matter may be posted on the walls and sold or given freely in homes so that men, women, and children can hardly avoid seeing it. The frequent repetition of the same idea tends to lead them to believe. It is said that people will not believe a new thing until they see or hear it at least five times. As a rule, they remember better what they see than what they hear, and if they both see and hear it, a new idea will soon win its way into the most resistant mind [Laubach, 1947, p. 21].

Although Laubach may be quite right about the efficacy of repetition and the combination of audition and vision—for some people, under some circumstances—his contentions are unacceptable as universal propositions. That literacy aids communication, nevertheless, is self-evident.

Africans who are illiterate, especially in urban areas, are at "a perpetual disadvantage" as their country enters the modern world at an accelerated rate. They must depend upon what is demonstrated to them. They cannot explain, amplify, or correct "erroneous impressions" through books. They are barred from certain occupations. They are duped by "literate rogues." They are unable to read materials which affect them vitally, such as labor contracts, railway tickets, road and safety signs, and government regulations. They are deprived of "the inspiration, recreation, and contact with a wider world which books afford" (J. Davis et al., 1945, p. 182).

Another potent argument for literacy is suggested by an official on the basis of his experience in the Eastern Province of Nigeria. "Even a slight degree of literacy," he says, has important effects on people's morale. They discover that there is "no great mystery and no unsurmountable difficulty" in learning to read, and then immediately they wish also to acquire for themselves more of "the comforts and benefits" of Western civilization (Chadwick, 1949). Literacy, it is thus contended, not only enables people to respond to printed media but also makes them seek out more of the modern media.

The attainment of literacy may also change the person's status within his own society since it brings him material benefits and also signifies that at least in this respect he has been able to place himself on the same level as Europeans. "In the eyes of the nonliterate man" among the Mende of Sierra Leone, "a 'civilized' individual is a 'book man,' 'one who knows books,' that is, one who can read." Such an individual may demonstrate pride in his accomplishment by reading a book or newspaper in public. At the same time he may be resented by illiterate people who characterize him as a "white man" and as a person to doubt and suspect. The latter view is sometimes substantiated by minor officials and clerks whose literacy enables them to defraud the illiterate (Little, 1951, pp. 209, 256, 262).

In order to determine on an empirical basis what factors are in fact associated with newly acquired literacy, the present writer conducted two exploratory studies in Northern Nigeria in the summer of 1959. One general hypothesis guided the work, viz., that literacy is positively correlated with behavior, knowledge, or attitudes suggestive of alertness. The results, it will be seen, tentatively confirm the hypothesis as well as the viewpoint of those who favor literacy for Africans in the modern world.

The site of the first study was a small Hausa community about twenty miles from Kaduna, the capital of the region. The chief there obtained the twenty-one adult males who were interviewed. He was asked to find all kinds of men, and the notion of a representative sample was roughly explained to him; in addition half were to come from those who had attended and half from those who had not attended adult classes for the teaching of literacy. In fact, ten were literate, eleven illiterate. The small sample, consequently, was not randomly selected; it cannot be called representative of the village; but probably the biases of the chief operated identically for both subgroups.

Each man was seen alone and questioned in Hausa through an interpreter. The separate parts of the schedule followed one another in this order: three census-type questions; the identification of eight straightforward pen-and-ink drawings taken from school textbooks in use in Africa and two fragments from photographs whose subject matter was thought to be most difficult to discern (a very poorly illuminated view of people huddled together and the section of an airplane wing); questions about news events, the mass media, and general beliefs; a request to recall the contents of the drawings and the photographs; the identification of two photographs; the identification of the content of a jigsaw puzzle as it was being assembled; and questions about literacy classes. In the course of the interview, two variables—warning vs. not warning the informant that he would be subsequently asked to recall the contents of the drawings and photographs; asking vs.

not asking leading questions about the content of the photographs —were randomly manipulated, the results of which are described elsewhere (IX.D.2.c).

Comparisons between literate and illiterate groups are summarized in Table 1. "Items" in the table refer to particular pic-

TABLE 1. *Comparison of Literates and Illiterates*

	Literates (n = 10)	Illiterates (n = 11)
PICTURES		
Number of items on which correct identification by group is greater	9	0
Mean number correctly identified	5.4	3.0
Number of items on which correct recall by group is greater	7	3
Mean number correctly recalled	4.7	3.3
NEWS		
Number of items on which complete ignorance of group is greater	0	9
Number of items on which greater contact of group with news sources is shown	4	0
SCIENTIFIC BELIEFS		
Number of items on which more in group hold scientific view	4	1
JIGSAW PUZZLE		
Number of criteria on which group shows poorer performance	0	3

tures or questions on the schedule; for example, the third row means that in seven instances a higher percentage of the literates than the illiterates recalled the drawings or photographs, and in three instances the higher percentage was found among illiterates. Without exception, the table shows, the performance of the literates is superior to that of the illiterates. More of the former than the latter could correctly identify nine of the ten pictures— the tenth figure turned out to be so ambiguous that no criterion for correctness could be applied. Only one of the differences on the separate pictures, however, is of sufficient magnitude to be statistically significant with such small groups, but the trend itself is significant, as is the difference between the mean numbers of pictures correctly identified. Differences with respect to the recall of the pictures, though in the same direction, are not significant. Similar trends emerge with respect to knowledge of news events (e.g., "What news have you heard last about Northern Nigeria?") and news sources (e.g., "When did you last hear a radio? What did you hear?"), although again the difference for each item is very small and not significant. There is also a slight tendency for more of the literates to have "scientific" rather than traditional beliefs (e.g., "Why do people get sick?"). Finally, the literates performed in a superior way as the pieces of the jigsaw puzzle were put in place.

The second study followed the same general plan as the first, with two differences. First other variables were manipulated—largely with inconclusive results (VIII.C.2). Secondly, an effort was made to see how quickly arrangements could be made to gather and then actually to collect information, since often the practical art of communicating to an audience demands that relevant data be gathered and processed with dispatch (XII.D.3). The chief of a village near Zaria selected the informants to be interviewed. He was asked to find men of all kinds, but there is no way of knowing how representative of the village his hand-picked sample was. Again the nineteen men who appeared were interviewed one at a time in Hausa through an interpreter. Each interview took no less than half an hour and no more than an hour. The schedule closely resembled the one in the first study; the precise items are indicated in the description of the results.

With such small groups it was not possible to obtain statistically significant differences on any of the individual questions. There is, however, a clear-cut trend; in comparison with the illiterates, a slightly higher proportion of those attending the literacy classes:

1. Heard a radio recently, had a radio in their homes, and remembered something specific from a broadcast.

2. Recently and specifically became acquainted with some news item that had appeared in the newspapers.

3. Claimed that they obtained items of news from friends or people in general as well as from the radio and newspapers.

4. Could reply specifically and meaningfully to the impertinent question, "What would you like to know about the world that you do not know?"

5. Could provide a scientific explanation of the moon's phases.

6. Were better informed about the use of a new chemical fertilizer which a government agency was trying to introduce.

7. Adapted themselves more skillfully to identifying the scene in a jigsaw puzzle which was gradually built up in front of them.

8. Were able to recall a communication that was read to them as well as other questions and items in the interview.

This trend, like that in the first study, might be said to reflect greater alertness concerning various aspects of the outside world. Likewise in another study devoted primarily to the perception of photographs and drawings (IX.D.2.c; $n = 20$) there were differences pointing in the same direction; virtually all of those who had been to school, for example, claimed to have fairly regular access to news through radio, newspapers, or other people, whereas less than one quarter of those who had not gone to school made the same claim. No one of these three studies is conclusive for at least two reasons. First, as already indicated, the groups being compared were much too small; and hence the trends can be considered only suggestive. Also, with this approach it is not possible to determine the cause-and-effect sequence that produced the tendencies. If the guiding hypothesis is valid, then it is possible that becoming literate increases people's alertness because they have access to more media of communication and perhaps to better jobs in the Western sense; and yet it is also probable that the more alert people in the community responded to the opportunity to attend the literacy classes. Or perhaps both sequences occurred: the initially more alert became literate and then, having become literate, they could become still more alert.

To determine how the informants themselves felt about the literacy classes, most of those in the first study were asked why they had or had not attended them and what benefits they had received or conceivably might receive from going. Of the nine literates so questioned, six maintained that they had wished to read news or in general to find out about events in the world, one gave a very general reason which he may have meant literally but which sounds intriguingly cosmic ("to get out of darkness"), and two mentioned very specific goals ("to be able to deal with Europeans," "to be able to read and write letters"). Five of the ten illiterates claimed they now planned to attend classes, and the rest stated they were too old or had no opportunity. Nobody, therefore, opposed the notion of becoming literate. The greatest benefit claimed from literacy was the ability to write and read letters from relatives. Except for a single reference to news, other advantages appear to be very general. Nor could most of the illiterates indicate how they would be specifically helped by becoming literate; but all stated that they want their children to learn to read and write.

VI.C.2 The final type of restriction stems from the *social structure* which regulates to some degree the relation between communicator and audience by assigning them roles to perform. As anthropologists repeatedly demonstrate each time they come upon a new society or analyze an old one more thoroughly, every society contains a web of groups in which people inevitably are placed. Males occupy a status different from females, and almost always distinctions are made on the basis of age. The family of origin affects the choice of one's associates during childhood and one's heirs after death. Since this social structure varies from society to society more or less singularly, it must be known or investigated in order to grasp the communications systems within a particular society. Just as the communicator has a particular status in the society and the group (I.A.1), so the audience has its assigned position (IX.C.1); hence the relation between communicator and audience is determined in part by the structure of the society. At one end of a continuum, no communication between the two may be permitted, at the other end there may be a constant, intimate, or interacting communication. The relation, it is said, is determined only in part by the structure because, although tradition, custom, and legal regulations always are of some significance—no man is ever completely free, libel laws in effect are omnipresent—there are bound to be at the same time some cracks in the structure.

The cracks in their turn come from a host of sources: from variations in personality, from conflicts within the society, and from the interaction of people. For this reason it seems desirable to distinguish between the relatively structured and unstructured relation of the communicator and the audience. By (a) *relatively structured* is meant that the norm for the relation is known and hence predictable by both communicator and audience and that their respectable expectations are likely to be confirmed. By (b) *relatively unstructured* is meant an unusual, deviant, "spontaneous," or unpredictable relation. There seems to be little doubt that few instances of communication involve one relation without the other; the social structure always restricts some but not all of what conceivably may be communicated.

In virtually any part of the world, the relationships between kinsmen that govern marriage, residence, and social affiliation of children are heavily reinforced and hence are among the last to undergo change. Two points must be noted concerning the social organizations to which these relationships give rise in Africa. First, they are especially important there because traditionally they have been intimately linked with economic, political, and religious institutions. In addition, their form tends to be somewhat uniform throughout the continent: related to the prevalence of polygyny already mentioned (V.B.2) are the dominant role of the male and the location of the family's residence among the husband's rather than the wife's relatives. For these reasons it may be anticipated that many of the really significant relations between communicator and audience in Africa for some time to come will be structured and restricted by these traditional forms of organization.

Relatively structured relations between communicator and audience are specified for some situations in any society. The intermediary communicator, for example, may be carefully designated. In early 1944, for example, the climax of the ceremony celebrating the coronation of a new king in a principality of the Fung empire in the Sudan was a fanfare from a special horn of a roan antelope that had been carefully preserved from the past and was "bound with human skin." The blast was blown by a herald from the king's household, who formerly would have been "obviously his chief slave or eunuch" (Disney, 1945). Among the Akan peoples of Ghana, drummers have a status higher than that of messengers; they are frequently sons or grandsons of the paramount chief; and they are expected to be acquainted with the heroic deeds of their ancestors and with their country's traditions so that they can thoroughly understand the verses they translate into the language of the drum (Danquah, 1928, pp. 51–2). Likewise an audience may be restricted to people with particular characteristics; thus among some of the Amhara in Ethiopia circumcision may not be witnessed by anyone who has had sexual intercourse within the last twenty-four hours (Bas-Work, 1957).

Unquestionably the structured relation between communicator and audience can sometimes provide extremely important information about the communication. A man and woman belonging to exogamous clans are not destined to exchange the prattle of lovers or the chatter of marriage, but that there must be some tendency to act and communicate in the forbidden manner is shown by the heavy sanctions imposed against incest. The same kind of suspicion must be voiced whenever communication is strongly taboo. Among the Ashanti, of Ghana, for example, "one of the most terrible sins" is to invoke a curse upon the king either directly with the use of words or indirectly through some symbolic act, such as compelling his son to build a path (a menial task performed by him only when clearing a way to the mausoleum of a recently deceased king). The offense, punishable by death, is considered so heinous that it can be referred to only by means of a euphemism or through circumlocution (Rattray, 1929, pp. 311–12). Why, undoubtedly, is the urge to curse the king so strong?

An examination of most institutions reveals how the relation of communicator and audience is structured only up to a point; then less structured communication takes place. Among the Tallensi of Ghana, "face-to-face communication and association" are heavily influenced by one's "genealogical relationships." Typically, for example, people are well acquainted with their own settle-

ment and those with which their clan has "close social bonds";
they know "more superficially" the area in which their mother
was born or in which close extraclan kin live; but they are almost
completely ignorant about settlements, even those near at hand,
with which their clan has no social bonds and with which they
have no personal kinship or friendship ties (Fortes, 1945, pp. 158–
9, 211). Within this rigid social context, which must markedly
determine the flow of communication in the society, however,
there is some flexibility. A festival, for example, celebrates the end
of the dry season, a fortnight or so after which communal fishing
expeditions begin. The owner of a particular pool "decides for
himself" exactly when he will fish his pool; thus the initiative
comes from him. He then is likely to use a formal channel to
communicate news of his decision, but simultaneously to rely
upon informal mechanisms for further transmission. A day or two
in advance he makes a public announcement "from the house-tops
of his settlement" and he allows the news to spread "from mouth
to mouth." Or he may resort to a completely informal method
within the established network of social relationships: on market
day he sends members of his family and neighbors "to inform
friends and acquaintances they meet" (Fortes, 1937, p. 133).

Even a very authoritarian political institution leaves some of
its communication relations relatively unstructured, apparently
for the sake of efficiency. Among the Ganda of Uganda, for example, chiefs are arranged under the king in a hierarchy of three
principal ranks. That hierarchy, for example, determines how
justice is administered; if a case cannot be settled at one level, it
must move formally in an approved manner to the next higher
chief. The system, moreover, regulates the flow of communication
between the king and his lesser chiefs. His own messengers cannot transmit his orders directly to people within "the domain of
the lowest chief." Instead they explain the problem to a principal
chief who sends *his* messenger to the next lower chief; and the
latter sends his messenger to the still lower chief under whose
jurisdiction the audience actually is. "Any attempt to short-circuit
this procedure" of communicating, it is said of the traditional
system, "would have been regarded as an unthinkable insult to
the dignity of a chief" (Mair, 1934, pp. 174–5). In contrast, in-

formation follows very informal channels when news rather than orders are involved. A chief seldom stays alone at home: he either receives visitors or makes visits. And so the following state of affairs prevails, or rather once prevailed before contact with Europeans:

> News travelled quickly. Many interesting subjects were discussed in a chief's house. The women met with their friends and talked about their gardens, and discussed any bit of gossip they could get hold of; they too had their own visiting circles. Women of the lower orders had not much to talk about beyond their gardens and their young children, i.e., those who were still too small to be taken away from them for education by members of their father's clan. The wives of chiefs living in the capital often received female visitors in their own quarters; scarcely a day passed without some friends coming to see them, and they were permitted to receive their male relatives [Roscoe, 1911, p. 8].

Similar cracks may appear in the communication patterns associated with polygyny. In theory the wives of a Moslem who are in purdah are in complete seclusion and can receive communications only from their husband and his specially selected servants. Among the Hausa of Northern Nigeria women escape from this formal restriction in various ways. In the first place, few men other than powerful emirs and wealthy merchants can afford to achieve complete purdah for their wives. Even these ostensibly lucky men, however, allow wives to visit relatives "at least every five years"; and the preadolescent children and women beyond the menopause who are permitted at any time to enter the women's quarters become "the bearers of news from one compound to another." For lesser people there is a modified form of purdah. In one the wife is confined only during the daytime; after dusk she may draw water from a well, bring in firewood, and also "greet her nearby kin and women friends." Finally, a "marriage of the ignorant" is also tolerated: women are subject to virtually no restraint and hence permitted to go as they please and especially to work even during the daytime (M. G. Smith, 1955, pp. 50–1).

This section showing the effect of social structure upon communication must be twisted at the end to suggest the reverse of the process: during socialization and thereafter the salient facts of that structure are, respectively, taught and reinforced through a series of communications. Among the Luo of Kenya, for example, the various sections of meat are distributed to people attending a ceremony in accordance with their position in the extended family; hence "when the Luo youngster of either sex begins to grasp why, on certain occasions, it receives a special supply of kidney or ribs to roast on the fire with its playmates, its education in the theory of lineage has begun." Similarly at the frequent beer parties the order of drinking from the pitchers is "strictly determined by lineage seniority." Since the ceremonial distribution of both the meat and the beer occurs on the family homestead, "the segmentary principles of the social structure" can be grasped in the appropriate context. No wonder, the anthropologist comments, the Luo themselves become acquainted, so painlessly and effortlessly, with "those principles of social organization which seem at first so intricate and confusing to the outsider" (Southall, 1952, pp. 36–8). The Luo, like all men, learn the restrictions they must and would impose upon themselves.

VII.   THE COMMUNICATION

Problems immediately burst out when the content of the communication is systematically planned or analyzed. The characteristics of communication media differ widely. The best technique imaginable to appraise a piece of prose cannot be used to describe a dance or the sound of a trumpet. Communicators and analysts approach no medium with standardized procedure. How, for example, should an analysis be made of a dance in which many people participate? Here there is no widely favored system to record the movements. Even when a system has received universal consent, as in music, all difficulties are not eliminated. The written notes that preserve a symphony do not specify how to reproduce its elusive, critically expressive qualities. Or "almost all" experts are said to agree that in African music rhythm is of "fundamental importance" and that it is frequently expressed "by the simultaneous use of two or more rhythms"; yet they do not agree concerning "the organizing principles upon which multiple meter is based" (Merriam, 1959, p. 65). To avoid these technical complexities and also to function within an extensively explored area, the present chapter concentrates almost exclusively upon verbal communications. Many of the points raised here can be applied, *mutatis mutandis,* to the other media. And what do those slick Latin words mean? Usually whoever uses them is either too lazy to demonstrate the modifications required by the other instances or incapable of doing so; this writer refuses to classify himself.

There are very definitely three conventional, well-tried, but important criteria which the analysis of *all* communication media, like any measure, must strive to satisfy. The analysis should be reliable, objective, and valid. *Reliability* and *objectivity* refer to the extent to which repeated measurements, respectively, by the same person over a period of time and by different persons at the same time yield similar results. *Validity* indicates the extent to which the measure agrees with some independent measure that is considered important or critical. Beneath the crisp, glib definitions are puzzling difficulties, especially in the field of communication. It is possible, for example, to achieve a high degree of reliability and objectivity by using measures that are rather meaningless and perhaps invalid. What is the man saying? What are the two dancers doing? One could count the number of words he speaks and then determine the proportion devoted to the indefinite article; and one could count the number of times the two dancers touch each other during the performance. The count in both instances would remain identical or almost identical if performed twice by the same person or once by two persons, but the information thus obtained undoubtedly would be useless. On the other hand a better kind of operation would be to determine how often the speaker is optimistic, how often pessimistic; and how often the dancers collide while in a friendly posture, how often in an unfriendly one. Optimism-pessimism and friendliness-unfriendliness are attributes much more difficult to detect than the number of indefinite articles or physical contacts; hence their reliability and objectivity are likely to be lower.

The really tricky problem arises in connection with validity: what is the important or critical "independent measure" which with the analysis must be correlated? Once more a trio presents itself, each member of which has noticeable defects. One measure may be derived from the *communicator:* does the analysis agree with what the communicator seeks to communicate? The communicator's intended goal, however, may not be the one he is likely to achieve or has achieved (II.B); his words, for example, may be at variance with the message conveyed by his involuntary gestures. A second measure comes from the *audience:* does the analysis agree with what the audience perceives in the communication? Such a psychological criterion is likely to be favored by anthropologists who are almost always interested in the interpretation placed upon a form of behavior by the people themselves. Usually such information is not easy to come by: if the investigator goes to the trouble of determining how people comprehend the content of a message, he might as well go a step further and investigate all their reactions, which would be a long cry from simply analyzing the communication as such. In addition, the data from one audience may not resemble those from another receiving the same communication. The third measure comes from the *analyst:* does the analysis agree with what the analyst believes to be the content of the communication? Such a criterion for validity is essentially redundant and hence superfluous, for it suggests only whether one operation of the analyst, such as a preliminary guess, agrees with another operation by him, such as the counting of categories. And yet if the analyst is competent and trustworthy, his analysis must be valuable, for with detachment he may note in the communication themes of which the communicator is unaware and to which a particular audience does not respond. Valuable, yes, but of unknown validity. Perhaps it is now clear why communication analysts prefer to worry about the reliability and the objectivity rather than the validity of their analyses.

———•———

The present writer finds it useful, in trying to comprehend the goal of communication in Africa, to try when possible to approach validity from all three standpoints. Concretely, here is an illustration from a booklet in English called "You and Your Country," issued by the Regional Adult Education Field Headquarters in Zaria, Northern Nigeria. The publication contains lucidly written questions and answers on various topics pertaining to government, disease, car-driving, conservation, etc. The explicit aim of the communicator is stated in the first two sentences: "This book has been prepared in order to provide the general public with information about what goes on around them. There is information about Government and the Native Authority, about your home and your neighbor." The dissemination of "information," then, is the goal of the communicator. Indeed, when the question is raised, "What are the chief diseases spread by polluted water?" and the answer given, "Dysentery, bilharzia, guinea worm, and diarrhea," the manual does seem to be on an informational level. But when the question, "Whom do the Premier, his ministers, and your representative at Kaduna serve?" is answered, "They serve you, the people of Northern Nigeria," the democrat from the West must politely but firmly chuckle a bit. "Yes" is the complete answer to the question, "Is it true that many of those who pretend to be witches are feeble-minded or insane?" (Northern Nigeria, 1958, pp. 1, 4, 31, 52). At this point it seems evident that more than information is being transmitted. Here are value judgments that Nigerians may or may not perceive, and here a deliberate if not necessarily successful effort is being made to change or at least affect feelings. A conference with the author of the manual revealed, of course, that he is most sophisticated and believes that a function of government is to strengthen loyalty toward the government and to weaken a few of the traditional beliefs which in his opinion interfere with the people's welfare. The categories of analysis must be obtained not by following the writer's own pronouncement but by probing beneath that utterance.

Three questions are being raised concerning verbal communications as such, only the first of which requires no elaborate apparatus to satisfy the criteria of reliability, objectivity, and validity. In what language does the communication appear and what are some of the attributes of that language? Next, what is the content of the communication, what does it say or attempt to say? Then, how is the message expressed, what is its style, and what rhetorical devices are employed?

VII.A

VII.A.1

Language Before analyzing or composing a verbal communication, it is necessary to know the language in which the communication, respectively, is expressed or is to be transmitted. *Identification of language,* though an obvious attribute in areas where a single language is spoken, cannot be overlooked when people with different languages inhabit the same geographical site. The present writer has had the experience of being addressed in the South Tyrol by a stranger in a voice so low that he first had to decide whether the language being used was Italian or German before trying to comprehend the words.

In a strict scholarly sense, information concerning the languages spoken in Africa is far from satisfactory. One writer has indeed attempted, on the basis of unspecified published sources, to list the "principal" languages of Africa: there are, he thinks, 8 European languages, 4 Asiatic, and 40 African, including Arabic and, as one group, the Berber dialects. For each language, an estimate is given of the number of indigenous speakers, the number of literates, and the very broad areas in which it is spoken. Another breakdown is by country: the languages therein, the percentages of people speaking them, and their status (whether used officially by government, whether serving as the medium of instruction in schools, and whether represented by a newspaper). This linguistic catalogue (MacDougald, 1944) has been termed "a disappointing effort" by an expert (Doke, 1945) because, according to him, many details are inaccurate. Under the auspices of the International African Institute the experts themselves have published a series of monographs in which they have classified African languages and supplied geographical and population figures for each of them (Westermann and Bryan, 1952; Guthrie, 1953; Doke, 1954; and Tucker and Bryan, 1956). Such scientific works give the impression that (a) scholars have not yet agreed concerning the most valid way of grouping African languages, and generally the number of groups grows less and less as more and more similarities on an abstract level are discovered; and that (b) the areas in which a language is spoken and the number of people speaking it indigenously or as a second language cannot be precisely specified. From the viewpoint of practical communication, however, the problem of classification may not be very relevant, just as it matters not whether English is grouped with French or German to a speaker of either of those languages who is trying to learn English. Also, in a broad sense quite a bit *is* known about the major African languages spoken in each meaningful locality. An expert's description of one non-Bantu language, Luo for example, illustrates the rough-and-ready adequacy of existing knowledge:

Where spoken: Kenya: Central Southern, and Northern Nyanza Districts, extending southwards into the northern part of Tanganyika. The Luo are also to be found scattered through Kenya in the larger towns (especially Nairobi, Nakuru, and Mombasa) in considerable numbers.

Number of Speakers: Kenya 725,585, Tanganyika c. 50,000.

Luo is a name applied to a great number of hardly distinguishable tribes speaking one language; in spite of the number of tribes, the language is remarkably uniform [Tucker and Bryan, 1956, p. 105].

Certainly such information could be more exact and certainly too it must be continually improved and brought up-to-date, but at the moment the crude guide seems exceedingly useful.

————◆◆◆◆————

In comparison with another language, each language possesses some *distinctive attributes* of its own which also must be known before an outsider can hope to communicate effectively or before an observer can evolve categories for a valid analysis. Reference is made to the fact that speakers of a language, if they are to be understood or frequently if they are merely to speak "correctly" from the viewpoint of the majority, have no choice except to use and to use properly the conventions within the language. In English, for example, the word describing the partaking of food by a human being or an animal is the same, *to eat;* but in German there is one verb for people, *essen,* and another for animals, *fressen.* Ordinarily an English speaker makes no distinction between the two actions, and a German speaker must. Without a knowledge of the verbal norms of a language, furthermore, the idiosyncrasies of a particular communicator may go unnoticed.

VII.A.2.a Each language has a more or less distinctive *vocabulary,* as illustrated above by the simple example from English and German. People are not likely to be aware of the distinctive words they use. Indeed those words are not set apart in dictionaries or lists. In English one *knows* a person and one also *knows* a fact, and most people do not notice that the knowledge is on two different levels until they learn another language (such as German, French, or Italian) in which such a distinction is made. The outsider or the analyst, therefore, cannot anticipate the precise nature and number of the twists within the language, but he can be sure that some, undoubtedly many, do exist.

VII.A.2.
a.i

A language, in the first place, has distinctive *meanings* attached to some words. Of course the word "meaning" raises perplexities in its own right, but here reference is made only to all the reactions provoked by a word. While it is perfectly true that the word for *cat* has as its referent the same animal in any language, it is probably not true that the connotations also attached to it are universally the same. What other languages besides English, for example, use the word as an adjective and refer to "catty women"?

———•———

In English a person's surname of course identifies the paternal family from which he comes, and his Christian name, besides almost always revealing his sex, distinguishes him from other members of that family. Sometimes more information may be conveyed; for example, the addition of "junior" indicates that the possessor has the same name as his father. Among the Ibo of Nigeria, a name has other meanings. At first a child is given two names, one by his father's line, the other by his mother's. The name finally selected usually comes from the more prominent side, but one set of progenitors may carry on a dispute with the other by using only the name of its own selection. Then, no matter which family originates it, the name conveys additional information: it may suggest circumstance relating to the child's birth or appearance; it may express a hope concerning his future; it may convey parental disappointment; it may reflect feelings of the mother; or it may even be a brief adage (Wieschhoff, 1941).

The operational meaning of a word or phrase presumably stems from values or beliefs within the society, although the connection may be impossible to determine. That German uses a different word to describe eating by people and by animals may suggest that Germans have a concern for the difference between people and animals, but is this really so? The concern may have once existed; the two different verbs, after being evolved, now persist within the language; and it would seem most probable that no difference between German and English speakers in this respect can be empirically ascertained. On the other hand, it looks as though some verbal differences can be traced to existing institutions with a high degree of confidence. Among the Tiv of Nigeria, the reply to the question, "Whose farm is this?" fluctuates from person to person. A man who himself does not cultivate that land names the lineage to which it belongs; a member of the lineage says, "It is ours"; and the head of the compound or the man or the woman actually cultivating the land all reply, "It is mine" (Bohannan, 1954, p. 31). The statements reflect the system of land rights in the society.

The modal meanings attached to words, and hence the responses likely to be evoked by them when they appear in communications, consequently, are to be found by ascertaining the significance attached to their referents within the society. Parts of the body, for example, are likely to be rich in associations, since they must play an important role in the life of everyone. To obtain adequate comprehension of the meanings of the words which represent them, therefore, an anatomical glossary ought to be at hand. Among the Bambara of the Mali Republic, four definitions suggest the prototype:

1. *Eye:* considered to be "a kind of mirror of the inner life"; hence "to have a sober eye" means to be sad; "to have a bright eye," to be cheerful; and "to have an eye that is old," to be beaten down.

2. *Head:* considered to be "the seat of decision, will, and pride"; hence "to have an ardent head" means to be active, or "to have a hard head" means to be tenacious.

3. *Heart:* considered to be the area where "all emotional life is concentrated"; hence "a good heart" means proper feelings, a bad man has "an evil heart."

4. *Liver:* considered, with the heart, to be the place where life is concentrated; hence to "take my heart and liver" means to destroy or annihilate me by removing these "two knots of life" (Monteil, 1924, p. 119).

In passing it must be emphasized that the meaning of nonverbal media can likewise be grasped by tracking down their referents within the society. Consider the following miscellany: a turban of glazed blue cloth; a sword; an alarm clock; two people cowering for half a minute or more; two people stretching out their fingers several times; bowing or kneeling low; the taking off of sandals; one man sitting slightly behind the other; squatting cross-legged; and pulling a sleeve or cloth over one's hands, while offering a gift. As discrete bits of behavior, they become intelligible when it is reported, first, that among the Nupe of Nigeria there is a "social gradation of remarkable thoroughness and indeed conspicuousness" and that the class barriers are communicated and enforced through etiquette and a system of symbols. The turban, the sword, and nowadays the alarm clock are worn or carried to signify high rank. When men of equal rank meet, they cower; if they know each other well, they stretch out their fingers several times. In the presence of superiors, men of lower rank bow or kneel low and remove their sandals; when sitting, they must be behind the others and, if the social distance between the two is great, they must sit cross-legged; when offering a gift, they must conceal their hands under a sleeve or a piece of cloth (Nadel, 1942, pp. 128–9). The content of the communications, indeed the fact that they are communications, thus becomes clear in the Nupe context.

————◆◆◆◆————

In most languages, specialized meanings are attached to certain words, and a somewhat unique vocabulary (which may or may not be accompanied by twists in the grammatical structure) is developed by particular groups; this is the attribute of language called *jargon*. As a form of purposive communication,
VII.A.2.   jargon usually conveys information concisely and
a.ii   accurately to members of the group; for example, physicians and lawyers in Western society have their own technical terms for communicating unequivocally among themselves. In addition the existence of a distinctive vocabulary helps to strengthen people's loyalty: it reminds them of the group's existence and values, and it may even change a verbal commu-

nication from an impersonal into a personal medium (III.A.5). As a form of consequential communication, jargon suggests to an outsider some of the practices and feelings of the group making use of it.

In Africa secret languages usually are institutionalized within a society and hence are employed by special groups, or in specific contexts. Among the Wolof of Senegal, each caste modifies the language of the society by adding words from some dialect or neighboring language (Leca, 1935, p. 23). Circumcised boys among the Mossi of the Voltaic and Mali Republics are said to learn a language that is unintelligible to the uninitiated (Delobsom, 1932, p. 267). The Rundi of Ruanda-Urundi have "special spiritual languages" for particular occasions; one is spoken, for example, during a ceremony by which admission to a cult is gained, another during "religious ecstasy" (Meyer, 1916, pp. 123–4). The people also consider it disrespectful to refer to the mundane activities of their king (eating, drinking, sleeping) with the usual words of their language; hence for him and for him alone they have a unique vocabulary to cover such referents (Pagès, 1933, p. 521).

Sometimes the reasons for the development of secret languages can be noted. Slang in Swahili—and slang of course is simply jargon that is popular in a particular group—is reported to arise in African towns and to reflect the interests of its inventors, young men, in money, food, drink, clothes, and women (Gower, 1958). Children at some of the courts of the more powerful Azande princes in the Congo and the Sudan learn to speak their language backwards with such speed that other people, except for pages raised at the court, cannot understand them. The boys, having few duties to perform, find it amusing to chat with one another in their own special language and also to "poke fun" at visiting commoners in their presence (Evans-Pritchard, 1954). At the other end of the social scale, illiterate shepherd boys among the Amhara of Ethiopia react to the secret phrases and riddles of literate contemporaries with a secret language of their own which they have devised "by interlacing letters between syllables and speaking rapidly" (Messing, 1957, pp. 446–7).

One language used by millions of Moslems in Africa is so secret that the speakers themselves do not know precisely what they ıre saying. The language is Arabic, in which the faithful offer prayers five times a day without understanding most of the words they have had to learn by rote. A Christian bishop, an African, reports that "there is no doubt that the foreignness of the language is a telling point for Islam in Nigeria at present" (Odutola, 1958, p. 66). In this instance, a foreign language is a medium not to convey meaning as such but to arouse the feelings and attitudes associated with its religion; it seems to be performing a function similar to that of specialized music.

VII.A.2. a.iii

Another important aspect of a language's vocabulary is *tabooed words*. Such words obviously are not completely taboo; unless they were used under some circumstances or by some people, they would drop out of the language. They are heavily sanctioned because they refer to behavior that is carefully regulated or considered thoroughly undesirable in the society. Often a word is taboo in some contexts but highly respectable in others. In the West, for example, the name of the Lord may not be used in vain, that is, in profane or secular situations, but it may certainly be uttered in prayer, during a church service, and as a forthright wish or blessing.

Among certain societies in the Congo, Nyasaland, and Northern Rhodesia (including the Aushi, Lala, Lamba, and Nsenga), each person has one or rarely two "spirit-names" and at least one "manhood" or "womanhood" name. Official registration is quite a problem. People prefer to be called by their manhood or womanhood names; but, aside from the fact that many have more than one name in that category, they may also change those names "for any or no reason, and according to who is addressing the owner."

In theory the spirit-name does not change and hence ought to be useful for purposes of identification. Such is not the case, however, for two reasons. First, there are so few names of this type that a dozen of them may be shared by the majority of the residents in an area. Then, truly to cap the climax of difficulties, there is a taboo against revealing the spirit-name, especially to strangers, and also against being called by it, because of the belief that "a witch may entrap a spirit more easily, if he knows its name" (Munday, 1948, pp. 29–41). Taboos regarding the use of names under specified circumstances seem fairly common in Africa. Among the Mende of Sierra Leone, for example, it is considered simply contrary to custom to address an ordinary man with his personal name, but it is "a serious offense" even to mention publicly the name of a chief, because "disrespect" is thus indicated as well as the suggestion that the speaker is "working some medicine" against the man (Little, 1951, p. 190).

The Mende also illustrate another point characteristic of most African cultures: in front of outsiders some topics are completely taboo, whereas others may be freely and eagerly discussed. At the taboo end of the continuum are the secret societies; at the other end are farms and techniques of farming. In between are genealogies, which are supposed to be mentioned only in "private conversation," and questions of land tenure, which are considered "delicate, but sufficiently topical and controversial to be introduced without fear of resentment" (ibid., p. 14).

VII.A.2.
a.iv
The vocabulary of a language, finally, may have certain *deficiencies:* there are no words for particular objects, actions, or ideas. Undoubtedly such deficiencies arise because the referents themselves are missing. Usually, however, circumlocution is possible when a translation is being made from another language: the missing word is replaced by a longer and perhaps awkward phrase. The question of psychological importance is whether people whose language is deficient in some respect are perforce correspondingly handicapped in some way that can affect their reactions to communications.

It is easy enough to understand that African languages lack the technical words employed by modern science and hence, until linguistic inventions occur or words are borrowed from a European language, speakers of those languages who would refer to scientific matters are handicapped by the deficiency. Less obvious is the fact that languages reflect people's mode of acquiring any kind of knowledge and hence may affect prevalent modes of communicating information about such knowledge. Each society, for example, has its own calendar and thus a method for charting the passing of time which its speakers simply must follow. Among the Nuer of the Sudan, people are said to be able always to indicate the season of a child's birth, but they cannot state the child's age with any precision. An outsider can estimate that age indirectly by the reply to specific questions: if he crawls, the child must be about one year old; if he has been weaned, about three; if he herds sheep, from eight to twelve. Instead of counting years, time may be linked to past events; something may have occurred either before or after "the boats of the air came" (Huffman, 1931, p. 84).

The fine nuances of a language are never more evident than when translations are attempted and do not quite succeed. "You can hear the creak of the European boots in every word uttered," one missionary comments upon most of the translations of the Bible into African languages which existed in his time. The early missionaries who did the work had not mastered the African language, nor did a revision of the translation by Africans necessarily eliminate the rough and awkward spots (D. Fraser, 1928, p. 94). How, for example, does one translate the phrase of the Old Testament, "a sure and steadfast anchor for the soul" for the Mossi of the Voltaic and Mali Republics who live near the Sahara Desert and hence know little of ships, and probably nothing of anchors? The literal translation as "a heavy, pronged piece of iron for the soul" would not convey the notion of spiritual safety or security. These people have, however, a device which in a sense serves the same function as an anchor: they tie their prized herds of horses and cattle to a "picketting peg" during the night; the animals are thus made safe and secure. The Biblical phrase in their language thus becomes "a strong and steadfast picketting peg for the soul" (Nida, 1952a, p. 46). Among the Bambara of the Mali Republic, the idea of redemption by Christ has been rendered as "Jesus Christ took our necks out." A man who had been captured during a slave raid in the past and who then had an iron collar around his neck could be rescued if a chief paid a fee and thus literally took his neck out of the iron collar (Nida, 1952b, pp. 8–9).

Other devices are employed to translate a word into a language that lacks the equivalent concept, in addition to that of finding, through one's own ingenuity or with the help of native speakers, a longer phrase or a different concept with similar connotations. The foreign word itself may be used, but of course at first it is both unpronounceable and unintelligible; it can be made at least pronounceable by literate speakers when it is spelled phonetically in the African language. A word may be invented which, according to speakers of the African language, may not seem completely foreign. In Northern Nigeria, equivalents are sometimes drawn from a third language (like Arabic for Hausa or like Hausa for Tiv) with which people already have some acquaintance. It is to be noted that for both historical and linguistic reasons Hausa has been able more readily to accept English words than other African languages in the same area (East, 1937, p. 100).

It is intriguing to note in the present connection that many Bantu languages from the standpoint of English and other European languages are deficient with respect to color terms. Colors that in English are given separate names—like black and blue— may be assigned the same name in an African language. It looks as though the African languages cut the color spectrum at different and fewer points. But do these linguistic deficiencies have any important effect upon the way Africans perceive the outside world and hence the contents of a communication?

First, it seems reasonably certain that color blindness is not the explanation for the absence of color terms in these languages. The language of the Ganda has such a characteristic deficiency, but an examination of 537 males from that Uganda society between the age of 7 and 32 reveals the incidence of red-green color blindness to be lower than the rate among Europeans; no instance of yellow-blue or complete color blindness could be discovered (Simon, 1951). Then, from a practical standpoint, again and again it is reported that Africans like colors; for example, as in the West, the publishers of printed media refer to "the great appeal color makes to the man in the street" (Shaw and Shaw, 1956, p. 27).

The present writer has conducted a series of surveys and experiments in an attempt to determine whether languages deficient in color terms affect the people who speak them. When African informants are asked to sort into piles having "something in common" sixteen pieces of cardboard which in fact differ with respect to color and other attributes such as size and shape; or when their responses to colored Rorschach plates are scored as color or noncolor responses, no significant or consistent differences appear between men from two societies having languages deficient in color terms (Ganda and Zulu) and those from a society having a language rich in color terms (Luo), nor also between Ganda and Zulu males with no knowledge of English and those with some knowledge. Zulu women having very little contact with Europeans, however, have a decided tendency to group colors together according to the common name assigned them in the Zulu language (Doob, 1960a, pp. 198–9).

Samples of Ewe children and adults whose native language is deficient in color terms have been asked to indicate the difference between pieces of cardboard that were shown to them in pairs. In fact, the members of each pair differed in size and color. Among the groups of children who knew English, half were addressed in English and half in their own language. Later the informants also named the colors of the cardboard. Again the results are not clearcut, largely it seems because the perception of color is a complicated process. No differences exist with respect to the perception of color in these situations, rather informants who knew English well could respond to colors more readily and more accurately. An illiterate old woman, for example, perceived the difference in the pairs of cardboard to be that of color, but each time she could not verbalize the difference. When shown a large yellow and a small blue piece, she said: "I see a difference between this, a red and a dark one." A large red and a small green piece: "A dark thing and a red one." And a large blue and a small black piece:

"I see the difference, this is dark; that too is dark, but it is like this; it puzzles me; I have lost the names of them." Subjects with a knowledge of English, even if addressed in Ewe, had a strong tendency to shift to English color terms; and indeed the English word "blue" has crept into the responses of people knowing no English (Doob, 1960b).

The investigator of color blindness among the Ganda has observed that "although the sky is blue, the African is more impressed by its brightness than its color and, unless particularly asked, will call it light or dark according to the time of the day" (Simon, 1951). After studying the reactions of audiences in four different and important societies of Nigeria to thirty-four different films, four of which were in color, an anthropologist concludes that "color seems to be of very little importance; many people failed to notice that some films were in color" and that color "did not in itself increase interest or enjoyment" (Morton-Williams, 1953, p. 45). The deficiencies of a language, in short, affect not only the phrasing of communications within that language but also to some degree the readiness of people to respond to the referents symbolized by them.

Readiness to respond, however, depends upon other factors than purely linguistic ones. The present writer, for example, has the impression that many Africans living under relatively traditional conditions are perhaps less accustomed to expressing themselves verbally than people in the West. Many of their day-by-day issues are settled not by discussion and argument but by customary action; hence their opportunities to practice verbal skills may be less numerous. Again and again, it appears, informants surprise themselves by discovering that they have an opinion, although perhaps the surprise is occasioned as much by the fact that they are stating their views in front of an outside investigator.

———◆◆◆———

Aside from a distinctive vocabulary, a language also has a distinctive *structure* that is relevant to communication. The rub comes not in discovering differences between the structures of languages—any schoolboy struggling with a new language can point out such

VII.A.2.b

differences by the score—but in knowing whether they are "relevant." Relevant means: do they make a difference in people's reactions? It is clear that word order is very important in English ("John killed Mary" vs. "Mary killed John"), but unimportant in Latin where declension rather than position determines the case of nouns. Is such a clear-cut difference reflected in people's mode of listening or their conceptualization of action? Or in English the meaning of a sentence rarely depends upon the last word or syllable, whereas quite often in German the meaning cannot be anticipated or, if anticipated, may be altered when the prefix detached from the verb finally puts in its appearance at the very end; again, however, does this signify that English sentences produce less tension or demand less attention than German sentences?

———•———

By exercising commendable restraint—at least for one paragraph—the present writer will use only a single illustration of linguistic structure in Africa and then suppress the other gems with which he is acquainted. In the language of the Ganda, there are two future and two imperfect tenses, each formed by distinctive infixes. One tense means the action will occur or has occurred within twenty-four hours, the other beyond twenty-four hours. To change from the present tense to the future or the imperfect tense, therefore, one of the infixes must be selected; if no infix is added, obviously the verb remains in the present tense. The speaker of the language is thus forced to make a temporal distinction that does not have to be made in English. This means that one cannot say "I shall go" in Luganda; the structure of the language requires the precision which is achieved in English not through the conjugation of the verb but by the addition of a word or phrase ("I shall go soon" or "I shall go the day after tomorrow"). Evidence, however, is needed to show that the Ganda are more conscious of the temporal distinction than speakers of English.

This section on language, however, must emphasize in yet another way and at some length the potential but tangled importance of language in affecting reactions to communication. Most educated Africans—certainly the elite who are now guiding the independent countries of the continent—are acquainted with and use at least two languages: their own and a European language. Does it matter whether they express themselves or are addressed in one language rather than another? The present writer has conducted a series of experiments in an attempt to find a preliminary answer to the question. The technique is fairly simple and straightforward. The subjects have all been secondary-school students acquainted with another language besides their own. They are given a written questionnaire consisting of twenty traditional or controversial statements, half in their native language and half in English; and they indicate whether they agree or disagree with, or have no opinion concerning each statement. After their papers have been collected and they have presumably assumed the session to be completed, suddenly and without previous warning they are asked to recall as many of the statements as they can. Half in each class must recall in their own language, half in English. Thus by means of a balanced design and samples selected at random, the effect of language upon the expression of attitude and upon the recall of material is noted. The procedure just outlined has been followed in schools among the Luo, the Ganda, and the Zulu; the experiment has also been repeated among Afrikaans-speaking European children whose acquired language is English and among Jamaican children where the comparison was made between standard English and the patois, with both versions of English communicated orally. In all instances, the accuracy of the careful translations has been checked by having a native speaker, other than the original translator, translate the translation back into English; discrepancies can thus be detected and eventually eliminated. Since the results have been reported elsewhere in detail (Doob, 1957a and 1958), a brief summary here will suffice.

The language in which a statement was originally presented to the pupils frequently but by no means always had a marked effect upon the expression of attitude. Among the three African groups and among the Afrikaners, there was a tendency for the native language to evoke more assent than English, but among the Jamaicans standard English rather than the patois (which probably more closely approximated their native language) had that effect. More Zulu children, for example, agreed with the following statement when it was presented to them in Zulu rather than in English: "A man with more than one wife can be a good Christian." Recall could likewise be affected; among the Zulu, where the effect was greatest, recall seems to have been best for statements both perceived and then recalled in English.

More recently the general design and procedure have once again been repeated, this time among Ewe secondary-school children in Ghana and Togo. Some variations were introduced: instead of one-sentence statements, there were three-sentence paragraphs; six rather than twenty topics were covered; half the paragraphs presented to each pupil began and ended with attribution to a source randomly called "good people," and the other three had the label "bad people" attached. Thus the statement concerning polygyny quoted above for the Zulu investigation now read as follows:

> *Many good people* think that a man can have more than one wife and yet be a good Christian. For to be a good Christian means that one is helpful to one's fellow men and worships God. The number of wives a man has he himself must decide. Do you agree with these *good people?* [italics represented by underscoring on the mimeographed questionnaire].

In Ghana the European language was English, in Togo French; 191 boys and girls were obtained in Ghana, 96 in Togo. One of the groups of Ghanaian children recalled, or tried to recall, the statements not immediately afterwards but one week later. The results are described here in some detail since they are being reported for the first time.

First, as Table 2 indicates, the language in which the statements were presented had no consistent effect upon the expression of attitude. Among the Ewe of Togo none of the differences are statistically significant. Among those in Ghana, however, two statistically reliable differences emerge (statements 4 and 5) and these lean in opposite directions: there was a higher percentage of agreement concerning the need to obey a chief "without argument" when the statement was in Ewe than in English, but the reverse occurred for a statement concerning the relation between

TABLE 2. *Percentage of Agreement*

| | LANGUAGE | | ATTRIBUTION | |
Statement	European	Ewe	good	bad
Ghana				
1	23	17	26 °	14
2	37	34	38	33
3	40	53	58 °	34
4	47 °	67	68 °	48
5	60 °	30	52 °	37
6	26	33	40 °	19
Togo				
1	50	47	63 °	38
2	52	46	60 °	38
3	35	36	41	36
4	56	55	71 °	41
5	69	60	75 °	50
6	27	40	40	28

° Differs significantly ($p < 05$) from figure to right.

"evil spirits" and "human sickness." The variable of greater significance was that of attribution (last two columns of Table 2); here, as might be anticipated, attributing a viewpoint to "good" people produced more agreement than attribution to "bad" ones for both groups. In this experiment, then, the effect of language upon the expression of attitude was not as strong as that of the source to which the statements were so arbitrarily and artificially attributed. In addition to conveying information, a statement evoked other responses among bilingual Africans, included among which *may* have been some kind of reaction to the language in which the statement is expressed. Perhaps that language served to remind them of one group to which they belonged rather than another or of the relation existing between groups. At any rate, this sort of response clearly was not always efficacious and it certainly interacted with feelings about the source of the communication.

Secondly, results concerning the recall of the statements are largely but not completely negative: rarely did the original language in which the statement had been presented, the language in which it was recalled, the relation between those two languages (they could be the same or different), the source to which the statements were attributed, or the initially expressed attitude have any significant effect upon recall. Typical are the figures for statement 1, the one on polygyny quoted above, that are shown in Table 3. But again even in this single instance one sig-

TABLE 3. *Percentage Recalling Statement 1*

| | GHANA | | TOGO |
	delay	immediate	immediate
LANGUAGE OF PRESENTATION			
European	85	64	80
Ewe	76	58	38
LANGUAGE OF RECALL			
European	84	62	60
Ewe	77	60	58
PRESENTATION AND RECALL LANGUAGES			
Same	83	60	65
Different	78	61	54
SOURCE			
Good	79	54	58
Bad	81	68	59

nificant difference appears for the Togo group: more statements could be recalled when the language of presentation had been French rather than Ewe. This particular finding may seem curious—Ewe of course was the native language of the children—until it is pointed out that under the French regime then in control of the educational facilities in Togo the language of the classroom was French.

To discover some of the complicating factors that together with language affect recall, additional information was gathered in these Ewe experiments. After they had recalled as many of the statements as they could, the children were asked to indicate the language in which they had seen the original statement and also whether it had been attributed to "good" or "bad" people. One way of analyzing the results is indicated in the four columns of Table 4 which contain figures representing the percentages of cor-

TABLE 4. *Percentage of Correct Recall*

Statement number:			(1) Statement	(2) Content [a]	(3) Language [a]	(4) Source [a]
1.	Ghana:	delay	61	75	35	58
		immediate	56	65	70	71
	Togo		36	69	46	55
2.	Ghana:	delay	62	96	45	29
		immediate	47	85	82	22
	Togo		36	67	40	26
3.	Ghana:	delay	21	81	44	38
		immediate	36	73	77	38
	Togo		21	80	33	16
4.	Ghana:	delay	33	95	45	52
		immediate	42	70	66	63
	Togo		24	77	43	19
5.	Ghana:	delay	10	67	— [b]	—
		immediate	31	72	62	34
	Togo		16	71	40	22
6.	Ghana:	delay	7	75	—	—
		immediate	36	68	70	44
	Togo		19	90	63	60

a. Based only on those recalling statement.
b. Number too few to compute.

rect recall. The base for column 1 is the total number in each group: of these, how many recalled the general scope of the paragraph correctly rather than incorrectly or not at all? The base for the remaining three columns is the number recalling the statement, whether or not the scope was correctly recalled: of these, how many recalled correctly details about the statement's content (column 2), the language in which the statement had been originally expressed (column 3), and its attributed source (column 4)? For the last two columns, chance alone could produce a correct reply 33 per cent of the time since there were three possibilities: one of two languages or sources and no recall. Judgments as to whether recall was "correct" or not were made independently by the present writer and an assistant, and then the few differences which appeared were peacefully reconciled.

In general, the table shows, if the scope of a statement could be remembered, other of its aspects were accurately recalled in the following order: content, language, and source. That the connection between source and content is quite quickly forgotten supports results obtained in the United States (XII.A.1.b), but here may be due to the nondescript character of the attribution. The finding that language is recalled less well than content confirms data obtained among the Zulu and the Jamaican samples: under the conditions created by these experiments, it is possible to recall information correctly without necessarily remembering the language in which the material was originally presented. Finally, in all four instances in which a meaningful comparison can be made between the one Ghanaian group recalling immediately after expressing their opinion and the other recalling after a delay of one week, the forgetting of the language occurred more rapidly than the forgetting of the source; for example, on the first statement, there was a drop of 35 per cent (from 70 to 35) for language but of only 13 per cent (from 71 to 58) for source. All these conclusions come from data in which the experimental variables (language of presentation, language of recall, and source) have been balanced. When the effects of these variables upon the last three columns of Table 4 are studied—the reader is spared the complications—it becomes evident, once more, that interactions occur in which language may play a role. Clearly, then, these experiments are inconclusive, except that they demonstrate the singularly fluctuating importance of language upon the expression of attitude and the recall of previously perceived material.

◄◄••►►

VII.B   *Content* After exploring the general properties of a language, the direct question may be asked: What does the communication at hand contain? Without doubt the concrete categories of analysis must be formulated on an ad hoc basis. A specific communication is likely to be singular, virtually any thought or feeling can be communicated, hence categories useful for a piece of poetry are not ordinarily very helpful in coding the contents of a laundry list.

On a more abstract level, however, there must be a system of categories applicable to all communications. The inspiration for such a set can be provided by many sources; here an unoriginal effort is made to distill the content of modern semantics and to emerge with a threefold classification:

(1) *Information:* verified or verifiable facts about any object, person, or event in the universe. An example: The moon revolves around the earth.

(2) *Values:* normative suggestions concerning the goodness or the desirability of judgments, standards, relations, information, or action. An example: The moon is more beautiful to behold than all the stars in heaven.

(3) *Action:* hortative suggestions concerning overt behavior to be initiated or completed. An example: Never plant when the moon is full.

Naturally beneath and around each of the categories lurk philosophical perplexities like demons that would devour their prey. When and how are facts "verified" or "verifiable"? What can possibly be meant by "goodness"? When is a suggestion "hortative" and when is it not "hortative"? These are proper questions, but they cannot be answered here. Each requires and indeed has received a treatise in its own right. Then the fine nuances simply cannot be taken into account if the content of communications is to be appraised, not for eternity but for theoretical or practical purposes. A very simple proposal is being defended: the content of a communication may be understood not only through a set of categories designed for the situation at hand, but also by referring it—or parts of it—to the trinity of information, values, and action. Admittedly it is not easy to decide whether a communication or one of its sentences is dedicated to presenting a fact or offering a normative or hortative suggestion; but taking up the challenge and trying to reach a decision, it is contended, provides significant insights.

There is by no means a one-to-one correspondence between this schema and the intended or unintended goals of the communicator (II.B). Much of the instrumental communication that occurs in connection with the attaining of primary goals may involve information ("The animal is over there"); yet certainly values are communicated ("Undercooked vegetables are better for you than overcooked") and action is urged ("Better use more fertilizer"). Likewise emotive communication usually stresses values ("She is beautiful, isn't she?") but can convey information ("She lives down yonder lane") or advocate action ("'Tis better to have loved and lost"). In addition, although the changes resulting from communication can also be conceptualized in identical terms (XI.A.1; XI.B), there may or may not be a direct relation between content and effects. Information to the effect that "the animal is over there" can alter not only cognition but also the evaluation of the site and immediate action.

What is the content of a story? The question can be answered in numerous ways. The plot may be briefly recapitulated. Mechanical details may be listed: the time covered by the tale, the number of characters, the emotions they portray, etc. But how can the decision be reached that the story contains values; and, if it does, what are those values? Previously one observer was quoted as saying that African folk tales provide a "release for pent-up emotions" and Akan tales were cited as illustrating the thesis (III.B.1.d.ii). How, then, does one gather evidence on the validity of this particular designation?

First, are the communicators, the tellers of the tales, expressing aggressive impulses? The observer really reports nothing about their motives except, as previously indicated, to say that someone with a grievance may relate or compose a story in front of the person whom he holds responsible. This criterion seems scarcely relevant: the stories are part of the tradition of the society; originally they may have expressed aggressive intentions, but now they may be repeated for some other reason.

When the reactions of the audience are examined, evidence appears in favor of the pent-up emotions theory. The stories are said to "call forth roars of laughter from all who witness them." Ordinarily, it may be presumed, the Akan peoples do not laugh at "an old woman dressed in rags and covered with sores" or at "a priest with an attendant carrying the shrine of his god," as they are reported to do when they hear the stories and when they see sections of them dramatically portrayed by actors. Even though the observer is giving only his general impression of these audiences and not a detailed or quantitative account, it seems possible tentatively to agree with him that the laughter indicates "a period of license" on such occasions. Here is one convincing bit of direct evidence:

> On one occasion—it was in connexion, I think, with a sketch depicting an old man covered with yaws—I asked some one seated beside me if people habitually laughed at persons inflicted by *Nyame* (the Sky-god) in this way, and I suggested it was unkind to ridicule such a subject. The person addressed replied that in everyday life no one might do so, however great the inclination to laugh might be. He went on to explain that it was so with many other things: the cheating and tricks of priests, the rascality of a chief—things about which every one knew, but concerning which one might not ordinarily speak in public. These occasions give every one an opportunity of talking about and laughing at such things; it was "good" for every one concerned, he said [Rattray, 1930, pp. x–xi].

Aside from the possible motives of the communicators and the reported reactions of the audience, what can be said about the content of the stories as such? The present writer, who is not a member of the Akan culture, bears witness to the fact that to him many of them sound aggressive. Three titles selected almost at random are: "How it came about that when Nwansana, the fly, settles on Kraman, the dog, he snaps at it, Kam! Kam!"; "How it came about that co-wives do not use the same hearth-stones"; "We do not leave an elephant behind to go and throw a stone at Aserewa, the wren" (ibid., pp. 165, 187, 269). There is a vast difference, however, between a story that "sounds aggressive" and one whose communicator would be aggressive or one which actually evokes aggression. It should be evident, therefore, that no certain verdict can be given concerning the categorization of these tales: the very best hypothesis, based upon available facts and intuition, supports the original interpretation that they communicate values and help displace aggression.

VII.C   *Style* The style of each communication, like its
          content, usually demands a set of specific categories
          to serve the purpose at hand. Once again, therefore,
          it is possible here only to propose very general ru-
VII.C.1   brics within which hopefully most styles fall. First,
          there are *figures of speech,* such as metaphors, similes,
proverbs, etc., the central characteristic of which is that they are
symbols further removed from the referents for which they stand
than the usual symbols of language.

Such figures, like any other aspect of language, must be referred
to a particular social context. Among the Ashanti of Ghana, for
example, there is the following proverb: "If you see one par-
rot, do not throw a stone at it, for there are many others." Undoubtedly, here is an observation whose significance is derived
from the fact that the Ashanti have a matrilineal structure and
that women confidently expect to be supported by their extended
family. Or the proverb, "If you wish to tell anything to the Supreme Being, tell it to the winds," must reflect the belief in the
omniscience of such a being (Rattray, 1923, pp. 79, 142). Likewise the metaphors in stories suggest the institutions of the society. Among the cattle-loving Nuer of the Sudan, for example,
one story relates that, when originally the beasts broke up their
community and went their own way, man slew the mother of
the Cow and the mother of the Buffalo. "Buffalo said she would
avenge her mother by attacking men in the bush, but Cow said
she would remain in the habitation of men and avenge her mother
by causing endless disputes about debts, bride-wealth, and adul-
tery, which would lead to fighting and deaths among the people"
(Evans-Pritchard, 1940, p. 49). The story thus describes, and offers a fanciful explanation for, the behavior of the Nuer with reference to cattle.

In fact, the analysis of the devices employed in the African literature raises problems very similar to those confronting literary
critics in the West. The following long sentence, though it is concerned with expressive devices among the Fulani of Nigeria which
such critics might disdainfully disregard, could well be used with

few changes in discussing, for example, the poetry, novels, and
dramas of modern European countries: "While Fula riddles and
proverbs, epigrams, tongue-twisters, and chain-rhymes are each
a distinct literary form, of varying merit, and there is no single
feature common to all, yet there are certain features common to
two or more—the comparison of like with like which underlies
proverbs, riddles, and epigrams, the word-play of tongue-twisters
and chain-rhymes, regularity of rhythm, grammatical anomaly,
and the various stylistic devices found in epigram and echoed elsewhere, even the frivolity of riddles, tongue-twisters, and chain-
rhymes, and the more serious nature of proverbs and epigrams."
The critic here feels, in brief, that he has discovered valid categories of analysis, for in the next sentence he makes the claim that
such common features "help to link together these varied types of
Fula oral literature as interconnected parts of a single literary tradition" (Arnott, 1957, p. 395).

Style includes a number of other devices which might be more
properly discussed in connection with the actual reactions of the
audience (VIII.C and D; X.A.2.e). They are listed here only to
be sure they are not overlooked when the categories for analyzing
a verbal communication are assembled:

> Forms of *allusion* to people, events, and the society
> VII.C.2–4   itself.
> *Temporal factors*, such as the position of particular
> themes within the communication, the use of repeti-
tion and redundancy, and the length of the communication.

Rhetoric, a most miscellaneous category that would include any
sort of device likely to lend emphasis to a communication.

The last category would provide for distinctive styles which,
though modal within the society, are not likely to be sufficiently
universal to be characteristic of all verbal communication. Two
examples must suffice. One of the impressive devices employed by
some African storytellers is the so-called descriptive radical or
ideophone. In the folk tale, the Tortoise manages to persuade his

friend the Vulture to carry him to the Vulture's high home but decides to talk to him en route; the Vulture is so startled that he lets go his hold, as a result of which the Tortoise falls *"pididi, pididi, pididi."* The sounds, according to the European observer, convey to Africans the notion of "down, unhastily, inevitably, inexorably down." They are accompanied, too, by changes in tone and appropriate gestures (E. W. Smith, 1946, pp. 149–50).

Another observer offers this description of a style prevalent among the Azande of the Congo and Sudan:

> The Azande are great chatterers, and can never state a fact succinctly. The narrator of any event will describe it at the greatest possible length, enlarging upon all details however remotely connected with it, whether relevant or not, and retailing the most unimportant conversations *in extenso*. His hearers will listen with avidity, and will show no signs of boredom at his repetitions or prolixity. He will talk in rather a loud voice, accompanying his words with unceasing pantomime, for he is quite unable to keep his hands still when speaking, and his gestures are often very expressive [Larken, 1927, p. 85].

Such singular explosiveness must somehow be captured by the analytic categories.

VIII.   MOOD

The audience so far has been considered only obliquely, because attention has been concentrated upon the communicator, the motives which inspire him, the media which he employs, the restrictions which he overcomes, and the communication which at length he finally delivers. Now the audience comes forward and hereafter occupies the central position in the analysis. The anthropological, sociological, economic, political, and even to a minor degree the historical boundaries have been boldly explored; psychology shyly approaches.

The people who are the audience bring to the communication a host of predispositions, some of which function as they arrive and others are evoked after perceiving that communication. Many but not all the predispositions are enduring tendencies of their personalities, and hence in the long run incline them to respond in a predictable manner. The concern of this chapter is with less enduring tendencies, with moods that come and go either regularly or irregularly. What are the principal factors likely to generate the moods that affect people's reaction to communications?

VIII.A

VIII.A.1

Time of Occurrence The time at which a communication reaches an audience can be viewed in terms of the conventional units of the clock and the calendar since those units are associated with forms of behavior. First there is the *hour* of the day. Ordinarily, for example, it is obvious that communication during sleeping hours is futile.

People may come to associate certain activities with particular hours of the day. Among the Fanti of Ghana, for example, communications portending bad luck are thought to occur more readily in the early hours than later on. A person who has not yet washed his face or is en route to the public latrine after arising brings misfortune to anyone he addresses. Loss of money in the morning is an omen that a worse evil has been in the offing, but later in the day it has no such significance and is just annoying per se (Lantis, 1940, p. 154). More usually, however, the significance attached to hours of the day depends upon people's normal routine. The kinds of communication cultivators can receive while working their fields must be very limited. The hours after dark when work is impossible are likely to be devoted to the communications involved in visiting and courting. In Africa, as elsewhere in the world, people gather in the lanes outside their homes after the evening meal and carry on informal conversations. The traditional stories among the Akan peoples of Ghana are "only permitted to be told after dark." If these tales really have the aggressive component previously attributed to them (VII.B), the time selected is propitious: people are available then, they are likely to be relaxed and in search of entertainment, and the darkness gives them protection as they are overcome by "roars of laughter." Only on one occasion is this temporal rule broken and in that situation other sanctions govern behavior: the stories may be related during the daytime at the funeral of a famous storyteller (Rattray, 1930, p. vi).

Changing the hour of communicating may affect the success of the communication. Only a few people in a small, isolated village in what was then French West Africa attended adult education classes; most of them had no wish to become literate, they could not spare the time from more pressing duties, and they were afraid they would be ridiculed for acting like children going to school. The response was much more favorable when the classes were held at night. Teaching materials could be projected upon a screen and thus an atmosphere of entertainment was created. Under cover of darkness people felt freer to attend and to participate (Terrisse, 1952).

The last anecdote suggests two important points about the hour of communicating. In the first place, the efficiency of the extending media may be affected. In the village the projector could not function well in broad daylight. Radio waves frequently travel farther and are received more clearly after sunset. Messages by "talking" drums are said to be transmitted best in the early morning or late evening: not only are there fewer noises in the village at that time but also air currents are rising (Carrington, 1949, p. 29).

Also, the reluctance of the villagers to spare time from work serves as a reminder of the fact that certain media of communication demand the full attention of people and cannot therefore be received unless the daily or the weekly routine makes provision for some degree of leisure. From the communicator's standpoint, if no favorable hours exist, they must somehow be created. Thus in the British Cameroons it was the Educational Department and not a department concerned with agriculture or health that once purchased corn mills to be distributed among African women who must grind corn for the evening meal after returning home from working in the fields during the daylight hours. The mills lightened their labor and hence, it was hoped, would increase the time that they could spend on "cultural activities" and the attending communications (Great Britain, 1958, p. 118).

The fact that an audience is available at a given time of day does not necessarily mean that communicators will seek to reach them. In Nigeria, for example, government offices begin work at 7 or 7:30, and then shut down at 9 or 9:30 for an hour before resuming again until closing time which is 2 or 2:30 P.M. During the late breakfast hour, consequently, a highly important audience, containing the very people likely to own a radio set or to subscribe to the radio-diffusion service, has the opportunity to hear local radio stations in their home. As of 1960, however, the stations in all three regions as well as the national one in Lagos ceased transmitting throughout that period: the staffs, too, breakfasted then.

———◆◆◆———

VIII.A.2   The next temporal unit having an effect upon mood is the *day* of the week. "Six days shalt thou labor, and do all thy work, but the seventh day is the sabbath of the Lord, thy God." Clearly when special significance is attached to a particular day of the week, people are in correspondingly different moods on that day and hence likely to receive and react favorably to some types of communication rather than others.

———•———

Only two points need be made for Africa in this connection. First, as in the West, many indigenous African societies establish mood-creating associations with specific days. Among the Tanala of the Malagasy Republic, for example, "lucky and unlucky days" are designated on a special calendar. During the second week of any month in the year, for example, the equivalent of Monday is considered to be "a good day for everything," whereas Tuesday is similarly "bad"; and Friday is a good day for funerals and for making tombs but not a good one for a wedding or a journey (Linton, 1933, p. 212). In many parts of Africa two different systems for regulating events by the day exist side-by-side. In West Africa people go to church every seven days, but some of their markets are on a three-, four-, or five-day cycle. Or in Ibadan, Nigeria, Christians attend church on Sundays, while the communal worship of pagan gods takes place at "most" temples every five days (G. Parrinder, 1953, p. 37).

———•———

VIII.A.3 After the day comes the week, the month, or—in broader terms —the *season*, with which are associated activities and ceremonials likely to have an influence upon people's moods. The most notable activities involve primary goals, since planting, harvesting, hunting, and fishing are determined in whole or in part by the season. Attached to, and also independent of such activities are holy days, holidays, festivals, special markets, political events, etc., which not only affect mood but which also bring people together to transmit and receive appropriate communications.

———•———

The fact that so much of Africa is located near the equator has some significance for communications from a strictly meteorological standpoint. For the hours of daylight are virtually the same throughout the year. The broadcaster who knows that people remain outdoors until sunset does not have to make seasonal adjustments in his schedule. The director of a mobile cinema van can begin projecting at an open site in a village at roughly the same hour all year round. The jolly cocktail party in East Africa can be very accurately and even formally called a "sundowner" at any season.

The year in most parts of Africa is divided at least into one dry and one rainy season. Even though the variability from year to year is great, there is usually a marked difference in the two seasons. The blowing of the harmattan from the Sahara makes people feel uncomfortable when, in some areas of West Africa, the air is filled with sand and the temperature falls. Among the Chaga of Tanganyika, "indoor conviviality" characterizes the rainy season. Stories are told then in the daytime when usually (except for beer parties and palavers) they are reserved for nights. "A bright fire is burning on the hearth" and visitors appear frequently, "bringing news and telling yarns" (Raum, 1940, p. 216). The differences in the seasons are so important that many African peoples, like the Ganda of Uganda (Roscoe, 1911, p. 44), count their years as roughly a six-month period, the time between one rainy season and the next.

Even within the same society details of the calendar may fluctuate, moreover, from region to region. The Nuer of the Sudan have two seasons, each of six months. Terminal months are allocated to different seasons in various parts of their territory because of minor climatic variations, because of "the marginal character of some months" that enables them to be included in either of two seasons, and because of the tendency of people to think of the division of time more in terms of social activities than physical conditions (Evans-Pritchard, 1939, p. 191). The functional character of a calendar is further shown by the fact that the peoples on Zanzibar and Pemba follow the Moslem system of reckoning for religious and most other purposes but not in sailing or in agriculture (J. Gray, 1955).

Hours, days, and seasons are relatively short periods of time and recur. The larger unit of the year may recur—in the United

States there is a presidential election every four years—but more useful for an analysis of behavior is the nonrecurrent fact of *age* based of course upon years. For age has an effect VIII.A.4 upon the person's status in society and hence upon the kinds of communications he is likely to transmit and receive. Admittedly the meaning of the word "mood" is now being stretched a bit—infancy or adolescence last too long literally to be grouped under such a category—but the phenomena associated with an age grade are transitory in two senses. First, the individual clearly goes from one period to the next. Then, for the society, the events of a year eventually end and hence represent a passing phase.

Some of the behavior associated with age is a function of physiological factors, such as the increased and then the decreased strength displayed during one's life or the glandular changes that come at adolescence. Equally important is the way in which age within a particular society is conceptualized. At what chronological points are people thought to pass from one age to the next? When is a child considered sufficiently old to assume adult responsibilities? Is the break between childhood and adolescence or between adolescence and adulthood accomplished sharply or gradually? As people grow old, does their prestige increase or decrease?

From the standpoint of both communication and change, it would be useful to know in detail how learning ability fluctuates with age. Differences in physiological receptivity and in alertness are so difficult to separate from motivational ones that a practical but not necessarily completely sound policy is to lay stress on the latter factors. This has been the approach of a UNESCO study which seeks to compare adults and children as students in formal school courses. First, adults are said to have one advantage: they are likely to be aware of the benefits to be derived from their studies, whereas children may not see a connection between their own interests and what they are learning. They suffer, however, from a number of disadvantages. Teaching must occur in the evening when they are fatigued. They are beset by the worries of everyday life and so are not as likely to become absorbed in their studies as children are. The fact that schooling for adults is completely voluntary may be good for their motivation, but bad for their attendance (UNESCO, 1958, pp. 5–6).

———•·•———

The age of a person is a datum of information that can be perceived directly but often somewhat crudely. People without a calendar or formal records can produce more accurate judgments and thus insure correct recognition of changing status through various mnemonic devices. Among the Ganda of Uganda, for example, the reigns of particular kings serve as easily remembered reference points, and also within a reign noteworthy events are singled out, such as a war or a plague. According to one competent observer, this system enables people to indicate "within a few weeks" the date of a person's birth or any other event (Roscoe, 1911, p. 37). The present writer, however, has the impression that the system orders events without quantifying the distance between them; three men can thus determine the order of their births but not necessarily whether the time separating the oldest from the middle one is greater or less than that separating the latter from the youngest. Among the Ibo of Nigeria, the age and to a certain extent the marital status of a female can be ascertained by looking at her clothing or the ornamentation she wears: "a slender cotton cord" around her waist means that she has had her first menstruation; the replacement of the cord by "a girdle of stronger material, the most common being a circle of coiled brass wire," that she is full-grown (about sixteen); and "a string of black round beads or flat discs of a particular pattern," that she is married. While her husband is alive, the beads are never removed except sometimes during purification ceremonies. Elaborate scarification indicates either approaching or actual marriage (Basden, 1938, pp. 205, 225).

Virtually any society provides evidence that communication patterns change with age. People, however, may focus not upon age as such but upon an event that is related to it either physiologically or culturally. As previously indicated (III.B.2.a.iv), the four front teeth of a Luo youth in Kenya are removed at puberty as a sign that he now has greater privileges within the society. A change in the avoidance pattern between him and his wife's mother is cued not to a physiological change within him but to an external event: after the birth of the first child, a ceremony is held and thereafter he is permitted to enter and to eat in her hut (Butt, 1952, p. 115).

Each generation in a society shares some experiences, if only those associated with having been children at the same time; as a result, bonds facilitating communication among them are established. In some societies, as among the Kikuyu of Kenya, this state of affairs may be institutionalized to a high degree. There a person's age is very important, for associated with each grade is a clearly specified series of rights and privileges which increase with age. Those circumcised during the same year constitute a meaningful group, and men "from all parts of the country," although their circumcision occurred "at places hundreds of miles apart," feel a sense of "fellowship and unity." They treat one another like "blood brothers," and they apply to themselves a distinctive name frequently derived from some important event at the time of their initiation (Kenyatta, 1938, pp. 2, 115–16, 134, 263).

For decades many young African males have been exposed to communications from the West because either temporarily or permanently they have left their rural homes for work in cities, in mines, or on European farms in order to earn enough money—in the European sense—to pay taxes, to buy Western articles like a metal roof or a bicycle, or to save enough money for a dowry. On the Firestone concessions in Liberia they usually remain two years before going back home; often they migrate periodically to achieve another financial objective (W. C. Taylor, 1956, p. 70). While the resulting turnover in the labor force decreases productivity, it increases the contacts which men at an impressionable age have if not always with other African societies (cf. I.A.1), then certainly with Europeans and their media. Radio-diffusion systems, motion picture theaters, and other appurtenances of the mass media are frequently located in labor compounds within or near cities and mines; government or private management sometimes organizes classes for instruction in hygiene, literacy, and other Western skills.

Both World Wars were also temporary emergencies producing

profound changes in the same youthful group which went off to fight in the battles of other men. In some instances they were taught to read and write because their officers believed that literacy would improve their efficiency as soldiers, and also because they themselves wished to communicate directly with their families as they were moved about Africa and, in World War II, Southeast Asia. The experience of seeing other peoples and of having more contact with Western devices and sometimes Western-type institutions provided many of them with an incentive to change.

VIII.B   *Unusual Conditions* Departures from normal existence result either from natural forces over which people have no control, or only partial control, or from social relationships which, being complex and hopelessly intertwined, cannot be easily regulated. Such unusual conditions, the proposition under discussion would state, affect people's moods and hence their communication systems. Previously the effect of *weather* on transportation related to communication and on communication media has been mentioned (VI.A.1.b); here reference is made to its direct influence on behavior. When the expected rains that "normally" end the dry season do not arrive, people are irritated by the high humidity and distressed to observe that their crops are parched or cannot grow. When a period is "unusually" damp, insects breed and make living uncomfortable.

VIII.B.1

The critical climatic factor for almost all African agriculture is rainfall. For by and large the continent does not suffer from the wide fluctuation in temperature characteristic of other areas and, with frost occurring only in the far south and at very high altitudes, plants can be grown throughout the year. "Viewed over the averages of a span of years, the rainfall regimes may appear regular enough," a geographer comments concerning Africa, "but few places enjoy an 'average' rainfall." "Instead," he notes, "there are violent fluctuations from year to year, serious differences in the dates when the rains come, violent spasmodic downpours rather than steady falls." Such irregularities from month to month and from year to year are especially characteristic of the very areas where rain is most precious, the widespread savanna regions which tend to have a low "average" rainfall. A locality with an average of 40 inches may have a fine harvest one year as a result of abundant moisture but suffer from famine the very next year when the rainfall drops to 20 inches (Stamp, 1953, pp. 62, 76).

Aside from affecting people's moods, it seems evident that the unusual conditions to which violent fluctuations in the weather give rise induce some forms of communication to begin functioning. The "big drum" found in every Thonga capital of Mozambique is struck only on important occasions, such as the approach of bush fires and floods (Junod, 1927, v. 1, p. 430). Religious observances during disasters are frequent. When plagued with droughts and epidemics, for example, the Bambara of the Mali Republic "promptly" offer sacrifices "to the manes and the gods of the place" (Monteil, 1924, p. 267). Unusual behavior, with correspondingly unusual communications, may also occur. Ordinarily the Tiv in Nigeria do not use a kinsman, a wife, or a ward as a form of currency. According to one informant, however, a famine was once so severe that "men sold their daughters to foreigners in exchange for food so that they could keep their sons alive" (Bohannan, 1955, p. 65).

VIII.B.2 *Food and drink* may create unusual conditions for receiving communications not only when they are in short supply but also when the supply is plentiful. The mood of a hungry person changes after eating an adequate meal. His mood changes, yes, but can one be more specific? At the extremes it seems reasonable to guess that he would be inattentive to a subtle communication if his hunger is so overpowering that he can only salivate or his satiation so complete that he must go to sleep, but the possible relations in between cannot be glibly formulated. Even the consumption of large quantities of alcohol produces marked variations from person to person, though the eventual soporific effect when it is ingested in big doses is predictable without exception. The partial or complete amnesia from which some drinkers suffer in the sober state suggests that some communication under conditions of intoxication has little or no lasting effect.

————•·•————

One learning problem in connection with food consumption can be succinctly illustrated. On the wall of the dining room in a mission school in West Africa were chalked "the reasons for a balanced diet and the cost in the local market of foods required" (J. Davis et al., 1945, p. 148). No doubt the children saw the information, and hence one of the problems in all communication, perception, was cleverly solved (IX.A.3.b). But did they learn what the communicator wished them to learn? If they disliked the mission food, it is quite possible that the gustatory prejudice may have unfavorably affected their reactions to the communication.

Figures on total food expenditures, though extremely difficult to collect in Africa and often of somewhat doubtful validity, suggest tempting speculation quite divorced from known facts. Thus the percentage of the expenditures allocated to meat is 17 in Accra and 32 in Kumasi (Johnston, 1961). If on the average people in one Ghanaian city spend almost twice as much for meat as in another, then surely their contacts at the markets where it is purchased must be different; and perhaps, too, they have differing interests or amounts of energy; or maybe they suffer from different kinds of diseases.

The drinking of alcoholic beverages on ceremonial and social occasions is probably as widespread in Africa as it is elsewhere in the world. One especially complete account demonstrates not only the rich association drinking has for people in the society but also suggests how many aspects of communication are influenced by the weak but steady supply of alcohol that enters the blood stream. Among the Bemba of Northern Rhodesia, beer is one of the "most important foodstuffs" and is also "the people's only kind of entertainment, the chief break in the monotony of their village life, . . . the common, and sometimes, the essential way of fulfilling social obligations, [and] the present of honor between kinsmen." The beverage accompanies all tribal councils, marriages, and initiation ceremonies. People from neighboring villages come together at huts of relatives in order to drink and "exchange gossip"; as many as possible crowd into one place; later singing and dancing are likely to occur. The brew is not strong, but is consumed in such large quantities that eventually people are affected. Samples tested at the start of an evening contained 4.4 per cent alcohol, but toward the end of the session the addition of hot water caused the percentage to sink by more than half. On a beer-drinking day, "very few" Bemba have anything else to eat. Chiefs, it is reported, "often subsist entirely" on beer "to the complete exclusion of solids." The Bemba themselves recognize that beer makes them "rejoice" and "warms" their hearts; it also induces a man to become "more talkative," to "quarrel," or to "indulge in illicit love-making." In the view of the anthropologist, people seem to be affected very quickly when they drink, except for chiefs who doubtless have developed a fine tolerance through practice (Richards, 1939, pp. 34, 76–9).

VIII.B.3 *Disease* is another source for change in mood. The ill person himself is affected; presumably he is less eager or able to attend to some communications, and is perhaps more attentive to others. Both the patient and people in his vicinity are likely to resort to two kinds of communications: through one they seek to explain why the disease has occurred, through the other they express or execute a theory of therapy. At this point another passing but respectful bow is made to the historical task of accounting for types of communication within a society: a connection tends to exist between the explanatory and therapeutic communications prevalent in many societies on the one hand and their socialization practices on the other hand (Whiting and Child, 1953).

It is almost impossible to exaggerate the problem of disease in Africa. Carriers like mosquitoes and tsetse flies; scourges like bilharzia and leprosy; gastrointestinal ailments like diarrhea and dysentery; or practices like vaccination or boiling water—these are topics of conversation not only among fearful Europeans but also among calmer Africans. Actual effects upon behavior, however, are not easy to specify, aside from the obvious fact that the patient is incapacitated and hence isolated from normal communication.

Kwashiorkor, which is widely prevalent in Africa, results from a protein deficiency in a diet containing enough calories for survival. When the deficiency is serious and a particular psychological syndrome clearly exists, both children and adults reveal "mental apathy" and "slowness and feebleness of movement." In particular, children lose "all the normal curiosity and desire for exploration that is natural to a child," and they seem to show "no interest in their surroundings" (Trowell et al., 1954, pp. 100–1, 256). It is not known whether a mild deficiency produces the same behavioral symptoms in a diminished form; but *if* it does, then conceivably people in an entire African society which taboos the eating of cattle or the drinking of milk and offers no protein substitute may be less keenly interested in the communications which reach them.

According to the society's own theory, a disease as such may be a consequential communication leading to action to prevent its recurrence. When a dozen children died during an epidemic of meningitis among the Fanti of Ghana in 1948, the catastrophe was attributed to sorcery exercised by two men and two young women who, consequently, had to throw themselves into the N'Tem River (Alexandre and Binet, 1958, p. 117). After contact with the West, an illness can sometimes produce a learning mood; according to the experience of a missionary to Nyasaland, "it is when things go wrong and people want to know how and why they have gone wrong that one first finds them interested to know how they work when normal and how they can prevent such trouble in the future" (A. Fraser, 1932, p. 50).

———◆◆◆———

The fourth unusual condition producing a change in mood involves the *relations* existing *within a group*. The relations between people may be temporarily satisfactory or unsatisfactory either because of their own actions toward one another or because of actions taken by an outgroup. The mood is joyful when a family is reunited after

VIII.B.4

someone's absence; it is sad when a member dies. A war, a contest, or a marriage with an outsider can also produce passing elation or depression.

———•———

Burial ceremonies have as their implicit goal the improving of a group's morale after the death of a member. Somehow in the face of the ultimate tragedy, communications must be transmitted that bring consolation and reduce the survivors' anxiety concerning their own mortality. Here if ever is a particularly important mood that affects, and is affected by, specially designed communications. Among the Nuer of the Sudan, the principal objective seems to be to convince people that they will not be disturbed by the deceased person's spirit or ghost, which is feared to such a degree that "death is a subject Nuer do not like to talk about." Only a man's age-set is permitted to dig his grave and attend his burial. Until the funeral has been completed, all young people, even those who were closest to him, must keep away from the homestead. The grave must be dug deep; if a hyena scratches a body from a shallow pit, the man's spirit will haunt those responsible. Almost always the earth on the grave is made level with the ground and there is no marker; hence no sign from the burial place can remind people of the deceased. Invocations during the funeral communicate the fact that the dead person is now gone by repeating the refrain, "Now you ghosts, you are finished with us, you are the people of God, you are the people of the other side." The ceremony ends when the participants carefully purify themselves and, to symbolize "the cutting off of the dead from the living," when they shave their heads. The latter rite, given the same name, also is performed during a wedding, when the hair of the bride is shaved to suggest "the cutting of the ties between her and her family and kin." These elaborate communications and rituals are considered to be so final and decisive that a man who returned to his village after having been thought dead and for whose soul a funeral had been held then had to be described as a living ghost; he could no longer be counted an active member of the society, and thereafter he could not participate in important ceremonies (Evans-Pritchard, 1949a; 1956, pp. 144–5). It looks as though the Nuer suppress their grief by having a counterirritant in the form of ghost-fear.

An outgroup probably affects people most dramatically in connection with war or the preparations for war. Prior to being subjugated by Europeans, for example, the Zulu in South Africa were extremely skillful fighters. Esprit was maintained by setting warriors apart as a special class from which regiments of 800 to 1,000 men were formed. Each regiment was made distinctive in a variety of ways, so that probably its members were frequently in a mood to respond to communications and other events only in accordance with their role in the group. The men in each unit were of the same age and had associated with one another since boyhood. They competed with other regiments not only with respect to military exploits but also in dancing at the royal kraal. They camped at a distance from other regiments. They had their distinctive songs, war cry, dress (especially headdress), and shields. In addition, within their own kraal they were served beer and also special kinds of food which were believed to strengthen them (Krige, 1936, pp. 262–6). Such an esprit, however, could not have been indefinitely sustained in spite of such ingenious devices if the Zulu had also not had enemies with whom they actually fought.

The Tallensi of Ghana likewise illustrate the ancient principle that hostility toward an outgroup promotes ingroup solidarity. The clans engage in feuds which are short and sharp and which are said to resolve tensions that build up from time to time. During the actual warfare "all personal interests" are subordinated to the clan, normal activity is suspended, and "clan patriotism" reaches "a pitch of fervor" evoked on no other occasion (Fortes, 1945, p. 242). In such a mood communications calling for self-sacrifice are more likely to be successful than during the drab periods of peace and interclan cooperation.

When relations are strained between groups but when one group fears the other, forms of communication may be evolved through which hostility can be expressed safely. The Yoruba of Nigeria were once reported to "delight in insulting Europeans without fear of reprisal by employing a complimentary form of address spoken in a tone which shows disrespect and contempt, but which the Europeans fail to recognize as insolence" (Bascom, 1942, p. 46). Communication regarding the outgroup among members of the ingroup may eventually become stereotyped if the relations between the group remain unchanged. The mood thus becomes semipermanent or even part of people's enduring predispositions. Toward some societies, the Mende of Sierra Leone feel contemptuous: one they think lives in "backward places" and has "degenerate" customs like filing their front teeth; another they regard as thieves and "flea-ridden"; another as "fools"; and another as "poverty-stricken and backward." Toward others they express admiration: one group they consider to be "aristocrats" and "clean"; another to be "aristocrats" and "dirty"; and Europeans to be people with prestige who "hardly ever break a promise" (Little, 1951, p. 73).

————◄••••►————

VIII.C	*Position* By position is meant the temporal relation between a communication or sections of a communication and succeeding events, including especially other communications or sections of the same

communication. For any message, any theme, is part of a long stream of communications; its effectiveness, therefore, depends to some extent upon the mood existing before and after its transmission. The first factor to be considered is that of

VIII.C.1	*prior communications.* In one sense predispositions result from communications in the past; thus people socialized in one way are set to react unfavorably to

communications containing contrary values. But in another sense the effect may be temporary, as when a person retains the advice that a speaker is biased only as long as he listens and then on another occasion forgets to be wary.

————•—•————

The Hottentots of South Africa have devised a series of actions which destroy the mood created by past communications and thus prepare the individual for new kinds. The procedure here seems to be to change his mental set by isolating him from the rest of society and then indoctrinating him with another point of view. "Transition rites" occur after an important experience, such as the birth of a child, marriage, remarriage, or the death of a relative. Not only is he then considered to be in a crisis and hence "exposed to danger on every side," but it is also thought that he is a peril to other people and "more especially to the animals and other living things on which the community depends." During the rites, therefore, he lives in seclusion and does not carry on his usual responsibilities. His contacts are limited to people who have passed through the stresses and strains of life, such as old men and women past childbearing age, or who have survived the crisis in which he now is. Next, part of the new group he would enter is literally injected into him; thus there may be an incision of his skin into which grease and dirt from the body of the initiating person is rubbed. The seclusion is finally ended when he renounces "all that represents his old life," has his body cleansed, eats an "expiatory" meal, purifies the hut in which he has been living, and puts on new clothes (Schapera, 1930, pp. 256–8).

The order of communications may be culturally established so that people know that a prior communication is likely to be followed by another communication whose content they can specify. Among the Nyakyusa of Tanganyika, for example, a quarrel between neighbors and its attending verbal assaults are expected to produce communications containing accusations of witchcraft. Under these circumstances, one family may be so certain that the accusations will be made and so convinced of the damage they may bring that they speedily move away in the interest of safety (M. Wilson, 1951, p. 153).

VIII.C.2 The *internal order* in which the various parts of a communication reach an audience undoubtedly affect people's reactions. If there are several themes within a communication, for example, which one will be more readily learned, the one coming first, last, or in the middle? Or, similarly, if there is a series of communications—conflicting or complementary—how will learning or recall be affected by the position in which they are presented? Considerable experimental work in the United States suggests that there are no simple answers to such questions since so many different factors may play a role. The side presented first by communicators with opposing messages may have the advantage of establishing a bias, but the one coming second may be remembered longer because it is the more recent of the two. The effectiveness of primacy is increased if members of the audience publicly commit themselves after hearing the first view. Indeed the whole problem of serial position has been found to be more important for people whose desire to comprehend is weak rather than strong (Hovland, 1957, pp. 130–8).

In one of the writer's exploratory studies in Africa—one concerned primarily with literacy in a community outside Zaria (VI.C.1.b)—an experimental variable was introduced which sought to determine whether a communication would be recalled more efficiently when its conclusion came at the end of a series of arguments rather than at the beginning. No significant difference emerged, largely, it was thought, because the experimental groups being compared were so small (total $n = 19$). It was decided, therefore, to repeat the experiment with larger groups of school children in two different communities of Northern Nigeria, Zaria and Kaduna.

The materials consisted of four items which pertained to telling lies, the need for forest reserves, the importance of luck and ability in producing success, and the prosperity of Nigeria in the future. Each item contained three sentences, two of which were alleged statements of fact and the third a conclusion. With very slight changes the sentence with the conclusion could be placed either at the start or the end of the item. In Form A the first and third items contained the conclusion at the start, and the second and fourth presented the conclusion at the end; in Form B the position of the conclusion in each of the items was reversed.

The experiment was conducted in four classes in different primary schools, two in Zaria ($n = 44$ and 38) and two in Kaduna ($n = 23$ and 37). The mean age of the children in each class was slightly over 11, but the range was from 7 or 8 to 14 or 15 (at least so they reported their ages). With the exception of four girls in each of the Kaduna classes, all were boys; over 75 per cent in each class were Fulani. The officials granting permission to conduct the research made every effort to find classes that were similar (both schools, for example, in each community were within the city limits), but they probably did not succeed since each section of a town in Northern Nigeria tends to be somewhat unique.

Except for a few introductory sentences by the investigator in English, which were immediately translated, all communication was in the Hausa language by an interpreter. The children were given pieces of paper with green and red numbers on them. Next to the green ones they wrote perfunctory information about their name, age, and society, so that they could become accustomed to replying to oral questions. Then they were told to listen to the statements that were read aloud and to write after the proper red number whether they agreed or did not agree with the viewpoint of each. After hearing the first communication, for example, they were instructed: "Do you agree or do you not agree? Write 'I agree' or 'I do not agree' after the red number one."

In the first class in Zaria, the interpreter committed an understandable error: in his zeal to be sure that the children had comprehended the first item, he repeated all three sentences; hence, for the sake of uniformity, the remaining three items in this class and all four in the other class in Zaria were presented twice. In Kaduna, the original plan was executed: the items were read only once.

Finally and unexpectedly the children were told, after their papers had been collected and after a very short pause, "to do one more thing. . . . Now try to remember as much as you can of the statements which I read to you a few minutes ago, the ones you said you agreed or did not agree with."

In passing it may be noted that the children, accustomed to obeying their Moslem teacher and elders in general, cooperated seriously and passively. In the Kaduna schools, for example, only two of them disagreed with a single statement. They wrote slowly and quietly.

The results have been analyzed in two different ways. With the first method, a comparison is made between the percentages of children remembering an item or its conclusion with that conclusion at the start or at the end. For the combination of the Zaria and Kaduna groups, only one difference is statistically significant: more children remembered the first of the four items when its conclusion came at the start (52 per cent) than when it came at the end (19 per cent). The difference for the second item is in the same direction, but is not quite significant. The position of the conclusion of an item had no effect on the recall of the remaining two items. When the Zaria and Kaduna groups are considered separately—since the procedure was slightly different for each—only one of the Kaduna differences is significant but three from Zaria are. Two of the latter differences come from the first item: 67 per cent of the children recalled it when its conclusion came at the start, 18 per cent when it came at the end; the corresponding figures for recalling the conclusion itself are 23 and 3 per cent. Then 67 per cent recalled the fourth item with its conclusion at the start, only 43 per cent with its conclusion at the end.

With the second method of analysis each child is placed in one of four categories: remembering more items with the conclusion at the start; the reverse; remembering an equal number of each kind; and remembering no items at all. For the four groups of children, the percentages are, respectively, 47, 12, 25, and 16. Thus more children tended to remember items with conclusions coming at the beginning. The first figure of 47 per cent would have been much higher were it not for an absolutely inexplicable and hence maddening reversal in one Zaria group, where only 9 per cent fell into the first category and 45 per cent into the category of equal number of recalls from each kind of item. For the other three groups, the percentages of those remembering more items with the conclusion first was high: 66, 65, and 62.

Under these very specialized conditions, no hard and fast principle emerges concerning the relative advantage of items whose conclusion appears at the start or the end. When the items were communicated twice as in Zaria, two with conclusions at the start had a decided advantage; but the result was not duplicated in the Kaduna study. With one exception, there was a marked tendency for the children as a whole to remember more items with conclusions at the start than items with conclusions at the end. It seems evident that no confidence in the obtained differences can be expressed, although the experiment serves one function: it warns that the position of the conclusion may possibly have an effect upon recall. It also demonstrates how a slight shift in a communication situation—the interpreter's error in repeating the items in Zaria—may have somewhat important consequences. Little wonder, therefore, that the singularity of each new situation must be respected and that generalizations from other societies must be cautiously applied to new situations.

VIII.C.3   The *recurrence* of the same or a similar theme which either occupies more than one position within the same communication or essentially an identical position in many communications over time serves a number of functions to be presently discussed (IX.A.2.b; IX.D.2.a; XI.C): the probability of perception, comprehension, and retention is thereby increased. Repetition and redundancy, however, also have certain disadvantages, included among which is the creation of an unfavorable mood through the boredom or indifference resulting from perceiving the theme again and again. In addition, a change in mood may call for repeating a theme which, though previously futile, then becomes effective.

Since the view is often held that mere repetition as such brings success inevitably, it is well to introduce the problem by firmly denying the contention. An African schoolteacher has declared:

> We people of Nigeria have not yet fully embraced the Communist doctrines. We are not sure just where they stand in regard to the Christian message, but if this Communist literature keeps flooding into the country we will have no other

alternative than to accept it—our minds will have been made up for us [Shaw and Shaw, 1956, p. 37].

The suggestion seems to be that the flood of communist communications virtually guarantees the eventual triumph of communism. But certainly the communist appeal must be perceived, must be comprehended, must be reacted to favorably before it can be influential; these processes depend on more than repetition, although repetition can be very helpful. The Nigerian just quoted, in brief, is assuming a host of circumstances that must be present before repetition alone is efficacious. Communists, however, are frequently shrewd communicators; when they repeat themselves, they do so not mechanically but to increase the probability of reaching and influencing their audiences. In this sense, the repetition of their communication in Africa may be considered a consequential communication: they at any rate must think their efforts are not being wasted.

The apparent fact that the mood must be "right" for repetition to be effective also indicates the more complete analysis required to assess the importance of that factor. In the field of health, for example, a lecture, a discussion, or a demonstration can be understood and can gain assent at the moment of perception, but people may forget the information when they really need it—when they are ill or some emergency arises. For this reason an experienced physician in Uganda is convinced that booklets are the best medium of health education: "Every booklet which is sold will be read and re-read many times" (Ladkin, 1956, p. 9). Of course literacy must be assumed.

VIII.D *Duration* Two temporal aspects of a communication can influence the mood of an audience. First there is (1) *actual length*. For an oral communication length means the passage of time between the beginning and end of the transmission as measured by a clock. For a visual communication, whether a leaflet or painting, some linear measure like number of pages or number of cubic inches can be employed. In both instances, the objective measures must be related to actual behavior if they are to be meaningful. Is the rate of transmitting the oral message adapted to people's ability to comprehend? How long in fact does it take people to read a page or understand a painting?

The other temporal aspect is (2) *attitude toward time.* As indicated, redundancy may increase the probability of comprehension, but it can also produce a mood of annoyance among those who are impatient or who like to hear the long and short of a message just once. Do people value time or are they indifferent?

The Director of Translation at the Nigerian Broadcasting Company in Lagos once mentioned informally to the writer that a five-minute newscast in English takes a little less time when translated into Hausa and a little longer when translated into Ibo and Yoruba. These differences he attributed to the structure of the languages; but should any additional significance be attached to them? Probably not, for it would be difficult to argue either that they reflect varying attitudes toward time or produce fluctuating tolerance of temporal intervals among the three societies. On other levels, however, people's attitude toward time may well be related to their way of life and affect their momentary appraisal of communications. Audiences in the West, it appears, prefer to have meetings and other scheduled events start punctually and, since they are allegedly in a hurry and time for them is supposed to be money, they demand communications that are relatively brief. In America, the tabloid newspaper, the digest magazine, and the quick news summary on the radio or television are thought of as symptoms of such an approach.

In contrast, the impression is gained that many, perhaps most Africans, even when they wear wrist watches and have alarm clocks in their homes, have a more lenient attitude toward time. They do not expect meetings to begin on time, and their expectations are usually fulfilled. They stand in queues for hours, and seem to voice no objection. These common views of course are hypotheses and may be just prejudices; at any rate, they require supporting evidence before being accepted. Years ago, for example, the senior master at Achimota College, in what was then the Gold Coast, stated that African children require specially written textbooks not only because they have a poorer background in the facts of world history but also for another reason:

> Neither the traditions themselves, nor the children that are to learn them, have any sense of time. The habit of counting years does not seem to exist. It is common to find that neither children nor adults have any idea of their own age [C. E. Ward, 1934, p. 191].

Such a statement, though reflecting experience that must be respected, exaggerates the situation to some extent: Africans, as indicated above (VII.A.2.a.iv; VIII.A.4), do seek to find ways to express age and to keep track of time in the absence of a calendar.

Indeed it may be a grave error to assume that Africans differ appreciably from Europeans with respect to their basic attitude toward time and especially toward the past. "From the beginning of my stay among the Ngoni," an anthropologist once reported from Nyasaland, "the chiefs and leading men impressed on me the importance of knowing about their past" (Read, 1936, p. 463). The point is important for two reasons. First, it suggests for this society the kind of allusion that a communication must contain if it is to fit not only people's moods but also their more enduring predispositions: the communicator, especially perhaps an outsider, must demonstrate to the audience his own awareness of their interest in what has occurred. With a knowledge of the past, any communicator can also make certain present points clear, for example, by means of a simile. "This man is as brave as old Mubakus"—the sentence communicates considerable information to people acquainted with the bravery of a legendary Mubakus. Then, secondly, the past is communicated to the present not automatically but through a series of culturally determined devices, such as songs and place names (ibid., pp. 465–6); historical knowledge must be constantly reinforced if it is not to be forgotten (XI.C).

Officials who have had experience with African audiences

generally emerge with some rule of thumb concerning the optimum length of a communication. Thus it was reported from what was then the Belgian Congo in the forties that "the best program for illiterate people should be made up of films with a simple script, the running time of which does not exceed thirty minutes." That there was nothing sacred about thirty minutes is shown by the next sentence: "Congo audiences are able to appreciate very well comedies of a longer duration than the usual short films, provided that the films are similar to those which appeal to the minds of juvenile audiences in Europe" (Film Centre, 1949, p. 95). Obviously, then, Africans like anyone else, whether "juvenile" or adult, are more tolerant toward a long program that interests or entertains them than they are toward one which bores them. When a mobile cinema van presents a single program of a series of films and a number of educational talks and when the program must be planned in advance, again some sort of rough guide may be needed. One officer suggests that "approximately 75 minutes" turns out to have been the best length in British areas of Africa, and he offers the following schedule of items in the indicated order: 4 minutes of music; 3 of an introductory talk; 8 of a film; 4 of a talk; 20 of a film; 5 of a talk by an influential local person; 15 of a film; 4 of a talk; 8 of a short entertainment film, and finally 1 of "God Save the Queen" (Sellers, 1955, p. 14). One must but note that 3 minutes are unaccounted for—and the good man is an optimist if he thinks that whatever piece of mechanical or electrical equipment breaks down during the performance, as some piece always does, can be repaired so rapidly.

◄•••►

VIII.E *Participation* A final category would call attention, in a very preliminary and inconclusive manner, to a set of factors which affect people's mood by inducing or compelling them somehow to participate, as it were, during the transmission of the communication. Two of these factors have been suggested by work on American audiences. When there are two sides to an argument, is an audience likely to be more successfully affected (a) when they hear only the side with which the communicator agrees or (b) when they hear that side and also a refutation of the other side with which he disagrees? Experiments among American troops suggest that for men poorly educated or poorly informed the one-sided presentation was more effective; but for the better informed, and especially for those appreciating the existence of counterarguments, the two-sided presentation was preferable (Hovland, Lumsdaine, and Sheffield, 1949, pp. 201–27). If the communication contains information that leads to a generalization or material which can produce a changed evaluation, is the audience influenced more when the conclusion is explicitly or implicitly drawn? Experiments here show that the explicit presentation is likely to be more effective but that other factors play a role, such as the prestige of the communicator, the theme of the communication, and the sophistication of the audience (Hovland, Janis, and Kelley, 1953, pp. 100–5). In both instances the participation of the audience apparently affects the outcome: people may or may not think of the opposing arguments that are unmentioned or they may consider the presentation fair which does mention both sides; and then they themselves are or are not called upon to see the point of what is being communicated to them. Likewise it has been suggested above (VIII.C.2) that public and hence active commitment to one point of view often prevents people from being affected by an opposing communication. And it may be that divergence from what is considered to be the conventional style (VII.C) either of a person or a medium causes members of the audience some perplexity, amusement, or distaste, and hence stimulates greater mental activity during the presentation.

———•———

Material on this category is hard to come by in the African literature since so far few efforts have been made to study the reaction of African audiences in sufficient detail or to carry on relevant experiments. On the one hand, the kind of protocol that is needed may be illustrated by quoting from a study already mentioned (VI.B.1.b); here is how a Yoruba (Nigeria) audience was observed reacting to the first part of a film on smallpox:

When the subject was announced, there was sudden hush, everyone's breath was caught. All watched intently. There were remarks like "He's getting ready" as Oke [a sanitary inspector] laid out his equipment on the table. Many who had never seen vaccination performed emitted sounds as "U-u-u!" [or] "A-a!," their attention wholly absorbed in Oke's work, as he vaccinated the child and the women. Some of the young men, among whom several had seen the film before, were more interested in admiring the young women. There were startled exclamations when Alabi [a character] refused to be vaccinated [Morton-Williams, 1953, p. 50].

Members of this audience, including the admiring young men, seem to have been participating vocally and actively; did this make the film more effective?

On the other hand, some observations are provocative but even more difficult to evaluate. When it is reported that "never or rarely does the Tussi say what he thinks; it has to be inferred" and that among these people in Ruanda-Urundi "lying is not only customary to strangers, but it is a deep-rooted vice practiced toward everyone" (Meyer, 1916, p. 15), the implication must be that normal communication in the society is quite a strain. People there always must be alert to try to discover the real meaning of the communication, if the report is really valid.

The hypothesis is suggested that euphemisms create a mood very quickly by demanding more than the usual effort by people who would comprehend their meaning. Among the Ashanti in Ghana a great man's name may "never be coupled" with the word for "death." The death of such a person, however, must certainly be announced or mentioned. And so circumlocutions like the following are used: "A mighty tree has been uprooted," "He is absent elsewhere," and "He has departed" (Rattray, 1927, p. 108). These expressions communicate the essential information but in a way that either obscures or almost contradicts reality. The reaction of the listener may not be quite so clear-cut as it would be to a blunt statement concerning the man's death, but eventually, by the activity of gently interpreting, the fact of the death is understood, and understood in the special way and with the respect that is intended. The Ashanti make an effort to have their leader's immortality extend not only into the future but also out of the past. When describing events in which his ancestors took part hundreds of years before his own birth, a chief speaks "in the first person as if he himself had been an actor in the drama" (Rattray, 1929, p. 221). Again some active participation is demanded of the audience before they can appreciate that he was not alive at the time, while simultaneously not altogether disbelieving the possibility.

IX. PERCEPTION

Now that the communication is actually approaching an audience in a particular mood, will people pay attention to it, will they perceive it, and will they understand it? A pragmatic way of classifying the factors affecting perception is to refer to those coming from the stimulus situation and those coming from the human perceiver. Actually there is almost always some kind of interaction between the two sets of factors. The object is seen because it is large, but it is seen only by a person not preoccupied with his own troubles. Similar interaction occurs in judging what is perceived. The diamond is considered large because in fact it is of a certain magnitude and because the person already has a certain concept of size in relation to precious stones; a watermelon of the same size he would call small. This distinction between stimulus situation and person is retained here: operationally it is possible to think of changing a communication to have more people perceive it, or of leaving the communication unaltered and finding another audience in a different mood. Information on a perceptual level, no matter how subjective, or rather for the very reason that it is subjective, inevitably increases understanding of communication. Size of audience, for example, is an objective fact that can affect the reaction of the audience (V.A); but the subjective estimate as to whether a group is considered large or small by its members is another fact to be taken into account.

IX.A *Devices of the Communicator* Often people pay attention to a communication involuntarily. They seek no information, they are satisfied with their values, and they are peacefully going about their own affairs. Then suddenly, unexpectedly, they perceive a communication which they have definitely not sought out. First this miracle, atrocious or not, can be wrought by a simple method, that of *compulsion*. Literally or figuratively the gong

IX.A.1   is sounded, and people assemble because they know that serious or trivial sanctions will be applied against them if they do not do so. Or else they are captured because the communication reaches them at a site which, for the moment, they simply cannot leave. An audience may thus be led to the meeting or sprayed with an unavoidable communication, but will they in fact perceive the message? In theory, although they can withdraw into a trance which the communication cannot penetrate, it is more likely that a certain amount of exposure under the postulated circumstances is unavoidable. Will the exposure necessarily then promote understanding and learning? The critical factor here may well be the audience's attitude toward the compulsion; thus the outlook for a permanent or drastic effect is not encouraging, from the communicator's standpoint, if people are enraged.

In Africa, as in the Western world, those concerned with the mass media are beginning to use captive audiences to solve the problem of perception. Reference will be subsequently made to the inclusion of educational talks and films in the midst of motion-picture programs which, having attracted audiences on the promise of entertainment, then take advantage of their presence for some other purpose (IX.A.3.b). A company in the Central African Federation has installed a tape recorder on one of its bus services so that its African patrons must hear continuous music on the trip. The initial reaction apparently was favorable, at least among nonpassengers: "When the bus left for Mtoko on its first trip with the recorder, an official of the company was prevented from getting near the bus by the large crowd of Africans dancing in the street" (Federation of Rhodesia and Nyasaland, 1959).

Traditionally, Africans have their own devices to compel people to perceive communications. Among the Hausa of Nigeria, for example, a type of roving singer finds a site from which the man whose praise he will sing and who is expected to provide a suitable reward is physically and socially helpless to withdraw. He may begin singing early in the morning before people have left their compounds or late at night when they have returned. He may function in a market since houses of traders and prominent people are close by and the site provides a good range for his voice. In the song he indicates to everyone within earshot just who it is that he is addressing by calling out the person's name. After chanting praise for a while, he begins his demand for gifts. The amount of the gift is publicly announced. If what he receives he considers adequate, he repeats briefly some of the praise and recommends the donor to Allah. But if he thinks it inadequate, he gradually changes the pattern of his singing to a staccato form which indicates his impatience and dissatisfaction. During this solo no one is supposed to make a conspicuous movement which would distract his attention and no one may silence him, although some forms of defamation or abuse are considered criminal offenses (M. G. Smith, 1957, p. 38). There thus seems to be no way for the victim to avoid the praise or, unless he can endure public shame, the presentation of the gift.

In fact, any kind of compulsory activity within a society is likely to affect communication patterns even when its goal as such has nothing whatsoever to do with communication. Among the Ganda of Uganda, for example, each district must contribute workmen to help in the construction of a new temple. The men work for two days, then rest two days, and usually the whole job takes from 14 to 16 months (Roscoe, 1911, p. 303). During such a long period the conscripts must have an opportunity to converse with one another which they would not otherwise have.

The device just discussed compels members of the audience to move their bodies to, or to keep them at, a site where they are exposed to the communication. The next method demands no such movement or restraint. Instead, people going about their normal affairs cannot avoid perceiving *penetrating* IX.A.2 *stimuli*. In this instance the weight to be attached to the factor of the stimulus in producing perception is overwhelmingly greater than that assigned to the perceivers. There are two principal ways of making

IX.A.2.a a stimulus so penetrating that some kind of perception is likely to occur: through intensity and redundancy. *Intense stimuli* can compete successfully with other stimuli confronting the potential audience. The sound is extremely loud. The sign is painted a brilliant hue different from its surroundings; or it is so big and at such a busy thoroughfare that it can be forever avoided only by a blind person. The large scar on a person's face is inevitably noted when people talk to him.

Among the Ashanti of Ghana, new legislation by the chief and his council of elders is communicated by town criers. A time at which an audience can reasonably be expected to hear the announcement is selected, viz., late in the evening after everyone has returned home from working in the forest or the fields. People there know when a public assembly occurs: their attention is "first arrested by the musical tinkle of [an] elongated bell-shaped gong" (Rattray, 1929, p. 315).

The decline in the importance of simple attention-getting media in African societies is often a symptom of profound social change. Like the Ashanti, the Yoruba of Nigeria also employ a town crier to proclaim new legislation by the king or an authorized chief. He is instructed to "go to every corner of the town, proclaiming and declaring the same in the hearing of the public" (Ajisake, 1924, p. 22). In more recent times, however, such communications are not heard by some members of the society who live in European-type towns and dwellings. Simultaneously traditional bonds between chiefs and followers are being broken by the disappearance of minor chiefs and of age-sets and by the weakening of lineage ties. Chiefs still meet as they formerly did, but there is only "token attendance" at the site where their decisions are communicated (Lloyd, 1953, p. 18).

Intensity may also alienate a communicator's potential audience. The publishers of a mission journal in Nigeria called *West African Christian* discovered that Moslems would not risk the reprisals they would receive from their contemporaries if they were seen reading "a paper whose cover page glaringly displayed the word 'Christian.'" The name, therefore, was changed to *African Challenge* (Shaw and Shaw, 1956, p. 26).

----••••----

IX.A.2.b   *Redundancy* produces an audience because when, either at a given moment or over a period of time, the same or a similar theme is presented frequently, it is likely to be perceived initially and repeatedly. A person may not notice the announcement on a sign as he passes by the first time, but later he pays attention to it when he happens to glance up or his mood changes. Or he receives the message when it is duplicated on another sign in a more favorable position.

----•-•----

Both to attract attention and also to serve another function mentioned below, that of increasing the probability of correct comprehension (IX.D.2.a), messages conveyed by "talking" drums are generally repeated. For people who are not listening must be made to listen, and ambiguity must be avoided. No message of course can be called typical, but here is one played on Ashanti drums in Ghana:

> Oh, Divine Drummer, I am scarcely awake and have risen up.
> I, the Ashanti porcupine chief's drummer,
> I am scarcely awake,
> I have made myself to rise up,
> I am about to sound the drum.
> If you have gone elsewhere and I call you,
> Come.
> The fowl has crowed in the morning,
> The fowl has awakened and crowed,
> Very early,
> They are addressing me and I shall understand.

The lines just quoted are the start of the message which is played every 43 days, while the chief is dressing, in order to announce the start of a religious ceremony (Rattray, 1923, p. 101). Two kinds of repetition thus seem to guarantee perception and comprehension: over the years the message as a whole is repeated and at a given moment the message as such repeats the central theme.

Songs, too, often repeat the same thought; the verse about a "splendid drummer" among the Hausa of Northern Nigeria begins as follows:

> The drum drums health,
> The drum drums wealth,
> He takes his wife six hundred thousand cowries.
> The drum drums health,
> The drum drums wealth,
> He takes his son six hundred thousand cowries.
> The drum drums health,
> The drum drums wealth . . .
> [M. F. Smith, 1954, pp. 57–8].

The listener who has not heard the references to drums, health, wealth, and cowries after these repetitions must be out of earshot.

———————

Another way to obtain an audience is through the use of what may be euphemistically called *seduction*. People are

IX.A.3 not interested in perceiving the communication as such but unavoidably perceive it because they are attracted to another stimulus which thus serves as seducing bait. If the experience proves to be rewarding, then in the future they probably seek out the communication which previously held no interest for them. Thus a guide for the teaching of illiterates in Togo, after recognizing the peculiar characteristics of adults as students, immediately emphasizes as its first general methodological principle, "to arrive at a tangible result in the very first lesson, thus awakening interest" (République du Togo, 1959, p. 5). Two initial modes of seduction are discernible when the device is viewed culturally, viz., the traditional and the novel. While following *traditional* or customary

IX.A.3.a practices, people unwittingly expose themselves to the communication. Upon returning from the fields, a man finds it rather impossible not to hear his wife's complaints during the evening meal.

The vast amount of communication that takes place during the socialization of people in any society cannot be used to illustrate a single perceptual device. For in the first place, children of course are a captive audience, the original captive audience, who must heed a set of communicators, parents and relatives. Then most children anywhere eventually want to grow up; for this reason they really would hear some of the communications (see IX.B, in just a moment). Finally they are trapped into becoming an audience by their primary drives: to eat, they must learn obedience and eventually the etiquette of eating. One observer, for example, indicates that the following "linguistic tools for directing childhood conduct" exist among the Chaga of Tanganyika: labeling all objects to be avoided with the same distinctive term; using a bull-roarer to imitate a lion or a snarl to imitate a tiger in order to make the child stop crying; telling stories with monsters to show the fate of children who disobey parents and, for older children, stories in which virtue triumphs; using proverbs, riddles, songs, and dances to summarize concisely the prescribed rules (Raum, 1940, pp. 212–23). The mere recital of the list is suggestive; for example, the bull-roarer and the snarl clearly are loud stimuli that attract a child's attention, and the stories teach him morality in an atmosphere of entertainment.

Indeed, when the methods of socialization of a society are considered in detail, it becomes clear that two series of communications are involved and interact: one seeks to communicate to the growing child the facts, values, and skills he must possess in order to be a functioning member of the society, and the other conveys to people and to the individual himself the progress he is making and, at a given point in his life span, the exact status which he has managed to achieve. Thus one observer has divided the "pre-European education for boys" among the Mbundu of Angola into two categories: rituals which make the boy a loyal member of his tribe and guild, and occupational experience which enables him to acquire the necessary skills and traditions. Rituals include: baptism, which first consists of having the village chief squirt sweet beer on the child's head and which later at puberty may take the form of filing his two upper middle teeth in a form resembling an inverted V; the bestowal by the mother of a secret name, which is later communicated to him as an inviolable secret; at the age of seven, admission into the men's palaver-house group, where he can observe directly correct speech and etiquette and where he can hear the older men discussing and recounting significant events in the history of the society; and, after acquiring such skills, further initiation marked by circumcision, physical endurance tests, and—under certain circumstances—admission into a status-giving guild. Vocational training is obtained in the following ways: the boy accompanies his elders on long caravan journeys which last from six months to two years, during which time he is assigned certain realistic responsibilities and expected to make observations of the flora, fauna, people, and natural phenomena en route; he learns bush lore from a particular guide; he acquires a specific craft as well as good manners; and he is specially tutored by a maternal uncle. Each step, it should be evident, requires that the initiate be induced to perceive and learn new forms of communication. Thus members are notified that a secret society is to hold a meeting by being sent a visual communication —holes pricked on a large leaf—which can be interpreted only by those belonging to the group (J. T. Tucker, 1954).

IX.A.3.b   People's attention may be gained by a *novel* event that is not customary or structured within the society. A stranger arrives; people wonder who he is, why he has come; then, as they cluster around him, he delivers a message.

Communications about events which, though unusual, can be anticipated within a society are likely to use unusual media to attract attention. A special signal—a wail or a particular drum beat—is transmitted and is perceived because its meaning is known, because it occurs infrequently, and also because it reaches people. Among the Mossi of the Mali and Voltaic Republics, for example, the death of a canton chief who owns horses is announced by sending one of the animals to the paramount chief. To make the

message unmistakable, branches from a particular tree are wound
with white rope and tied to its tail (Delobsom, 1932, p. 63).

Whenever an examination is made of the communications that
outsiders transmit to Africans, it is difficult to avoid finding an illustration of how a communication is perceived by being added
as a novel element to a situation in which the evoked drive is
serving a different purpose. The most innocent glance at textbooks used in African schools reveals that irrelevant judgments
are displayed, perhaps unwittingly and certainly not devilishly,
by European authors who thus indoctrinate after evoking students'
interest in education. In a reader for the first form, for example,
lesson 2 is as follows:

> This is the house of Henry and Kate. They live in this house
> with their father and mother. In the house there are a bed,
> a table and a chair, and a mat. Mary sits on the stool. James
> sits on the chair. Henry and Kate sit on the mat [Travis,
> 1957, p. 9].

Here is clearly a monogamous family with Christian names. The
bed, the table, and the chair in the accompanying drawing follow
European patterns; the mat, the stool, and probably the clothes
on the four people are African; the house itself must be considered
a compromise between a European and African structure. Likewise a book of drawings accompanying a text for teaching English in Nigeria is permeated by sketches of European scenes and
artifacts (French, 1955). While African children learn English
in the school, consequently, they must inevitably perceive material favoring European institutions and practices.

Another outside group, missionaries, often also succeed by utilizing drives directed toward a goal different from that of the
communication at hand. It is the impression of this writer that
those missionaries in Africa who insist that the church must not
be inflexible but must adapt itself to African conditions, whether
or not they utilize the mass media (II.B), advocate such a technique to obtain people's attention. One of them writes:

> In many instances an audience gathers on Sunday [to attend
> church services] in numbers that cannot be reached during

the week, and during times of epidemics and local out-breaks of disease, simple explanations of the methods of infection and preventive measures that might be taken are surely not out of place among the disciples of a Master whose teaching was so often interrupted by the arrival of some needy sufferer.

The same missionary also reports that other "opportunities" may be seized to deliver communications concerning health which the audience has not assembled to perceive: the real causes of disease can be discussed with patients seated in the waiting room of a clinic; explanations of sepsis can be given to the spectators who are watching the delivery of a child "in a native hut" (A. Fraser, 1932, pp. 28, 29, 32).

"We had not come to Africa," two journalists who founded a Christian newspaper there wrote subsequently, "just to express the Christian viewpoint, just to hurl religious phraseology through printed words at the man in the street." Such an approach they seem to have rejected not because of a Respectful Attitude toward African sensibilities or even an Attitude of Respect-with-Reservation (I.B.3), but for pragmatic reasons derived from their Useful Understanding: hurling phrases could not attract an audience. What they did, therefore, was to offer nonreligious features, such as a monthly summary of world news, which they knew their readers did not receive through other sources. In addition they sought to make the religious theme attractive by printing the following: serials and short stories in which Christian truth was applied to practical life; photographic stories; special sections for women, children, ministers, and students; a personal testimony section ("Horrors of Polygamy Exposed: Never Would I Raise My Child in a Polygamous House"); and contemporary features like "The Christian and Communism" (Shaw and Shaw, 1956, pp. 35–8, 49). Besides inducing people to buy and read the paper initially, such devices may also have encouraged the growth of favorable feelings toward the medium as such (X.A.2.c) and hence have led to repeated patronage (XI.C). Gently, not necessarily skeptically, the question must be raised again (II.B): Does such a Policy of Flexibility, inspired as it is by the mass media of the West, make good Christians out of Africans?

Perception via seduction likewise is used to achieve other goals of missions. Like colonial officials and the leaders of newly independent countries in Africa, some missionaries postulate a fundamental incompatibility between many African and Western institutions and hence they try to combat "tribalism." One mission school in the former Belgian Congo forced its students, as it were, to recognize the virtues of other clans by assigning members of diverse origins to the same dormitory and then by promoting competitiveness between the dormitories. "At the end of each week the dormitory which has excelled that week proudly raises its flag beneath the Belgian flag as a symbol of the joint endeavor of the group." It was hoped that through such devices "lasting friendships" could be formed between students from different clans; and some success toward that end was claimed (Nida, 1952b, p. 33).

One other outside group may be briefly considered: information officials in Africa. Whenever they discuss their craft, the present writer feels, they eventually raise a fascinating problem: Can an audience be attracted without the lure of entertainment? With relation to motion pictures, for example, some believe in "the concealing of the lesson within a story," whereas others assert that "the sugaring of the pill is unnecessary and that the appeal of the cinema itself is sufficient to ensure the interest of the audience in the subject matter" (UNESCO, 1952, p. 11). When attention is paid to mobile cinema vans in bush areas, however, there seems to be agreement that audiences, attending a performance for the first time or very infrequently, need no other attraction than the films themselves; thus at the outset the problem of perception is easily solved. But thereafter, the question goes, how much entertainment must be mixed with education in order to be sure that members of the audience will reappear in the future? A report from the Congo, previously cited (I.C.1; VIII.D), suggests that "the program should finish for preference with a cartoon of a character affording mental relaxation," and elsewhere also states that "the program which captured the permanent attention of the largest number of spectators" consisted of a news

film, an animated cartoon, a short comedy, and a film dealing with
African life (Film Centre, 1949, p. 95). An official from the same
area states that African soldiers during World War II were pleased
by anything during their first contacts with motion pictures; but
after the novelty wore off, they began to lose interest, at least
in films which they could not understand (Bever, 1952, pp. 59–
60).

No one denies, consequently, that films deliberately designed
or selected for their entertainment value can gain the attention
of the audience. The question is whether people who are being
entertained are in the right mood to comprehend, learn, and retain the information the communicator would transmit to them.
To lower the appalling accident rate in one African country, another official told the present writer, a safety film from the West
was widely exhibited; but the audience, he claimed, paid much
more attention to the four-lane highways, the skyscrapers, and
the volume of the traffic than they did to the rules being explained. The animated cartoon at the end of an educational performance appeals to people, causes them to relax, but may also
make them forget the lesson in public health contained in the previous reel. "How many times," the same film officer has angrily
stated in print, "have I seen the whole effects of teaching disappear in the gusts of laughter greeting Charlie Chaplin" (Spurr,
1952, p. 38). There is no end to the controversy in sight, and unfortunately there are no sound principles sufficiently specific to
suggest the best procedure for each situation, which, as ever,
must be considered more or less singular.

IX.B   *Drives of the Audience* Perception dependent
upon the devices of the communicator results from
the nature of the communication or from the interest
of the audience in some other activity. People, however, are not always passive perceivers or the victims—or bene-
ficiaries—of seduction. They seek out situations which they would
perceive and experience. The problem here is one of motivation:
what sorts of drives directly induce audiences to perceive communications?

First there are the *routine drives* involved in normal primary and social goals. People actively desire
IX.B.1   instrumental communications to attain primary goals
and they engage in purposive communications to
reach social ones (II.A). The drives themselves may be evoked
by situations (or their symbolic substitutes) in which satisfaction has been previously attained; hence familiar materials ordinarily are likely to elicit warm responses and to lead to perception.

In any area, it seems, an effort is made to arouse the interest
of Africans by presenting them with materials that are distinctly
African rather than European. The latter may be rejected not
necessarily because they are incomprehensible but because they
are simply not appealing. Thus a publisher of school texts, Longmans, Green and Company, issues general books on arithmetic
but also has special ones for particular regions; even *Central African Arithmetic* has a Swaziland edition and a Basutoland edition. The book for the Western Region of Nigeria, according to
a 1959 catalogue, is "full of bright illustrations in color, but the
use of color throughout the text and pictures has been planned
strictly as an aid to teaching." Such books of course must be approved by local authorities and hence must cover slightly different arithmetical material, but evidently they also evoke interest by keeping the appeal as specific as possible. As suggested
later (X.A.2.e), however, some African adults are offended by
communications deliberately designed for them, for these they
interpret as a slur on their ability to comprehend the European
version.

The next category of drives includes primary and sometimes
social ones that are actually or potentially *unreduced*.
A person who is dissatisfied seeks some way to ease
IX.B.2   his tension and hence may be ready and eager to perceive communications that appear as though they
might assist him in doing so. After the machine breaks down,

the owner reads a book of instructions concerning repairs or consults an expert. From a reverse standpoint, sometimes communications are avoided when the individual thinks that perceiving them may lead to frustration, dissonance, or simple unpleasantness. Research in the West has substantiated the common-sense finding that people incline to expose themselves only to a congenial point of view and that therefore the members of an audience are often composed largely of the converted, who may be of less immediate interest to the proselyting communicator than are the unconverted (e.g., Festinger, 1957, pp. 48–52, 138–49).

The welfare of any society is associated with ceremonies and customs that are repeated over and over again and that therefore appear efficacious. People appreciate and utilize the solutions at hand to meet many of their difficulties; they do in fact consult the mechanic or the physician when they are in trouble. The satisfaction brought by a religious ceremony or by conformity to a moral code cannot be weighed objectively, in the manner of assessing the mechanic's skill when the machine runs again or the doctor's pill when the pain ceases. In part such conformity is promoted by communications which clearly indicate the social or legal penalties attached to nonconformity. Among the Hausa of Nigeria, for example, special "songs of ridicule" are usually leveled at people committing sexual offenses, the principal ones being premarital pregnancy, incest, and the inability to perform sexual intercourse (M. G. Smith, 1954, p. 275). A "very beautiful" girl once suffered from what was apparently a vaginal obstruction. Her disability became known and, although she herself was undoubtedly not responsible, sanctions were applied against her. According to a sympathetic Hausa informant, children would continually tease her with a song containing these words:

> She's blocked up, she's only looked at,
> Without a door, without a path.

"It was a pitiful thing," the woman continued, but "they kept on and on; we told them, 'For shame, to behave so unkindly to her!' . . . She used to come to our house to grind grain for us,

the children were plaguing her" (M. F. Smith, 1954, pp. 147–8).
Presumably the children thus disposed of pent-up energy and
also demonstrated their attachment to elders who must have encouraged them in the first place to sing the cruel songs; and the
parents reduced somewhat the anxiety which they felt consciously
concerning departures from the norm and less consciously concerning the possibility that they themselves might have had such
a defect. Nothing further is reported about the poor girl, whose
subsequent mood could have led her to feel submissive toward
any communication likely to appear to help her.

IX.B.3

Finally there are what may be called *drives* to perceive *communications:* under some circumstances
people seek to be informed because the information
as such brings satisfaction. The satisfaction is intrinsic, for the information does not necessarily lead to the attainment of some other goal. As ever, no sharp categorization of drives
can be made. Thus the person who must hear the latest newscast,
read the latest edition of the newspaper, or question the most recently arrived stranger in the community may think consciously
that he wants only to be informed; in fact, though, he may be
seeking unconsciously to attract the attention of his contemporaries by passing on to them the information that he reaches out
to perceive. Such a drive plays a different role and its scope varies
from person to person. For some the seeking of information occurs only rarely, and then in connection with particular topics
or areas, whereas for others the seeking and obtaining of information is a central preoccupation. Perhaps a distinction between
(a) a *casual* and (b) a *central* communication drive may prove
useful.

In many, perhaps most societies at least a casual communication drive functions in some contexts. When people meet, for example, a perfunctory inquiry concerning each other's health occurs and often the general question is also asked, "What's new?"
The give and take may be quite conventionalized—often, one is

not supposed to report bad health—but the established norm may demand the transmission of really new information. Among the Mende of Sierra Leone travelers pausing on a road to talk are not supposed to part until they have listened to each other's news. When a visit has been previously arranged, people do not settle down to discuss the real problem at hand until they have communicated "all that has happened since their last meeting (Little, 1951, p. 131). Such a quest for information must be quite central.

A somewhat exotic illustration of a communication drive is offered by the Tumba in the Congo. Upon the death of a chief, the eldest member of the community becomes the successor if the newly selected chief dies before he has been installed or if for some reason that man decides to withdraw from the position offered him. This "normal" procedure, however, may be altered. If another man dreams that he himself should be the chief, he thereby immediately acquires the right of succession. Would a man fabricate a dream to obtain the post? The Tumba themselves say that no one would dare lie: "any man so doing would be sure to die, and the fear of death would deter him from such baseness" (H. D. Brown, 1944, pp. 432–3). Thus the man's conscious drive to express and communicate an ambition is skillfully regulated, but his unconscious impulses in the same direction are presumably left unchecked.

"Primitive man lives in a smaller world than ours" (Goodwin, 1937, p. 230) is fairly typical of assertions that are made concerning the scope of the information that Africans traditionally are supposed to seek. It may very well be that, when life centers so solidly around the local community and contacts with the outside are few, people are less interested in what they cannot perceive directly. One interesting theory (Wilson and Wilson, 1945, pp. 28, 40) is herewith reinterpreted to mean that the amount of communication by people everywhere is roughly the same, only the depth and scope vary. Originally Africans communicated a great deal about a limited number of topics; now, as they widen their contacts, they communicate much less about a larger number. Certainly one finds, as will be indicated subsequently, that samples of Africans have little interest in, or knowledge of, events somewhat distant from them (X.A.2.c); but it is also necessary to inquire whether people in the West, for all their verbal agility, have more than surface information about what are called the great issues of the day.

———————◀••••▶———————

IX.C   *The Audience* At the moment of perception the communication is affecting people and hence it becomes possible and necessary to indicate who in fact that audience is. Frequently more than one group simultaneously observes the same communication: different strata of a society are among those watching a ritualistic ceremony or hearing a radio program. A minimum of two observations can be made concerning the real audience or audiences. Their (1) *status* within the society may be indicated, and under this category any attribute can be included which is important within the society and which also characterizes the group. Secondly, note can be taken as to whether or not the audience actually reached is the one intentionally sought by the communicator in the first place; this factor can be referred to as (2) *realization* or nonrealization of an audience.

———————◀•▶———————

In many situations the observed status of the audience gives an important clue concerning the probability that the communicator will in fact achieve his goal. Special efforts should be made to improve the formal education of African girls, according to one observer, because both "educationalists" and "anthropological research" indicate that "in African society it is the woman who holds the key to future progress rather than the man" (Evans, 1952, p. 583). A communicator with such an objective in mind must note the number of women in his audience or the number of girls at school; he must reach this particular group to be successful. At the same time, though an audience like women may be important, their status in the society cannot be neglected. A home economist functioning as a missionary in Angola observes that decades of teaching in schools and of visits to villages did not produce improvement in food and living habits, especially in comparison with changes in dress and general education. "We began to see," she reports, "that we were not gaining ground because we were too often reaching only one member of the family." The correct audience had received the communication, but the relation of women to their husbands in a male-dominated society had been neglected. "We may have persuaded the wife, for example, as to the value of having beds for the children but, if the husband wasn't present for the same lessons, she couldn't carry out the plan because he did not see any sense in it" (Dille, 1957, p. 84).

As a result of their status within the society, some groups are more likely to be the audience for a given set of communications than others. Among the Nupe in Nigeria, for example, there is "a separate leisure class" of people whose occupations as traders, teachers, landowners, and public officials require them to work only half as long as the majority of the population. They devote some of this extra time to "recreation and aesthetic pleasures," including various forms of social communication (Nadel, 1942, p. 360). For this and other reasons, therefore, communications from the outside may reach them rather than their otherwise burdened contemporaries.

————◆◆◆————

IX.D *Comprehension* After their attention has been gained, how does the audience comprehend the communication? What is the relation between the communicator's intention and their comprehension? Since that intention is embedded in a communication, the problem really becomes one of highlighting the relation between the content of the communication as analyzed from some standpoint other than that of the audience (VII.B) and people's own decoding or interpretation of what they perceive. The issue can be phrased in various ways, depending upon the jargon of the analyst. One term undergoing a fashionable revival at the moment is "cognition," which apparently refers to all of an individual's activated moods and predispositions as well as to his comprehension and other reactions; thus "cognitive structure" covers a multitude of processes. Modern information theory is especially concerned with the relation between input and output in a communication system, since the relation has implications for a variety of fields ranging from engineering and cybernetics to physiology and psychology. Comprehension in such a conceptual scheme is a process intervening between input and output. For the kind of human communication considered here, it seems reasonable to assume that some kind of *discrepancy* between input and comprehension is always present.

IX.D.1 Undoubtedly such a discrepancy is likely to be greater when the communicator is an outsider than when he is an insider, if only because, as already indicated (I.A.1), the former is less aware of the communication restrictions confronting him. In fact, a fairly marked discrepancy seems unavoidable when two people from different cultures are communicating, not only because their different languages can produce misunderstandings but also because they speak, as has been previously suggested (III.B.1.a and c.ii), different "silent languages": coming from diverse cultures, they unwittingly and simultaneously use other media besides speech, such as gestures, which the other person may not comprehend. And beneath the surface they are likely to be seeking different goals without realizing it. When an American and an Arab begin to bargain in a market place of the Middle East, for example, more than the price they are discussing is at issue. The American bargains not only to save money and to avoid being cheated, but also to arrive at what he assumes to be the real asking price. The Arab, on the other hand, bargains for more money of course but, in addition, he views haggling as "a means of passing a day" and "a technique of interpersonal relations"; in his mind, furthermore, there is not a single price, rather there are several prices to be achieved contingent on circumstances. Such basic differences are reflected most inadequately by the language floating at the surface (Hall, 1959, p. 129).

The very word "rumor-mongering" in English suggests the distortions that frequently arise when information is transmitted through a channel composed of a chain of people. What may begin as a slight discrepancy between the original communicator and the person constituting his audience or between the original observer and an event becomes larger and larger as the number of recipient-disseminators increases. It has been shown that the changes resulting from such distortions, both in laboratory studies and in real life, follow the same principles as those originally devised to describe very general forms of perception (Allport and Postman, 1947).

Illustrations of misunderstanding between Africans and Europeans can be found for virtually every medium. One European observer, for example, reports himself perplexed by a gesture noted in Ruanda-Urundi: "If a Tussi approaches a European, he covers his mouth and nose with his hand." People from two societies that are subjects of the Tussi do not behave in this fashion. Do those covering their mouth and nose fear that they will be poisoned by strangers? Do they regard their "protruding mouth as ugly"? Since they themselves are "pomaded and perfumed with rancid butter," do they dislike the odor of Europeans, who consequently remind them of corpses? No answer to these breath-taking hypotheses is provided (Czekanoswki, 1917, p. 126).

Misunderstandings by Africans rather than Europeans are more likely to be reported since the observers are usually Europeans who can quickly note frailties in others. In addition, Africans may in fact react exotically to the mass media with which they have had only limited experience. In Ghana, for example, the writer was told by a most reliable social scientist of one African who thought that a historical film on Anthony and Cleopatra was a newsreel; further inquiry revealed that he did not know that the camera had not been invented in antiquity. Certain impressions have been noted from a six-month tour of Northern Rhodesia and Nyasaland by a mobile propaganda unit of the East Africa Command during World War II (III.B.1.e). "Nearly all Africans" were puzzled by a film containing a short sequence in which the King of England inspected naval, military, and air detachments: they could scarcely believe that they were seeing the same man, since in each instance he was shown wearing the appropriate uniform of the service, and even a king they knew could not change clothes so quickly. A Chaplin film, *The Tramp*, made Africans believe Europeans to be magicians who can restore life since a character therein is hit on the head with a sack and survives without any indication that he has been the least bit hurt. The simple technique of "the camera leaping from the shell to the breech, from the gun muzzle to the gunner's outstretched hand, backwards and forwards, with demoniac speed" in order to suggest rapid fire is "a waste of celluloid" for an African unacquainted with a gun or a shell (Dickson, 1945, p. 16). Similarly an official from the former Belgian Congo believes that "the primitive African" connot comprehend ordinary travel films or those in which scenery is featured. When the camera shifts, "he thinks he is watching trees moving, buildings increasing or decreasing in size, and objects which are normally stationary changing their position" (Bever, 1952, p. 60). And the Fundamental Education Committee of Experts attached to UNESCO recommended in 1948 that documentaries be produced in "slower tempo" because "the idiomatic techniques and rapid episode of changes of usual 'documentaries' are clearly unsuited to unsophisticated minds" and also because "many audiences" cannot easily absorb both sight and sound when they are simultaneously presented (Film Centre, 1949, pp. 93–4). Many of these generalizations about Africans evidently stem from intriguing but unsystematic impressions.

It is in the area of language, especially in translation, that misunderstandings are most frequent, undoubtedly because language is used more extensively than any other medium. Some of the reasons have already been indicated: like languages everywhere, each African language tends to have its own distinctive vocabulary and structure, which make translation difficult (VII. A); knowledge of nonindigenous languages by Africans and of African languages by Europeans is not widespread (VI.C.1.a). Missionaries are especially sensitive to this kind of difficulty since they themselves must appear before their congregations and translate into an African language the Bible, prayers, and other parts of a normal church service. One linguist, who is devotedly interested in missions, provides a bushel load of faulty translations that have been used in Africa, sometimes "for more than a century." It appears to the present writer that the faults can be traced to two principal sources: incorrect pronunciation and a failure to appreciate the connotations of the translated word or phrase.

Incorrect pronunciations can easily occur in tonal languages: "Our Father God" became "Our Mother God" because only a slight rise in the first syllable distinguishes the two words. Or the speaker had not learned to pronounce the distinctive phoneme in the language: the benediction, "O Lord, dismiss us with Thy blessing," emerged as "O Lord, kick us out gently." The wrong connotation of a word or phrase was conveyed either because a slightly different referent is used in the African language or, when the referents in both languages are roughly the same, they evoke quite different reactions. "*We* have all sinned and come short of the Glory of God": the missionary meant by *we* both Europeans and Africans, but by using the exclusive rather than the inclusive form of that pronoun in the African language he was referring in effect only to the sins of the Europeans and not to those of his audience. The literal translation of "Behold, I stand at the door and knock" did evoke in the African audience the correct image of someone knocking on a door, but for them the image is unpleasant: only thieves knock on a door to discover whether the occupants are at home. Since honest men in that society call out both the name of the occupant of the house whom they would see and also their own name, the translation thus had to be: "Behold; I stand at the door and call" (Nida, 1952b, pp. 3–9).

The same writer indicates that such misunderstandings could go unnoticed since the Africans, not knowing of course the original text, simply accepted what they heard. Sometimes, however, they were puzzled by a faulty translation and then they altered the meaning in accordance with their own beliefs. During the communion service in East Africa, for example, missionaries used the wrong intonation for the word *blessing* in the sentence, "This cup of blessing do we bless," as a result of which *blessing* became *poison*. Members of the audience, however, reinterpreted the sacrament. The minister, they thought, had placed poison in the cup and then blessed it during the service. No one obviously died from drinking the poison; hence the Christians must have been using this device to try "to demonstrate their innocence" (ibid., p. 4).

The way a communication is comprehended is more likely to resemble its intended or actual content when it contains certain perceptual *aids* or when the communicator provides them.

IX.D.2.a

Once again *repetition* is invoked as a device but combined this time with variation. Previously repetition has been mentioned in connection with the moods of an audience (VIII.C.3) and the gaining of their attention (IX.A.2.b). Now by assuming that the communication has been both prepared and received, stress is placed upon comprehension: the more frequently a theme is repeated or the more varied the ways in which it is transmitted, other things being equal of course, the greater the probability that comprehension will more closely resemble input. On an elementary level, for example, simple redundancy corrects potential errors: repeat the word "now" in a telegram and it is less likely to be transmitted as "not" or "nor." A theme in one form may be misunderstood but, when repeated in a somewhat varied form, it can perhaps be more easily grasped.

———·—·———

The subtleties of communication presumably occur so frequently in a society that insiders comprehend them quickly and without error. From this standpoint idiomatic expressions are very economical because they convey in condensed form information or values which, if expressed explicitly, would require a much longer communication. Outsiders, however, experience difficulties. One observer indicates the rather typical perplexity of the outsider who is confronted with proverbs easily comprehended by the people themselves; he is writing of the Ibo of Nigeria:

The Ibo has a generous store of proverbs which are continually brought into use. They are so profuse that often it is impossible to understand the full meaning of a conversation without knowing some of the more common ones. Frequently, a question is asked to which no direct answer is given; instead a proverb is quoted. It is always very apt to the occasion, but quite confusing to a person not acquainted with either the words or their interpretation [Basden, 1938, p. 436].

Likewise any culturally stereotyped behavior is not likely to be misunderstood since people grow accustomed to a uniform interpretation. One of the taboos for a community among the Ashanti in Ghana has included, for example, the following: "A woman during her 'periods' might not address a priest or any of the . . . palace attendants" (Rattray, 1929, p. 315). Sudden silence by a woman, after weeks of addressing these authorities, must have conveyed to them the fact of her menstruation. The type of social learning on which communication is based is shown in Dahomey. There brass figures and appliquéd cloths are used to decorate the homes of chiefs, priests, and others in the upper class who do not have to perform manual labor. Both the objects and the cloth serve no other function and, since they are beyond the means of commoners, they therefore stamp their owners as "persons of means as well as of taste" (Herskovits, 1945, p. 30). Undoubtedly the art becomes associated with status in this society since its connection with the class of owners is so frequently observed.

The difficulties which Africans allegedly have in understanding film techniques from the West decrease as more mobile cinema vans arrive in their communities or as they have increasing opportunities to attend regular performances in established theaters. During the transition from naiveté to sophistication various pedagogical devices are suggested. The commentary on a film, for example, should not occur during an exciting scene since Africans are not supposed to be accustomed to receive simultaneously an idea in both visual and oral form. Educated people in the West "focus their eyes at a point a few feet from the screen" and hence presumably appreciate an entire scene at a glance; whereas illiterate Africans, it is asserted, allow their eyes to travel from one part of the picture to another, as a result of which they may not grasp the entire representation. Scenes in films for Africans, therefore, should last long enough for the audience to comprehend the details (Sellers, 1955, p. 14).

The next device to be considered that aids comprehension is *simplification*. Metaphysically the argument could be advanced that, since no communication ever reflects all of reality, some degree of simplification is inevitable. Let the argument be accepted forthwith without a quibble: nonconsequential communication is likely to be more easily understood when distracting, unnecessary details are deliberately removed.

IX.D.2.b

A society's proverbs, it was said a few pages ago, are difficult for an outsider to comprehend. From the viewpoint of those who use them correctly, however, they represent simplified summaries of approved rules of conduct and of the society's explanations of those rules. Instead of preaching a sermon, as it were, or laboriously recalling the reasons for acting in a particular way, the communicator can quote the traditional injunction or explanation and be certain, or reasonably certain, that his audience comprehends the communication. Among the Fanti of Ghana, for example, many of the rules of the society are conveniently expressed in proverbs: the collective responsibility and cooperation associated with clan and lineage membership ("If you are getting your hair cut by your mother's child, you do not look into a looking glass"); prestige and authority of elders ("We follow the words of the mouth of an elder, not his thoughts"); child-rearing ("The child who provokes his mother and father eats food without salt"); and general values, like doing the proper thing ("If water is not near you, you go near it"). Noteworthy is the fact that for one subject, the power of the chief, on which the society has no unequivocal policy, proverbs can be quoted on either side of the proposition: one type stresses his ultimate power ("One cannot make the same tracks as an elephant"), the other his limited power ("When the chief has good advisers, he reigns peacefully"). In this society proverbs are so popular that they are used as a form of entertainment: contests are staged in which two men seek before a panel of judges to cite one proverb after the other (Christensen, 1958).

The Fanti, like many other African societies, also use proverbs in judicial proceedings, even as precedents are quoted in courts in the West. Thus a request for postponement of a case may be supported by this proverb: "It takes time to make a dress for a hunchback." Among the Mbundu of Angola, "No advocate would weary his audience and the jury of elders by quoting a proverb in full, but contents himself with giving the first word thereof" (J. T. Tucker, 1954, p. 208). Here, then, is simplification of a simplification.

Nonverbal media may also serve to simplify aspects of communication after being continually associated with a particular meaning. Reference has been made above to the custom, among the Hausa of Nigeria, of having one or more musicians sing the praises of a particular person who usually is expected to reward them with a gift (IX.A.1). Musical instruments may accompany the singing, but only kings may be praised with trumpets, only certain vassals with double gongs, and only officials who have reached the rank of district head or its equivalent with wooden horns or reed instruments. Similarly a particular cult summons, entertains, and praises its spirits with the help of a special type of guitar or violin; during their ceremonies women resort to an upturned half-calabash standing in a bowl of water or in an empty vessel. Some type of double-membraned "talking" drum is struck by individual men while complimenting one another (M. G. Smith, 1957, p. 28). At a distance, therefore, the Hausa must be able to infer from the instrument the status of the person being praised even without hearing the words of the song.

The practical people, the ones who are seeking to change Africans quickly, especially Europeans, almost always include among their treasured rules of thumb some injunction to simplify for the sake of intelligibility. Thus the five suggestions of a former Congo official regarding the production of films for African audiences all involve some simplification. Each film, he says, should be "simple" in the sense that it "faithfully reproduces what is seen by the human eye." It should have "the greatest possible continuity." It should have the principal character appear in the foreground and be the only person in motion during a sequence. It should offer "the smallest number of actions" at a given instant of time. And it should make frequent use of "close-ups and semi-close-ups" (Bever, 1952, pp. 61–2).

Printed media supply distinctive forms of simplification for African audiences with a shaky ability to read. In Northern Nigeria, for example, the aim of the North Regional Literature Agency is "to provide vernacular reading material in support of the literacy campaign and in the general interest of public enlightenment." Within two years after its inception in 1954, this group published thirteen newssheets, six in different dialects of Hausa and the remaining in other African languages. To attract attention, each sheet has a distinctive title that is "printed boldly" across the top of the front page and often supported by a symbolic device that is immediately grasped by the local audience. To increase comprehension, typography has been simplified: there are only four columns to a page; an effort is made to have each line contain enough words "to encourage smooth reading"; whenever possible, words are not broken at the end of lines; spacing between lines is liberal; "straightforward roman type" is used" and items are separated by brief headlines (Jeffries, 1957, pp. 24, 30).

———————

IX.D.2.c Another aid to comprehension is what may be called *pointing*. In effect, the communicator says to his audience, "Look at this, it is important." As suggested previously (VIII.E), experimental evidence indicates that under some conditions people are more influenced when conclusions are explicitly rather than implicitly drawn. Instead of actively participating and perhaps drawing a different conclusion, they are led directly to note at a minimum the communicator's standpoint. On a simpler level, it is being said that the composition, an arrow, or a caption in a drawing or photograph draws attention to a significant component.

———————

Many authorities insist that the best way to teach people to follow certain procedures, especially in the fields of health, agriculture, and the household, is to provide concrete exhibitions or demonstrations and at the same time to permit the audience to ask questions. With maximum feedback (XII.A.1.a), the communicator can perceive whether his explanation has been understood and, if it has not, he can repeat himself and then indicate by pointing what should be done or where the difficulty lies. More than common sense is needed to use the technique effectively; demonstrators are supposed to be carefully and deliberately trained in advance. After the attention of the audience has been gained, after a note of welcome has been sounded, and after the precise purpose of the session has been explained, communicators working with women on domestic problems are advised by an experienced Ghanaian bureau to proceed as follows (anon., 1959b):

1. Explain each step as you work, in a clear, deliberate voice.
2. Speak slowly and distinctly.
3. Use simple words.
4. Face the group at all times.
5. Avoid talking when using noisy equipment or if you have to turn away from your group for a short while.
6. Avoid unnecessary pauses.
7. Clean up as you go along . . . see that stray bits of material, crumbs, and dirty utensils are cleared away at once.
8. Work quietly and with as little noise as possible.
9. In concluding the demonstration it is necessary to summarize briefly.

In demonstrating "personal cleanliness" to women, for example, the best thing to do is actually to "bathe a toddler" in front of the audience: "inspect hair, nails, etc. before bathing" and "treat sores, etc. after bathing" (Department of Social Welfare and Community Development, 1958, pp. 2, 34). It is easier, no doubt, to point to and then bathe an *etc.* than to describe one.

To highlight the present discussion of comprehension, it seems desirable once again and at some length to return to the problem of whether or not Africans having little contact with the West can comprehend photographs and drawings. This time, let the first word come from a missionary who early in the century reported point-blank: "Take a picture in black and white and the native cannot see it." Tell them that they are looking at "a picture of an ox and a dog" and they will immediately "consider you a liar." If one concentrates upon the young boys in the group and points out to them the horns of the ox and the tail of the dog, however, this specialized audience will respond correctly and soon "the old people will look again and then they clap their hands and say, 'Oh! yes, it is a dog.' " The report concludes by asserting that such tutelage-by-pointing has permanent repercussions: "When a man has seen a picture for the first time, his book education has begun" (quoted by Beach, 1901, p. 468).

In spite of the fact that photographs have been widely distributed in Africa during the intervening sixty years, some European and African officials still report in personal conversation anecdotes and impressions like the one just quoted. In previous studies devoted to other problems, however, the present writer incidentally noted that all African informants seemed to comprehend stereoscopic photographs and that the ability to comment upon vague drawings tended to be positively associated with education in the Western sense (Doob, 1960a, pp. 297, 311). Education undoubtedly provides repeated and varied contact with all types of visual media. In addition, two very limited pilot studies were more recently conducted in order to try to discover more systematically not only whether small samples of Africans do have difficulty comprehending photographs and drawings but also whether their perception can be affected by experiences during a brief interview and testing period.

The first study was made in a Fulani community about 20 miles outside of Kaduna, the capital of Northern Nigeria. The chief of the village agreed to obtain 20 informants who in his opinion were "typical" and who had attended school a varying number of years. No better sampling method was feasible during the short time at the investigator's disposal. Of the 20 men thus selected, 12 had never been to a school of Western type; 5 claimed to have attended such a school four years, 2 six years, and 1 eight years. Each man was interviewed alone and, by means of an interpreter, in his own language. He was told that the visitor from America wanted to learn more about his country from the answers he would give to questions and from the way in which he would use his imagination. Then eleven photographs, one after the other, were shown, and the informant was asked to report what he saw. There followed a few questions pertaining to the man's age, schooling, literacy, etc. Next, and without prior warning, he was asked to recall verbally as many of the photographs as he could. Finally, he was shown nine pen-and-ink drawings, one at a time, and asked to identify them.

Both the photographs and the drawings were arranged in order of difficulty as previously rated by Europeans who had worked intimately with Africans. Some of the photographs were obtained from the United States Information Office, the remainder from the Nigerian Ministry of Information. The least clear photograph showed three vague figures who were illuminated only by a fire they were watching. Toward the middle of the series was a photograph of Africans clustered about a scale and receiving money; at the end was a straightforward photograph of an airplane. The drawings, taken from primers in use in African schools, began with a detached nose, progressed through a simple and realistic drawing of a face, and ended with the sketch of an entire dog. One experimental variable was introduced into the interview: half the subjects reacted to the photographs in order from "difficult" to "easy," and the other half in the opposite order. Within each group, the order of difficulty of the drawings was reversed: those who saw the easiest photographs first were presented first with the most difficult drawings, etc. This experimentally manipulated variable, it was thought, would affect the confidence and experience gained while responding to a series of photographs or drawings.

In analyzing the results, photographs and drawings are considered to be "correctly" identified when the replies agree with the captions originally given by the government agencies from which they were obtained or when they seem appropriate in the African context. There is, then, a significant relation between the order of difficulty suggested in advance by Nigerian officials and the number of correct identifications in the case of the photographs (rho = +.69) but not in the case of the drawings (rho = +.38). No relationship exists between the ranks of the photographs with respect to correct identification and correct recall (rho = +.26).

Results bearing on the hypotheses being tested are summarized in Table 5. In the first two columns the small sample is divided

TABLE 5. *Identification and Recall of Photographs and Drawings*

| | EDUCATION | | ORDER | |
| | | | *complex-to-simple* | *simple-to-complex* |
	none (n = 12)	*some* (n = 8)	(n = 10)	(n = 10)
PHOTOGRAPHS				
Number of items on which correct identification is greater	1	10	2	7
Mean number correctly identified	2.9	4.9	3.1	4.3
Number of items on which correct recall is greater	1	10	7	4
Mean number correctly recalled	2.7 °	5.5	4.4	3.6
DRAWINGS				
Number of items on which correct identification is greater	0	8	2	6
Mean number correctly identified	5.4 °	7.1	6.1	6.0

° Differs significantly (p <.05) from figure to right.

into those with no and those with some education. One of the three differences between the means is not statistically significant; but otherwise the trend of the items (as appraised by a sign test) and the significant differences themselves indicate clearly that education is related to correct identification and, in the case of photographs, to correct recall. In interpreting these findings, however, it must be noted that age is confounded with education: the uneducated group happens to be in the late thirties, the educated one in the early twenties. In the second two columns of the same table, the sample is divided by experimental treatment, that is, those receiving the photographs and drawings in the order of complex-to-simple are compared with those subjected to the order of simple-to-complex. Here neither the differences nor the trend is significant: the varying experience during the interview was not an effective determinant.

Additional results relate to the process of perception. First, these particular African informants, whether educated or not, were not baffled by the task of identifying the photographs and drawings. Out of twenty men, the highest number unable to identify a photograph was four, and that photograph was the most difficult one; and no more than one person on each of the remaining ten photographs was dumbfounded. Likewise trouble occurred only in connection with the first and the fourth drawing in order of assumed difficulty, on each of which five men could not respond; otherwise the remaining drawings were understood by all or almost all the men (two men were unable to respond to two of the drawings and one man to one of them; the other four were correctly labeled by everyone).

Without exception, human beings were noted in the photographs when they were in fact present, but most of the time the activity in which the figures were engaged was not indicated. Thus the photograph of Africans watching a game was so described by only one person; four said simply that they saw "schoolboys" and four that they were looking at "a crowd." A very clear photograph of Africans beside a scale being paid money which was quite visible was reported simply as "men" by half the sample.

Those who responded like the majority of the group to a photograph (the "modal response") were also able to recall the particular photograph better than those in the minority: in ten out of eleven instances, more of those conforming to the mode recalled a photograph than those not conforming. This finding is not easy to interpret. Perhaps under the circumstances men who unwittingly conformed were less baffled by the task and hence less likely to forget what they had seen.

Why, though, were some photographs and drawings identified correctly more frequently than others? As a hypothesis it is suggested that the critical factor may have been not familiarity with their content but with the technique of presentation. Thus the three photographs identified correctly by fewest of the informants portray very familiar scenes: human figures illuminated by a fire, African schoolboys watching a football game from behind a protecting screen of wire, and Africans (Nigerians in fact) in a commonplace financial transaction. The lighting in the first photograph, however, is dim, and the figures are difficult to separate from their dark background; in the second, no other section of the stadium and no part of the playing field are shown; and in the third so many men are present that the scale and money tend to be overshadowed. The difficult drawings are of a detached nose, the outline of a face with no features, and—third in order but comprehended by many more—a detached foot. The argument, however, loses some force when one wonders why a detached nose caused more trouble than a detached foot and why a detached hand turned out to be easy to identify.

Only an occasional response seems to provide a basis for the belief that Africans sometimes experience unusual difficulty in identifying photographs or drawings. One man, for example, called an extremely clear photograph of an airplane "a fish." Perhaps the exotic or atypical response is remembered by European observers rather than the more mundane, typical ones.

A second study, conducted in the same community and dealing primarily with the subject of literacy, has already been described (VI.C.1.b). In the midst of a long schedule, the ten literate and the eleven illiterate men tried to identify eight rather simple pen-and-ink drawings taken from textbooks in use in Africa and two fragments from photographs which were thought to be very difficult to identify (a poorly illuminated view of people huddled together and the isolated section of an airplane wing). Later on they were also shown two straightforward photographs. During the interview two variables were manipulated which, it was anticipated, would affect recall or perception. The first consisted of a verbal warning to half the men that they would subsequently be asked to recall the series of drawings and photographs; the other half were not so warned. The second variable was the form of the question concerning the identification of the two clear photographs: half were told merely to report what they saw, the other half were asked pointed questions about each picture ("Show me the fire in this photograph").

The warning about recall had no effect either on perception or recall. The second variable, however, was decisive both in an absolute and a statistical sense. In the first photograph, one out of ten informants reported voluntarily the fire there portrayed, but nine out of eleven correctly pointed to it when asked to do so. In the second, two out of ten spontaneously referred to the weighing scale, but ten out of eleven in the other group correctly pointed to it. It is thus clear that the verbal warning was not efficacious but that tutelage by inquiry was.

Additional findings can be briefly reported. Once again, as in the previous study, the informants had no difficulty in responding: in connection with only four of the ten drawings and photographs did more than two men say they could not identify what they saw. These particular pictures, after the fact, seem difficult: the detached airplane wing, a wall isolated from the rest of the house, a window likewise isolated, and a very dim photograph of people. There was a general tendency, too, to make a brief reply and thus not to mention many of the objects in the picture. One sketch, for example, shows many objects, including a desk, books, chair, and other furniture as well as a dog and a blue handbag inside the room; a goat, a chicken, a bird, grass, and hills are visible outside. What most of the men did was to mention some of the animals or objects either inside or outside the room but not those in both places; and the animals were reported much more frequently than the objects. Virtually nobody included the blue bag on his list, though it was the only part of the sketch in color. When it was used, the simple pointing question, "Do you see anything else?" was sufficient to elicit a fuller report.

One general conclusion emerges from the two studies which seems to jibe with a previous discussion on the perception of colors (VII.A.2.a.iv): Africans at this level of education and contact with Western media either perceive more than they report or else easily can be made to perceive more when they are requested to do so. If anything, they suffer from a lack of experience with drawings and photographs, but this difficulty they can quickly overcome. Without doubt they do not readily express what they perceive.

IX.D.2.d

One other condition promotes comprehension: *diminished egocentrism and ethnocentrism* on the part of both communicator and audience. The very label here sounds like pious preaching, but the empirical fact seems to be that patience on the part of either the communicator or the audience or both is likely to promote understanding and that patience in turn is cultivated by lessening the degree of egocentrism and ethnocentrism of either party. If the communicator knows that the manual gesture he would employ has exactly the opposite meaning in the society of the audience, then he will modify it. Similarly if members of the audience realize that the gesture already employed by the communicator has the opposite meaning for him, they will not become indignant but instead will understand, maybe even forgive, the error. The well-prepared diplomat, businessman, or tourist anticipates the unusual situations or people he will meet abroad and hence, it is hoped, will behave a little less unwisely. The same process functions when antidotes to rumor-mongering are provided: uncertainty and insecurity are reduced, facts are offered, or warnings against rumors as such are given in order to induce people to be a little less egocentric and a little more objective.

Incident after incident involving misunderstanding between outsiders and Africans arises from the ethnocentrism of both sides. A mission in West Africa is reported to have constructed their principal station "on an attractive hill top." They disregarded the protests of the Africans because, from their ethnocentric viewpoint, they "wished to enjoy the lovely view." But years later they discovered that the equally ethnocentric Africans kept avoiding them: for traditional reasons the particular hill was considered to be taboo (Nida, 1952b, p. 15).

Without expressing anything more than a bias it is impossible to say whether Europeans or Africans are more ethnocentric, but certainly each side, assuming the sanctity of its own value system, believes that the other is less tolerant. In fact, both groups rarely suspend judgment. A revered figure like Livingstone is reported to have shocked some Africans by sleeping in the same wagon as his wife after their son's birth (E. W. Smith, 1926, p. 50). An anthropologist was disturbed when a good friend among the Gusii in Kenya met him one day, glared, and barked, "What are you doing, tramping around here? Go away! Or shall I hit you?" For the moment he failed to remember that the Gusii believe that "those who abuse one another and are not angry are those who love one another." The "playful insult" is a sign of affection and friendship used between good friends of the same age and also in certain structured relationships, such as between grandparents and their grandchildren (Mayer, 1951, pp. 27–34).

Ethnocentrism on a verbal level seems especially persistent. After once finding or achieving a translation for a word or expression, the outsider is likely to rest content and never again challenge its accuracy. "It is possible to live years in Africa," one observer states, "before making the discovery that direct and simple phrases, apparently referable to everyday, material objects with the ordinary surface meanings of the individual words employed, may have totally unexpected values." He mentions as an illustration an occasion when he heard people refer to their community as "a good village." From his standpoint the village was far from good: it was littered and dusty, and many of the huts needed urgent repairs. A blatant conflict in evaluation made him ask the headman what he meant by a "good village"; the reply was:

A good village is where the headman and the elders are respected by all; and where they too have regard for all, even for the children. It is a good village where the young respect parents and where no one tries to harm another. If there is even one person who belittles another person or works harm, then the village is spoiled [Young, 1934, pp. 89–90].

To be able to view with both understanding and tolerance another person's or another society's conception of the good different from one's own is virtually a superhuman feat.

X. REACTIONS

Strong though his impulse may be, the analyst cannot rip people apart or probe them with a fluoroscope to discover directly how they react internally and privately to a communication. He is dependent upon what they report to him; and of course they may or may not be able or willing to tell the truth. Or he can make inferences concerning their reactions either from antecedent factors in the communication or consequent changes in their behavior. If the wave length of the light falls within what is conventionally called the red part of the spectrum, it is reasonable to believe that most people perceive red and not green. Or if people halt when they see one light rather than another and if halting in the society is associated with a red rather than a green light, a similar inference is possible. In this chapter attention is focused exclusively upon the very internal, private reactions of the audience to the communication. At times the tone may suggest that the writer can perform surgery or has a fluoroscope in his possession which reveals what occurs. Such is not the case, it is confessed; in each instance the indirect procedure of depending upon people's reports, antecedent conditions, or consequent behavior is assumed.

X.A *Evoked Predispositions* People do not usually perceive and comprehend a communication passively. For one thing, they almost inevitably are in a passing mood which, it has been emphasized (VIII), has some effect upon their reactions. Then the very drives inducing perception in the first place, whether they stem from the artifices of the communicator (IX.A) or the audience (IX.B), persist while reactions to the communication occur, and they may play an influential role in the ensuing responses. At this point, moreover, other forces begin also to function: people react to the communication as such. They now know, or think they know, how the communication would have them feel or what it would have them learn or do, as a consequence of which their predispositions from the past are evoked.

X.A.1 The *quality* of these predispositions is the first attribute to be observed. More specifically, (a) what *feelings* do people have toward the communication as a whole or toward some of its components? Any pragmatically useful set of categories can specify that attitude, such as the trio of favorable, unfavorable, and neutral. Other questions can be asked. For example, (b) what *prestige* do aspects of the communication have? Prestige here can be broken down in the same way as the communicator's attitude toward the audience (I.B.2): high, medium, and low. Again the problem at hand must determine how minute the divisions should be. Thus sometimes prestige may be thought of as general or specific: a communicator has high prestige as a person (he is respected as a human being) but low prestige as a communicator (his delivery is considered poor).

X.A.2 Next the *content* of the predispositions must be described. Consciously or unconsciously people are likely to have feelings toward all components of a communication, and to attribute to those components varying degrees of prestige. At a given moment or for a specific person the feeling may be vague and have little effect upon the communication, but that means only that its weight which happens to be low in the present could be high in the future. The audience is so interested in the message that they pay little attention to the communicator; then the sudden appearance of another communicator toward whom their inclinations are definitely positive or negative alters their reactions.

X.A.2.a The first component of the predispositions is the *communicator:* how does the audience feel toward the person or persons whom they believe to be responsible for what they perceive? Characteristics associated with the communicator which facilitate his influence, at least among Americans, include his authority, his affiliation with the audience, and his fairness and impartiality (Janis and

Hovland, 1959, pp. 11–12; Weiss, 1957). That influence can pertain to the perception or the acceptance of the communication, or to both. A communicator considered untrustworthy, for example, may not attract an audience or, if he appears after they have assembled, he may not be believed.

In traditional African societies the prestige of established leaders is carefully maintained so that in their normal roles as communicators their communications are likely to evoke approval. One recurrent device is the use of special terms or linguistic forms in the presence of important people or even in referring to them (VII.A.2.a.ii; VIII.E). The prestige of medicine men and others who practice magic must be especially high if their performance is to be believed or if their advice is to be followed. "Props" may help reinforce the impression to be conveyed. One of the three ordeals to determine whether a person among the Fang in the Gabon and Cameroon Republics is guilty of a crime consists of having the "practitioner" listen to "mysterious voices" which seem to come out of the earth. Three people are named by the voices as possible culprits; this dramatic communication "probably" is produced by ventriloquism, for it is known that practitioners have mastered that art. The three people so designated must each bring a fowl; after the birds have been slaughtered and the practitioner has examined their entrails and observed how their blood falls upon the ground, he is able to announce which person is the criminal (Trilles, 1912, p. 562).

As individual Africans learn Western ways, the display of what they are learning constitutes for their contemporaries a consequential communication concerning their new status. That information may lessen their general prestige as upholders of the traditional within the society, but it is likely to add to their specific prestige as communicators about the new world. Indeed, sometimes their general prestige may also be affected. The symbolic value of literacy in this context has already been suggested (VI.C.1.b). During the last war, according to one report, a soldier from the Gold Coast was asked what he thought of his East

African "brothers." He replied: "These men be no brother, they be bush men." And why did he consider them so backward? "They no proper black men," he stated, "they no speak English at all" (Hodson, 1941, p. 304). On the other hand when Africans pursue Western ways and are unable to acquire the proper symbols, their prestige as communicators is low and their communications may be ineffective. Many "bush schools" in tropical Africa, for example, are reported to employ very poor grade-school teachers. Salaries are inadequate; hence teachers may not be well qualified, in fact may enter the profession only after having failed to achieve a more attractive post (Batten, 1953).

Outsiders like Europeans must come to evoke favorable attitudes if they are to function effectively as communicators. The same problem faces an investigator who cannot easily communicate to naive Africans his scientific interest in their actions and values. Like so many others who preceded and followed him, one anthropologist reports that his best approach initially among the Mende of Sierra Leone has been through educated adults, whether they be chiefs or commoners. After being convinced that his intentions are sincere, many of them allay "traditional suspicions" among their countrymen, and some have gone "out of their way to seek out fresh channels for me even though they may thus lay themselves open to the charge of 'betraying the country.'" European missionaries have also been helpful (Little, 1951, p. 14).

Often the prestige of missionaries as communicators is increased not by their communications concerning men's spirit but by their conscientious efforts to help men's bodies through teaching, medicine, nursing, and agriculture. For this reason most of them in modern times have another skill besides that of spreading the gospel. The respect they win with their earthly work presumably is generalized to their religious role, which of course is not to maintain that their motive for rendering material assistance is only the communication gain.

Europeans possess—or once possessed—general prestige in Africa, but they must often win prestige in connection with specific roles, since uneducated Africans probably have no idea concerning their overseas status or are unimpressed by it. In the West, for example, laymen usually obey quite uncritically most of the advice they obtain from a physician on medical matters, especially after having voluntarily consulted him. In Africa, however, the orders of a Western physician or of an African trained in the medical techniques of the West are not necessarily followed. Africans in western Uganda are reported to have had faith in injections; but for diseases not so treated they seldom accorded the skill of the European physician higher value than that of their own medicine men (Goodchild, 1936). Medical outsiders, therefore, usually know that, unless they are entering a region already acquainted with Western medicine, they must establish their own reputations as effective healers whose prescriptions should be heeded. Unfortunately, Western medicine obviously cannot always be successful. The unavoidable death of an African while undergoing treatment may be ascribed to the physician, who thus, from the African standpoint, demonstrates his incompetence to receive patients in the future. Here is a very neat ethical-medical dilemma. Most physicians and nurses, this writer feels, proceed with Africans as if they were Europeans: they try desperately to help them even when the odds at succeeding are slim; and then if they fail they explain, often to no avail, what has occurred. One nurse in Ruanda, however, has stated a solution to this problem which shockingly departs from medical practice in the West but which is immediately intelligible in terms of the greatest good that can be achieved by effective communication and existing facilities in most parts of Africa:

> Surgically we treat anything that comes along . . . anything in which we are pretty certain of achieving a satisfactory result. . . . For example, if an old woman came in with carcinoma of the abdomen and begged us to operate on her, we would not do so if we thought she would die during the operation or soon after. . . . News travels fast in Africa . . . and patients would immediately become superstitious and tell their friends to refuse operations [Walker, 1936, p. 135].

X.A.2.b A second component of the communication is its *perceived goal:* what is the attitude of the audience toward the goal they themselves ascribe to the communicator or his communication? Prestige here may have a slightly different meaning from the one it has in connection with the communicator: it often includes a conception of the importance of the goal to the audience. Two people may heartily approve of a goal but for one the interest is a central one, for the other quite segmental.

A missionary group in Africa once concentrated its preaching "on negative pronouncements against the drinking of beer, the wearing of beads, and dancing." The African audience, however, could see no connection between religion or morality on the one hand and beer, beads, and dancing on the other. For beer in that society was a staple food and did not often if ever lead to drunkenness. Beads were a form of clothing for the men and had "practically no religious significance." And certainly dancing had "no moral implications" (Nida, 1952b, p. 28). People reacted unfavorably, therefore, first because they were predisposed in favor of the practices being condemned and, secondly, because they did not grasp the relation between such activities and the goal of the missionaries who must have been guiding themselves by an Inflexible Policy which in turn was based on Little or No Understanding.

X.A.2.c Next is the attitude of the audience toward the *medium* in which the communication appears. If an item is reported by a newspaper, must it *therefore* be true or must it be false? Can one trust one newspaper more than another? Do the gestures and facial expressions of the man really speak louder than his words? Evidence in the United States indicates that people have preferences for some media rather than others and that *perhaps* those less well educated are influenced more by aural than visual media (Janis and Hovland, 1959, p. 12).

Occasionally in traditional African society it seems perfectly clear that a medium of communication must have prestige because it is surrounded by a set of respected symbols. Among the Nkole of Uganda, the royal drums, the only drums in the society, receive daily offerings of milk from a herd of sacred cows. This diet is varied with beer or cattle which a man provides after the birth of a son or after some other joyful occurrence, such as promotion to office or a successful expedition. The drums have their own special guardians and their own sacred spears. In addition, in earlier times, when the skins were changed upon the accession of a new king, they were rubbed with papyrus ashes as well as with the blood of a young boy deliberately sacrificed for that purpose. If they are moved, they are greeted by smaller drums (also royal) and by the handclapping of assistant guardians. They have special ceremonies in their honor when the king goes to war. They may offer sanctuary to those in need—for instance, people condemned to death for committing some crime—and anyone so helped thereafter becomes their "perpetual servant." They are not used as a form of music; instead they function rarely, and then on special occasions that include the appearance of a new moon and the ceremonies accompanying the crowning of a new king (Roscoe, 1923, pp. 44–8, 56, 79). Such well-fed, well-attended, well-revered drums must indeed have prestige as a medium when they are sounded.

The traditional media, like many other practices from the past, tend to persist in most African societies because they symbolize important values. Africans are in contact with them from infancy on and often express and achieve through them significant primary and social goals. Some of the media, moreover, are quite compatible with new developments. A highly sophisticated leader can convey to a public meeting or to a television audience his tribal membership and his respect for the African way of life by appearing in tribal dress. Modern mass media and the extending channels can transmit communications initially produced by basic media, such as speech or gestures.

Without doubt new media, especially the extending ones, have accompanied the missionary, the trader, and finally the colonial official into Africa. Government in particular has needed these media to achieve its objectives of community development, mass education, improved agricultural practices, etc., as well as the more general goal of retaining power through transmitting information concerning its good deeds and its policies (I.C.1). Each new extending medium from the West, even if it seems on the surface to depart only slightly from the traditional form, then, must acquire prestige. Many Africans are accustomed to attend meetings in their traditional society, for example, but such sessions are likely to follow fairly formal rules of some sort. The medium of lecturing to disseminate knowledge, however, may be quite strange to them and may not at first evoke attitudes conducive to learning. In the words of one missionary:

> Any approach to lecturing is rather a hopeless way of dealing with pupils who have never been trained in sustained mental effort. Perfect silence and eyes fixed on the teacher's face are no indication of rapt attention. The minds behind the eyes may be a perfect blank or may be absorbed in the interesting speculation of how long the *Dona's* hair would be if she let it down. There must be question and answer and exchange of ideas to keep their brains working [A. Fraser, 1932, p. 37].

The gentle lady is sweetly deluded if she imagines that only African women thus behave at a lecture, as everyone who has ever taught a class anywhere could quickly tell her. She is indicating, however, that the give-and-take technique is one to which Africans are probably more accustomed; that feedback helps communication; and that her own lectures enjoyed low prestige.

A more radical innovation from the West is radio. Officials responsible for introducing that medium into what was then the Gold Coast sought deliberately to fit it into an African framework. They believed that its initial prestige depended in large part on the kind of translation that was used, since people allegedly had confidence only in "the deep vernacular . . . a highly figurative and allusive form of language which requires a knowledge of the doings of mythical figures, the traditions, the folklore, the proverbs, and rough country humor passed orally from one generation to another." A format was used which resembled the pattern of the linguist who transmits messages between the chief and his people (I.A.2.b), although of course on radio the communication goes only one way. A "signature drum" announced the start of a transmission, the way a drum in the village assembles the people; programs began, as linguists open a meeting, by greeting dignitaries (such as the paramount chief and the village headman) and by offering good wishes for the sowing and protection of crops (Williams, 1950, pp. 45–6). So skillful an adaptation of a new medium to the traditional society requires rather complete decentralization of broadcasting. Each society must in effect have its own station or program, and this may be impossible for purely financial reasons (VI.B). In addition, listeners in other societies, of which there are always many within the range of a radio transmitter, may become bored or hostile while the society in question is being wooed.

Africans struggling to learn European ways of behaving bestow upon Western media special symbolic value. To be seen reading a book or to possess a small library of books is considered a source of prestige (VI.C.1.b). The present writer once spent a week traveling with a bright, ambitious African university student in an adjacent country. Each evening he would insist on hearing the BBC summary of the news rebroadcast by a station in his home capital. We would interrupt a leisurely stroll by the sea along a magnificent promenade or, once, a reasonably important interview with an African informant in order to return to our hotel rooms to hear that particular broadcast. Often as the signal would fade away from the transistor set (VI.A.1.c), he would place his ear close to the speaker in order, presumably, to miss not a phrase. Through subtle and unsubtle questions, the writer sought again and again to discover whether he retained any of the news. Nary a trace of it was evident. He had not forgotten what he had heard, rather he had not really paid attention in the first place. He may have been attempting to impress the writer, but this possibility is not likely. To be in the presence of the sounds from the BBC at 7 P.M. was important to him.

Often one finds in Africa that experiences from the West are repeated, naturally after Africans have acquired appropriate Western values. Many Africans, for example, have come to accord less prestige to a free gift than they do to something that must be purchased. "Generally," one student of missions writes, the Bible is sold to Africans, though at a financial loss: "The one who buys appreciates the Book immeasurably more than if it were given." Another advantage besides prestige is suggested for selling: the so-called *colporteur* ("Bible peddler"—the present writer takes no credit for the definition; it comes from the man to be cited at the end of the sentence now interrupted by these parentheses) has "a wonderful opportunity," while conducting the transaction, "to speak extensively with his customers in order to persuade them of the importance of the Book and the need of the message" (Nida, 1952a, p. 166).

Exploratory studies by the present writer in West Africa suggest that, although Africans in rural areas may have little contact with the modern mass media, they generally express a favorable attitude toward them. It must be emphasized, however, that quantitative figures on contact as such are not very significant. Less than one-fifth of the people in two small samples of rural Ghanaians (XI.B.2), for example, had attended traditional markets on the previous day; but this does not mean that the market as an economic institution and also as a source of information was unimportant to them. All of them knew the obvious fact that a market had occurred; all of them named someone who had been to the market; and all of them undoubtedly could have reported some sensational piece of news disseminated there, if one had indeed been disseminated.

Relatively few of the Fulani males interviewed in the pilot study of literates and illiterates conducted near Kaduna in Northern Nigeria (VI.C.1.b) claimed to have direct or even indirect contact with the modern mass media. Only a single informant had seen a film within the past week; most had attended at least one performance at some indefinite time in the past but could recall nothing of what they had allegedly perceived; and a handful, all illiterates, had never watched a motion picture at all. Two men signified that they had read a newspaper within the last few days and could recall specific contents. The modal response of literates was to claim vaguely that they had seen a newspaper within the past month and to report equally vaguely about its contents; and the modal response of illiterates was either to state that no one ever reads newspapers to them or relays their contents, or else to be unable to remember anything they might have heard about newspapers from others. Radio, too, was not perceived by most, or at least not perceived in a way that could produce conscious memories: a handful could recall specific items, and a few claimed they had heard some program recently without being able to recall its contents.

During the interview almost nobody showed an awareness of what was occurring outside the community, whether in Northern Nigeria, elsewhere in Africa, or in Russia. By and large, very few could voluntarily recall news items about those areas. Of the 21 interviewed, however, 16 had heard of the Soviet satellite around the moon, a news item which apparently impressed the Hausa mightily. On the other hand, although the press and radio at the time of the study, like the governments of Nigeria and other West African states, were protesting violently against the plans of the French Government to test an atomic bomb in the adjacent Sahara Desert (from which the harmattan winds reach Nigeria during part of the winter), only 5 of the 16 men interviewed showed any familiarity with that plan. Nine knew when Nigeria would achieve independence within the British Commonwealth; still the one bit of news about their country that they could name was the fact if not the time of this pending independence. It seems likely that their ignorance not only resulted from, but also led to, few contacts with the mass media. If knowledge had been greater, interest would have been stronger; and the reverse must have been true too.

The impression gained from most traditional Africans is that they remain interested in their most immediate affairs, for they can always reply to questions about events occurring close by. The meaningful political unit for them is their community, tribe, or society. From the standpoint of the West, what is sometimes still quaintly called public opinion concerning broader issues and concerning the nation as a political unit is in the process of being formed.

At the same time it is important to note that Africans, perhaps almost everywhere, have a tremendous interest in the mass media and are certainly willing to perceive them if they are made conveniently available. The writer, like anyone who has had the experience, can testify to the shouts of joy which go up in a village when a mobile cinema van arrives; and virtually everyone turns out for the performance. In a somewhat remote area of Northern Nigeria, essentially naked pagans, members of the Gbari society, expressed keen interest in having a radio; and indeed they knew the price of a set as well as of the batteries required to operate it. In another Nigerian community previously described (VI.C.1.b), almost everybody in a very small sample claimed to have heard a radio program fairly recently and many could recall specific details: there the government had installed its system of rediffusion and hence radio was readily available. In addition, most of these people, whether literate or illiterate, differed from those in the other Nigerian community just mentioned: within the last few days they had either read a newspaper or had heard news that had appeared in one. Such people do not have a strong drive to learn about events in the world, as indicated by the fact that few of them could give a sensible reply when asked directly and crudely what gaps in their knowledge about that world they would like to fill. They unabashedly say, as do people in America and Europe, that they want to be entertained by the mass media. Obviously in being entertained they inevitably will perceive news and receive additional information. They themselves wish to open Pandora's box.

X.A.2.d The medium, it has been said (V), reaches the audience at a particular *site:* what sorts of responses are consequently evoked? It seems useful to distinguish two effects: (i) those arising as a result of the prevailing *atmosphere* and (ii) those associated with the *group* to which the audience refers their behavior. Atmosphere includes the host of feelings, beliefs, and satisfactions which stem from the arrangements at the site: the size of the audience, its composition, the interaction, and the kind of communication likely to occur there. By "reference group" is meant the group to which people at the moment feel they belong and whose standards therefore they are likely to employ, in this instance, to judge the communication. At a given moment, does a man think of himself as a member of his family, his occupation group, his church, his club, or his nation? The site can help determine the selection of the particular reference group for two reasons. First, those present constitute a group and hence serve as a physical reminder of its existence. The man undoubtedly is conscious of his family as he watches television at home in the presence of his wife and children. Secondly, the site itself is so clearly associated with a group that by itself it can reinstate people's sense of membership. The man watching television alone in his home may still use the values of his family to judge what he views since the very house and its furniture emphasize that group rather than some other.

The feelings associated with a site depend upon factors operating before and then during people's actual presence there. A distinguished committee once investigated rural education in West Africa and the Congo, and reported that adults "were reluctant that their children should go to school, lest they be weaned from the land, while others sent their children to school with the intention of their leaving the farm to become wage earners" (J. Davis et al., 1945, p. 154). The parents of course first determined whether or not the children could attend, and probably affected their attitudes and learning moods. When once in the classroom, however, the pupils may have been more influenced by the atmosphere there than by their parentally induced predispositions regarding education.

The practical problem of determining to which group people in the audience refer their behavior at a given moment is quite staggering. Certainly, as suggested two paragraphs back, sensible inferences can be made from a knowledge of the site. The inference, alas, can go awry as a result of the communication itself. The regularly scheduled meeting may be taking place at the clubhouse, and therefore members are reacting as members of the organization; but suddenly a speaker reminds them—or some of them—of another group to which they belong ("as good family men, you should . . .") and they then use other standards of judgment. Under these circumstances, the only practical solution for the communicator is at least to be acquainted with the groups to which people belong, with the importance of these groups, and with the sites likely to be associated with them.

For Africa this phase of people's reactions to any communication can be anticipated through obtaining, at a minimum, information concerning the society's social structure and the groups functioning there. The latter information is not easy to come by, especially in countries that are changing rapidly. In Nigeria, for example, there are—or have been—various kinds of cooperatives (Haig, 1950); "Young Farmers' Clubs" among the Yoruba (Faulkner, 1953); Boy Scout groups among the predominately Moslem youth of the North (A. Brown, 1947); and a variety of associations ranging from boys' boxing clubs to adults functioning as a community council, all organized by the Department of Social Welfare (Federation of Nigeria, 1959, pp. 2–6). There is no guarantee that at a given moment Nigerians will be present at the sites of such groups or that, whether present or absent, they will judge a particular communication in terms of that group's standards. A knowledge of the existence of these groups, however, suggests at least as a preliminary hunch the possibility that the sites and standards of judgment may be employed. This section thus ends on the practical, empirical note that needs to be struck many times in Africa.

X.A.2.e   The *form and content* of the communication obviously evoke predispositions that can exert an important influence upon people's reactions. The two are combined for the usual reason offered by many literary critics: they are likely to be so intertwined that a separation is painful and artificial. Members of the audience, it is simply being stated, are induced to perceive a familiar face, phrase, or value from the past within the communication, and they react appropriately. In the Anglo-Saxon world and elsewhere, a sharp distinction is often made between what are called arguments based upon "reason" and those that allegedly appeal to the "emotions." Intuitively most people believe the division to be valid: facts, evidence, and logic are part of reason, whereas loaded words, flag-waving, and chest-thumping are very emotional. The point here is not to argue—reasonably or emotionally—concerning the operational criteria of the dichotomy but to state firmly that those who make the distinction are likely to judge a communication favorably if they throw it into the category which they themselves favor. To a man who prides himself on his intellect and the control he exercises over what he dubs his emotions there can be nothing more damaging to the credibility of a communication than for him to say to himself or his associates, "Oh, that's just emotional." The reaction to the categories, however, should not obscure the real empirical problem of determining whether the effectiveness of a communication is affected by the inclusion or exclusion of certain appeals that pragmatically look "emotional," or at least are so judged or experienced by the audience (Hovland, Janis, and Kelley, 1953, pp. 56–98).

Reference has previously been made to the ability of Africans to comprehend motion pictures (VI.B.1.b; IX.D.1). The issue at this point involves not comprehension but the way they allegedly react to the content of the medium. Here, too, outsiders report that audiences in Africa are often different from those in the West. Reasonably representative of such generalizations is one mentioned to the Audio-Visual Deputation of the National Council of the Churches of Christ as they were visiting what was then the Belgian Congo:

> The African with little background for interpreting the motion picture tends to take what he sees literally. He does not always get the message intended by the producer. The motion picture, especially scenes of violence therein, tends to excite him, and often such violence strikes him as humorous [RAVEMCCO, 1953, p. 16].

Such a statement is not very precise; it does not indicate who "the African" is, under what circumstances it is possible for the audience to "get" or not "get" the producer's message, or whether the African is so different from audiences anywhere when witnessing "scenes of violence." The views thus expressed, nevertheless, cannot be lightly dismissed; they require empirical investigation. To the extent that an African audience differs psychologically from some other audience, their reactions to films may possibly also be different.

A specific question arises in connection with the form and content of films: Are certain African audiences at their present stage of contact with the medium more or less likely to generalize from one aspect of the film to another or to the film as a whole? An African audience, it is reported, reacted favorably to a film on the preparation of animal hides for market because it contained a wedding sequence which they knew to be true. Presumably there can also be generalization in reverse when a section of a picture is judged to be untrue or otherwise faulty. The same officer reports that in a film on tree-growing he did not show how the small trees that were the subject of the picture would look when mature, simply because the task of transplanting trees to a compound, which he would have had to do to achieve the effect, he found "too formidable." The Africans, however, noted the omission and were disturbed by it (Spurr, 1952, pp. 37, 41); were they consequently unable to accept the educational message?

In printed media, there is often a curious, amusing, and also pathetic conflict between the demands placed upon form and content by the need for intelligibility on the one hand and by the sensitivity of some Africans on the other. Intelligibility is increased by simplicity, for example, but Africans may find a simple style insulting. Thus the Associate General Secretary of the World Council of Churches has noted that most Africans require books that are "rather shorter than the ordinary English textbook, and couched in simple English style." Writers must express themselves "plainly" and they must try to avoid "that allusiveness that has been characteristic of English style since the Romantic movement." Without question such a view is sound as far as comprehension is concerned (IX.D.2.b). And yet the same source must also note that Africans reveal "extreme reluctance" to admit the possibility that they should have books different from those supplied to Europeans; simplicity they are likely to suspect as "something inferior and second-rate." In fact, he adds—without exaggeration, or without much exaggeration in the opinion of the present writer—"if you wish to make sure that a book will not sell in West Africa, all that is needed is to print on the title page, 'For use in West Africa'" (Neill, 1950, pp. 22, 27–8). Unfortunately, such suspicion regarding a simple style, though now largely groundless, stems from bitter, valid experience in the past; but it seems probable that African officials of the newly independent governments may consider the unhappy symbols associated with simplicity less important than the goal of efficient communication.

Just as membership in a group may or may not be salient during a communication, so the responses that can be expected to accompany a particular aspect of that communication are not necessarily evoked. The meaning of a word, for example, may be well known to a person, and it may have influenced him in the past, but its subtlety can easily remain unnoticed in a specific sentence. Likewise the social significance of any stimulus, profound as it is or has been, may have little relevance in a particular communication. Consider, for example, the name of a man's wife among the Tallensi of Ghana. An anthropologist points out that the prevailing rule of clan exogamy requires that she be addressed by a name which in fact indicates something about the clan of her parents. The appellation may refer to that clan's place-name, to an important spot in her natal settlement, to a custom or belief distinguishing her clan from her husband's, or to some office vested in the clan or the maximal lineage. Thus, the anthropologist concludes, the method of addressing a wife "shows how, without explicit formulation, the notions of locality, lineage, sacred attributes of the Earth, distinctive customs, and politico-ritual office—the major themes of Thale social and political organization—are linked together in a single ideological configuration" (Fortes, 1945, pp. 165–6). To understand communication between a husband and wife in this society, however, such a lucid, valid, anthropological description is insufficient: it is absolutely necessary also to know the extent to which either the man and the woman are in fact momentarily and consciously aware of the significance of her name when they are carrying on a normal conversation. Certainly the custom of addressing a wife in this manner must be, or must have been at some time, a function of the society's rule of exogamy; possibly, too, exogamy has been facilitated and in a given generation reinforced by the verbal tradition. If an unsubstantiated hypothesis may be offered, moreover, it seems highly unlikely, when the husband must quickly attract his wife's attention during a crisis, that he thinks of the societal connotation of her name. In this instance the responses that may and sometimes really do accompany the name either are not evoked or, if evoked, undoubtedly play a minor role in the reaction to the communication.

<hr />

For theoretical and especially for methodological reasons, the predispositions that are aroused by a communication must somehow be anticipated. Their *location*, it is felt, can be charted in two dimensions. First, do they reflect some general tendency within the society, within a group of that society, or within specific people or even a single person? Secondly, have they been or are they privately or publicly expressed? Obviously the two continua are not intended to be mutually exclusive.

X.A.3

The first dimension, then, may be called (a) *culture-personality,* for at one extreme are the phenomena of culture representing marked tendencies toward uniformity and at the other extreme, variations ascribable to personality. Attention is now turned to *culture.*

X.A.3.a.i

<hr />

The problem to be explored here is the following: How can the predispositions likely to affect the reactions to the content of the communication be anticipated? An assumption may be made that the basically important, the heavily reinforced, values of a society are evoked in a great many situations: by definition their central role within people has in fact such an operational meaning. Are there, for example, distinctively African values that appear in almost every African society? The prevalence of polygyny throughout the continent, according to one anthropologist, has already been mentioned (V.B.2). Another anthropologist believes that for all of Africa no other question is "of greater importance" than that of land, including land tenure: "it has special significance that goes beyond its economic value; it permeates every aspect of life— religious, emotional, and cultural" (Herskovits, 1959). Just as a knowledge of a society's organizations gives a preliminary indication of the sites at which people are to be found and of the groups to which possibly they may refer their judgments (X.A.2.d), so insight into such transcending values offers important clues to behavior. Once again, however, investigation is needed, in this instance to determine in some detail how the values are expressed in the society in which the communication occurs. Thus polygyny is declining in some areas more rapidly than others, either because men cannot afford to purchase additional wives or because conversion to Christianity tends to lead to the rejection of the practice.

The really critical part of an ethnography that contributes to an understanding of communication, therefore, is the section on the values of the society. Among the Tussi in Ruanda-Urandi, for example, it is reported that a man wants others to recognize his power and his courage; he wants the respect which comes from having many children; he wants to own cattle; he wants to display self-mastery; he wants to be known as a person who keeps his promises, who is generous toward his friends, and who is liberal toward the poor; and after his death he wants to be remembered as a great warrior or a powerful cattle-owner (Maquet, 1954, pp. 178–80). There is of course no guarantee that responses reflecting those particular values occur whenever a Tussi communicates or receives a communication, and indeed it is wise perhaps to retain a certain skepticism concerning the crisp statement of a society's values which a competent anthropologist is able to pull out of his field notes.

More specific ethnographic insight into values can be sought. Attitudes toward a communicator, for example, may reflect the general and the specific traits attributed to the ideal person in the society. Very frequently it is possible to indicate, or to try to indicate the nature of those traits. Thus the Mende of Sierra

Leone are said to approve the following qualities in themselves: "open-handed generosity," "extreme secrecy over personal affairs," "boisterousness," "friendly behavior," "nonchalance in the face of difficulty or danger," and "bravado." One consequence of this constellation is said to be that "a person, even an adventurer, may be courted and flattered so long as his success lasts; but, once unfortunate, he is likely to be reviled or forgotten, whatever past service he has rendered" (Little, 1951, p. 74). If this be so, then clearly the prestige of the communicator has a marked effect upon the reaction of an audience to his communication.

Like simple statistical material, information concerning any aspect of culture must be kept up-to-date. Probably anyone who has conscientiously prepared himself to work in an African society by reading its standard ethnographies before leaving home has been shocked to discover in a specific community that people do not behave the way they are supposed to. The ethnographies may have quite validly indicated the modal tendencies of the society, but the community at hand is not typical or has changed in the meantime. The present writer, for example, once watched the leaders of an Ewe community in Ghana perform a traditional ritual whose climax was the beating to death of two chickens. Everyone seemed to know that the ceremony was scheduled to occur, but the gongs had to be sounded again and again to assemble a small number of spectators. Those who finally did appear seemed indifferent or in a jocular mood as they watched the rite. Christians reported that they deliberately boycotted this pagan survival from the past. Of course the more basic values of a society are likely to persist, but an empirical check is necessary.

Any generalization about a society's evaluation of some specific component of communication is perhaps more practical and useful. People, for example, seem to have culturally determined associations with various colors, the kinds that appear especially in the extending media. For color itself, regardless of the terms through which it is expressed (VII.A.2.a.iv), is an omnipresent fact of life, hence likely to be affected by experiences more or less different in each society. One writer has sought to summarize "the mystical significance" of colors among people in the Malagasy

Republic. With *black*, he says, words like the following are associated: inferior, unpleasant, evil, suspicious, disagreeable, undesirable. With *white:* light, hope, joy, purity. With *red:* power, might, wealth. Even on this island, however, some variability is noted; for example, *blue* is "the favorite color of the Hova," but among the Sakalava it is "the color of mourning" (Leib, 1946, pp. 129–31).

Perhaps the most specific way to anticipate predispositions is to investigate directly those people who are likely to be the audience for the communication. This is the equivalent of market research in the West. Again the exploratory studies of the present writer in West Africa may serve as an illustration of the potentially useful information to be obtained by interviewing people. In the community about twenty miles from Kaduna, Northern Nigeria, the very small panel of 21 males who were the subjects in the first literacy study (VI.C.1.b) were asked questions about the subject of disease. "Why do people get sick?" "Allah" was mentioned by most people, usually as the sole explanation and otherwise in conjunction with other causes, such as water or dirt. In response to the very next question, however, one-third of the sample referred voluntarily to the role of the mosquito in the genesis of malaria. And then at the same time about one-third likewise had the unequivocal belief that "charms" alone can prevent disease, and another third qualified that belief by claiming that charms are efficacious only with Allah's consent or in connection with certain diseases. Clearly, then, if inferences may be made from such a small sample, these particular Fulani may be expected to respond to a reference to disease with a mixture of traditional, religious, and scientific beliefs.

For a communication reaching a large audience, it is important to know whether or not there is a modal practice, value, or form of knowledge in the community—that is, is there a tendency for most people to agree? Thus the description given above of the color associations of people in the Malagasy Republic indicates some variability from place to place. The second study on literacy near Zaria in Nigeria (see again VI.C.1.b) tentatively established for the very small sample of 19 males modal tendencies in some verbal areas but not in others. Most or all of the informants tended to approve of a chemical fertilizer promoted by the government (though virtually no one uses it); to possess very adequate scientific knowledge concerning "what causes crops to grow well"; to be unable to explain the phases of the moon except through a reference to Allah; to consider "dirt" an important cause of disease; to feel uncomfortable when attempting to employ polar categories, such as honest-dishonest or short-tall, in describing the same person; and to believe that money, food, property, and health are the most important goals in life. Simultaneously there was very little or essentially no agreement concerning each of the following: the reasons for not using the chemical fertilizer mentioned above; the credibility to be given "different sorts of people who tell you the news"; the kind of information it would be desirable to have "about the world that you do not know now"; and the explanation for the "troubles" that plague people. Again the findings are not world-shaking, but they suggest the degree of dispersion possibly to be anticipated in connection with specific communication themes.

X.A.3.a.ii Predispositions of specific people are discoverable at another level, that of the *subculture:* modal tendencies within the groups which compose the society.

The need for considering meaningful segments of a society is often shown in ethnographic reports which suggest marked variability from region to region within the same society. Among the Amhara of Ethiopia, for example, two seasons are distinguished, but the terms used to subdivide them "differ locally," no doubt as a result of variations in topography and hence climate (Messing, 1957, p. 7). Then, regardless of whether or not an adequate explanation has been or can be provided, a deviation has significance for communication at the moment. Anyone wishing to understand or employ the graphic signs, usually a series of vertical lines, to represent numbers among the Bambara of the Mali Republic, must know that the system "varies with regions and sometimes from one village to another" (Paques, 1954, p. 16).

A subgroup in every African society having distinctive predispositions, and hence usually requiring special forms of communication, is that of women. Moslem women are often in purdah and hence cannot be easily reached. Far fewer women than men attend school. Women, from the standpoint of change in the direction of the West, tend to be more conservative and perhaps more retiring. Frequently, in part because of polygyny, they must discharge a role in society subservient to men. Anyone who has worked with African women, consequently, emerges with suggestions for improving communication with them. One female missionary, for example, advocates that the teaching of hygiene, child welfare, or any aspect of public health be done for women by women teachers, for then the timid students can think, "If we are slow and stupid, we'll not tell anyone outside." (A. Fraser, 1932, p. 69). And yet women, let the sensational news be spread again (IX.C.2), are important in Africa too. In the mid-twenties the International Missionary Council issued this clarion call:

> One thing is certain: Africa will never be won for Christ until her women are won. Their sorrows, which are many, call for relief. A wise strategy would seek to enlist them for Christian Mission. Gain the women, and you will gain the men—the reverse is not so certain [E. W. Smith, 1926, p. 45].

A solution satisfactory from the mission standpoint, however, has not been forthcoming.

As indicated above (X.A.2.d), the existence of clubs and associations in a society in effect suggests, though tentatively, the kinds of predispositions which possibly can be evoked by a communication. Likewise a specific attribute of a group, such as its formal education, can serve the same function. When the curriculum of a particular school covers certain subjects, what can be said about the knowledge and hence the predispositions of its students? The "syllabus" of a famous school of community development in Kenya, for example, once consisted of "the history of Kenya; the economy of Kenya; the government of Kenya; some special social studies, e.g., family life, land tenure, pastoral customs; a general review of Kenya agriculture; hygiene; physical culture; music and drama; religious studies." Clearly the titles of the courses are by themselves insufficient. More details are needed, like the following: "In government the syllabus traces the growth of representative forms of local and central government during the period of British rule, and studies in detail the functions of local government institutions and the activities and responsibilities of the central government" (Porter, 1954, pp. 355–6). But even this is not enough, for it indicates only what graduates of the school in theory have been exposed to, not what they once learned, not what they now retain, not their idiosyncratic reactions to the materials and the particular instructors.

For Africa, however, the point cannot be sufficiently repeated, preliminary insights dare not be completely discredited, for even a crude guide to possible predispositions is usually better than intuition. "In the Eastern Region two out of every five children have a school place," a report from Nigeria states, "in the Western Region one out of every three, and in the Northern only one in twenty, with girls given less preference than in the two other regions which have declared a universal primary educational policy" (Pilkington, 1956, p. 220). If one knows absolutely nothing else about the three regions of this country, it may be tentatively assumed that differences in the school enrollments play some role in the reaction to many kinds of communications. As previously indicated (VI.C.1.b), education is also an index to literacy, which has important implications for communication in its own right.

The discussion of subcultural groups must end on a note of warning. Almost always the extending media, and sometimes, too, the basic media, reach not a single group but a number of groups simultaneously. From one standpoint everyone watching a ritualistic dance constitutes the audience, but in fact more than one group is likely to be present (for example, males and females, or nobles and commoners), each of whose predispositions may be somewhat distinctive. Perhaps, therefore, it would be safer always to use the word *audiences*—in the plural—in order to emphasize the subcultural variability.

Finally some predispositions are so unique that they must be
considered idiosyncratic or peculiar to the *personality*
X.A.3.   of someone in the audience. Almost any aspect of
a.iii   behavior of course is influenced by culture. In some
instances, however, it appears that the explanation
can be more profitably sought not in the culture or in the subculture but in the peculiar combination of events and influences
which compose the life history and hence the personality of a
particular individual. Ordinarily, at least in mass communications, idiosyncratic predispositions may be disregarded, but when
the audience is a single person and especially when that person
is important, because, for example, he is a leader, the nuances
must be taken into account. Personality traits which vary considerably from person to person, moreover, have been shown to
affect responses to communication. A general attribute of "persuasibility," for example, seems to characterize some but not other
Americans who have been used as subjects in experimental situations; and persuasibility itself is related to more general personality traits such as self-esteem and, to a lesser degree, aggressive-
ness (Hovland and Janis, 1959, pp. 225–34). The same investigators have summarized evidence indicating that such traits need
not be "bound" to particular aspects of the various communications received by people (such as certain types of communicators
or content) and hence may be relatively influential over a correspondingly wide range (Janis and Hovland, 1959, pp. 6–13).

The enormous or the slim differences which inevitably exist
between two people suggest why all communication is difficult
or, in another sense, why no communication is ever perfect. Even
the intimate communication between two lovers must somehow
manage to bridge the solipsistic gulf between them. By locating
dispositions as close as possible to the individual person, the observer increases the probability of successfully communicating
with a smaller audience; by locating them in the direction of the
modal tendency in the society, he decreases that probability but
increases the chances of affecting a larger audience.

What at first glance appears in a small group or in a single individual to be an idiosyncratic departure from culture or tradition

may turn out to be almost completely socially determined; hence the communication must be considered relatively structured rather than unstructured (VI.C.2), and no explanation in terms of personality has to be provided. Why, for example, does this Sotho woman call the grain "flower of the corn" (*chake*) instead of employing the customary, straightforward term "corn" (*poone*)? Or why does this pagan Hausa man never use the name "Friday" to refer to the day of the week and instead consistently calls it "the day of Gwarzo" (i.e., the chief market day of the town of Gwarzo, which happens to be Friday)? The word "corn" is not taboo among the Sotho, nor is "Friday" among the pagan Hausa—for most people. But these two individuals are not following personal whims to be traced to early childhood experiences. Among the Sotho a woman may not pronounce the name of her father-in-law; if his name has as one of its referents a common object to which she frequently refers, she is then forced to substitute another name for that object by borrowing one from a foreign language like Zulu or by inventing or adapting one; in this instance, since her father-in-law has the name of "corn," she uses a completely different word that refers to the grain's flower and yet conveys the intended meaning (Laydevant, 1946, p. 84). Similarly among the pagan Hausa the name of a child may not be spoken in communicating with others; the father of a boy called "son of Friday" has found an adequate substitute for the name of that day (Greenberg, 1946, p. 21).

Deviant behavior in a society may communicate the fact that some systems of communication have been unsuccessful. Such cases, however, are usually presented in a tantalizing manner: only the fact of the deviation is mentioned, not the reasons for it. The importance of the age or circumcision group to the individual among the Kikuyu of Kenya has already been mentioned (III.B.2.a.iii; VIII.A.4). Each group there names its annual festival after some event around the time of the original initiation ceremony. The group initiated in 1898 referred to "the year of the jigger or the burrowing flea," 1901 to "the year of the hyena," and 1907 to "the year of lying on back." The last title was derived from a "rare occurrence" in the society: one of the boys ran away to avoid being circumcised and so had to be "forcibly operated upon in that attitude," which was commemorated in the group's label

(Routledge and Routledge, 1910, pp. 10–11). Nothing more is
said about the rebel.

The second dimension along which predispositions can be located would indicate whether they have been previously or are
at the moment being *expressed privately* or *publicly*.
Such information is useful for two reasons. First,
public expression provides data concerning the existence of the predisposition: a man who shouts loudly
the praises of a communicator and who also attends continually to
him reveals a predisposition more plainly than one who broods in
silence about his attachment and shyly avoids the display of his
feelings. Also, shreds of evidence in the West suggest that people
who commit themselves publicly to a point of view are less likely
to be affected by a contrary communication than those whose beliefs and feelings have remained private (VIII.C.2).

X.A.3.b

A person who takes an oath that he is telling or will tell the
truth (for example, at a trial) is in effect communicating a message which suggests that in the future he will never be able to
forget any falsehood he may be tempted to utter. He usually
swears the oath in the presence of an audience and of an object
such as a sword, a skull, a tree, a tool, a book, or ashes. The human witnesses, he knows, may enforce the oath or apply sanctions
in the future if he fails to carry out his promise; the very appearance of these people and of the objects will always remind him
of the oath and of the punishment that transgression will bring.
During the oath-taking, therefore, he also communicates to himself the nature of the punishment as well as the identity of the
enforcement agencies and the symbolic reminders. The oath itself may contain a reference to symbols such as lightning, ancestors, or gods who can make their presence felt, the man tells himself, suddenly and without warning. Learning during the oath can
be made more impressive by some unusual action; thus among the
Malabu of Nigeria a man avers that disputed land belongs to him
by eating a piece of earth as he says, "If this is not my earth, then

may I never eat the fruits thereof and live" (Meek, 1925, v. 1, pp. 264–5). Among the Bachama in the same country a man who publicly swears a false oath believes that the spirits of a hillock which he sees every day "will cause him to swell as though with child till he dies" (Kirke-Greene, 1955, p. 49). He must realize privately that he will never be able or allowed to forget the pending punishment, and he is thus provided with a powerful motive to tell the truth.

------◆◆◆◆------

In concluding this section it is well to emphasize once more a point that has been previously suggested, especially in connection with voluntary movements of the human body (III.B.1.c.ii): there is no certain method of decoding communications which might enable an investigator to attach similar significance to one of its components in different cultures and hence to anticipate from the communications the kind of predispositions likely to be evoked. In the area of language, although research on "phonetic symbolism" suggests the possibility that certain sounds as such may have a meaning transcending a particular culture (R. W. Brown, 1958, pp. 111–39), no crude—and certainly no subtle—idiom is likely to be comprehended directly by anyone unacquainted with the language. How do people react to the fact that in some societies an African man always walks along a path ahead of his wife and in others he always walks behind her? The order of march does not necessarily reflect and hence consequentially communicate information concerning the status of the two sexes in the society, as it might in the West, rather its significance may be different in each society: in one, the man goes first in order to defend her in case an enemy attacks, in another he follows her because he has little confidence in her integrity and hence would keep her in full view (Driberg, 1932, p. 404).

Any type of communication, no matter how simple it appears on the surface, is likely to convey subtleties that are immediately intelligible only within a particular culture area. When someone says "no," does he really mean "maybe"; or does "tomorrow" really imply "never"? Is it permissible to ask a direct question to elicit information? When one person addresses another person in a

loud voice or in an excitable manner, is he himself disturbed or
calm? How far away from each other should two people stand
when they are carrying on a formal or business conversation?
The answers to questions like these, it has been suggested, involve nuances of communication which show vast cross-cultural
fluctuations. Thus a speaker conveys the quality of sincerity to
an Anglo-Saxon when he talks calmly but to an Arab when he
talks loudly (Hall and Whyte, 1960). Since such variability occurs
in people's reactions to the same component of a communication,
the communicator must either understand beforehand the culture of his audience or else obtain—through feedback (XII.A)
—some information in the course of communicating. In the same
sense, however, variability exists not only between cultures but
among people of the same culture. Each man attaches slightly
different meanings to the words, the postures, the products, and
the actions of others. Differences resulting from personality, consequently, loom large in the analysis of communication. The singularity of every situation and every man again must be trumpeted.

X.B
Interplay People in a mood react to a communication: to some extent they comprehend or fail to
comprehend its message and then various predispositions within them are evoked. Some sort of interplay
occurs between their comprehension on the one hand and their
mood and predispositions on the other. The interplay of these
tendencies can be conceptualized in terms of harmony-disharmony and comfort-discomfort.

X.B.1
First, an expository paragraph about *harmony-disharmony.* Harmony suggests congruence, on the conscious or unconscious level, between understanding
and the other tendencies; the message is in accord
with the philosophy, viewpoint, credo, values, desires, impulses,
etc. of the audience, however one wishes to summarize their prior
and immediate reactions. "To find the man, turn left after passing the tall cottonwood tree"—harmony here means that the listener comprehends the referent of each word and of the entire
sentence, that he has no contradicting information concerning
the location of the man, that he trusts the person giving the direc-

tion, that he has no fear of cottonwood trees, and that in truth he wants to find the man. Fancier modern terms for disharmony are *conflict, incongruence,* and—above all—*dissonance.* Research on the consequences of disharmony indicates not necessarily the form of behavior which ensues but, most significantly, that some reduction or solution will occur, in large part because people almost always find such a state of affairs intolerable and unpleasant. The communication concerning the left turn at the tree would produce disharmony if the recipient had been previously told by someone else that the man could be found by turning to the right near the skunk-cabbage patch. Obviously there can be various forms of harmony and disharmony. The individual, for example, compares his own goal with what he believes to be that of the communicator or the communication; this goal of his, moreover, may be structured in individual or in group terms. If in individual terms, he considers himself out of social context or at least in a generalized context: Shall I vote for this man? If in group terms, he is concerned with what he and fellow members of a group seek: If I vote for him, what will my friends think? Research in the United States has shown that individuals tend to respond to communications in a manner that makes the various components of their attitudes as consistent as possible under existing conditions (Rosenberg et al., 1960); and that, when a discrepancy is noted between the standards of a reference group and the communication goal, the influence of the communication depends in large part on the prestige of the reference group (Hovland, Janis, and Kelley, 1953, pp. 139–44).

———•———

Disharmony is avoided in many situations simply by interpreting an event in terms of an acceptable principle. The converse of a proposition may not be true from the viewpoint of formal logic, but calling it true brings comfort in real life. Thus if it is believed that A produces B, thereafter B may be attributed to A and to nothing else. The temptation to do this is especially great when B is disturbing and when a reference to A cuts off further discussion or when A itself cannot be easily tested and hence disproved. A dramatic illustration is provided by a Hausa woman in her own words. First she states the general proposition that B follows A, and then she ascribes two cases of B to A:

> The thing that causes a person to be ill in this way is that his mother has not been careful when she is suckling him; she should always cover her other breast with her cloth, so that no milk shall fall on her child's genitals. If milk falls on them, they will die. If the child is a boy, he won't be able to do anything with women; if a girl, there will be no entrance, it will be blocked up, or her genitals will die. Her husband will send her away, she won't be able to bear children. If a man, he will not seek after women. . . . Some of [those to whom the misfortune occurs] work very hard at farming, we had one in our *rinji* [place where slaves worked] at Karo, he worked very hard indeed, but he did not go after women, he had no power. . . . Then there was a girl who was not healthy, she came to New Giwa, she came from the south; her name was Shekara. She was beautiful with light reddish skin. [A particular man] desired her, she was very beautiful with her firm round breasts, but after a short time she left his compound. At first it was said to be a lie, but indeed it was true. Closed up, who would touch her? [M. F. Smith, 1954, pp. 147–8].

A harmonious reaction to a communication is likely when a culturally stereotyped response is evoked that is also in accord with the impulses of the audience. According to his son, one African goldsmith among the Malinke living in Guinea often required a special communication before he would set to work to smelt gold and produce a delicate trinket. A female client would employ an official praise-singer who, while playing on a harplike instrument, heaped so much praise on the smith's ancestors that "my father's vanity" became "inflamed" and he would set to work. The communication of praise continued. As the jewelry took shape, the singer reached a high point of ecstasy. At the very end, as the completed product was about to emerge, he intoned "the great chant" reserved only for celebrated men (Laye, 1954, pp. 32–9).

A discrepancy between the goal of the communicator and the

audience usually reflects differing experiences in the past and hence diverse values. All missionaries in Africa begin their work by assuming correctly some disharmony between the church's views and those of potential converts; otherwise they would not be motivated to proselyte. A communication advocating blouses for females among the Bwaka of the Congo, who, as previously indicated (III.B.2.b.ii), think that only prostitutes wear clothing above the hips, must perforce seem discrepant to that audience. On a more cerebral level, missionaries are concerned with differences between their own religion and the religion of potential converts. To attain a higher degree of Useful Understanding, a distinction has been made between Africans "who are of the opinion that all things have been in existence all the time and were not made by anyone outside themselves" on the one hand and those who "are in agreement that there is a Maker" (E. W. Smith, 1946, p. 31). The opinion is expressed that "most" Africans fall into the second rather than the first category; hence relatively little disharmony originally exists between their views and those of Christianity.

Naturally, in establishing the degree of harmony between the two forms of religion, more is involved than the attitude toward creation. For the missionary's arsenal contains many other central beliefs, such as a sense of sin, shame, or guilt; a conception of the soul or spirit; and the certainty of everlasting life. Whether or not Christians and Africans have harmonic views on such basic issues is not easy to determine, either in advance or sometimes after years of proselyting communication. The existence of a taboo in an African society, according to one observer, by no means indicates that people have a sense of sin from the Christian viewpoint. For them the taboo is "essentially an amoral restriction" in an animistic sense, whereas for the Christian sin involves a "moral code." Likewise a belief in spirits does not bring people closer to Christianity; among the Grebo of Liberia, more concern is shown in "placating bad spirits than supplicating good ones" (Nida, 1952b, p. 25). On a less basic but practical level—that of Useful Understanding—parallels in the content of African religions and that of Christianity can be discovered which then may be utilized in communicating with African audiences (I.B.3).

Disharmony in religious beliefs, however, need not be resolved. Among the Hausa of Nigeria, for example, some people continue to believe in the existence of pagan supernatural beings long after adopting a monotheistic religion like Islam (Greenberg, 1946, pp. 67–8). In this instance, perhaps in all such instances, the disharmony is perceived by the outside observer and not by the audience: they may keep the two seats of beliefs in different compartments and hence not experience disharmony.

Sometimes the communicator assumes disharmony between himself and his audience when none exists. One missionary, for example, attempted to have a group of African mothers give their babies a daily bath. She felt that she had "almost persuaded" them to accept this standard practice from the West. Finally one of them told her that she could see merit in the new plan: "It would save so much trouble compared with washing them three times a day as we do now" (A. Fraser, 1932, p. 15).

Besides creating some harmony or disharmony, the interplay between comprehension and mood or predisposition produces feelings and drives that fall along a continuum here called *comfort-discomfort*. Under discomfort appears

X.B.2   a long list of human miseries: anxiety, fear, frustration, insecurity, etc. There is no consistent relation between harmony-disharmony on the one hand and comfort-discomfort on the other. A man being given directions may understand what he has been told and have complete faith in the communication, but he can be thrown into terror by the thought of the person who dwells to the left of the tall cottonwood tree. Likewise discrepant information need not produce discomfort: a contradiction can be intriguing and can be resolved without feeling psychologically disturbed. Discomfort, whatever the particular form, drives people to action, not only to perceive a communication (IX.B.2) but also to change and to adopt new forms of behavior.

One of the principal tenets of officials engaged in what is called "community development" in Africa is the concept of "felt need."

People, it is said, are more likely to change their community when the initiative comes from themselves rather than from government. They are willing to make sacrifices which they would reject from interlopers. They are thus in a mood to be instructed, that is, to receive and react favorably to communications. There is no discrepancy between their comprehension and their predispositions or needs; those needs, being unreduced, lead to the actions involved in improving or developing their community. The present writer, for example, once observed the following sequence in a Ghanaian community: the elders wanted to improve teaching in the local school; they decided they would have to attract a more competent teacher, and that such a person might agree to come if a good residence could be placed at his disposal; the chief and some of his advisers consulted government officials regarding the financing of the project and building techniques; then men from the village took turns working on the house until it was completed.

The idea of the "felt need," however, appears to be a pleasant fiction most palatable to people with democratic, grass-roots leanings, but not an entirely accurate reflection of reality. First, according to some experts, it is "naive" to think that people will spontaneously feel and then express the needs which, from an outsider's standpoint, are being unsatisfactorily reduced. In Ruanda-Urundi, it is said, the Belgian Administration took the first step by deciding upon the measures that would promote social welfare and then allegedly Africans agreed and were ostensibly happy (Elvin, 1957). Also people may feel the need to achieve a particular goal (e.g., abolishing a disease), but find the means proposed not in harmony with other habits. If that is so, then the task becomes one of strengthening the felt need and deliberately changing preferences concerning means.

Indeed at some point the proponents of the doctrine indicate that action by government rather than the spontaneous expression of a popular need is the decisive factor. One writer, for example, states that the aim of community development is to "help people reduce some of the tensions that they have so far failed to reduce." Fine, but he also adds another goal which people themselves cannot possibly be anticipating: to assist a community "better to resolve the new tensions that further change may bring."

If the changes cannot be foreshadowed, people must have only the glimmering of a "felt need" to reduce the consequent discomfort. The kinds of intervention proposed by the same writer sound sensible and reasonable: "stimulating people to decide exactly what it is they want and then helping them to get it"; "introducing people to new kinds of satisfactions and ways of realizing them"; and "maintaining existing groups or developing new ones to ensure that each individual has opportunities of developing his personality" (Batten, 1957, pp. 223–4; italics omitted). These proposals, however, depend not on the felt needs of people but on the wisdom of the communicators. Another writer comes closest to a realistic statement when he states that those officials who toil in the vineyard of community development are in truth "vitally concerned in the task of translating an unrealized need into a felt one" (Jackson, 1956, p. 9). Let not the impression be gained that only a verbal quibble is involved here; for at issue is the question of the extent to which Africans and therefore human beings can control their own destiny through the discontent that inspires action.

XI. CHANGES

The final boundary of a communication as such usually involves some kind of change. Most communicators seek either to change their audiences or to prevent them from changing; or unintentionally or consequentially some innovation is induced. New information that has been perceived and comprehended is likely to produce further repercussions within people. Even when old information is received or old values reaffirmed, the context or the site may be different; the ensuing reinforcement alters the strength of that old tendency quantitatively if not qualitatively; and the audience if only by growing older reacts somewhat differently with the passing of time. The changes are conceptualized in this chapter under two headings: the nonovert, which must be inferred, and the overt, which can be directly observed.

XI.A *Nonovert Changes* Since action originates from tendencies within people, changed tendencies precede changed action. The nonovert changes can be conceptualized by indicating their type and content.

XI.A.1 With respect to *type*, terminological diversity abounds; and so recourse is made again to two of the terms previously employed to describe the content of

XI.A.1.a the communication, information and values (VII.B).

Information refers to people's beliefs, knowledge, opinions, or stereotypes. These are the propositions which everyone holds about certain aspects of the world, including himself. The question implicitly asked about information is: "Is this true?" or "What grounds are there for accepting or believing this?" The inquiry may be nothing more than a fleeting flutter, but at a minimum the reliability of the communicator or the medium is established. The siren sounds, and instantly those acquainted with its assigned meaning formulate, as it were, a proposition concerning

313

the imminence of danger in a somewhat new context which they must also grasp.

A number of problems occur in connection with the receipt of information. Clearly people hold beliefs with (i) varying *degrees of certainty*, which they themselves are often able to specify with little difficulty. Then knowledge has (ii) a *temporal aspect*, which here seems divisible into the categories of *present* and *anticipated*. People's beliefs pertain to propositions which they now know to be true or which they think will be vindicated in the future. At the present time the sun definitely has not risen, for it is dark; but its eventual rise above the horizon can be anticipated with supreme confidence.

The other kind of nonovert change, involving people's feelings and attitudes, can be summarized by a reference to their *values*. The telling question here pertains not to truth but to goodness and badness: "Is this good?" or "Is it good for me?" The problem arises on a mundane or lofty level when people ask themselves whether the information or advice in the communication should alter the support they give to some proposition or cause. As already indicated in other connections, attitudes may be scaled, and on the scale three points may be singled out: (i) *favorable*, (ii) *neutral*, and (iii) *unfavorable*.

XI.A.1.b

Varied relations exist between knowledge and belief. Knowledge of an event, for example, can affect people's attitude regarding the occurrence or the participants. A favorable attitude toward a person may induce an audience to acquire more information about him. As a result of such interplay, the content of a communication may or may not produce the anticipated nonovert or overt changes. A message appearing to involve only the knowledge of the audience may in fact change some of their values and induce them to take unanticipated action.

─── • • ───

People can learn to behave differently toward a person when they have received information about his changed status through an extending or a basic medium of communication: his skin is scarred, he wears different clothes, he displays insignia, a public announcement is made, etc. It is quite possible that elaborate ceremonies to signal a change in status serve the function of communicating the change so dramatically that forgetting is not likely. Among the Lele of the Congo, people's knowledge concerning a so-called "village wife" at first is gradually but later is decisively altered. About one-tenth of the women in the society occupy this polyandrous position that is held in high esteem. During a trial period whose duration can be from a few months to a year, the woman has intercourse with a different man in her hut every two nights; and anyone in the village has access to her when she goes into the forest during the day. But then her position is regularized at a special ceremony: she prepares for the men whose common wife she will thereafter be a meal which is eaten in the middle of the village; presumably in this way everyone is made acquainted with her new status. The men also pay a substantial dowry to her father and mother, as a result of which they can recover damages from anyone who sleeps with her in her house, but not from males of the village who may continue to have sexual relations with her in the forest (Tew, 1951, pp. 3–4).

New information must likewise be acquired by Africans after increased contact with the West. Sometimes outside communicators seek to change their knowledge along certain lines because changed information, they feel, will engender changed values. Missionaries, for example, are interested in education per se and also as a way of reaching and influencing their audiences. Here is how one missionary, reporting from the area of Lake Nyasa at the start of the century and following a Policy of Flexibility for educational rather than religious matters, suggested that the two forms of communication be combined:

> The first lesson was "A watch and how we divide time." The division of the day into hours was explained to them on a large blackboard. . . . The watch was then compared with the world, and it was shown that the latter must have a maker as well as the former. The second lesson was "Cotton and its uses," from which the people were shown the necessity of a change in the natural heart before it can be useful. The third was "How we communicate with each other," and from

this they were taught how God communicates to us His love
and grace [Beach, 1901, p. 464].

The technique here seems direct and straightforward. The interest
in the lessons as such enables the communicator to reach his audience, that is, to have them perceive the rest of his communication (IX.A.3). The new information on world affairs serves as an
analogy for information on spiritual and religious matters. The
implicit suggestion, which must have been explicitly expressed,
is that true information on both levels is good or that the form
of religion being communicated is as inevitable as the natural
phenomena.

It should be obvious that a communication can change or influence the information of an audience without affecting their
values. In an experiment previously described in part (VI.A.5),
the present writer read a communication on soil erosion to a
sample of 98 Ganda males and one on nutrition to a sample of
61 Zulu. Prior to receiving the communication and again a half
hour afterwards the men's opinions on the issue were obtained.
For the Ganda the before-question was: "What should be done
with people who do not cooperate with the government in check-
ing soil erosion?" And the after-question: "A person who does not
cooperate with the government in preventing soil erosion should
be put in prison for a year; do you agree or disagree?" Almost
20 per cent in each sample shifted their view in the direction of
the communication. But can the conclusion be drawn that the
communication produced the shift? No, for almost as many in a
control group of 27 Ganda and 36 Zulu, who were randomly selected, who replied to the same before- and after-questions, but
who were not presented with the communication, shifted too;
hence the changes in the experimental groups must be attributed
to chance or to imperfection in the questions seeking to ascertain
values. In spite of the fact, then, that no significant change in
values occurred, the communication had an effect upon the samples: over three-quarters of the Ganda and exactly two-thirds of
the Zulu could recall some aspect of the communication when,
without previous warning, they were suddenly asked to do so
about two hours after originally perceiving it. Thus knowledge

about soil erosion or nutrition improved without a change in values (Doob, 1957b).

The reverse situation can also occur: people's values can be changed without a corresponding effect on their knowledge. A film on smallpox which was shown to audiences among the Yoruba in Nigeria, according to a well-documented investigation, "did not affect their belief that spiritual forces have a part in the transmission of smallpox, but it seems to have persuaded some of those who saw it that vaccination was a protection for the individual, possibly analogous to a charm." The value of vaccination advocated by the film was apparently learned but for the wrong reasons. In addition, another item of information in the picture was discredited: members of the audience could not believe that vaccination is "painless and harmless," because a man known to them personally had apparently suffered unfortunate after-effects from that inoculation (Morton-Williams, 1953, p. 27).

XI.A.2   Little time, space, or energy needs to be devoted to the *content* of the nonovert changes resulting from a communication, for the same categories must be involved as those utilized to describe the evoked predispositions: (a) the *communicator*, (b) the *goal*, (c) the *medium*, (d) the *site*, and (e) aspects of the *communication* itself. Undoubtedly a change in one component is followed by a change in one or more of the others. A communicator who discredits himself, for example, is likely to make his communication less acceptable; and a discredited communication undoubtedly has negative effects on the prestige of the communicator and his medium.

It is possible to show that some institution in a society, through communication, alters people's information and values about any one of the components just mentioned. Here one instance is considered, a ceremony in which the participants apparently seek to change the reactions of an audience to themselves as people and potential communicators. Among the Fulani in Northern Nigeria, there is an annual flogging contest, in which youths between the ages of 10 and 17 are the communicators. With large switches pairs of age-mates beat each other's bare backs in turn until one of them withdraws or shows signs of feeling pain. By these actions, young unmarried boys convey their physical prowess, especially to women who demand that husbands possess this attribute; and newly married men demonstrate their fitness to attain the status of full manhood in the community (Whitting, 1955).

XI.B *Overt Action* Almost always the critical question eventually asked about a communication involves the action of people to which it may lead. For the communicator wishes his communication to have social significance, and significance is appraised by behavior or conduct. After being exposed to a communication and after changing nonovertly, then, does the audience change overtly?

XI.B.1.a The *occurrence* of the action can be viewed variously. First, there is the logical possibility that changed action *"never"* occurs. Quotation marks enclose the word to call attention to its connotation of finality and hence to warn that the concept must be cautiously employed. The communication advocates a declaration of war and there is no declaration; can it be said that the indicated action "never" occurs? At the moment it is easy to observe whether war has started, but it is another matter to determine the role of the communication in a series of events leading to some future conflict. And then there may never be a war, but still the original communication can affect some related or unrelated form of action.

Of all the possible kinds of communication, those with emotive goals seem least likely to lead to significant action and yet on occasion of course they may do so. The hypothesis has been advanced, for example, that in Africa the so-called ancestor cult "forms the most important soil for the growth of figure sculpture." According to the theory, the figures are carved as a resting place for wandering souls, which remain dangerous until they come to rest there. They are iconic so that the souls may be attracted by dwelling places similar to the ones they have left. The sight of the figures, consequently, reminds the living that the souls of their ancestors are not moving about and, as a result, anxiety on that score is presumably reduced. Up to this point, then, there is communication without action. But action does occur: the figures are the sites at which sacrifices are made and other tokens of respect are displayed in order to keep the souls within their new residences (Schmalenbach, 1954, pp. 108–14).

XI.B.1.b   Perhaps the category of *unascertainable* brings one closer to the truth concerning action which appears "never" to occur. Here the analyst or the communicator is limited by the fact that he can make only a small number of observations at a given time, and also by the fact that the actions take place later when observations are no longer possible. Then, too, the forces producing action may be so numerous and intertwined that the effect of a single communication cannot be isolated.

The role of specific communications in producing change after contact with the West seems especially difficult to ascertain in Africa. A very simple event may be so inadequately reported that a connection between the communication and the action cannot be inferred with any confidence. The following incident comes from a Daily Vacation Bible School in the Congo:

> Shortly before noon each day the children were given a Bible picture to color which represented one of the stories told that day. The use of crayons was a novel experience for them and many were hesitant. However after an initial try they were thrilled with it and the teachers were amazed with the results [Burkett, 1954, p. 14].

Very little about this device is mentioned beyond the fact that the children learned to use the crayons. Was the message of the Bible picture communicated to them more effectively *because* they colored it? How much of an increment in knowledge was there over what they may have learned from only hearing the story? What effect did the experience have upon their immediate and subsequent feelings about Christianity and—finally—upon their overt actions? The effect is unascertainable and, from the mission's standpoint, not worth investigating, for the assumption seems to be that faith is constructed and then reinforced by a long series of communications and actions.

Through sheer will power and steady observation, an attempt can be made not to isolate the role of a particular communication but to seek to ascertain the effect of a complicated pattern of communication upon general modes of behavior. Among the Soga of Uganda, for example, traditional villages were neither isolated nor self-sufficient, since they were bound together through a central authority and since they had contacts with other societies, especially by way of Arab and other traders. The coming of the British produced many changes. A European town, a large one, has grown up as the seat of European government and as a place for Europeans to live. Nearby is another town for African local government. Roads have been built over which people travel in buses, cars, and bicycles. A railroad passes through Soga country. Postal and telegraph services are available. What have been the effects upon people of these modes of transportation and hence of communication? All conceivably relevant details are lacking, but the hypothesis has been proposed that "without these technological innovations, lineage structure would be even more effectively shattered" in particular areas. The structure has been weakened by the fact that people's neighbors no longer tend to be lineage-mates; but the improved transportation facilitates visiting, especially on weekends, so that lineage ties can be retained through contact and direct communication (Fallers, 1956, pp. 59–61, 115–16). It should be evident that the nexus between one set of facts (changes in the lineage structure) has been boldly made by the observer, but of course it remains only a reasonable, unprovable hypothesis. For perforce there is no comparable society that can serve as a control case.

XI.B.1.c

Obviously there is a temporal dimension to *ascertainable* action: the action may be (i) relatively *immediate* or it may be (ii) *delayed*. Other things being equal, the connection between communication and action is probably more certain and easier to determine if the action is immediate. "The animal is behind the third bush," the scout says, and the hunter quickly fires in that direction. The radio listener who again and again hears tales about a particular subgroup but who behaves no differently toward its members until he thinks the appropriate moment arrives is exercising his privilege to delay but is playing havoc with research.

———•———

The reason for the delay in carrying out an action can often be traced to practical matters rather than to the absence of nonovert change. In Kenya it was once reported that "very little propaganda is needed to induce natives to build better houses"; the principal obstacles to overcome were "ignorance of the methods of building something better than the old round hut and inability on the part of the man who wished to build to provide the necessary funds for the purchase of material" (Gilks, 1935). The first obstacle suggests only the failure to receive communications, which apparently after being perceived would have been successful; the second one, insufficient money, of course is not peculiarly African. Action may not follow effective communications for other mundane reasons. The Community Development Department in what was then the Gold Coast, for example, sought to persuade farmers to spray their cocoa trees in order to combat a devastating plant pest. The campaign succeeded so well that the demand for sprayers quickly exceeded the available supply, and the interest of 3,000 farmers had to be maintained until new stocks arrived from overseas (anon., 1955).

In any society the most significant delay between communication and ensuing action is connected by and large with the process of socialization. Over a period of years the growing child receives communication after communication which affects him not only immediately but also later when he matures. Of course there are complicating factors: what the adult does also depends upon his physiological maturity and upon the communications he subsequently receives, but significant portions of his predispositions and hence of his personality have been shaped previously. For this reason the communications accompanying socialization can be said to be successful determinants of action merely because they occur; without their occurrence socialization would be different and adults would be different.

Close examination of the communication aspect of socialization in a society reveals the techniques with long-term consequences (II.A.2.b.i; IX.A.3.a). Among the Tallensi of Ghana, these purposive communications have been reduced by one anthropologist to three "fundamental learning processes." First is imitation. After hearing his sister call out a message to another child at some distance, the boy of five, "equally interested in the other child," repeats the message in the same words and tone. The boy acts as a recipient-disseminator of the communication: like his sister he seeks to attract the attention of the distant child; he evidently understands that her communication is likely to achieve its objective; he echoes the message as best he can; and he is in a position in which any errors in transmission—for example, the mispronunciation of a word—can be quickly corrected. Secondly, the child models his values, aspirations, and conduct after the parent of the same sex. Here the parent must have prestige and the child probably a favorable attitude toward him or her; and the parental communicator administers appropriate and tangible rewards and punishments. A third technique is cooperation, an illustration of which is:

> The little girl who goes with her mother to the water-hole and is given a tiny pot of water to carry is making only an infinitesimal contribution to the household's water supply. Yet it is a real contribution. She learns to carry her little pot of water in relation to a real need of the household [Fortes, 1938, p. 48].

The media of communication here seem to be the mother's action and the miniature pot; the "real need of the household" is also felt by the child, who undoubtedly is rewarded symbolically for playing her role.

--------◆◆◆◆◆--------

XI.B.2 Since the ultimate aim of most communication is to affect action, it becomes necessary at some point to consider the *relation* of that action *to the communicator's original goal.* The point selected is here and now. Certainly a distinction must be made between (a) *achievement* and (b) *nonachievement,* and the latter can be broken down into subcategories such as (i) complete *rejection* and (ii) *rejection* but the *attainment of some other goal.* Such concepts must be immediately clear, except for the last one, which refers to goals either in opposition to those of the communicator or to ones which are just different. An advertisement, for example, reminds people that they need a particular product, and then they go out and buy one from a competitor of the communicator who set off the impulse.

Achievement or nonachievement, however, cannot be glibly determined. For at one end there is the problem of determining the precise goal of the communicator, and it has been strongly emphasized that some of the goals he seeks or attains (or both) may be different from the ones he consciously would reach (II.B). At the other end is the problem regarding the occurrence of action, already mentioned in the previous section and to be discussed in the next chapter during a review of the methods of appraising feedback, viz., the determination of a causal connection between communication and action (XII.D). Both ends meet, too, in connection with analyzing the content of a communication (VII.B). No certain solution exists for this recurrent problem, other than being alert to its significance and expecting singular solutions in each situation.

A communicator can achieve his goal with one audience, but as a direct result may unwittingly alienate another group. Those reacting negatively in effect say they can have no respect for a man who attracts such followers, or for the communication which succeeds in doing that. Here other people become the medium of transmitting a consequential communication (IV.B.3.g).

The achievement or nonachievement of a goal can be assessed more easily sometimes when nonovert change rather than action is involved, but only by assuming that the meaning of the information being conveyed is universally recognized by virtually everyone in the society. When a person says, "The grass is wet," his precise motive for transmitting the information may be debated, but anyone familiar with the language must understand the content or the reference of the statement. Other media besides language can be just as unequivocal. "If one met a group of young girls" among the Zulu in South Africa, it has been observed, "one could tell immediately which of the group had recently fallen in love, and which were too young for love affairs." That vital information is conveyed by beads. Until maturity, for example, a Zulu girl wears only one string of beads around her waist, ankles, and wrists. When she falls in love, she announces this fact both to her lover and the community by changing the beads on her body (Twala, 1951, p. 114). Now the goal of the Zulu girl, like that of the observer of grass, cannot be determined with dispatch, nor can the actions of her lover and the rest of the population, but a high degree of success for part of the communication undoubtedly can be presumed.

In many instances, especially when an objective index of behavior is available, it may be possible to skip from the communication to the action and ignore the intervening processes. An example can sharpen the issue. Traditionally among the Ibo of Nigeria unmarried girls wear nothing except a string of beads around their hips, for only those who are pregnant would seek to conceal their condition; clothes, consequently, are reserved for married women. In one community the executive committee of a welfare association considered the practice immoral, but they as well as the Native Authority Council believed the tradition too strong to be affected by direct action. Instead they issued an appeal, they circulated rumors to the effect that the police would arrest unclothed girls who appeared in the government station, and they publicly ridiculed girls who did not cooperate. The observer reports: "The campaign, really directed at the parents and future husbands of the girls, was on the whole successful" (Ottenberg,

1955, p. 20). Such a conclusion is based on a leap from nudity-be-fore-the-campaign to nonnudity-after. No evidence concerning the actual reactions of the girls, their parents, or their future hus-bands is offered. Obviously, all three groups must have been ex-periencing some kind of conflict, for they knew the traditional views and also the new proposal. The success may very well have depended also upon simultaneous changes in the direction of Eu-ropean culture, which, among other things, postulates a connec-tion between morality and clothes. Certainly the campaign played a role, but only in conjunction with other previously established dispositions; it may be called a pragmatic success, nevertheless, since that role must have been a major one.

The success of a communication can sometimes be inferred even when the precise action is not specified. The application of severe sanctions by a group, besides showing that past communications have been effective, suggests the likelihood of significant changes in action for the future. Once a youth among the Tallensi in Ghana died of dysentery after being served porridge that was cold rather than, in accordance with established custom, hot. The old woman who had broken the tradition was accused of bewitch-ing the young man and thus causing his death. She was sent for and found guilty by a diviner; according to an anthropologist who was present throughout the episode:

> In vain she protested her innocence. The head of the youth's maximal lineage told all his people to mock her . . . with a derisive chant. Neighboring clans took up the chant, as she passed on her way home, and some weeks later it was made the theme of one of the dance songs [at a festival]. "Wherever she goes," my informants said, "men, women, and children look askance at her and jeer at her for being a witch. Shame and grief will dog her, and she will pine away and die" [Fortes, 1949, p. 34].

It is not reported whether or not the lady did die, but there can be no doubt that this barrage of communications must have af-fected some of her overt behavior.

The difficulty with many traditionally stereotyped messages is that, without the kind of investigation which no one really wishes to undertake, it is not possible to say how seriously they should be analyzed as forms of purposive communication. Among the Mende of Sierra Leone, for example, a girl receives her first name three days after birth during a brief ceremony. The woman whose name the child is to bear "takes her out in the early morning, faces the sun, spits on the child's face, and says, 'Resemble me in all ways and deeds, because you are named after me.'" Now will or will not the child, after she comes to realize the significance of the name and perhaps sees a similar ceremony performed for other infants, model her behavior, consciously or unconsciously, after her namesake? No answer can be given; and the mystery becomes denser when it is pointed out that this original name is abandoned at adolescence, after the girl has been initiated into a secret society. In addition, whatever action may persist from the spitting ritual becomes enmeshed in other influences if the girl attends a mission school: there she not only changes her style of dress, her coiffure, and her ways of expressing herself verbally but she also acquires a Christian name after being baptized (Little, 1951, pp. 113–14, 117). The message from the woman to the infant undoubtedly serves a purposive function within Mende society and provides a consequential communication concerning its social structure, but the decision as to whether the expressed goal—"resemble me in all ways and deeds"—is or is not achieved at some time must be left unmade.

To account for the total or partial failure of communications is also not easy. A critic of present missionary work in West Africa, himself a minister and an ardent supporter of missions, has speculated concerning the reasons for the greater successes recently achieved by Islam in comparison with Christianity. He says, "we have to face the fact that, if we rely wholly on spiritual methods, Christianity will not be spread abroad, for we must remember that our conception of religion and secular spheres is alien to the African's conception of the unity of spirit and community." Africans, in effect, do not possess the predispositions to which Christian doctrine often appeals. In this situation, he recommends two Flexible Policies. First, like Islam, Christianity must offer material inducements: "Conversions in general take place not because of new insight into reality but in direct ratio to their immediate utility." Then, Christianity in effect must become less egocentric (IX.D.2.d): "May it not be that the true mission is not 'conversion,' with its implication of religious superiority, but 'dialogue,' a mutual communication and encounter which leads to mutual growth and understanding?" (Trimingham, 1955, pp. 42, 50). An authority like the author just cited is arguing ex cathedra; he knows that Islam has been gaining more converts than Christianity and he is appalled, too, by the loyalty which Moslems show to their religion; and he then offers intelligent, well-informed speculation as the explanation.

So often communications in Africa fail not because members of the audience have responded unfavorably but because they are prevented from carrying out the relevant action by restrictions they themselves cannot overcome (VI.C.2). Newly independent nations in former British areas have been calling in their colonial currency and issuing new notes and minting new coins in the old form of pounds, shillings, and pence. Like educated people in the United Kingdom and the United States, African officials appreciate the greater utility of the metric system not only for currency but also for weights and measures; yet the introduction of a completely new system, after using the British method for so many years, is expensive and awkward. Another example involves a different type of innovation. Moslem men in Northern Nigeria may become convinced that drinking water ought to be boiled and filtered. Within their homes unboiled, unfiltered water, however, may continue to be drunk since the kitchen is not their domain and their wives, especially those in purdah, cannot be easily reached by adult-education officers and, if reached, are likely to find the extra work onerous.

One final caution regarding the achievement or nonachievement of the goal of a communication: the action following receipt of the message, being dependent on predispositions, may vary considerably from group to group within the same society. Among the Amhara of Ethiopia, for example, men greet public announcements with "respectful silence." Women, on the other hand, indicate "actual or pretended joy with their joyshout"—and by "joyshout" is meant a distinctive expressive sound (Messing, 1957, p. 520). Among the Hausa in Nigeria, women but not men "wail" when they receive the news of someone's death (M. G. Smith, 1954, p. 264).

At the conclusion of a communication campaign it is usually important to know not only whether the immediate objective has been attained but also whether people have changed in other respects that are important either in their own right or else, conceivably as a form of feedback (XII.A.1.c), have implications for future communications. In an Ewe village of the T.V.T. (Trans-Volta/Togoland) region of Ghana, the local authorities once staged a campaign to wipe out malaria. With the aid of the World Health Organization, people were given information about malaria and were also persuaded to swallow weekly doses of an antimalarial pill. The taking of the pills followed a simple routine: each week an official distributed them to clan chiefs, who in turn gave them to families. From the standpoint of action as such, the campaign was most successful: the incidence of the disease was reduced almost to zero. The present writer in 1959 tried to determine whether people of this experimental village had learned anything more than that pills prevent and help cure malaria.

To investigate the problem, another village was needed in which the people were roughly the same but in which no antimalarial campaign had been staged. Outside the psychological laboratory or in the absence of the captive subjects found usually only in schools and armies, perfect control groups are not easy to assemble. As a result of the splendid cooperation of the authorities, the two villages eventually studied seem at least to be superficially similar: they are the same size, located off a main road, and adhere to traditional forms of agriculture and social organization. They are not identical, however, in at least one respect: the control village is less than ten miles from Ho, the capital of T.V.T. (in which Western influence tends to be strong), and the experimental village is twenty-five miles away.

In a brief time only samples in each village could be interviewed, and indeed the two samples had to be selected in different ways. In the control village the chief called people together and, following the tradition of the palaver, explained to them that the European sitting in front of them was carrying on an investigation and he urged them to cooperate. A prolonged, cordial give-

and-take occurred, during which the chief talked to his people and they to him through his linguist and the writer to the chief and the people—and vice versa—through his interpreter, who thus fitted perfectly into the role of the linguist (I.A.2.b). At the end of the friendly discussion people readily, even eagerly, agreed to receive the stranger. Under such favorable circumstances it was hoped to obtain a random sample. A chart of the dwellings in the village was prepared, and houses were selected in accordance with a systematic sampling procedure. In each house one person was to be interviewed: in the first, the husband; in the second, the senior wife; and so on in alternation. The time chosen for interviewing was right after marketing days when people are likely to be at home. In spite of a strenuous effort on two different occasions to find or make appointments with the 30 selected potential informants, the result was quite disappointing: out of 15 males, only 9 were successfully interviewed; out of 15 females, only 3. In the experimental village, the chief produced 12 males of unknown representativeness and an African government official dragooned 9 females who were haphazardly selected from her adult-education class for women.

Each informant was interviewed alone, in the malaria-rife village within or close to his home, in the other village at a central and somewhat isolated place out-of-doors. The questions themselves on the whole were open-ended and straightforward. They began with the perfunctory greeting, "Are the children well?"; proceeded to census-type requests ("Roughly how old are you?"); shifted to the area of disease; continued with a projective problem about race relations; and ended with inquiries concerning crops and the differences between living and nonliving phenomena. An interview lasted between 15 and 45 minutes and was conducted in Ewe.

Few significant differences between the two villages appear when the results are analyzed, but of course with such small samples the differences must be extremely large not to be attributable to chance. In each instance, nevertheless, slightly more of the sample from the experimental village than from the control possessed knowledge that may be related to the communication campaign. More of them mentioned (a) the mosquito as the exclusive cause of malaria and (b) pills as the exclusive cure for malaria. The campaign, furthermore, may have had repercussions of two kinds. Significantly more experimental than control informants flatly denied that "spirits" can affect the growing of crops; and, secondly, more of them expressed favorable attitudes toward Europeans in replying to a projective question asking them to imagine what an Ewe and an European might be talking about if they were seen together on a road. In absolute terms, however, four facts suggest that the campaign clearly did not influence everyone in the experimental village:

1. About one-quarter of the sample still thought that the traditional remedy for curing malaria—drinking a concoction made from certain leaves and herbs which have been boiled—effectively combats malaria either alone or in combination with the pills.

2. "Sun and heat" were mentioned as the cause of malaria by more people than any other cause.

3. About one-third believed that "spirits" affect crops, but every informant in both villages saw a connection between crops and the fertility of soil and rainfall.

4. Finally, there is no relation between the belief that pills and only pills can cure malaria (an avowed objective of the campaign) and the possibly related belief that plant growth is unaffected by "spirits" on the one hand, and various ambitions, the tendency to seek distant rather than immediate rewards, and the degree of contentment on the other hand.

Aside from demonstrating the difficulty of conducting clear-cut research in a limited time, this study suggests that a campaign on a community level can be immediately effective in terms of action without necessarily affecting people's beliefs and attitudes either on very relevant or distantly related matters.

It is always important to note, when possible, who has understood or responded favorably to a communication and who has not (IX.C). In a miscellaneous group of adult males whom the chief of a small village in Northern Nigeria once hastily assembled as this writer and his friends suddenly appeared, only one old man could be found who had any knowledge about world affairs, including some recent developments in the field of atomic warfare.

To all the rest it seems the mass media had failed to communicate such information, but with him they had been successful, undoubtedly because he alone in the village had a radio. Under some circumstances such as a crisis, this limited success might be crucial: the man could pass on information and, if his status were high—in fact, it did not appear to be—he could become an influential recipient-disseminator.

———◄••••►———

XI.C   *Reinforcement*   The changes resulting from a communication, whether they be nonovert or assume some form of action, eventually lead or do not lead to the reduction of whatever drives have been evoked. There follows harmony or disharmony, comfort or discomfort. When the audience is thereby satisfied, activity for the moment ceases, or rather people engage in some other activity. The goal of the communicator and his communication is achieved if the changes producing a satisfactory state of affairs are the very ones that have been sought. Then similar conditions in the future are likely to reinstate a similar series of events: when the appropriate drives have been evoked, a similar communication is sought, the communication is similarly comprehended, similar values are evoked, and similar action takes place. The repeated word obviously is *similar*, not *identical*, since some variability can always be detected.

From the standpoint of the communicator, satisfactory reinforcement is necessary when he must frequently transmit a communication. In carrying on psychological warfare against a specific enemy unit, the goal is to communicate successfully once and only once. Here the communicator wants that unit to surrender or to become so demoralized that it loses the battle and hence never again can be his audience for such a communication. Even in this instance, however, the more usual problem is to be effective on one occasion without appreciably damaging one's credibility as a communicator in the future: the unit does not surrender or is not wiped out; instead it must be pounded with communications day after day (Doob, 1949–50). The latter in fact is the prototype for most communication which must recur regularly or irregularly, since the communicator wishes repeatedly to be understood and have his advice heeded.

The permanence of the change produced by a communication depends upon many factors, which can be sorted out into those originating outside and inside the audience. Directions for reaching that man who still lives to the left of the cottonwood tree may be comprehended and followed successfully, but the visit is not repeated. The change in knowledge and the consequent effect on action are thus impermanent; why? External circumstances, on the one hand, may not demand a repetition of the visit: the person receiving and following the directions moves away from the tree or, if he remains in the neighborhood, he avoids the man only because the occasion for seeing him a second time does not ever arise. On the other hand, he may be unable to recall the route when he wishes to repeat the visit, or he may just never wish to see the fellow again after an unfortunate experience with him during the last visit. Naturally, more realistic situations cannot be so blithely analyzed, but it seems evident that once more the factor of repetition must be considered in connection with the internal circumstances of forgetting and disliking.

Repetition, let it be repeated, affects the mood of the audience (VIII.C.3) as well as the probability of the audience's perceiving (IX.A.2.b) and comprehending (IX.D.2.a) the communication. Now it is being said that the communication will be forgotten or disregarded unless there is repetition that reinforces. The last clause is the important one: the communication may be repeated again and again, but it may not be perceived and comprehended and it certainly will not reproduce overt action unless somehow people's drives are satisfactorily reduced. At least retention is much more difficult and forgetting correspondingly more likely in the absence of reinforcement. Although the directions past the cottonwood tree may be shouted from the housetops or flashed in neon lights upon the firmament, they will go unheeded by those who need them not or, having followed them, find them to be either incorrect or to lead to a disagreeable experience. Research on communication in the West suggests that memory for communications follows roughly the same course as almost any other kind of behavior (Hovland, Janis, and Kelley, 1953, pp. 241–53).

For effective communication, therefore, activity is important. By being active people may create within themselves a mood that affects their initial reaction to the communication (VIII.E). By doing what the communication tells them to do, they may come to appreciate its value to them. "It is a recognized fact," a UNESCO report states without documentation, "that people retain an average of only 20 per cent of what they hear, 30 per cent of what they see, 50 per cent of what they both see and hear, and 70 per cent of what they actually do for themselves" (UNESCO, 1958, p. 9). The statement may exaggerate the state of affairs and certainly there are cultural and individual variations in the effects, but without doubt the action stemming from a communication may effectively promote its retention.

The sparsity of extending media of the preserving type, especially writing, in traditional African societies; the difficulties that thus arise in keeping a record of the past; and the consequent efforts to devise media and techniques that can perform such a function have been noted in other contexts (IV.B.2.c; VI.C.1.b). In effect, consequently, Africans have not had objective models which could reinforce, positively or negatively, their conception of what either they themselves or their ancestors have experienced. Under these circumstances memory of the past is likely to be dependent less on facts and more on fantasy. That fantasy, an anthropologist cogently argues, is directed by present needs requiring satisfaction: "pre-literate peoples only take pains to preserve versions of their historic past which explain their existing social grouping and institutions," indeed "these versions of the past may have scant relation to the actual sequence of events in the case of the tribe concerned." She herself noted, after returning to the Bemba in Northern Rhodesia twenty-three years later, that fewer names of great chiefs in the past could be recalled; when old men were shown her photographs of a late paramount chief, they exclaimed, "The chief himself! We had forgotten how he looked! That was the way he folded his cloth! That was how he leant on his staff!" At the same time, each generation must face the problem of distributing "political rights" to people and to groups on the basis of claims originating in the past. To establish the claims legitimately and thus avoid and resolve social conflict, functional fantasy alone is insufficient. The prevailing version of history must be sustained through a "mnemonic system" that provides realistic reinforcement to people again and again. Devices like the following are employed: kinship terms, which indicate conveniently the important social relations in the society; the inheritance of name and status, which helps people to retain past associations with a particular position; the formal recital of names and events on ceremonial occasions; assigning "ownership" of a genealogy or historical event to one group, which is thus motivated to preserve its "property" in memory; and deliberately teaching the facts of lineage and political power during socialization (Richards, 1960).

Conformity to any significant institution within a society is likewise learned through a long and continuous series of communications that serve to reinforce both meaning and action in appropriate situations. At the outset, for example, the audience may be compelled to undergo a profound experience which will make them grasp the meaning of the communication; later reminders are provided to prevent forgetting. Among the Azande of the Congo and the Sudan, the establishment of blood brotherhood between two men is a very important act which affects the future behavior not only of the pair but also of all members of their clans. A pact is concluded under solemn circumstances that are likely to be remembered: the two men, alone or in the presence of relatives, soak pieces of special wood or groundnuts in each other's blood, which flows from incisions especially made for that purpose. Forever after each man knows that he has inside himself some blood from his new brother; and blood, according to conventional symbolism, has various properties which function as reinforcing agents. Blood can "act of itself" under certain circumstances. If one of the men has sexual relations with the other's wife, and even if he keeps the deed a secret, he and his kin can be destroyed by the brother's blood inside him. In addition to such heavily reinforced self-reminders, there are public forms that can be employed to preserve the pact. When one man feels injured, he may utter a spell which can cause his blood to avenge the injury, perhaps even by exterminating the blood brother and his relatives. Public censure may be added, for a person not fulfilling the obligations of the pact becomes "an object of contempt to his neighbors and of shame to his kinsmen" (Evans-Pritchard, 1933).

It may very well be that a significant index to the importance of an institution is the type and frequency of the communications which are associated with it. Among the Jie of Uganda, for example, there are at least fifteen different ceremonies before, during, and for a few years after a wedding. The first takes place when the girl's family is approached to give their approval to the marriage. The tenth follows the birth of the first child: to indicate his own pleasure and that of his kinfolk over the success of the union and simultaneously to "ensure its further success and fertility," the wife's father kills an ox in his kraal and gives her its hide. And the fifteenth and final ceremony admits the woman and her children into the husband's clan: her father again supplies a ritual ox to signify his complete approval of the marriage and, after prayers for the permanence of the marriage and for her continued fertility, the wife is led through the cattle gate of the central cattle kraal into the husband's homestead. It comes as no surprise, after noting the period of time covered by these ceremonies and their elaborate symbolic character, to have the anthropologist point out that marriage is considered by the Jie to be "not just the act of making a girl the wife of a certain man" but a ritual whose aim is "to found and establish the legal, social, and spiritual elements of the marital union between the man and the woman, to ensure and maintain the fertility of the wife and the welfare of her children, and to produce and strengthen the vital affinal relationships" (Gulliver, 1953).

The one institution which always reflects and affects reinforcement patterns within a society is language: words occur frequently and they economically remind people of prevailing practices and values. Among the Amhara of Ethiopia, only noble women are not considered to be basically inferior to men, nor are they treated as such; but they and all other women are thought by men to be "psychologically" inferior. The weakness is regarded as "biological, intellectual, and moral." Expressions within the language, consequently, cast aspersions upon women. The term for "vulgar language" is literally "woman's language," whereas that for "polite language" is "man's language." A talkative man can be insulted by calling him "womanish." There are proverbs which make the same point: "Women and donkeys (must be trained) with a stick"; "Even if a woman has knowedge, (only a) man knows how to hold on to it" (Messing, 1957, p. 422).

Learning by doing rather than by listening or watching is a theme that appears very often in connection with significant changes being introduced into Africa from the West. "It is one thing to give a lesson on malaria," a missionary has written, "another to set out to drain off puddles of water and scatter paraffin on the breeding places of mosquitoes," for in general terms "a pupil will learn and remember better by doing than by memorizing from a book" (D. Fraser, 1928, p. 144). Or in the specific view of a medical missionary writing from Angola: "Demonstrations, teaching, and visual education are of doubtful value if not accompanied by creative activities." In fact there may be resistance:

> Every time we repeated the story of hookworm and its toll of broken health there was just that much less desire on the part of the hearers and viewers of Disney's "Lazy Joe" to get busy and dig latrines. . . . There seemed to be a bell in men's minds sounding: "Tell us something new; we've heard this before" [Gilchrist, 1957, p. 67].

Evidently insufficient reinforcement comes from passive learning so that, without appropriate action, medical information is forgotten.

Likewise a skill imported from the West needs to be exercised again and again under satisfying conditions if it is to be retained. After adult Africans have painfully become somewhat literate, they must be provided with interesting and important materials to read. Otherwise they occupy themselves in the traditional ways or succumb to competitive distraction from the outside such as radio or motion pictures. In the West, the mass media that do not require an ability to read arrived after the literacy rate had become high; but often in Africa and in similar areas they precede universal education. Reading matter for Africans tends to be scarce and not especially attractive. As already indicated (VI.B.2), the production and distribution of books and pamphlets in vernacular languages are generally so expensive that they are beyond the means of private enterprise. Libraries exist in the larger cities, and "library vans" travel into the countryside. "Mobile sales vans" are recommended, but they are not "an economic proposition." Efforts are made to have government announcements of public interest appear in the relevant African languages on posters so that people may be induced to read them (Mullane, 1956; Du Sautoy, 1956). Newspapers and magazines are often published in African languages, although usually the efficient, fast-moving organ is in a European language. When Africans acquire a desire to keep informed, and especially if they live in relatively inaccessible areas, they usually depend upon radio and not printed media for the latest news, or rather the latest tidbits of news.

Still another way to assess the reinforcing value of a system of communication is to examine a doctrine that has come into Africa from a different culture and has become a durable part of many African societies. Such a doctrine is Islam, which has appealed tremendously to millions of Africans and, at the present time, is gaining more converts than competing forms of Christianity. Unless otherwise specified, the analysis here stems largely from that provided by a Christian minister who is an outstanding scholar of Islam and whose friendly criticisms of the approach by Christian missions has been quoted in the previous section of this chapter (Trimingham, 1955). Certainly religion—any religion—involves more than a system of communication, but just as certainly each religion offers frequently exercised modes of communication.

In the first place, the clergy who communicate the Islamic faith are easily recruited and instructed, and as a result they are widely scattered through the African population. Only "the minimum of training" is required: sufficient is "the merest smattering of the Qur'an [Koran] and a knowledge of the regulations of Islam." Under these circumstances, a Moslem village is likely to have a number of part-time clergymen who also carry on as cultivators and traders while simultaneously serving as "representatives of the vast heritage of Islam." In contrast, Christian clergymen usually must study for years at a theological seminary and must pass examinations. Being fewer in number, those finally ordained are assigned to areas containing many actual or potential parishioners with whom they, unlike their Moslem counterparts, cannot usually be on intimate terms. In addition, most Islamic clergymen are lay Africans, whereas even now virtually all the professionally trained Christian missionaries and the majority of Christian clergymen are Europeans. It is not surprising, therefore, that "Christianity is still identified with the West" and that Islam is considered by Africans to be "the religion of the Blacks." In brief, in comparison with Christians, Moslem clergy are more likely to have their message perceived because they are more numerous, because they are more strategically located, and because as Africans they probably possess more prestige.

Secondly, communications from Islam have been hospitably received by so many Africans for cultural reasons: they reflect a really Respectful Attitude toward traditional African customs and hence demand relatively little change. Obvious and important is the harmony between Moslems and Africans with respect to polygyny. Similarly Islam has no objection to other traditional African customs which Christianity has also rejected, such as the bride-price system and many so-called "animistic" practices.

Also, it appears as though Islam strengthens many African institutions while simultaneously and gradually changing them in a manner that favors the new faith. The naming ceremony in West Africa, which often occurs eight days after the birth of a child, has been accepted by Islam but transformed: "The local cleric is always present to name and shave the child and sacrifice the ram." Christianity, on the other hand, has ignored this rite and instead has substituted another ceremony, baptism, which turns out to be "entirely extraneous" from an African standpoint. A Moslem clergyman almost always is at hand for every African ceremony, including those in the home, as a consequence of which "the worship of God belongs to the routine of daily life and does not involve a Sunday suit and perhaps a long walk to the edifice of a particular sect." Or, as a conference of Christian missionaries has observed: "It is the secret of the marvellous success of Islamic propaganda that it brings the Africans a more sure knowledge of the God of whom they are already aware" (E. W. Smith, 1926, p. 42). The changes advocated in the communications and the doctrine of Islam, moreover, can occur without disrupting the everyday existence of Africans.

Islam, like every great religion, offers its adherents a complete philosophy and system of ethics. When people have been brought up in the Moslem tradition or converted to its spiritual doctrines, therefore, the favorable predispositions are so strong that they are likely to resist basic changes from the outside. Thus material innovations from the West may be accepted by devout Moslems because they do not conflict with those predispositions, but the "deeper cultural and spiritual traits of Western civilization" are not perceived or, if perceived, they are rejected. Faith in Islam is made more durable because of the information which action communicates. "The African," an African Christian once stated, "knows that he is welcome in any mosque, and he also is aware that there are Christian churches into which he cannot enter—simply because of his color."

Finally, it appears that the all-embracing, powerful faith in Islam is communicated to Africans in a form that by and large demands and hence receives from them no critical evaluation. Most Moslem towns have schools or at least a teacher, a *malam,* who transmits a knowledge of the Koran, of moral duties, and of correct rituals. Parents may send their children to such schools at a very early age, even at three or four. Both boys and girls ordinarily receive an hour of instruction before and also after sunset so that they may perform their normal duties (such as working in the fields for boys) during the day. Virtually none of the pupils ever learn Arabic, instead they are taught to recite in unison and thus memorize long passages from the Koran without understanding the meaning. Long ago it was noted that this system of indoctrination prevents African disciples from having access to the liberal aspects and achievements of modern Islam (Meek, 1925, v. 2, pp. 8–9).

The experience of Islam in Africa, a swift summary can state, supports a variant of a well-documented hypothesis of modern social science: significant changes are induced by communication when they repeatedly and ultimately provide meaningful rewards.

XII. FEEDBACK

The special kind of communication through which the communicator becomes acquainted with the fate of his communication, including its transmission and the reactions of the audience, is called "feedback": information about his own efforts is fed back to him. In this sense there is zero feedback when the poet dies before anyone reads his sonnet, or quite complete feedback when the speaker knows immediately whether he has been understood by observing his good friend's facial expression. Usually a communication provides some feedback, however imperfect. The poet does not die, he hears people report pleasure, pain, or nothing at all as they read his creation. The moment a communication is transmitted through an extending medium like print or stone there can be subsequent feedback even in the absence of the original creator. After the death of the poet, his heirs or his publisher decide whether past sales justify a new edition. Feedback is especially important when a series of communications, rather than a single communication, appears, for the experienced communicator has not only practiced the art of communicating by exercising it frequently in the past, but also has been able to judge which of his efforts have been successful and which unsuccessful. A new communication thus is likely to depend heavily upon the communication fed back from an old one.

XII.A   *Occurrence* The *temporal relation* between the communication and feedback is relatively easy to specify. For it is necessary only to know when the original communicator or his agent makes an observation or an analysis. In the first place, feedback may be almost *simultaneous:* while the communication is in progress, the communicator himself receives information concerning the transmission of his message or the reaction of the audience; as a result, he is able to adjust his communication accordingly. The speaker at a meeting notes that people at a distance cannot hear him; he signals to his associate to step up the volume of the public address system.

An instance of feedback is reported by a team surveying missionary work in Africa:

> In the homiletic classes, we frequently found that the sermon-pattern of the West was being followed slavishly, with the familiar introduction, three main points with the subheadings, and application. The interesting and revealing thing was to see how, very often, a sermon outline in writing was made to follow this pattern and accepted by the teacher; but the actual sermon preached, not in English but in the vernacular, would instinctively move completely away from the outline pattern; it would usually sound more relevant to the congregation than the suggested outline [Neill, 1950, p. 47].

The changes made by the student-ministers undoubtedly came about not "instinctively" but as responses to cues provided by the congregations, such as symptoms of restlessness or boredom. Conceivably, too, the communicators, being Africans, functioned as their own audience before appearing in church: they could feed back to themselves dissatisfaction with the conventional pattern of the sermons and then plot the changes in advance.

XII.A.1.b Another temporal form of feedback is *subsequent*: after the end of the communication, the communicator receives relevant information about the transmission and people's reaction. The information may arrive relatively soon or be long delayed. Such feedback obviously cannot affect the communication concerning which it conveys information, but it can contribute to the education of the communicator and hence perhaps increase his skill in the future. Subsequent information of some sort is essential to be able to detect the appearance of so-called "sleeper" effects, viz., changes that occur after the perception of the communication. Evidence in the United States suggests that, since people tend to forget the source of a communication unless it is deliberately reinstated, a communication from a source with low prestige is likely to prove as effective as one from a source with high prestige after time has elapsed (Hovland, Janis, and Kelley, 1953, pp. 253–60).

XII.A.1.c — Subsequent feedback from one audience is *antecedent* feedback for the same or similar audiences in the future. The methodological question here is straightforward: to what extent can it be assumed that the same audience remains sufficiently unchanged or another audience is sufficiently similar to enable information from the past to be used in the future? The identical sampling problem occurs when, in the absence of suitable subsequent feedback, information concerning a communication is collected in advance by staging a rehearsal or by pretesting the message on a smaller but similar audience.

Since instances of subsequent and antecedent feedback are given later in this chapter under Methods (XII.D), only one incident is reported now to show how modern market-research techniques are being employed in Africa. The editors of a religious journal in Nigeria describe how they pretested photographs:

> Before each subsequent issue we submitted different series of group photographs to a panel of Africans chosen because of their diversity of intellect and occupation. One by one they considered the groups, not realizing the great importance we attached to their reactions of delight or lack of interest. We found that photos of most appeal were those of human interest. Never once did anyone in this panel choose a scenic photo such as would appeal to European taste [Shaw and Shaw, 1956, pp. 42–3].

Although details are lacking, the procedure at first glance seems ideal: the evidently representative informants were permitted to react spontaneously to the photographs. It would be interesting to know how their cooperation was obtained; why, for example, did they think they were being asked to look at the materials? The validity of the procedure is reported a bit vaguely: photographs selected by the panel "appeared in the next issue and appealed to all readers, well-educated and new-literate alike." Without carping, it must be said that information is needed concerning the way that appeal was ascertained. And without appearing rude, or very rude, it seems necessary to add that the style of reporting—"never once," "all readers"—makes the results of the feedback sound a little too journalistically sweeping to be convincing or credible.

———————

XII.A.2 The *frequency* with which feedback occurs may also be noted. No necessary connection exists between the amount of feedback and the validity of information thus conveyed, for a single report may be better than a long series of inaccurate impressions. Three points along a continuum of frequency can be quickly indicated. Feedback, in the first place, is provided (a) *once or very rarely*. There may be no more than a single opportunity to procure the information: the equivalent of a market survey is completed and then funds for this sort of research are exhausted. Or the communication itself may occur only once: the author writes a single book, the criticisms of which make him devote his energies to other activities. Or the communicator, after obtaining the desired information, feels so confident that he no longer seeks to check his own efforts. Then, in the second place, feedback may be (b) *sporadic*, when opportunities arise from time to time or when the communicator believes that occasional probes suffice. Finally, there is (c) *continuing* feedback: information flows in regularly, and the communicator presumably profits from the yield. Indeed the effectiveness of a communication may be dependent upon continuing feedback not because the communicator thereby obtains relevant information, rather because the audience becomes favorably disposed by being provided with some means to express and thus also to commit themselves. Under some circumstances not yet well understood, for example, audience participation in a decision sought by a communicator is more likely to lead to the appropriate action or to nonovert changes than a direct communication accompanied by little feedback; at least this finding emerges in American investigations (Hovland, Janis, and Kelley, 1953, p. 217).

———————

Only a simple instance of feedback is usually necessary to determine whether a particular translation evokes the desired or valid response, provided that the person serving as the audience is a competent speaker of the language. The statement by Jesus that "my sheep follow me" can be expressed for the Kpelle of Liberia in three ways: "follow me, but at a great distance"; "stalk" or "chase after me," with the implication of evil intent; and "follow behind me, your leader" (Nida, 1952a, pp. 49–50). A single Kpelle assistant can immediately indicate the distinctive connotations of each translation and can thus feed back to the missionary the information that the third one conveys correctly the Biblical meaning.

Again and again throughout this book references have been made to the shifting Attitudes, Understandings, and Policies of missionaries in Africa. The principal changes during the century have been from a Disrespectful Attitude to an Attitude of Respect-with-Reservation, but not to forthright Respect; from Little or No Understanding to Useful but not to Pure Understanding; and from a relatively Inflexible to a relatively but not completely Flexible Policy. Why, the question may legitimately be asked, have there been such significant shifts? With the passing of time, it would appear, more and more information has been fed back from Africans to these outside communicators, as a result of which the modern missionary is not only more skilled in the use of communication media and techniques but also more sensitive to the needs and feelings of his audience, provided that they do not conflict violently with his own significant religious principles. The sensitivity comes from firsthand observation of Africans and of the effects of proselyting and also from the codified wisdom of previous generations of missionaries, whose experience is handed down by reports, by word-of-mouth, and eventually by teaching in mission schools.

Many of the earliest European missionaries did in fact enter the continent for the first time a century ago with No Understanding and hence a Disrespectful Attitude and an Inflexible Policy. In an imposing *Cyclopaedia of Missions*, it is first stated that "though debased by their heathenism, yet the inhabitants of Western Africa are not to be ranked among the lowest of the human race." A paragraph after that faint compliment, the peoples are thus objectively described:

> Selfishness, the controlling principle of the heathen heart, has full sway here. The principles of justice, the rights of individuals, the rules of decency, the voice of humanity, the ties of kindred and friendship, are trampled under foot. Theft, falsehood, fraud, deceit, duplicity, injustice, and oppression, are favorite agents and constant companions. Intemperance, licentiousness, gluttony, and debauchery furnish the ailment upon which it feeds. It is almost impossible . . . to say what vice is preeminent among these degraded natives. Falsehood is universal. . . . Theft, fraud, and intemperance are considered as praiseworthy acts. Chastity is an idea for which they have no word in their language, and of which they can scarcely form a conception. . . . Their intellectual faculties are obtuse and circumscribed, almost beyond conception. Beyond a few local associations, the ideas of the most intelligent native on the coast of Africa are not one particle above the speculation of a child in this country of two or three years of age. And over such minds, superstition reigns with absolute sway. . . . Even *cannibalism* prevails to some extent, in connection with punishment for witchcraft. A man's importance in society is regulated by the number of his wives; but between them and himself there exists no affection [Newcomb, 1854, p. 59].

Now, after more than a century of feedback, one observer from the mission world admits without hesitation that "Western ideals of morality rarely apply to African institutions" (Trimingham, 1955, p. 39); and an International Missionary Council Conference in Ibadan, Nigeria, in 1958, has made the following declaration in the preamble to a section called "Christian Marriage and African Tribal Customs":

The early missionaries, when they encountered the tribal patterns of the people to whom they preached the Gospel, realized that many of the established practices conflicted sharply
with Christian standards. This is still true. However, it is more
clearly recognized today that the wholesale abandonment of
some of these practices, without the provision of adequate
equivalents, can lead to a breakdown of social organization
which creates new evils as damaging as the old. Moreover, it
is now acknowledged that there are features of tribal practice
which are consistent with Christian principles and therefore
worth preserving [Carpenter, 1958, p. 26].

The last sentence of the quotation suggests the shift in Attitude:
African customs are no longer completely rejected, they are partially accepted. It is "still true," nevertheless, that no amount of
feedback can modify some sections of Christian belief. Missionaries, it once again appears, never allow themselves complete license to commit the "naturalistic fallacy" for the sake of expedi-
ency. Feedback provides only relevant data, whose implications
are then evaluated. The section immediately after the preamble
just quoted, for example, lists "Practices the Church Should Dis-
courage," and the first to be discouraged "actively" is "female circumcision or clitoridectomy." Now it happens that many Africans
just as actively support that practice: "This operation is still regarded as the very essence of an institution which has enormous
educational, social, moral, and religious implications, quite apart
from the operation itself" (Kenyatta, 1938, p. 133).

More important than the issue of clitoridectomy is the practice
of polygyny. On this point the Christian Church has always been
officially adamant. In contemporary Africa, however, there are
reports of missionaries who try to avoid noticing the plural wives
of some of their converts, especially the strategically important
ones; but then a tender point is raised when the second or third
wife presents her children to be baptized. Information fed back
from Africans, moreover, has caused a few Europeans with long
experience in Africa to question timidly the Christian crusade
against the African custom: "In such a matter," the great Lugard

once wrote, "there is much to be said from the point of view of the wife as well as of the husband, provided that it is regulated and restricted" (Lugard, 1926, pp. 152–3). Recently a Christian clergyman in South Africa has courageously wrestled in print with the question of whether Christianity really must demand monogamy (Helander, 1958).

XII.B   *Categories*   What kind of information is fed back to the communicator? The answer must be: information
XII.B.1   tion concerning any aspect of the communication process. First of all there is *background information* about the audience, including (a) *broad cultural information* about them, such as a competent anthropologist, traveler, or any outsider on occasion may possess about a group of people. Then there is (b) *general technical information* more closely related to the communication: information bearing on the media of communication (III, IV), the site at which communications are received (V), the restrictions that are imposed upon communicators (VI), and modes of communicating (VII). This latter kind of information is usually a form of antecedent feedback, although sometimes relevant data are obtained through simultaneous feedback: right *in medias res,* for example, the communicator unhappily notes how inadequately trained his assistant is.

The broad cultural information that must be fed back to communicators concerns the values, the groups, and the deviant behavior of a society that have already been discussed in connection with the reactions of the audience to the communication (X.A.3.a). Here the same methodological problems recur but in a slightly broader context. Illustrative of the background information that would be extremely useful in designing communication programs in Africa, *if* the information were valid, are the following observations of a journalist from the Netherlands, who suggests that both the British and the French have been "about equally successful in impregnating their wards in Africa with their particular way of life and their political philosophy." This means that African "wards" have been "educated" to subscribe to different beliefs (Huizinga, 1959, p. 29):

French Africa	*British Africa*
The revolutionary and originally supranational credo of equality, liberty and fraternity, belief in the rights of men regardless of race, color, or frontier.	The belief in the right of people, collectivities, to dispose of themselves; a belief in equality and liberty and freedom as between peoples and not as between men.

The contrast is exciting and perhaps reasonable from an historical standpoint; but, the skeptical question must be asked, is the assertion really useful? First, who are the wards to which reference is made? They could be the mass of Africans, since the colonial offices of France and England have dominated the educational systems of their areas until the countries achieved independence. They could be only the elite, including many of the present political leaders, who were trained in the mother country's traditions while being educated overseas. After specifying the audience, empirical investigation is required to know just how well Africans have absorbed the values and beliefs of their former colonial teachers. It seems likely that some of the hypotheses of the journalist cited above would be substantiated in qualified form, since modern African nations most tenaciously function within the old boundaries which, though arbitrarily established by Europeans at the outset, continue to determine many local loyalties and most national policies.

Other background information is likewise needed but must be cautiously employed as a guide to effective communication. In the Portuguese areas of Africa, for example, five types of elite are distinguished: white Portuguese; "natives" who have achieved the status of being considered assimilated and their children; detribalized Africans who have learned some European ways but are not considered to be assimilated; African chiefs; and other racial minorities, viz., Indians and Chinese (Moreira, 1956). The group to which a potential audience belongs thus seems to affect their ability to comprehend Portuguese and other aspects of European culture, the kinds of goals they seek, the restrictions regulating their lives, etc., all of which provide valuable clues for communication. Of course it would be desirable to have many more details concerning each group. Also, group membership is only one of the factors determining the actual prestige or ability of people; it has been argued with reference to another section of Africa that careful investigation and expert advice are needed before a health educator is selected either from the elite or the general population (Conacher, 1957).

Even specific cultural information can be utilized only after ascertaining details in a specific locality. At first glance, it is important to be able to designate the areas in Africa where large sections of the population are followers of Islam. Closer examination, however, reveals considerable variability in actual practices. In Nyasaland and Uganda customary law prevails almost completely in local courts, but in Tanganyika and Kenya Islamic law is used in some instances and has affected customary law in others (Anderson, 1951).

Feedback can provide not only general background information but also *specific information* about the communication itself. The obvious route to follow here is that of the audience itself: perception (IX), reactions (X), and changes (XI). First there is *perceptual information*. Note can be taken of the size and composition of the actual audience that assembles; the devices that attract and retain their attention; and their ability or lack of ability to comprehend the communication.

XII.B.2

XII.B.2.a

Again (IX.D.2.c) reference can be made to the perception of photographs, this time in the form of subsequent feedback concerning the Azande in the Congo and Sudan:

A picture is always looked at upside down; it seems to be the natural way for an Azande to do it, and if it is placed the right way up, in a very short time he will have reversed its position.

The natural Azande cannot take in the representation of a landscape, and it is only after a considerable amount of time has been spent in contact with white people that he begins to be able to do so [Larken, 1927, p. 96].

If these observations were really valid, then here indeed was valuable information concerning the perceptual habits of these people, which, as antecedent feedback, could have enabled a communicator to anticipate that pictures would be viewed upside down and that landscapes would cause trouble.

XII.B.2.b *Information about the reaction of the audience* in effect evaluates the assumptions that have been made, wittingly or not, by the communicator as he originally planned and delivered his communication. If he has thought people servile and then observes that they turn out to be belligerent, clearly he must alter his communication to conform to this newly discovered state of affairs. The communicator thus tests his hypotheses concerning the audience in all respects, including what he has believed to be their feelings toward himself.

Information about predispositions, to be really useful to communicators, must be up-to-date and precise; for this reason simultaneous feedback is very desirable. But in real life, especially in Africa, what is usually available are data from the past which, if stretched, can be considered to be a form of subsequent or antecedent feedback. What, the question must be asked again (VI.C.1. b; X.A.3.a.ii), shall one do with such data? Once more some statistics from Nigeria may be taken as illustration. In 1945, of the 350,000 children in school in what was then a British colony, 320,000 were in mission institutions of the Christian faith, including the Roman Catholic (J. Davis et al., 1945, p. 61). The children of 1945 are now adults, and many of them must be occupying important positions in an independent Nigeria. The fact that the missions since 1945 have been playing a less important role in Nigeria probably has no retroactive effect upon this generation. But exactly how much mission influence survives from that time? To what extent are the predispositions of certain unspecified Nigerians still affected by the schooling they once had? They remember parts of the Bible perhaps, yet are their ethical attitudes basically Christian? Such questions are unanswerable, *but* the fact of the mission's critical role in the past must somehow be cautiously taken into account in planning or assessing communications to educated adults of Nigeria in the present day. At the very, very least it may be safely assumed that they possess some knowledge concerning Christian beliefs and practices, whether or not they wholeheartedly subscribe to them.

XII.B.2.c Specific *information about changes* includes both nonovert changes and changes in action. Often feedback supplies only the type of information which comes from direct observation, in contrast with information about perception and reactions that must be inferred. The leap from the observation to the conclusion that the communication has played the decisive role, however, must be inhibited until, as pointed out previously (XI.B.1.b), evidence of a connection is forthcoming.

In order to achieve the objectives of government, "demonstration teams" in Uganda frequently stage educational exhibitions which, externally at least, resemble the traditional American fair. An official describes the kind of feedback such a device produces:

> There are signs that their peacetime work is also of positive value. The chiefs certainly say they are introducing new ways of life (but of course chiefs are sometimes prone to say what we want to hear!). Yet there are other signs which suggest that some of the lessons are being learned—in one or two places better houses and latrines are appearing, and better cattle are being produced by better feeding and care and so on [anon., 1949, p. 19].

According to this experience, the validity of deeds is greater than that of words. But is it really? The chiefs may tell their superiors what they want to hear, but the fact that they do so suggests at least what their attitude is toward the communicators. And independent evidence is needed to show that the better houses, the better latrines, and the better cattle are in fact the consequence of the demonstration and not of other events or communications.

Among the Mende of Sierra Leone, a sample of roughly 200 Creoles and "literate native persons" has been surveyed in order to determine the "popularity" of various cultural traits from the West. The most widely adopted characteristic or habit turns out to be style of dress, which is followed in descending order by "religion, profession, leisure-time activities—including games and club affiliations—marital status (i.e., monogamy as distinct from polygamy), food-taking habits, style of house decoration, and marriage ceremonies" (Little, 1951, p. 264). As a form of subsequent feedback the survey suggests how the Mende have reacted to Western culture and to communications concerning that culture: they have responded more favorably to dress than to marriage ceremonies. The inference is very general and very tentative, for the precise interaction between the millions of communications from Westerners regarding their culture on the one hand and the predispositions of generations of Mende on the other are of course unknown. Then, secondly, the survey as a form of antecedent feedback indicates the kind of communication which in the present or the future is likely to be received with favor or disfavor. Obviously, for example, a political leader is not going to win applause by attacking the traditional marriage ceremony or the traditional style of house decoration.

XII.C   *The Collector*   Information of course does not automatically flow in to the communicator: someone must collect it, or at the very least set up the apparatus, if there be appropriate apparatus, to do the recording. In many instances it is the *communicator* himself who performs this function. The speaker with the audience in front of him is able to combine the communicating and the feed-

XII.C.1

back functions, provided he can observe his listeners while arranging and expressing his own thoughts. The feedback need not
be simultaneous for one person to assume the dual role. After the
communication has been transmitted, the communicator may deliberately seek to ascertain whether the audience was pleased, and
he himself can observe their subsequent deeds. He probably can
more easily and successfully be his own collector when he is a
member of the same society or group as the audience, for then as
a result of the experience he shares with them he can respond
simultaneously or subsequently to slight cues which an outsider
may fail to detect (I.A.1).

———— • ————

In teaching African women various aspects of public health, a
missionary devised the following method of simultaneous feedback:

> It is advisable . . . to ask a native to go over each lesson at its
> close. Let one of the most intelligent listeners know that she
> is expected to sum up and make clear to the others what you
> have been teaching. . . . What is worth hearing can bear
> repetition and is more easily assimilated when it comes from
> the familiar tongue of one of themselves. It is very profitable
> for the teacher to listen to her understudy. It helps you to see
> where you have failed to make any point clear. On the other
> hand, if the repetition shows an intelligent grasp of what you
> have said, you learn by listening to the language in which it
> is restated fresh and idiomatic ways of expressing your ideas
> [A. Fraser, 1932, pp. 52–3].

Ingenious as the technique is, it produces imperfect feedback since
it seeks simultaneously to achieve other objectives. Alerting the
listener who will provide the summary makes her self-conscious,
perhaps more attentive, and so not representative of the audience.
She is also deliberately selected because of her atypical intelligence. The communicator does not know whether the students
have comprehended the communication, although the repetition
of course increases the likelihood that they have. Clearly, though,
the teacher receives some feedback: if she has failed with the

alerted, more gifted child, she probably has been unsuccessful with the rest. And certainly her own mode of communication will be improved not as a result of feedback from the entire audience but from the kind of translation provided by the African giving the summary.

XII.C.2

If information is not fed back directly to the communicator, then some *intermediary* serves the function. The intermediary may be either attached or unattached to the communicator: (a) an *attached* intermediary is someone deliberately utilized to provide the feedback, such as a market-research organization in modern society; (b) an *unattached* intermediary is someone who unwittingly collects the information while seeking another goal—thus a trader in the course of his regular activities may obtain information concerning people's feelings toward their leaders.

In traditional African society, the use of intermediaries to convey to communicators information about people's reactions to specific communications or about public opinion in general has usually not been noted by anthropologists and other observers. It is impossible to state, consequently, whether African leaders do or do not employ such informers because, as indicated in the Prologue to this book, the absence of a report can mean either that the phenomenon is absent or that its presence has been unnoticed. Some instances, however, do appear in the literature. As an official announcement is proclaimed among the Amhara of Ethiopia, for example, "paid listeners" are known to "mix with the public" in order to trace to their "sources" negative reactions, which are expressed by "murmuring in a delayed stage whisper" (Messing, 1957, p. 520). Since the function of this information-collecting is to prevent the kinds of rebellions that have occurred in the past, it seems probable that the listeners are acting more like secret police than public-opinion pollsters. Among the Hausa in Zaria Province, Northern Nigeria, intermediaries perform two roles simultaneously: they collect information about public reaction and they transmit information. The communicator in this instance is the village chief, who is subject to pressure from two sides: his primary loyalty is to the district head who has appointed him, and he must also control people within his own community so effectively that they do not compete for his office or complain to the head. Each chief retains some persons whose duty it is to keep him informed concerning "local affairs and reactions" and to "deal with his commoners individually or in groups as occasion requires" (M. G. Smith, 1955, pp. 6–7, 11).

Outsiders from the West may be aware of the need for audience research through intermediaries, but so often they find the problems of communication themselves so pressing that little time remains to organize and then supervise a staff to conduct that research. A "UNESCO Field Counsellor for Audio-Visual Aids" sought to supplement his own impressions of how Egyptian audiences were reacting to educational films by having students and technical assistants carry on informal interviews under conditions that he describes as follows:

> Unfortunately we always had to give our shows to about 800 people. The only time we tried to do some experimental screenings to a small audience the rest of the village created a minor riot and nearly broke the doors down. So my picture of the Egyptian village and its attitude to films is a broad one.

"Broad" knowledge so impressionistically gathered apparently did not prevent the official from arriving at sweeping conclusions, such as the assertion that "the pill of knowledge must . . . be sugar-coated" (A. Shaw, 1952, p. 20).

XII.D *Methods* Whoever collects the information that is fed back to the communicator, whether the communicator himself or an intermediary, employs some technique or method that is part of the repertoire of modern social science. No extensive, exhaustive analysis is attempted here. Instead, after a paragraph about validity, a simple classification of methods, together with illustrations, is offered. Since many sharp words, perhaps too many, have already been directed against methodologically unsound observations and conclusions, the flavor of this section can be anticipated.

Ultimately the validity of the information fed back to the communicator must be determined by someone, or the experience cannot be properly utilized in the future. Any form of feedback has its own peculiarities in this respect, and there is no sure-fire route to salvation unless a controlled experiment can be approximated. Again and again, therefore, the problem is approached from a purely pragmatic standpoint: if feedback provides data which, according to the belief of someone, especially the communicator, contributes immediately or ultimately to the success of the communication, then the information and the method of obtaining it are considered to be valid. Of course the fact of the matter may be that the information is quite false; and yet, if the communicator—deluded or not—has his self-confidence thereby increased, the feedback obviously has assisted him and may indeed lead to successful communication. Here is no tongue-in-cheek solution to a difficult problem, rather a polite reminder of the possible value of unfounded convictions and half-truths.

The system of classifying methods of feedback is based on the relation between the collector and the audience. First, no ostensible relation is established; the collector employs what may be called without a sneer the method of *intuition*. On the basis of his broad knowledge of people or their culture, or as a result of specific knowledge which he may possess because, for example, he himself is a member of the group to which the communication is being transmitted, he quickly and effortlessly anticipates how the communication will fare or he similarly gauges its success or failure afterwards. If he is gifted and skilled, he easily utilizes cues from a variety of sources—to be discussed below—without being systematically dependent on any one of them. Clearly the technique is risky, but it may yield interesting, sometimes valid information.

XII.D.1

———————

In the absence of data which observers must consider too obvious to report, it seems reasonable to suppose that communicators in traditional African societies employ intuitive methods very extensively. Such societies tend to be relatively small or to function on the level of communities and, under these conditions, the chief must know his followers so well that he need only glance at them to perceive their mood or to determine whether they have comprehended his command. The newer media, especially the extending ones, however, demand the creation of feedback techniques which, being novel, are more likely to be noted and described. "All typographical problems" concerning news sheets published in Northern Nigeria, according to one observer, are "put to the General Manager of Gaskiya Corporation, who arranges for specimens to be prepared which illustrate his professional advice and from which selection can be made by eye" (Jeffries, 1957, p. 30). Clearly the General Manager of this government-sponsored publishing house must be an experienced man. The selection technique, "made by eye," may or may not be the best under each circumstance. In a relatively fast-moving publishing operation, however, there often is no time for elaborate pretests. Somehow, intuitively accumulated experience serves as the guide.

XII.D.2 Close to but removed somewhat from intuition is *direct observation*. Here the collector does not talk to people, does not make inquiries of them concerning their reactions. He observes, and what he can observe directly is the number and composition of the audience, their attentiveness, perhaps their understanding and approval, and their overt action. Some of the data so observed can be objectively ascertained; often, for example, it is a simple matter to count the number of people at a meeting. But other data are based upon inferences which may or may not be valid. Have people, for example, comprehended the communication? Intuitively the experienced collector will see whether their faces are "blank" or whether "stars" seem to come out of their eyes; the relation between blank looks and starry eyes on the one hand and comprehension on the other by no means can be easily established.

Once more, the guess may be hazarded, here is a method, with or without accompanying intuition, that is probably used so extensively in traditional African societies that reporting it seems superfluous. But observers are aware of the device in connection with media from the West. One official, for example, suggests that he checked the view that Africans like only films in the cowboy tradition of the American West by observing their reactions:

> The audience sat either silently bored or occupied in conversation on quite extraneous matters with their neighbors through the long stretches of meaningless dialogue, waiting for something to happen. At last someone drew a gun and shot—here at last was something the audience understood and it reacted noisily [Izod, 1952, p. 48].

Intuitively the observation seems valid; when research standards are applied it becomes necessary to wonder why a noisy reaction to the shooting demonstrates comprehension and to ask what in fact Africans "understood" while witnessing this sample of Western civilization.

———————◄••••►———————

XII.D.3   Subsequent feedback can be arranged through *interviewing the audience* or a sample thereof. By questioning people an effort is made to determine either some of their nonovert reactions which cannot be directly observed or their overt actions which in this manner are catalogued more easily than by direct observation. In the first instance, for example, they may be asked to express their feelings about the communicator or his medium; in the second, they may be requested to specify what they did after perceiving the communication. Ordinarily the method cannot be employed simultaneously while the communication is being perceived since the audience is of course occupied with the communication itself. This difficulty is circumvented somewhat in market research in the West when a sample, during an actual or simulated performance, indicates their feelings by pressing one of two or three buttons to signify their private reactions. The interviewing may be either (a) *systematic* or (b) *unsystematic*. The former pays more attention and the latter less to technical problems like sampling; the establishment of rapport with informants; the type, order, and number of questions; and the eventual processing of the data.

One kind of information most desperately needed in contemporary Africa is a record of the changes that are occurring within people. Without such a record, communicators cannot know whether they have achieved short- or long-run effects; government officials cannot state with precision how people are reacting to changes and contacts with the West; journalists, historians, and other serious observers cannot transmit a valid analysis to people elsewhere and to future generations. An important technique to obtain significant data could be the panel: the repeated interviewing of a carefully selected sample of people over a period of time. Unfortunately so little polling occurs in Africa that most investigators must rest content with simple probes, which obviously provide no knowledge of trends.

Very frequently relevant technical details are missing from reports describing feedback obtained by interviewing members of the audience. An official of what was then the Gold Coast pronounced his conviction that the successful producer of radio programs must keep "as closely in touch as possible with the audience" destined to enjoy, profit from, or simply react to his programs. "Toward that end," he states, "from time to time one or another broadcaster was sent out to spend a fortnight or so amongst the audience." Since the sojourn undoubtedly involved interviewing, it is necessary to wonder whether persons trained in broadcasting techniques could be expected to have either the temperament or the talent to collect information concerning the reactions of the audience, even when they came from the same society. In the report, moreover, nothing is said about how the information was collected. Suspicion is aroused by the honest statement that a really important gain was one having nothing whatsoever to do with feedback: "An audience liked to know its broadcasters personally and as a result listened with more pleasure and attention" (Williams, 1950, p. 46).

Interviewing in any area that is unaccustomed to the practice is not easy or rapid, especially if an effort is made to find a random sample of informants. Obtaining permission from local authorities, after one's identity, credibility, and trustworthiness have been established, can be by itself a lengthy affair. Then the approach to the interviewees must be gentle and tactful. People must be greeted in the required way and other etiquette must be observed. Their justified curiosity concerning the purpose of the interview must be satisfied, and whatever hostility or anxiety they evince toward the stranger must be reduced if valid replies are to be obtained. The view is perhaps a trifle extreme, but the dictum of an anthropologist who worked in North Kavirondo in Kenya may serve as a warning:

> My experience was that to visit only 50 native homes and to ask questions in each concerning a few points only would take the better part of three months, as the visit must appear casual and as many houses require one or several preliminary visits before any valuable information would be forthcoming [Wagner, 1938, p. 99].

Painfully aware of such problems from experience in the past, the present writer once sought—in Northern Nigeria in the summer of 1959—to see whether it would be possible for an outsider in a very brief time to gather data on a problem related to communication. A short chronology can be given. He arrived in Zaria shortly before noon on a Friday. A European official then facilitated initial contacts so that before tea that afternoon arrangements had been made to hire a car, the permission of the relevant Nigerian official to carry on surveys had been granted, and still another official had promised to cast about for an interpreter. By Saturday evening an excellent car and a submediocre interpreter had been obtained, and the schedule of questions had been planned and translated. The work began in a village a short distance from Zaria on Sunday morning, after a delay of about two hours when the chief in the village asked that permission from additional authorities be secured. Interviewing was carried on also on Monday and Tuesday mornings. Actually, then, less then three half days were consumed; the elapsed time could have been shortened by interviewing during the torrid afternoons, but that much energy and ambition the interviewer—and maybe also the potential interviewees—simply lacked. Each interview took at least a half hour but never more than an hour. In all, nineteen interviews were completed. The experience proves only that one can push oneself into a community and into interviewing if the way has been cleared by prior arrangements; under such circumstances, however, the questions that can be asked, as the description of the results has doubtless shown (VI.C.1.b; VIII.C.2), are not commendably subtle.

An inconclusive finding from the quick survey, however, warns that valid feedback depends upon the technical aspects of interviewing. Not a single informant of a group of eleven mentioned "spirits" when asked about the causes of disease; but three of eight men gave an affirmative reply to the direct question, "Can spirits cause disease?" The form of the question may have a marked effect upon the replies.

In this writer's opinion, one of the greatest difficulties that arises in interviewing Africans is the inability of many of them to report their own impressions, feelings, and even actions. They may be perfectly willing to provide information but be simply unable to express themselves through lack of practice in situations resembling the interview. In one of the exploratory studies previously mentioned (XI.B.2), a handful of Ewe informants—seven in all—were questioned concerning the "latest news" they had heard concerning the principal city close by, the capital of Ghana, Ghana itself, and the world outside Ghana. Only one at the spur of the moment could report any news about the capital and nobody could report a single item concerning the other places. A few days previously the writer had arranged for the entire community to see three motion pictures that had been projected from a mobile cinema van. When asked generally whether they liked or did not like the films, six of the same group of seven spontaneously said they had liked them, but only three could mention any specific film or item without considerable coaxing. When asked in particular what they had learned from a film on disease and another showing the differences between living and nonliving matter, each mentioned something different. And yet the possibility must not be excluded that these people had heard news which may have influenced them or that they had been more definitely affected by the films than they were able during the quick interview to indicate. Perhaps only a genuine experiment—with an experimental group receiving and a strictly comparable control group not receiving the communication, and with behavioral rather than verbal measures both before and after the delivery of the communication to the former —could provide a valid measure of effectiveness to be fed back to a communicator. But experiments in Africa, where comparable groups in real communities are not easy to find and where repeated measurements of behavior are tortuous to arrange, can seldom be carried out.

A more specialized form of interviewing involves the administration of standardized tests to samples of informants. Through the highly popular Rorschach plates or some modification of the Thematic Apperception Test, for example, an attempt is made to discover people's predispositions, their interests, or their modes of perceiving. Such research falls under the heading of antecedent feedback and ought to be able to provide basic information relevant to many types of communications in the future. At least a brief word of caution, however, is necessary: within one society the predisposition thus measured may vary markedly as a function of the particular test item that is employed, but in another no such variability may occur. In one study, for example, a higher proportion of Ganda males expressed a favorable attitude toward Europeans when, in the tradition of the T.A.T., they were asked to describe what "a European" and an "African" were doing in an ambiguous drawing than when they were asked directly, "What do you like and what do you not like about Europeans?" Among the Zulu, on the other hand, the same questions produced virtually identical scores; in either case, the number expressing a favorable attitude was very low (Doob, 1957–58).

The interviewing of people need not occur literally; their opinions can be inferred by noting the content of a communication they produce for a related or unrelated purpose. The observer can listen to what people say in normal conversation, and perhaps innocently inject a question or two of his own. He can analyze the kinds of letters which people write to newspapers and radio stations—and it is the present writer's impression that African officials rely heavily on this ready and convenient source of information. Children in school can be asked to compose essays on a relevant subject, a device that has been used to very good advantage in a study of adolescents in the copper belt of Northern Rhodesia. From her analysis of four essays on assigned subjects by over 100 boys and girls, the anthropologist draws a number of provocative conclusions, one of which can serve as illustration: "The image of Europeans as inhospitable and greedy, making all guests (including relatives) pay for hospitality, was as strongly held as the opposite one of African hospitality" (Powdermaker, 1956, p. 809). From another area of Africa, here are the first and last paragraphs written in June of 1959 by a Ghanaian boy, age 18 and in the last form of a first-rate secondary school, in response to the teacher's assignment to write on "The Problem of the Intellectuals in Ghana":

> Nationalism is a thing that is now well established in the modern world. Its main driving force is patriotism, a sense of devotion to a society to which one belongs and in which there is an awareness of oneness. The major demand of this sort of society is duty, a willingness to serve the nation. The demand of duty is present in Western democracies and is well pronounced in Communist countries. Ghana is a new nation of the world, much faced with the difficult task of making herself stand on her legs. And if we believe in building up as a means of progress, then our country requires the maximum amount of duty from us. . . .

> In the field of politics, the evolution of the type of government we want will rest on the shoulders of the intellectuals, who in this field must be prepared to do their duty faithfully and even to be martyrs. The rest of the duty they owe to Ghana can be majorly termed the responsibility of education. The intellectuals must carry on the education of the citizens from age to age. It is on this that the ultimate place of Ghana in the world depends; whether that it will be economically and politically strong, whether that it will be virtuous and whether it will be in the vanguard of the workers for the perpetual, peaceful coexistence of all people of the world believing in "Justice and Freedom" which undoubtedly is the key to tranquility and order.

The boy's knowledge of English, his desire and ability to clothe his thoughts in elaborate words, the extent to which he has absorbed clichés of the West, or at least expresses them in an essay at school, the emergence of a philosophy which suggests the need for self-sacrifice—these and other clues are evidently provided by such a composition. Naturally his essay must be carefully evaluated, and compared with the products from other students. But here is subsequent feedback from the secondary school and from the West; and also antecedent feedback for anyone, including teachers, who would communicate with an educated African minority.

<hr />

XII.D.4   *Interviewing* can be focused upon *critical people* who, though not members of the audience, have special knowledge of what might occur or has occurred as a result of a communication. Such leaders, observers, or experts may base their information on intuition, direct observation, or the interviewing of the same or similar people as compose the audience. It is necessary thus to evaluate their information in two respects: do they validly convey what they know, and is what they know valid? As indicated in the previous section, moreover, the opinions of persons occupying strategically important positions in a society often have special value in their own right.

<hr />

Virtually all Europeans and almost as many educated Africans are self-styled experts on Africans, and especially on their reactions to the West. The writer feels that many of them are indeed so experienced that they are able to provide invaluable, valid information. The rub comes when one tries to separate such information from sheer prejudice. Is the European merely disguising his own feeling of superiority when he asserts that Africans, "through no fault of their own, don't you know?" are allegedly inferior in some respect? Or is the African who has been to Oxford merely displaying inverted snobbery when he maintains that Africans can "jolly well" do what other people can? The General Secretary of the International Committee on Christian Literature, for example, has written:

> It is my conviction that churches and missions will have a greater impact upon the masses in Africa through the use of illustrated magazines than through the use of books and booklets. . . . The illustrated magazine is for large numbers; if well edited, it has the chance of being read over and over again each month—with a greater impact than the author of a book can ever achieve [de Mestral, 1956, p. 95].

Unfortunately this authority does not indicate the source of his "conviction." Common sense might agree that photographs can be understood by illiterates and books cannot be, but what is meant here by "impact"? Photographs may be seen and understood, but what will their influence ultimately be? Or how can that influence be compared with that of a book read by a few people who belong to the elite and pass on part of its content to a larger audience? Obviously, much also depends upon the kind of information being transmitted; does the author cited above think that medical knowledge or agricultural techniques should be broadcast through illustrated magazines rather than through lectures, demonstrations, or community projects? The questions are raised more in grief than in anger, since the very kind of advice needed by anyone interested in African welfare at the present moment seems to be contained in the quoted statement. Ex cathedra convictions should not be brushed aside perhaps, but they certainly have to be challenged.

In most contemporary African countries, the opinions and attitudes of an extremely small elite group are particularly important since they control government as well as other institutions in large part created by, and certainly now regulating, contact with the West. In a pilot study during August of 1959, a political scientist succeeded in interviewing 26 Africans who occupy positions of medium importance in government, in political parties, and in the professions of the Eastern Province of Nigeria (Bretton, 1959). The men were addressed and answered in English since they had had at least an elementary-school education and some had attended institutions of higher learning in England. With few exceptions, they were quite aware that their replies were being recorded. Their reactions to particular communications were not assessed, rather attention was focused upon general predispositions created among them by what must have been a whole series of unascertainable political communications in the past. Data from this small, haphazardly selected sample do not permit sweeping generalizations, but they provocatively demonstrate the value of systematically interviewing strategic people. Two concrete illustrations from the results are offered; the present writer, having selected them from the investigator's original notes, is alone responsible for what follows.

Toward the middle of the interview, respondents were asked: "Considering the difficulties facing your country, would it not be better if you had a dictatorship for a while to get things done? Can progress be made without a dictatorship?" The replies may be categorized regarding attitude toward dictatorship:

Disapproval	11
Approval	7
Qualified approval	4
Question not asked	4
	26

After two other questions pertaining to Nigerian politics, a personal question, and a question on a current event, the men answered the following: "Should a person with dangerous ideas, such as communism or fascism, be permitted to stand for office?"

Yes	3
Qualified yes	2
No	5
No, but may vote	4
Don't know	4
Question not asked	8
	26

As so frequently happens, the crude categories conceal the richness of the material from which they are derived. An acting labor officer, age 28, with ten years of education and a fluent knowledge of English, replied to the question about dictatorship in these words:

Dictatorship will not give us stability. We are essentially democratic. In order to have a stable government we have to give people what they have been used to. The people here have been democratic for a long time. They have had a democratic form of government under their traditional system.

On the other hand, a judge, age 45, with six years of education and a fair to fluent knowledge of English, stated: "For a start it may be necessary to have a virile, unifying force, more or less a form of dictatorship." The following answer was given to the other question concerning communism and fascism by a divisional secretary of a political party, age 44, with ten years of education and a fair knowledge of English: "We don't know what a communist is. Is foreign to us. I can't define it until I know which is which."

At the very least it may be said that these leaders were responding to ambiguous English words in the questions such as *dictatorship, progress, communism,* and *fascism* to which, like people in the West, they also attached a variety of connotations. Communications from the past had not taught them a single meaning or a single attitude; communications in the future which employ the words are likely to produce diverse reactions. Noteworthy, in addition, is the fact that all other political and social questions on the interviewer's schedule also elicited diverse responses among the same informants as well as in another small group of noncritical people, such as taxi drivers and fishermen.

————◄••••►————

XII.D.5   Finally, feedback can come through a series of *indices:* data from direct observations gathered for a different purpose are employed as the basis for making inferences concerning the people who have given
XII.D.5.a   rise to them and whom they therefore in some way reflect. First, there are *behavioral artifacts* that provide knowledge about people's reactions to communications. Statistics on attendance may suggest the popularity of a medium or a type of communication without indicating the reasons therefor. In parts of West Africa local theaters have a library of pictures which,

since they attract an audience, are repeated at irregular intervals.

XII.D.5.b

External conditions sometimes offer a clue to the kind of mood (VIII) likely to characterize people who are exposed to a communication. If the weather has been or is about to be unusual, for example, it may be possible to risk certain statements about an audience's feelings of well-being. Statistics on an area's

XII.D.5.c economy can serve a similar function.

The analysis of the *content of past communications,* especially when the success of the communications with similar audiences is known, may suggest, however tentatively, the factors that are responsible for the communication's fate. Such a procedure is risky because the categories of analysis may be different from the factors influencing overt behavior. Thus, if the sales of a magazine fluctuate markedly from issue to issue, it may not be easy to decide which features attract and which repel leaders, and the decision may have to be validated through the equivalent of an experimental procedure.

―――――・―――――

From the really embarrassingly abundant materials of the past, reference is made here only to radio logs, which, in the manner of the West, appear in African newspapers and special radio publications; attention is directed to the schedule of programs for a specific day (perchance August 3, 1959) in Nigeria. Differences in programs appear from region to region of that country. The Northern Region opened its broadcasting with "Reading from the Holy Koran" for 15 minutes; then the day's programs were briefly reviewed. The Western Region began with the same two features but reversed their order. The Koran was not read at all in the Eastern Region. At 2:15 in the afternoon the station at Lagos, the capital, broadcast "Egun Music by Omoruose Alamu and his Group" and "Bata Music by Laisis Alijonu and his Group," a program carried by none of the regional stations. In the North, the broadcast was "regional news" in English and Hausa; in the East, a program called "Our Kind of Music"; and in the West a "Western Band." From 7 to 8 P.M. all four transmitters sent out the same programs: world news, national news, and a quiz program called, in the British manner, "The Brains Trust" (*Nigerian Radio Times,* August, 1959).

What kind of information does such a schedule feed back to potential communicators, or to anyone interested in Nigeria? There are in fact variations from region to region, with Moslems being located predominantly in the North and to a lesser degree in the West; hence the reading of the Koran undoubtedly conformed to regional preferences. The conformity, however, stemmed not from systematic feedback but from valid intuition. For at the time, stations in Nigeria conducted virtually no audience research; only through hit-and-miss impressions gained by personal contact and through fan mail could the operators of the stations gauge the success of their programs. Also, the directors and producers, with few exceptions, were Africans, and many if not most of them came from societies located in the region of their specialty. Presumably they could estimate sagaciously whether people wished to hear readings from the Koran at all or, if so, at the very start of the day. Presumably, but evidence of course is lacking. The present writer received the impression that the technicians in the radio stations, perhaps like their governmental counterparts everywhere, were interested in broadcasting not merely what people wished or found entertaining, but also material which, in the broadcaster's own opinion, would benefit them. Radio—they who had a virtual monopoly said—has an important educational function to perform. It is quite possible, too, that regional directors, in accepting or rejecting programs for rebroadcast from the national station, were reflecting not the tastes of their audiences but the political policy within the region to assert its independence from the central government around which the Federation of Regions is loosely organized. Economic considerations may also have played a role; it is sometimes less expensive for a regional station to rebroadcast a national program than to originate its own, and—as an official told the present writer—the national station frequently uses BBC features not because they are especially desirable but because they are "cheap and available." Under all these circumstances, the conclusion must be, the day's log could not have been a sensitive form of feedback from Nigerian audiences. It did indicate the programs people tolerated without overtly rebelling—a very wide operational margin indeed—and can also be said to reflect the well-informed guesses of the officials concerning both the tastes and needs of their listeners.

More dangerous and hence more intriguing than old communications or schedules as a source of information must be *history* in general. Does historical analysis of past

XII.D.5.d   situations feed back into the present or the future? This is no new question of course, but it needs to be repeated with reference to communication. At what point, for example, does a community or a society in a developing continent like Africa begin rapidly to abandon traditional media of communication and to adopt modern mass media? If there were a series of complete case histories on the growth of communications in particular areas (IV.A), could one have similar expectations for other areas? Perhaps, too, there are generalizations about communications from history; for example, is it true that in modern times no government, no matter how authoritarian, has ever been able to prevent its people from receiving and then being affected by communications from the outside? Undoubtedly past situations, like present ones, are singular and hence do not easily give rise to transcending generalization, but somehow they must provide significant hints.

EPILOGUE

The entire circle of communication has now been traversed. The journey may have seemed long, and in fact was long, but there have been no detours. Seemingly small points have been mentioned and illustrated because in some more or less singular situation in the past they have been decisive and hence may be not small but critical in the future. What has been accomplished?

Human communication, it has been shown, cannot be analyzed speedily if all its boundaries are to be explored. Principles operate only within a very narrow, arbitrarily selected, but useful section of the circle. The operational kit of the communicator and the conceptual one of the analyst contain many tools. At a given moment only a handful of these tools needs to be employed, and it is usually possible to see at a glance which ones are inapplicable and hence to be kept in reserve for some other communication in the future.

The diversity and the complexity that have been emphasized should not be the least bit discouraging. Rather it is false simplicity that ought to produce dismay, for ruin can come when the understandable but foolish attempt is made to comprehend behavior with too few variables. Diversity and complexity, furthermore, are not synonyms for chaos. Only the intellectually weak give up the struggle and say that nothing about people is lawful just because everything about them is likely to be diverse and complex. Of course principles never produce absolute certainty, of course there are exceptions to every generalization, of course the unexpected may happen—what straw man ever proclaimed otherwise? If the boundaries of communication must include as many factors and subfactors and subsubfactors as this book has emphasized, then so be it: more lawfulness can be attained by being aware of their number and their interrelations. When understanding of these numerous factors has been gained, it is possible to look about the village or the world with greater skill and satisfaction: the cry of the baby, the exhortation on the television screen, the ribbon in the hair, the masterpiece in the gallery, the facial tic, the plowed field are observed abstractly and concretely to serve similar functions and therefore they can be grasped within a single unified intellectual framework.

The search for the boundaries of communication has been carried on with the help of African materials. Perhaps, therefore, greater insight into Africans and contemporary Africa has been proffered. It must now be perfectly evident that Africans themselves, living in a wide variety of societies, have evolved their own forms of communication, which for them at the time were adequate (except perhaps for the almost complete absence of the permanent, flexible record provided by writing). As they accept more and more practices and values from the West, they come to be intimately dependent upon the extending and especially upon the mass media of the culture they absorb. Modern Africa contains a mixture of traditional and novel communication systems because those systems so sensitively reflect and affect the changes in progress.

Communication could not be discussed without referring slyly or blatantly to almost all behavior. The sweep has had to be broad in order to locate the boundaries. Likewise, communication in Africa could be appraised only by mentioning most of the significant aspects of African society. For people in general, for Africans in particular, consequently, communication is a critical problem at the very center of existence. May our struggling African friends eventually emerge with satisfactory modes of communication; if wholly by chance or wondrously by design they do, they thereby will have also achieved a better life.

REFERENCES

An asterisk indicates that the original reference could not be conveniently obtained; the citation is based on a summary provided by *African Abstracts.*

AJISAFE, A. I. C. *The laws and customs of the Yoruba people.* London: Routledge, 1924.

ALEXANDRE, Pierre and BINET, Jacques. *Le group dit Pahouin.* Paris: Les Presses Universitaires de France, 1958.

ALLPORT, Gordon W. and POSTMAN, Leo. *The psychology of rumor.* New York: Holt, 1947.

———— and VERNON, Phillip E. *Studies in expressive movement.* New York: Macmillan, 1933.

AMES, David W. Wolof co-operative work groups. *In* William R. Bascom and Melville J. Herskovits (eds.), *Continuity and change in African cultures.* Chicago: University of Chicago Press, 1959, pp. 224–37.

ANDERSON, J. N. D. Islamic law in African colonies. *Corona,* 1951, *3,* 262–6.

Anonymous. A demonstration team in Uganda. *Mass Education Bulletin,* Dec. 1949, *1,* 18–19.

———— The cocoa campaign. *Advance,* July 1955, no. 7, 1–8.°

———— Aids in the cocoa campaign. *Advance,* Oct. 1956, no. 12, 10–14.°

———— Summary of discussions held at senior officers' conference, 1958. *Advance,* April 1959a, no. 22, 23–4.

———— Visual aids in women's work. *Advance,* April 1959b, no. 22, 4–8.

ARNOTT, D. W. Proverbial lore and word-play of the Fulani. *Africa,* 1957, *27,* 379–96.

ARNOULD, Charles. Les fêtes au Yatenga. *Notes Africaines de l'Institut d'Afrique Noire,* 1949, *42,* 38–45.°

BARNES, J. A. The village headman in British Central Africa: III. The Fort Jameson Ngoni. *Africa*, 1949, *19*, 100–6.

BASCOM, William R. The principle of seniority in the social structure of the Yoruba. *American Anthropologist*, 1942, *44*, 37–46.

—— Yoruba food. *Africa*, 1951, *21*, 41–53.

BASDEN, G. T. *Niger Ibos*. London: Seeley, Service, 1938.

BAS-WORK, Terrefe. Birth customs of the Amharas of Sawa. *University College of Addis Ababa Ethnological Society Bulletin*, 1957, *7*, 41–55.*

BATES, M. Searle; BAËTA, Christian G.; MICHAELI, Frank; and SUNDKLER, Bengt G. M. *Survey of the training of the ministry in Africa: Part II*. London: International Missionary Council, 1954.

BATTEN, T. R. The status and function of teachers in tribal communities. *Yearbook of Education*, 1953, *15*, 76–94.

—— *Communities and their development*. London: Oxford University Press, 1957.

BEACH, Harlan P. *A geography and atlas of Protestant missions*. New York: Student Volunteer Movement for Foreign Missions, 1901.

BEIER, H. U. Yoruba vocal music. *African Music*, 1956, *1*, No. 3, 23–8.*

Belgian Congo. Information and cinema in Africa south of the Sahara. *Monthly Bulletin*, 1958a, No. 9, 1–5.

—— A survey of the Congolese press. *Monthly Bulletin*, 1958b, No. 11, 9–13.

BEVER, L. VAN. The cinema as a means of education in the Belgian Congo. In *Visual aids in fundamental education*. Paris: UNESCO, 1952, pp. 59–67.

BIRKETT, J. D. Cattle immunization camps in Northern Nigeria. *West African Review*, Sept. 1952a, *23*, 896–99.*

—— The trade cattle of Northern Nigeria. *West African Review*, April 1952b, *23*, 326–29.*

BLOOMHILL, G. Africa's bead language: religious and social symbolism among primitive peoples. *African World*, Nov. 1957, 15–16.*

BOHANNAN, Paul. *Tiv farm and settlement*. London: Her Majesty's Stationery Office, 1954.

———— Some principles of exchange and investment among the Tiv. *American Anthropologist*, 1955, *57*, 60–70.

———— Beauty and scarification amongst the Tiv. *Man*, 1956, *56*, 117–21.

———— and BOHANNAN, Laura. Tiv markets. *Transactions of the New York Academy of Sciences*, 1957, *19*, 613–21.

————, ———— *Three source notebooks in Tiv ethnology*. New Haven: Human Relations Area Files, 1958.

BRETTON, Henry L. Pilot study, Eastern Region of Nigeria. Unpublished report, August, 1959.

BROWN, Arthur. The development of the scout movement in Nigeria. *African Affairs*, 1947, *46*, 38–42.

BROWN, Godfrey; Barton, OWEN; and Spurr, NORMAN. Village drama: a discussion. *Advance*, April 1959, No. 22, 9–14.

BROWN, H. D. The *Nkumu* of the Tumba. *Africa*, 1944, *14*, 432–46.

BROWN, Roger W. *Words and things*. Glencoe: Free Press, 1958.

BROWNLEE, Frank. "Uncanny." *Journal of the Royal African Society*, 1937, *36*, 452–60.

BURKETT, Ruth. Successful D.V.B.S. initiated in the Ubangi. *Congo Mission News*, 1954, No. 166, 14.

BUSIA, K. A. *The position of the chief in the modern political system of Ashanti*. London: Oxford University Press, 1951.

BUSSE, Joseph. Nyakyusa-Rätsel. *Zeitschrift für Phonetik und Allgemeine Sprachwissenschaft*, 1957, *10*, 108–19.°

BUTT, Audrey. *The Nilotes of the Anglo-Egyptian Sudan and Uganda*. London: International African Institute, 1952.

BUXTON, D. R. The Shoan plateau and its people: an essay in local geography. *Geographical Journal*, 1949, *114*, 157–72.

CARNELL, W. J. Sympathetic magic among the Gogo of Mpwapa district. *Tanganyika Notes*, June 1955, *39*, 25–38.°

CARPENTER, George Wayland (ed.). *The church in changing Africa*. New York: International Missionary Council, 1958.

———— *The way in Africa*. New York: Friendship Press, 1959.

CARRINGTON, J. F. The drum language of the Lokele tribe. *African Studies*, 1944, *3*, 75–88.

———— *Talking drums of Africa*. London: Carey Kingsgate, 1949.

CHADWICK, E. R. The anatomy of mass education. *Mass Education Bulletin*, 1949, *1*, 30–6.

CHRISTENSEN, James Boyd. The role of proverbs in Fante culture. *Africa*, 1958, *28*, 232–43.

CLARKE, Roger T. The drum language of the Tumba people. *American Journal of Sociology*, 1934, *40*, 34–48.

CONACHER, D. H. Health education and anthropology. *Health Education Journal*, 1957, *15*, 125–30.*

CORY, A. Figurines used in the initiation ceremonies of the Nguu of Tanganyika Territory. *Africa*, 1944, *14*, 459–64.

CORY, Hans. The ingredients of magic medicines. *Africa*, 1949, *19*, 13–32.

CUST, Robert Needham. *Clouds on the horizon*. London: Elliot Stock, 1891.

CZEKANOWSKI, Jan. *Forschungen im Nil-Kongo-Zwischengebiet*, Vol. 1. Leipzig: Klinkhardt and Biermann, 1917.

DAIFUKU, D. and BOWERS, J. B. Museum techniques in fundamental education. UNESCO *Educational Studies and Documents*, 1956, No. 17.

DANQUAH, Joseph Boakye. *Gold Coast: Akan laws and customs and the Akim Abuakwa constitution*. London: Routledge, 1928.

DAVIS, Jackson; CAMPBELL, Thomas M.; and WRONG, Margaret. *Africa advancing: study of rural education and agriculture in West Africa and the Belgian Congo*. New York: Friendship Press, 1945.

DAVIS, J. Merle. *Modern industry and the African*. London: Macmillan, 1933.

DELOBSOM, A. A. Dim. *L'empire du Mogho-Naba*. Paris: Loviton, 1932.

DE MESTRAL, Claude. Epilogue. *In* Trevor and Grace Shaw, *Through ebony eyes*. London: Lutterworth Press, 1956, pp. 92–6.

Department of Social Welfare and Community Development. Extension campaigns. Accra: mimeographed memorandum, 1956.

―――― Family and community living. Accra: mimeographed memorandum, 1958.

DICKSON, A. G. Studies in war-time organization: III. The mobile propaganda unit, East Africa Command. *African Affairs*, 1945, *44*, 9–18.

DIETERLEN, Germaine. *Essai sur la religion Bambara*. Paris: Les Presses Universitaires de France, 1951.

DILLE, Lois L. Schools for better family living. *In* I. W. Moomaw (ed.), *Deep furrows*. New York: Agricultural Missions, 1957, pp. 84–7.

DISNEY, A. W. M. The coronation of the Fung King of Fazoghli. *Sudan Notes and Records*, 1945, *26*, 37–42.

DOKE, C. M. Book review of Duncan MacDougald, Jr., *The languages and press of Africa*. *African Studies*, 1945, *4*, 103–5.

―――― *The southern Bantu languages*. London: Oxford University Press, 1954.

DOOB, Leonard W. *Propaganda: its psychology and technique*. New York: Holt, 1935.

―――― *Public opinion and propaganda*. New York: Holt, 1948.

―――― The strategies of psychological warfare. *Public Opinion Quarterly*, 1949–50, *13*, 635–44.

―――― Goebbels' principles of propaganda. *Public Opinion Quarterly*, 1950 *14*, 419–42.

―――― Information services in Central Africa. *Public Opinion Quarterly*, 1953, *17*, 6–19.

―――― The effect of language on verbal expression and recall. *American Anthropologist*, 1957a, *59*, 88–110.

―――― An experimental approach to the press in underdeveloped areas. *Gazette*, 1957b, *3*, 17–26.

―――― An introduction to the psychology of acculturation. *Journal of Social Psychology*, 1957c, *45*, 143–60.

―――― Psychological research in nonliterate societies. *American Psychologist*, 1957d, *12*, 756–8.

―――― The use of different test items in nonliterate societies. *Public Opinion Quarterly*, 1957–58, *21*, 499–504.

―――― The effect of the Jamaican patois on attitude and recall. *American Anthropologist*, 1958, *60*, 574–5.

—— Becoming more civilized: a psychological exploration. New Haven: Yale University Press, 1960a.

—— The effect of codability upon the afferent and efferent function of language. Journal of Social Psychology, 1960b, 52, 3–15.

DRAKE, St. Clair. Communications survey: the village communications structure. Unpublished questionnaire, University College of Ghana, Department of Sociology, 1959.

DRIBERG, J. H. The status of women among the Nilotics and Nilo-Hamitics. Africa, 1932, 5, 404–21.

DU SAUTOY, Peter. The organization of follow-up literature for mass literacy campaigns. Colonial Review, 1956, 9, 137–8.

EAST, Rupert M. Modern tendencies in the languages of Northern Nigeria. Africa, 1937, 10, 97–105.

—— (ed.). Akig's story: the Tiv tribe as seen by one of its members. London: Oxford University Press, 1939.

ELVIN, L. Education and community development: some recent trends in Africa. Fundamental and Adult Education, 1957, 9, 59–66.*

EMA, A. J. Fattening girls in Oron, Calabar Province. Nigeria, 1940, 21, 386–9.*

ENEMO, Eleazar Obiakonwa. The social problems of Nigeria. Africa, 1948, 18, 190–8.

ESTERMANN, Carlos. O problema do homicidio ritual no sul da Africa. Portugal em Africa, 1958, 15, 69.*

EVANS, P. C. C. British African tropical dependencies. Yearbook of Education, 1952, 14, 550–86.

EVANS-PRITCHARD, E. E. The dance. Africa, 1928, 1, 446–62.

—— Zande blood-brotherhood. Africa, 1933, 6, 369–401.

—— Witchcraft, oracles, and magic among the Azande. Oxford: Clarendon, 1937.

—— Economic life of the Nuer: cattle. Sudan notes and records, 1938, 21, 31–77.

—— Nuer time-reckoning. Africa, 1939, 12, 189–216.

—— The Nuer. Oxford: Clarendon, 1940.

—— Burial and mortuary rites of the Nuer. African Affairs, 1949a, 48, 56–63.

—— Nuer curses and ghostly vengeance. *Africa,* 1949b, *19,* 288–92.

—— Marriage customs of the Luo of Kenya. *Africa,* 1950, *20,* 132–42.

—— Nuer spear symbolism. *Anthropological Quarterly,* 1953, *26,* 1–19.°

—— A Zande slang language. *Man,* 1954, *54,* 185–6.

—— *Nuer religion.* Oxford: Clarendon, 1956.

FALLERS, Lloyd A. *Bantu bureaucracy.* Cambridge: Heffer, 1956.

FAULKNER, Donald. Young farmers' clubs in Lagos colony. *Nigeria,* 1953, *40,* 328–40.°

Federation of Nigeria. *Annual report of the Federal Department of Social Welfare for the year 1957–58.* Lagos: Federal Government Printer, 1959.

Federation of Rhodesia and Nyasaland. Music for bus passengers. *Newsletter,* Oct. 23, 1959, p. 7.

—— Regional radio service for Nyasaland. *Newsletter,* March 4, 1960, p. 9.

FENN, William P. Christian colleges and the future. *Occasional Bulletin from the Missionary Research Library,* March 25, 1960, *11,* 1–3.

FESTINGER, Leon. *A theory of cognitive dissonance.* Evanston: Row, Patterson, 1957.

FIELD, M. J. *Search for security: an ethno-psychiatric study of rural Ghana.* Evanston: Northwestern University Press, 1960.

Film Centre, London. *The use of mobile cinema and radio vans in fundamental education.* Paris: UNESCO, 1949.

FISHER, W. Singleton. Burning the bush for game. *African Studies,* 1948, *7,* 36–8.

FORTES, Meyer. Communal fishing and fishing magic in the northern territories of the Gold Coast. *Journal of the Royal Anthropological Institute,* 1937, *67,* 131–42.

—— Social and psychological aspects of education in Taleland. *Africa, Supplement,* 1938, *11,* No. 4.

—— *The dynamics of clanship among the Tallensi.* London: Oxford University Press, 1945.

———— *The web of kinship among the Tallensi.* London: Oxford University Press, 1949.

FRASER, Agnes Kenton. *The teaching of healthcraft to African women.* London: Longmans, Green, 1932.

FRASER, Donald. *The new African.* New York: Missionary Education Movement of the United States and Canada, 1928.

FRENCH, F. G. *The new Oxford English course (Nigeria): Book I.* London: Oxford University Press, 1955.

GAMBLE, David P. *The Wolof of Senegambia.* London: International African Institute, 1957.

GARLANDA, U. Vita primitiva dei pigmei. *Universo,* 1957, *37,* 687–98. °

GHANA, Government of. *Handbook of commerce and industry.* Accra: Ministry of Trade and Industries, 1958.

GILCHRIST, W. Sidney. Adult schools in Angola. *In* I. W. Moomaw (ed.), *Deep furrows.* New York: Agricultural Missions, 1957, pp. 66–9.

GILFAND, Michael and SWART, Yvonne. The Nyora. *Native Affairs Department Annual,* 1953, *30,* 5–11. °

GILKS, J.L. The relation of economic development to public health in rural Africa. *Journal of the African Society,* 1935, *34,* 31–40.

GOODCHILD, R. T. S. News from Kabale. *Mission Hospital,* 1936, *40,* 137–40.

GOODWIN, Astley J. H. *Communication has been established.* London: Methuen, 1937.

GORER, Geoffrey. *African dances.* New York: Knopf, 1935.

GOWER, R. H. Swahili borrowings from English. *Africa,* 1952, *22,* 154–7.

———— Swahili slang. *Journal of the East African Swahili Committee,* 1958, *28,* 41–8. °

GRAY, John. Nairuzi or Siku ya Mwaka. *Tanganyika Notes,* March 1955, *38,* 1–22. °

GRAY, Robert F. Sonjo bride-price and the question of African "wife purchase." *American Anthropologist,* 1960, *62,* 34–55.

Great Britain, Colonial Office. *The Cameroons under United Kingdom Administration, 1957.* London: Her Majesty's Stationery Office, 1958.

—————— *Somaliland Protectorate, 1956 and 1957.* London: Her Majesty's Stationery Office, 1959.

GREENBERG, Joseph. *The influence of Islam on a Sudanese religion.* New York: J. J. Augustin, 1946.

GRIAULE, M. and LIGERS, Z. Le bulu, jeu bozo. *Journal de la Société des Africanistes*, 1955, *25*, 35–7.°

GULLIVER, P. H. Jie marriage. *African Affairs*, 1953, *52*, 149–55.

GUTHRIE, Malcolm. The lingua franca of the Middle Congo. *Africa*, 1943, *14*, 118–23.

—————— *The Bantu languages of western equatorial Africa.* London: Oxford University Press, 1953.

GUTMANN, Bruno. *Das Recht der Dschagga.* Munich: C. H. Beck, 1926.

—————— *Die Stammelslehren der Dschagga.* Munich: C. H. Beck, 1932.

HAHN, Theophilus. *Tsuni-Goam: the supreme being of the Khoi-Khoi.* London: Trübner, 1881.

HAIG, E. F. G. Cooperatives in Nigeria. *African Affairs*, 1950, *49*, 41–50.

HAILEY, Lord. *An African survey—revised 1956.* London: Oxford University Press, 1957.

HALL, Edward T. *The silent language.* Garden City: Doubleday, 1959.

—————— and WHYTE, William Foote. Intercultural communication: a guide to men of action. *Human Organization*, 1960, *19*, 5–12.

HAMBLY, Wilfrid I. The Ovimbundu of Angola. *Field Museum of Natural History, Anthropological Series*, 1934, *21*, 89–362.

HARRIS, John. Notes on book preservation in West Africa. *West African Library News*, 1956, *2*, 102–5.

HELANDER, Gunnar. *Must we introduce monogamy?* Pietermaritzburg: Schuter and Shooter, 1958.

HENRY, Joseph. Les Bambara: l'âme d'un peuple Africain. *Bibliothèque-Anthropos*, 1910, *1*, No. 2.

HERSKOVITS, Melville J. *Background of African art.* Denver: Denver Art Museum, 1945.

―――― *The human factor in changing Africa.* Draft of forth-coming book, mimeographed by Food Research Institute, Stanford University, 1959, pp. 1–3.

HOBLEY, C. W. Eastern Uganda. *Anthropological Institute of Great Britain, Occasional Paper,* 1902, No. 1.

―――― Anthropological studies in Kavirondo and Nandi. *Journal of the Anthropological Institute,* 1903, *33,* 320–59.

HODSON, Arnold W. An account of the part played by the Gold Coast Brigade in the East African campaign, August, 1940 to May, 1941. *Journal of the Royal African Society,* 1941, *40,* 300–11.

HOPGOOD, C. R. Language, literature, and culture. *Africa,* 1948, *18,* 112–19.

HOVLAND, Carl I. Summary and implications. *In* Carl I. Hovland (ed.), *The order of presentation.* New Haven: Yale University Press, 1957, pp. 129–57.

――――; Janis, IRVING L.; and KELLEY, Harold H. *Communication and persuasion.* New Haven: Yale University Press, 1953.

―――― and Janis, IRVING L. Summary and implications for future research. *In* Irving L. Janis, Carl I. Hovland, et al., *Personality and persuasibility.* New Haven: Yale University Press, 1959, pp. 225–54.

――――; LUMSDAINE, Arthur A.; and SHEFFIELD, Fred D. *Experiments on mass communication.* Princeton: Princeton University Press, 1949.

HOWELL, Paul Philip. *A manual of Nuer law.* London: Oxford Unversity Press, 1954.

HUBBARD, Hugh W. *Filmstrip and slide evaluations.* New York: World Council of Christian Education and Sunday School Association, 1959.

HUFFMAN, Ray. *Nuer customs and folk-lore.* London: Oxford University Press, 1931.

HUIZINGA, J. H. Unique experiment in French black Africa. *African Affairs,* 1959, *58,* 25–33.

HULSTAERT, Gustave E. Le mariage des Nkundo. *Institut Royal Colonial Belge, Sections des Sciences Morales et Politiques, Mémoires,* 1938, *8,* 1–519.

IZOD, Alan. Fundamental education by film in Central Africa. In *Visual aids in fundamental education*. Paris: UNESCO, 1952, pp. 45–58.

JACKSON, I. C. *Advance in Africa: a study in community development in Eastern Nigeria*. London: Oxford University Press, 1956.

JANIS, Irving L. and HOVLAND, Carl I. An overview of persuasibility research. In Irving L. Janis, Carl I. Hovland, et al., *Personality and persuasibility*. New Haven: Yale University Press, 1959, pp. 1–26.

JEFFREYS, M. D. W. The bull-roarer among the Ibo. *African Studies*, 1949a, *8*, 23–4.

——— Funerary inversions in Africa. *Archiv für Völkerkunde*, 1949b, *4*, 24–37.

——— The winged solar disk. *Africa*, 1951, *21*, 93–111.

JEFFRIES, W. F. Vernacular newspapers in Northern Nigeria. In *Periodicals for new literates: seven case histories*. Paris: UNESCO, 1957.

JOHNSON, Samuel. *The history of the Yorubas*. London: Routledge, 1921.

JOHNSTON, Bruce F. Personal communication, 1961; his computations are based upon Gold Coast, Office of Government Statistics, *1953 Accra survey of household budgets*, p. 22; and *Kumasi survey of population and household budgets*, 1955, pp. 48–9.

JUNOD, Henri A. *The life of a South African tribe*, 2 vols. London: Macmillan, 1927.

KENYATTA, Joma. *Facing Mount Kenya*. London: Secker and Warburg, 1938.

KIRK-GREENE, A. H. M. On swearing—an account of some judicial oaths in Northern Nigeria. *Africa*, 1955, *25*, 43–53.

——— A Lala initiation ceremony. *Man*, 1957, *57*, 9–11.

KITCHEN, Helen. *The press in Africa*. Washington, D.C.: Ruth Sloan Associates, 1956.

KRAEMER, Hendrik. *The communication of the Christian faith.* Philadelphia: Westminster Press, 1956.

KRIGE, Eileen Jensen. *The social system of the Zulus.* London: Longmans, Green, 1936.

—— and Krige, J. D. *The realm of a rain-queen.* London: Oxford University Press, 1943.

LABRECQUE, Ed. Le marriage chez les Babemba. *Africa,* 1931, *4,* 209–21.

LADKIN, R. G. Health education in Uganda. *African Women,* 1956, *2,* 9–10.

LANCOUR, Harold. *Libraries in British West Africa.* Urbana: University of Illinois Library School, 1958.

LANTIS, Margaret. Fanti omens. *Africa,* 1940, *13,* 150–9.

LARKEN, P. M. Impressions of the Azande. *Sudan Notes and Records,* 1926, *9,* 1–55; 1927, *10,* 85–134.

LAUBACH, Frank C. *Teaching the world to read: a handbook for literacy campaigns.* New York: Friendship Press, 1947.

LAYDEVANT, F. La coutume du Hlonepho. *Africa,* 1946, *16,* 83–91.

LAYE, Camara. *The dark child.* New York: Noonday Press, 1954.

LEAKEY, L. S. B. *Mau Mau and the Kikuyu.* London: Methuen, 1952.

LECA, N. *Les pêcheurs de Guet N'Dar.* Paris: Librairie Larose, 1935.

LEDDEN, W. Earl. *"Nobody works like him."* New York: Board of Missions of the Methodist Church, 1959.

LEIB, Arthur. The mystical significance of colours in the life of the natives of Madagascar. *Folk-lore,* 1946, *57,* 128–33.

LEWIS, I. M. Modern political movements in Somaliland. *Africa,* 1958, *27,* 244–60, 344–62.

LEWIS, L. J. Africa. *Yearbook of Education,* 1949, *11,* 312–37.

LINTON, Ralph. The Tanala: a hill tribe of Madagascar. *Field Museum of Natural History, Anthropological Series,* 1933, *22,* No. 317.

LITTLE, Kenneth L. The Poro society as an arbiter of culture. *African Studies,* 1948, *7,* 1–15.

—— The sociological implications of the film in colonial areas. *Colonial Review,* 1949, *6,* 15–16.°

—— The Mende of Sierra Leone: a West African people in transition. London: Routledge and Kegan Paul, 1951.

LLOYD, P. C. Some modern changes in the government of Yoruba towns. Mimeographed report, West African Institute of Social and Economic Research, Annual Conference, March 1953.

LODS, Jean. Professional training of film technicians. Paris: UNESCO, 1951.

LUGARD, Frederick. Progress in Africa. In Edwin W. Smith, The Christian mission in Africa. London: International Missionary Council, 1926, pp. 148–53.

MACDOUGALD, Duncan, Jr. The languages and press of Africa. Philadelphia: University of Pennsylvania Press, 1944.

MAES, J. Notes sur les population des bassins du Kasai, de la Lukenie, et du Lac Léopold II. Annales du Musée du Congo Belge, 1924, 1, No. 1.

MAIR, Lucy P. An African people in the twentieth century. London: Routledge, 1934.

MAQUET, J. J. The kingdom of Ruanda. In Cyril Daryll Forde (ed.), African Worlds. London: Oxford University Press, 1954, pp. 164–89.

MASON, I. Notes on book distribution. Books for Africa, 1951, 21, No. 1, 9–11.*

MAYER, Philip. The joking of "pals" in Gusii age-sets. African Studies, 1951, 10, 27–41.

MEEK, C. K. The northern tribes of Nigeria, 2 vols. London: Oxford University Press, 1925.

MERCIER, Paul. The social role of circumcision among the Besorube. American Anthropologist, 1951, 53, 326–37.

MERRIAM, Alan P. African music. In William R. Bascom and Melville J. Herskovits (eds.), Continuity and change in African cultures. Chicago: University of Chicago Press, 1959, pp. 49–86.

MESSING, Simon David. The highland-plateau Amhara of Ethiopia. Ph.D. thesis, University of Pennsylvania, 1957.

MEYER, Hans. Die Barundi. Leipzig: Spamer, 1916.

MIDDLETON, John. The central tribes of the north-eastern Bantu. London: International African Institute, 1953.

MONTEIL, Charles. *Les Bambara du Ségou et du Kaarta.* Paris: Larose, 1924.

MOOMAW, I. W. *Deep furrows.* New York: Agricultural Missions, 1957.

MOREAU, R. E. Suicide by "breaking the cooking pot" (Usambara). *Tanganyika Notes,* Dec. 1941, *12,* 49–50.°

MOREIRA, Adriano. As élites das provincias portuguesas de indigenato. *Garcia de Orta,* 1956, *4,* 159–88.°

MORRIS, Charles W. *Signs, language, and behavior.* New York: Prentice-Hall, 1946.

MORTON-WILLIAMS, P. *Cinema in rural Nigeria.* Zaria: Federal Information Service, n.d. (1953).

MULLANE, Barbara. The role of the public library in African mass education programmes. *Colonial Review,* 1956, *9,* 11–12.

MUNDAY, J. T. Spirit names among the Central Bantu. *African Studies,* 1948, *7,* 38–44.

MURDOCK, George Peter. *Africa: its peoples and their culture history.* New York: McGraw-Hill, 1959.

NADEL, S. F. *A black Byzantium: the kingdom of Nupe in Nigeria.* London: Oxford University Press, 1942.

NEILL, Stephen. *Survey of the training of the ministry in Africa: Part I.* London: International Missionary Council, 1950.

NEWCOMB, Harvey. *A cyclopaedia of missions.* New York: Scribner, 1854.

NIDA, Eugene A. *God's word in man's language.* New York: Harpers, 1952a.

——— *How the word is made flesh: communicating the gospel to aboriginal peoples.* Princeton: Princeton Theological Seminary, 1952b.

Nigerian Radio Times. Programme journal of the Nigerian Broadcasting Corporation. Lagos, August, 1959.

NKETIA, J. H. Modern trends in Ghana music. *African Music,* 1957, *1,* No. 4, 13–17.°

——— The contribution of African culture to Christian worship. *In* George Carpenter, *The church in changing Africa.* New York: International Missionary Council, 1958, pp. 59–65.

Northern Nigeria, Director of Information Services. *Social and economic progress in the Northern Region of Nigeria*. Kaduna: Government Printer, 1957.

Northern Nigeria, Government of. *You and your country*. Zaria: Regional Adult Educational Field HQS, 1958.

ODUTOLA, S. O. Islam as it affects life in Nigeria. *In* George Carpenter, *The church in changing Africa*. New York: International Missionary Council, 1958, pp. 65–7.

OGDEN, C. K. and RICHARDS, I. A. *The meaning of meaning*. New York: Harcourt Brace, 1936.

OTTENBERG, S. Improvement associations among the Afikpo Ibo. *Africa*, 1955, 25, 1–28.

PAGÈS, G. *Un royaume Hamite au centre de l'Afrique*. Brussels: Libraire Falk, 1933.

PAQUES, Viviana. *Les Bambara*. Paris: Les Presses Universitaires de France, 1954.

PARRINDER, E. G. Divine kingship in West Africa. *Numen*, 1956, 3, 111–12.*

PARRINDER, Geoffrey. *Religion in an African city*. London: Oxford University Press, 1953.

PAULITSCHKE, Phillip. *Beiträge zur Ethnographie und Anthropologie der Somali, Galla, und Harari*. Leipzig: Eduard Baldamus, 1888.

PHELAN, Nancy. How to make your own film strips and how to use the kerosene projector. *African Women*, 1956, 2, 23.

PICKERING, A. K. Village drama in Ghana. *Fundamental and Adult Education*, 1957, 9, 178–83.

PILKINGTON, Frederick. The problem of unity in Nigeria. *African Affairs*, 1956, 55, 219–22.

PORTER, John L. Adult education at the Jeanes School for Community Development in Kenya. *Yearbook of Education*, 1954, 16, 351–6.

POWDERMAKER, Hortense. Communication and social change, based on a field study in Northern Rhodesia. *Transactions of the New York Academy of Sciences*, 1955, 17, 430–4.

—— Social change through imagery and values of teen-age

Africans in Northern Rhodesia. *American Anthropologist*, 1956, *58*, 783–813.

PROSSER, A. R. G. An experiment in community development. *Community Development Bulletin*, 1951, *2*, 52–3.

RATTRAY, Robert S. *Ashanti proverbs*. Oxford: Clarendon, 1916.

────── *The Ashanti*. London: Oxford University Press, 1923.

────── *Religion and art in Ashanti*. Oxford: Clarendon, 1927.

────── *Ashanti law and constitution*. Oxford: Clarendon, 1929.

────── *Akan-Ashanti folk tales*. Oxford: Clarendon, 1930.

RAUM, O. F. *Chaga childhood*. London: Oxford, 1940.

RAVEMCCO (Radio, Visual Education, and Mass Communication Committee, National Council of the Churches of Christ). Africa: Audio-Visual Survey and Training Deputation. New York: mimeographed, 1953.

READ, Margaret. Tradition and prestige among the Ngoni. *Africa*, 1936, *9*, 453–84.

────── Native standards of living and African culture change. *Africa, Supplement*, 1938, *11*, No. 3, 5–56.

────── *Children of their fathers*. New Haven: Yale University Press, 1960.

République du Togo, Ministère du Travail des Affairs Sociales. Education des masses. Lomé: mimeographed, 1959.

RICHARDS, Audrey I. *Land, labour, and diet in Northern Rhodesia*. London: Oxford University Press, 1939.

────── (ed.). *Economic development and tribal change*. Cambridge: Heffner, 1954.

────── *Chisungu*. London: Faber and Faber, 1956.

────── Some mechanisms for the transfer of political rights in some African tribes. *Journal of the Royal Anthropological Institute*, 1960, *90*, 175–90.

RILEY, Oliver L. *Masks and magic*. New York: Studio Publications and Thomas Y. Crowell, 1955.

ROSCOE, John. *The Baganda*. London: Macmillan, 1911.

────── *The northern Bantu*. Cambridge: Cambridge University Press, 1915.

────── *The Banyankole*. Cambridge: Cambridge University Press, 1923.

ROSENBERG, Milton J.; HOVLAND, Carl I.; McGUIRE, William J.; ABELSON, Robert P.; and BREHM, Jack W. *Attitude organization and change.* New Haven: Yale University Press, 1960.

ROUTLEDGE, W. Scoresby and ROUTLEDGE, Katherine. *With a prehistoric people.* London: Edward Arnold, 1910.

ROUX, Edward. Easy English for Africans. *African Studies,* 1942, *1,* 261–9.

RUESCH, Jurgen and KEES, Weldon. *Nonverbal communication: notes on the visual perception of human relations.* Berkeley: University of California Press, 1956.

SARMENTO, A. Contribuiçào para o estudo das mutilaçòes etnicas dos indígenas de Angola—Huambo e Sambo. *Trabalhos de Antropologia e Etnologia da Sociedade Portuguesa de Antropologia,* 1951, *13,* 10–15.*

SCHAPERA, Isaac. *The Khoisan peoples of South Africa.* London; Routledge, 1930.

SCHMALENBACH, Werner. *African art.* New York: Macmillan, 1954.

SELLERS, W. Mobile cinema shows in Africa. *Colonial Review,* 1955, *9,* no. 1, 13–14.

SHAW, Alexander. Visual aids for the Egyptian villager. In *Visual aids in fundamental education.* Paris: UNESCO, 1952, pp. 15–24.

SHAW, K. C. Some preliminary notes on Luo marriage customs. *Journal of the East African and Uganda Natural History Society,* 1932, No. 45–6, 39–50.

SHAW, Trevor and SHAW, Grace. *Through ebony eyes: evangelism through journalism in West Africa.* London: Lutterworth Press, 1956.

SIMON, K. Colour vision of Buganda. *East African Medical Journal,* 1951, *28,* 75–9.

SMITH, Bruce Lannes; LASSWELL, Harold D.; and CASEY, Ralph D. *Propaganda, communication, and public opinion.* Princeton: Princeton University Press, 1946.

SMITH, Edwin W. *The Christian mission in Africa.* London: International Missionary Council, 1926.

————— The function of folk-tales. *Journal of the Royal African Society*, 1940, *39*, 64–83.

————— *Knowing the African*. London: United Society for Christian Literature, 1946.

SMITH, M. F. *Baba of Karo: a woman of the Muslim Hausa*. London: Faber and Faber, 1954.

SMITH, M. G. Notes. *In* M. F. Smith, *Baba of Karo*. London: Faber and Faber, 1954, pp. 257–90.

————— *The economy of Hausa communities of Zaria*. London: Colonial Office, 1955.

————— The social functions and meaning of Hausa praise-singing. *Africa*, 1957, *27*, 26–45.

SOUTHALL, A. Lineage formation among the Luo. *International African Institute*, 1952, Memorandum 26, 1–43.

SPURR, Norman F. "Pamba." *Empire Cotton Growing Review*, 1950, *27*, 172–6.*

————— Some aspects of the work of the Colonial Film Unit in West and East Africa. *In Visual aids in fundamental education*. Paris: UNESCO, 1952, pp. 37–44.

STAMP, L. Dudley. *Africa: a study in tropical development*. New York: Wiley, 1953.

STAUB, Jules. *Beiträge zur Kenntnis der materiellen Kultur der Mendi in der Sierra Leone*. Solothurn: Vogt-Schild, 1936.

SWAYNE, H. G. C. *Seventeen trips through Somaliland and a visit to Abyssinia*. London: Rowland Ward, 1900.

TAUXIER, L. *Le noir du Yatenga*. Paris: Larose, 1917.

TAYLOR, JOHN. *Christianity and politics in Africa*. London: Penguin, 1957.

TAYLOR, Wayne Chatfield. *The Firestone operations in Liberia*. Washington: National Planning Association, 1956.

TEMPLE, O. *Notes on the tribes, emirates, and states of the northern provinces of Nigeria*. Lagos: CMS Bookstore, 1922.

TEN RHYNE, William. *A short account of the Cape of Good Hope, and of the Hottentots who inhabit that region*. Cape Town: Van Riebeeck Society, 1933.

TERRISSE, André. Combatting illiteracy in a French West African project. *Fundamental and Adult Education*, 1952, *4*, No. 4, 32–5.*

—— Broadcasting services and education. *Fundamental and Adult Education*, 1959, *11*, No. 1, 5–18.*

TESSMANN, Günter. *Die Pangwe*, Vol. 1. Berlin: Ernst Wasmuth, 1913.

TEW, Mary. A form of polyandry among the Lele of the Kasai. *Africa*, 1951, *21*, 1–12.

TRAVIS, I. M. *New English Course: Reader 1A*. London: Longmans, Green, 1957.

TRILLES, R. P. H. *Le totémisme chez les Fân*. Münster: Aschendorffsche Verlagsbuchhandlung, 1912.

TRIMINGHAM, J. Spencer. *The Christian Church and Islam in West Africa*. London: S.C.M. Press, 1955.

TROWELL, H. C.; DAVIES, J. N. P.; and DEAN, R. F. A. *Kwashiorkor*. London: Edward Arnold, 1954.

TUCKER, A. N. and BRYAN, M. A. *The non-Bantu languages of north-eastern Africa*. London: Oxford University Press, 1956.

TUCKER, J. T. Pre-European education for boys in an Angola tribe. *Yearbook of Education*, 1954, *16*, pp. 206–14.

TWALA, Regina G. Beads as regulating the social life of the Zulu and Swazi. *African Studies*, 1951, *10*, 113–23.

UN. *United Nations Statistical Yearbook, 1958*. New York: UN, 1959.

UNDERWOOD, Leon. *Masks of West Africa*. London: Alec Tiranti, 1948.

UNESCO. *Press, film, radio*. Paris: UNESCO, 1951.

—— *Visual aids in fundamental education*. Paris: UNESCO, 1952.

—— The use of vernacular languages in education. *Monographs on Fundamental Education*, 1953, No. 8.

—— Education for journalism. *Reports and Papers on Mass Communication*, 1954, No. 8.

—— *Catalogues of short films and filmstrips*. Paris: UNESCO, 1955.

—— World illiteracy at mid-century. *Monographs on Fundamental Education*, 1957, No. 11.

—————— Adult education groups and audio-visual techniques. *Reports and Papers on Mass Communication*, 1958, No. 25.

U. S. Foreign Broadcast Information Service. *Broadcasting stations of the world, Part I*. Washington: U. S. Government Printing Office, 1959.

UPPER NILE, Lucian. Out with an Acholi hunt. *African Affairs*, 1946, *45*, 178–84.

WAGNER, Günter. The study of culture contact in its practical applications. *In* B. Malinowski (ed.), *Methods of study of culture contact in Africa*. London: Oxford University Press, 1938, pp. 92–105.

WALKER, Sister A. M. W. Medical work at Gahini. *The Mission Hospital*, 1936, *40*, 134–7.

WARD, C. E. The writing of history text-books for Africa. *Africa*, 1934, *7*, 191–8.

WARD, Ida C. Practical suggestions for the learning of an African language in the field. *Africa, Supplement*, 1937, *10*, 1–39.

WEISS, Walter. Opinion congruence with a negative source on one issue as a factor influencing agreement on another issue. *Journal of Abnormal and Social Psychology*, 1957, *54*, 180–6.

WELSH, Anne. *Africa south of the Sahara: an assessment of human and material resources*. Cape Town: Oxford University Press, 1951.

WESTERMANN, Diedrich. Introduction. *In* Ray Huffman, *Nuer customs and folk-lore*. London: Oxford University Press, 1931, pp. v–xi.

—————— *Die Glidyi-Ewe in Togo*. Berlin: Walter de Gruyter, 1935.

—————— and BRYAN, M. A. *Languages of West Africa*. London: Oxford University Press, 1952.

WHITELEY, Wilfred H. *Bemba and related people of Northern Rhodesia*. London: International African Institute, 1950.

—————— The changing position of Swahili in East Africa. *Africa*, 1956, *26*, 343–53.

WHITING, John W. M. and CHILD, Irving L. *Child training and personality*. New Haven: Yale University Press, 1953.

WHITTING, C. C. J. Fulani floggings. *West African Review*, 1955, *26*, 1–12.*

WIESCHHOFF, H. A. The social significance of names among the Ibo of Nigeria. *American Anthropologist*, 1941, *43*, 212–22.

WILLIAMS, J. Grenfell. *Radio in fundamental education in undeveloped areas.* Paris: UNESCO, 1950.

WILSON, G. H. The Northern Rhodesia-Nyasaland Joint Publications Bureau. *Africa*, 1950, *20*, 60–9.

WILSON, Godfrey and WILSON, Monica. *The analysis of change: based on observations in Central Africa.* Cambridge: Cambridge University Press, 1945.

WILSON, Monica. *Good company: a study of Nyakyusa age-villages.* London: Oxford University Press, 1951.

YOUNG, T. Cullen. A good village. *Africa*, 1934, *7*, 89–96.

INDEX

The names of African societies or tribes are followed by an asterisk. The pages on which an author is listed in the References (pp. 373-93) are not indexed.